D1077507

FIONN DAVENPORT

DUBLIN
CITY GUIDE

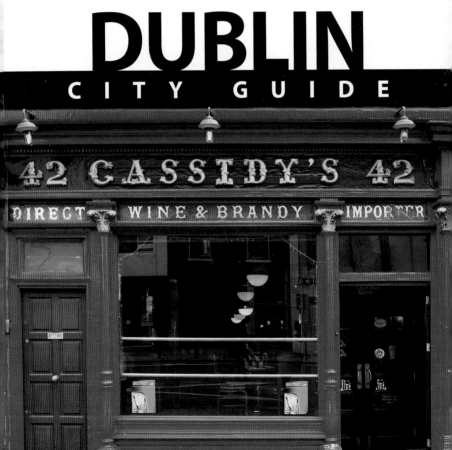

Crossing distinctive Ha'penny Bridge (p133) would once have cost you said ha'penny

OLIVIER CIRENDINI

Decadent, delightful and full of surprises, Dublin packs a punch that, delivered correctly, will leave you reeling but still wanting more. That's big talk for a small capital.

Dubliners don't mind a bit of hyperbole, especially if it's to 'big up' their own beloved burg. Yet Dubs can also be brutally unsentimental about the place, which mightn't come across as sexy or as sultry as other European capitals, but aren't pretty things as easy to like as they are to forget? Dublin, they'll tell you, has *personality,* which is way more important than good looks, and will last far longer.

Which isn't to say that Dublin can't do pretty. An amble through the landscaped parks corralled by the city's rich Georgian heritage is enough to make anyone's head turn, while even half a peek at the city's myriad cultural offerings will show that it has pedigree too, these days expressed as much through its recently acquired multicultural cosmopolitanism as through its own traditional forms.

Yet Dublin's most enduring quality can be found in Dubliners themselves, both native-born and blown-in. Garrulous, amiable and witty, Dubliners at their ease are the greatest hosts of all, a charismatic bunch whose soul and sociability are so compelling and infectious that at some point during your visit you could find yourself wondering if you could possibly figure out a way of staying here permanently. And if you can't, don't worry: it'll still be here when you come back.

CITY LIFE

Crash, bang, wallop. The party that was the Celtic Tiger came to a shocking, sudden end in late 2008, leaving Dubliners to deal with the consequences of a debt crisis that has far too many numbers in it to seem real. The dust has settled somewhat, but Dubliners are still pissed off – at the banks, the government and the developers who promised a better life through bigger houses, newer cars and a wardrobe full of pricey junk, but then delivered a hefty bill that nobody seems able to pay.

Dublin is in the midst of the worst financial crisis in a century or more. There are fewer jobs and plenty of pay cuts. Negative equity is the albatross around the city's neck, with tens of thousands who bought a home in the last ten years desperately trying to figure out a way to pay the mortgage in the face of dropping house prices and growing unemployment. 'Staycation' is the new fad for many Dubliners, who once took four foreign trips a year for granted but are now put off by the cost.

Yet Dubliners are a determined and resolute lot. Half of them have been here or hereabouts before, having grown up in the grey decades that preceded the boom. The other half, the under 35s, might find it all a bit shocking and confusing, but the children of the Celtic Tiger aren't just about bling and brand new BMWs – they are the generation that grew up believing that everything is possible and that innovation, intuition and hard work will deliver the goods.

Despite common belief to the contrary, this smiling optimism is very much at odds with Dubliners' traditional fatalism, which has always been the fuel for their expertly delivered gallows humour, a necessary tool for getting through the tough times. Those tough times are back, but Dublin is no longer the same. The Celtic Tiger is well and truly dead, but its legacy will be more than just a bucket-load of debt.

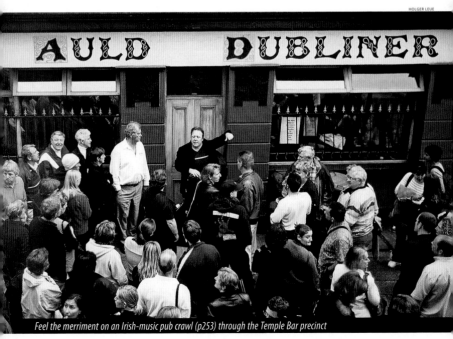

Feel the merriment on an Irish-music pub crawl (p253) through the Temple Bar precinct

HIGHLIGHTS

OLIVIER CIRENDINI

JONATHAN SMITH

ARTY FACTS

Dublin's collection of canvases and other arty bits are signed by some of the world's most famous names, both classic and contemporary, and can be found in galleries and museums on both sides of the Liffey.

THE IRISH IMAGE COLLECTION/PHOTOLIBRARY

❶ National Gallery
The home of the Great Masters and Ireland's own Jack B Yeats (p82)

❷ Irish Museum of Modern Art
Outstanding examples of the best of contemporary art (p98)

❸ Russborough House
A collection so stunning that various thieves tried to steal it – four times (p237)

❹ Dublin City Gallery – The Hugh Lane
A priceless collection including Francis Bacon's actual studio (p104)

❺ Douglas Hyde Gallery
Trinity College gets a dose of cutting-edge contemporary art (p70)

❶ Hill of Howth
Climb through the gorse and bracken for stunning views (p227)

❷ Phoenix Park
A huge park for everything from a stroll to a proper game of polo (p118)

❸ Grafton Street
Brilliant buskers guarantee top-class music... for free (p74)

❹ The Forty Foot
It doesn't have to be Christmas Day for you to take the plunge in this traditional swimming spot (p17)

❺ Glasnevin Cemetery
As poignant a reminder of the bloody cost of determining history as any in the city (p125)

OLIVIER CIRENDINI

DIY DUBLIN

Slow down. Take a moment and keep your hand in your pocket to enjoy some genuine Dublin experiences.

EOIN CLARKE   STEPHEN SAKS

1 Croke Park
The home of Gaelic games and the spiritual home of an important tranche of Irish culture (p124)

2 Fairyhouse Racecourse
Come for the Grand National on Easter Monday (p207)

3 Shelbourne Park
A night at the dogs is one of the best experiences in town (p207)

4 Dalymount Park
Home of the Bohemians Football Club, aka the Gypsies, pride of the north side (p206)

5 Royal Dublin Society
Provincial side Leinster plays at this handsome ground in Dublin 4 (p208)

A SPORTING CHANCE

Dubliners are passionate about their sport, whether it's supporting the Blues playing Gaelic football or watching the dog in trap four take their betting dreams and crush them against the rail.

DWIMAGES IRELAND/ALAMY

COURTESY OF DAVE MOORE

MARKET GOODNESS

Dublin has always had traditional markets, but in recent years they've been given an organic, exotic spit 'n' shine.

JACQUE DENZER PARKER/PHOTOLIBRARY

❶ Moore Street Market
Where the genuine Molly Malones sell their flowery, meaty and fishy wares (p145)

❷ Dublin Food Co-op
Make up your own picnic at this wonderful bi-weekly organic market (p154)

❸ Meeting House Square Market
Organic foods and tastes from everywhere at this weekend fair (p145)

❹ Coppinger Row Market
Organic, exotic goodies for home cooking or on-the-fly eating (p154)

❺ Howth Fishermen's & Farmers' Market
Best in the city for fresh fish, organic meats, and jams, cakes and breads (p228)

DUBLIN DESIGNS

Dublin's beautiful architecture is not just about the Georgian city – there are buildings both old and new that will make you stop in your tracks and pull out the camera.

DOUG MCKINLAY

DENNIS GILBERT/ALAMY

MANFRED HOFER

① National Museum of Ireland – Decorative Arts & History
The British army was loath to leave this extraordinary former barracks (p106)

② Berkeley Library
Brilliant, brutalist building in a thoroughly modern style (p70)

③ St Patrick's Cathedral
Ireland's largest church is also the city's most impressive (p93)

④ Royal Hospital Kilmainham
A stunning example of the pre-Georgian Anglo-Dutch style (p98)

⑤ Leinster House
Ireland's parliament is a suitably magnificent Palladian mansion (p83)

1 JJ Smyth's
Nod your head approvingly at the best jazz sessions in town. Nice (p193)

2 Cobblestone
Superb nightly music sessions performed by traditional musicians (p196)

3 Whelan's
Dublin's spiritual home of the intimate rock and folk gig (p195)

4 Twisted Pepper
Live acts and top-class DJs fill this multi-tiered room with terrific sounds (p189)

5 Vicar Street
Soul, jazz, blues and other sultry sounds for discerning audiences (p195)

COURTESY OF TERREL STAFFORD

A MUSICAL NOTE

Whether it's jazz or rock, traditional or totally experimental, Dublin's musical scene is one of the unavoidable highlights of any trip to the city – you'll hear music everywhere.

DOUG MCKINLAY

COURTESY OF AISLING O NEILL

KIM HAUGHTON/ALAMY

A PINT OF PLAIN

As the world discovers the exported Irish pub, the traditional boozer is becoming something of an endangered species in Dublin, but there are still enough of the real deal to quench your thirst for a genuine experience.

❶ Mulligan's
Tourists aside, it's what a traditional pub should look and sound like (p176)

❷ Long Hall
A Victorian classic that has retained its integrity (p176)

❸ Kehoe's
Atmospheric, beautiful Kehoe's is popular with Dubliners and visitors alike (p176)

❹ Grogan's Castle Lounge
The favourite pub of Dublin's artists and writers (p175)

❺ Gravediggers
This unreconstructed treasure is worth the trip to the suburbs (p183)

WERNER DIETERICH/ALAMY

KEVIN FOY/ALAMY

HOLGER LEUE

RICHARD CUMMINS

JUST FOR KICKS

'Dublin can be heaven/with coffee at 11/and a stroll in Stephen's Green.' Or so goes the old song. Test the theory with some aimless ambles that will prove to be not so aimless after all.

1 Temple Bar
Look for the zaniest hen party or the largest group of visiting students (p86)

2 South Wall
Great views along the South Wall to Poolbeg Lighthouse (p114)

3 Grand Canal
Be inspired: follow in the footsteps of poet Patrick Kavanagh (p121)

4 Phoenix Park
Winter football at the Fifteen Acres: at least it's not you (p120)

5 Killiney
Be on Bono Watch in the neighbourhood of the stars (p230)

SCULPTURE BY JOHN COLL/PHOTO BY TONY WHEELER

OLIVIER CIRENDINI

RICHARD CUMMINS

PSST. TELL NO ONE

Some of the city's most memorable attractions have escaped the tourist hordes and the marketing hype – for now.

❶ Marsh's Library
A magnificently preserved scholars' library next to St Patrick's Cathedral (p95)

❷ James Joyce Museum
Martello tower, where James Joyce's *Ulysses* kicks off (p230)

❸ Iveagh Gardens
The 'forgotten' gardens of the city's Georgian parks (p78)

❹ Shaw Birthplace
The restored birthplace of one of Dublin's Nobel Prize winners (p77)

❺ War Memorial Gardens
Hardly anyone visits these Lutyens-designed gardens to the west (p100)

OLIVIER CIRENDINI

CONTENTS

**INTRODUCING
DUBLIN**   **2**

HIGHLIGHTS   **4**

THE AUTHOR   **15**

GETTING STARTED   **16**
When to Go   16
Costs & Money   19
Internet Resources   20
Sustainable Dublin   20

BACKGROUND   **22**
History   22
Arts   33
Architecture   48
Environment & Planning   53
Government & Politics   54
Media   55
Language   56

NEIGHBOURHOODS   **59**
Itinerary Builder   62
Grafton Street & Around   66
Merrion Square & Around   79
Temple Bar   86
Kilmainham &
the Liberties   90
North of the Liffey   101
Docklands   114
Phoenix Park   118
Beyond the Grand Canal   121
Beyond the Royal Canal   124
Walking Tours   128

SHOPPING   **135**
Grafton Street & Around   137
Temple Bar   143
Kilmainham &
the Liberties   144
North of the Liffey   144

Docklands   146
Beyond the Grand Canal   146

EATING   **149**
Grafton Street & Around   152
Merrion Square & Around   159
Temple Bar   161
Kilmainham &
the Liberties   163
North of the Liffey   163
Docklands   166
Phoenix Park   167
Beyond the Grand Canal   167

DRINKING   **169**
Grafton Street & Around   172
Merrion Square &
Around   177
Temple Bar   178
Kilmainham &
the Liberties   180
North of the Liffey   180
Docklands   182
Phoenix Park   182
Beyond the Grand Canal   182
Beyond the Royal Canal   183

**NIGHTLIFE &
THE ARTS**   **185**
Clubbing   186
Comedy   190
Film   191
Karaoke   192
Live Music   192
Theatre   197

**SPORTS &
ACTIVITIES**   **201**
Health & Fitness   202
Activities   203
Spectator Sport   204

SLEEPING 209

Grafton Street & Around 212
Merrion Square & Around 215
Temple Bar 216
North of the Liffey 218
Docklands 220
Beyond the Grand Canal 220
Beyond the Royal Canal 222

EXCURSIONS 223

Howth 227
Malahide 228
Dalkey 229
Brú na Bóinne 230
Glendalough 233
Powerscourt Estate 236
Russborough House 237
Castletown House 238

TRANSPORT 240

DIRECTORY 246

BEHIND THE SCENES 258

INDEX 266

GREENDEX 275

MAP LEGEND 276

THE AUTHOR

Fionn Davenport

Half-Italian and a lifelong supporter of Liverpool Football Club, Fionn is the ideal Dubliner – a native son in love with the city of his birth but one eye forever on somewhere else. He's left the city many times – usually looking for warmer weather or a job, but he always returns – because too much sun is bad for you and all jobs get boring. But the reason he loves Dublin so much is that it treats gallows humour as high art: why look for a straight answer when a funny one is far more satisfying. Lonely Planet has kept him busy for the last 15 years or so, but he also hosts his own radio show on Newstalk 106-108 (you can listen to Culture Shock online at www.newstalk.ie) and makes the occasional foray into television.

FIONN'S TOP DUBLIN DAY
All good days in Dublin begin with a read of the *Irish Times* and a hit of caffeine. It's sunny and warm (of course) so a stroll up Grafton St and into the calm of St Stephen's Green (p73) sets me up just right for a day in pursuit of idleness, surely a Dubliner's ulti-

mate ambition. I'll check out the newly refurbished Natural History Museum (p83) before ambling up to my favourite museum of all, the Chester Beatty Library (p72), a treasure chest of beautiful books, ancient scrolls and objets d'art. Lunch is a piadina loaf stuffed with Italian goodies from the totally fabulous Bottega Toffoli (p158) just around the corner, after which it's time to meet a friend who's taken a half-day off as a moral obligation: we make our way west, past the Guinness brewery to the exquisite grounds of the Irish Museum of Modern Art (p98) and then on to the War Memorial Gardens (p100) in Islandbridge, a marvellous open secret that few ever bother to visit. We sit by the lovely Liffey and, momentarily inspired by a bit of Joyce, 'riverrun, past Eve and Adam's, from swerve of shore to bend of bay' we make our way to the South Wall. I time our walk out to the Poolbeg Lighthouse (p114) with the setting of the sun – there's surely no more romantic spot in Dublin. Dinner with friends follows at Coppinger Row (p156) before a drink in the Long Hall (p176) on South Great George's St. Lovely.

Dublin is a cinch in virtually every respect. The city is small, easy to get around and offers no greater challenge than struggling to be cultural the morning after the night before. That is, of course, if you don't care about the gridlock or the fact that nightclubs are calling chucking out time when their equivalents in southern climes are just getting going. Otherwise, just get stuck in.

WHEN TO GO

You don't like the weather? Wait 15 minutes. So goes the old refrain about a city where it's virtually impossible to predict the climate other than to make vague generalisations about it being warmer in summer than in winter – which are true, at least most of the time. From June to August, the days are reasonably warm and – most importantly – very long. At the height of summer you won't need to turn on lights until after 10pm. It is also peak tourist season, which means there are far more people pretty much everywhere and prices are at their highest.

Not surprisingly, most of the yearly festivals occur during these times so as to take advantage of the crowds and the more favourable weather. Spring (March to May) and autumn (September to November) are usually good times for a peek, although the city's popularity as a tourist destination can often blur the lines between mid- and high-season tourism. Still, you have a better chance of some peace and quiet and the weather can be surprisingly better in April and September

than in mid-July – again, it's all part of the uncertainty principle.

Winters are dark, wet and cold, with December the wettest of all (an average 76mm of rainfall), but hey, it's Christmas and everyone is high-spirited; plus, you can enjoy indoor pleasures and you won't feel as guilty lounging in the pub. January is the only time the city's not really itself, when it's a little quiet and cranky after the festivities, and the days seem interminably gloomy.

See p246 for more information on Dublin's climate.

FESTIVALS

Dubliners' need to justify their propensity for celebrating stuff – 'it's Wednesday!' – just doesn't work for some, so the city's party planners have conveniently laid on an ever-changing menu of festivals and events for everyone to feel better about their hangovers.

January
NEW YEAR'S CELEBRATIONS
Experience the birth of another year with a cheer among thousands of revellers at Dublin's iconic Christ Church Cathedral (p96).

February
JAMESON DUBLIN INTERNATIONAL FILM FESTIVAL
☎ 872 1122; www.dubliniff.com
Local flicks, arty international films and advance releases of mainstream movies

---

ADVANCE PLANNING

From Easter to September, queues can be horrendous at popular attractions; arrive early. Most fee-paying sights offer discounts to students, the elderly, children and families. If you're serious about sightseeing, buy the Dublin Pass (p247) as soon as you set foot in the airport – it'll give you a free ride on the Aircoach.

Two Weeks Before You Go
Advance purchase is a must if you want to take in a hit play at the Abbey (p197) or the Gate (p198). A couple of weeks ahead should be plenty of time. Ditto if you want to watch a game at Croke Park (p124), especially for the latter stages of the championship, which runs from April to September.

Three Days Before You Go
The very best of Dublin's restaurants can be pretty tough to get a booking in for the first few months of business, but you shouldn't have any problems a couple of days in advance.

ONLY IN DUBLIN

All-Ireland Finals (☎ 836 3222; www.gaa.ie) The climax of the year for fans of Gaelic games; the season's most successful county teams battle it out for the All-Ireland championships in hurling and football, on the second and fourth Sundays in September, respectively. The capital is swamped with fans from the competing counties, draped in their colours and swept along by their good-natured, family-oriented exuberance.

Bloomsday (☎ 878 8547; www.jamesjoyce.ie) Every 16 June a bunch of weirdos wander around the city dressed in Edwardian gear, talking nonsense in dramatic tones. They're not mad – at least not clinically – they're only Blooms-dayers committed to commemorating James Joyce's epic *Ulysses* through readings, performances and re-created meals, including Leopold Bloom's famous breakfast of 'kidneys with the faint scent of urine'. Yummy.

Christmas Dip at the Forty Foot Possibly the most hardcore hangover cure known to man, this event takes place at 11am on Christmas Day at a famous swimming spot below the Martello tower – made famous by James Joyce in *Ulysses* – in Sandycove, 9km from the centre of Dublin. A group of the very brave, and certifiably insane, plunge into the icy water and swim 20m to the rocks and back. With heads cleared after their frozen frolics, each heads home for Christmas lunch.

Handel's Messiah (☎ 677 2255; Neal's Music Hall, Fishamble St) *Messiah*, Handel's most highly esteemed composi-tion and one of the most renowned works in English sacred music, was performed for the first time at this site (in today's Temple Bar) on 13 April 1742, an event commemorated with a special gala-style performance each April.

Liffey Swim (☎ 833 2434) Since 1924, at summer's end (late August/early September), hundreds of swimmers – or lunatics, as they're colloquially known – traditionally dive into the Sniffy Liffey for a swim through 2km of mud and murk in the centre of Dublin, from Rory O'More Bridge to the Custom House. There are separate handicap races for men and women and it's fun to line the bank and watch the competitors trying not to swallow a drop. You can see it depicted in Jack B Yeats' famous *Liffey Swim* painting in the National Gallery (p82).

make up the menu of the city's film festi-val, which runs over the last two weeks in February (see the boxed text, p192).

SIX NATIONS RUGBY
☎ 647 3800; www.irishrugby.ie
Ireland, winners of the 2009 Grand Slam, play their three home matches at the brand new Aviva Stadium in the southern suburb of Ballsbridge. The season runs from Febru-ary to April; see p207 for more.

March
ST PATRICK'S FESTIVAL
☎ 676 3205; www.stpatricksfestival.ie
The mother of all Irish festivals. Hundreds of thousands gather to 'honour' St Patrick on city streets and in venues throughout the centre over four days around 17 March. Events include the three-day Guinness Fleadh music festival in Temple Bar.

May
INTERNATIONAL DUBLIN GAY THEATRE FESTIVAL
www.gaytheatre.ie
A fortnight at the beginning of May de-voted exclusively to gay theatre – plays by

gay writers past and present that have a gay or gay-related theme.

June
CONVERGENCE FESTIVAL
☎ 674 5773; www.cultivate.ie; 15-19 Essex St
A five-day festival on sustainable living that takes place at the end of the month, with a diverse program of workshops, exhibitions and children's activities in Temple Bar.

DIVERSIONS
☎ 677 2255; www.templebar.ie
Free outdoor music, and children's and film events occur during weekends from June to September in Meeting House Sq.

DUBLIN WRITERS FESTIVAL
www.dublinwritersfestival.com
Four-day literature festival in mid-June at-tracting Irish and international writers to its readings, performances and talks.

WOMEN'S MINI-MARATHON
☎ 670 9461; www.womensminimarathon.ie
A 10km charity run on the second Sunday of the month that attracts up to 40,000 participants (including some poorly dis-guised men).

MARDI GRAS

☎ 873 4932; www.dublinpride.org

Dublin's Gay Pride event has turned into a weeklong festival of parties, workshops, readings and more parties at gay venues around town, although these are just to warm up for the parade that takes place – and takes over – on the last Saturday of the month.

July

OXEGEN

☎ 0818 719 300; www.oxegen.ie; Punchestown Racecourse, County Kildare

Music festival over the July weekend closest to the 12th; manages to pack a few dozen heavyweight acts into its four-day line-up. Strictly for the young or the young-at-heart.

August

DUBLIN HORSE SHOW

☎ 668 0866; www.dublinhorseshow.com

The first week of August is when Ireland's horsey set trot down to the Royal Dublin Society (RDS) for the social highlight of the year. Particularly popular is the Aga Khan Cup, an international-class competition packed with often heart-stopping excitement in which eight nations participate.

DUN LAOGHAIRE FESTIVAL OF WORLD CULTURES

☎ 230 1035; www.festivalofworldcultures.com

A colourful multicultural music, art and theatre festival featuring up to 200 different acts is held on the last weekend of August in the southern suburb of Dun Laoghaire.

September

ELECTRIC PICNIC

www.electricpicnic.com

Our favourite festival of all is in the grounds of Stradbally Castle, County Laois, about 80km southwest of Dublin; this three-day experience at the beginning of September combines top-class acts with organic food and a mind-body-soul area. Let your good vibes flow.

DUBLIN FRINGE FESTIVAL

☎ 1850 374 643; www.fringefest.com

This excellent theatre showcase precedes the main theatre festival with 700 performers and 100 events – ranging from cutting

edge to crap – and takes place over three weeks. It's held in the Famous Spiegeltent, which has been erected in different positions in recent years; for more, see the boxed text, p198.

BULMERS COMEDY FESTIVAL

☎ 679 3323; www.bulmerscomedy.ie

Big laughs over three weeks from an ever-widening choice of comic talents, both known and unknown. It takes place at more than 20 venues throughout the city.

October

DUBLIN THEATRE FESTIVAL

☎ 677 8439; www.dublintheatrefestival.com

This two-week festival at the beginning of the month is Europe's oldest and showcases the best of Irish and international productions at various locations around town.

DUBLIN CITY MARATHON

☎ 677 8439; dublinmarathon.ie

If you fancy a 42km (and a bit) running tour through the streets of the city on the last Monday of October, you'll have to register at least three weeks in advance. Otherwise, you can have a lie-in and watch the winner cross the finishing line on O'Connell St at around 10.30am.

DUBLIN ELECTRONIC ARTS FESTIVAL

DEAF; ☎ 872 8933; www.deafireland.com

A must for anyone into the cutting edge of music, DEAF showcases the work of some truly innovative musical – and visual – talents, both home-grown and international. From moog to movies, this is the future, now. Venues vary; check the website for details.

HARD WORKING CLASS HEROES

☎ 878 2244; www.hwch.net

The only showcase in town for unsigned Irish acts, this three-day music festival features 100 bands and musicians playing at venues on and around Camden St on the south side of the city.

SAMHAIN/HALLOWE'EN

Tens of thousands take to the city streets on 31 October for a night-time parade, fireworks, street theatre, drinking and music in this traditional pagan festival celebrating the dead, end of the harvest and Celtic new year.

November

FRENCH FILM FESTIVAL
www.irishfilm.ie
Organised by the French embassy and sponsored by Carte Noir, it showcases the best of French releases for the year.

JUNIOR DUBLIN FILM FESTIVAL
www.irishfilm.ie
A weeklong showcase of the best efforts of the world's young filmmakers, the Irish Film Institute screens an exclusive selection of movies from all over.

December

LEOPARDSTOWN RACES
☎ 289 3607; www.leopardstown.com
Blow your dough and your post-Christmas crankiness at this historic and hugely popular racing festival at one of Europe's loveliest courses. Races run from 26 to 30 December.

FUNDERLAND
Royal Dublin Society (RDS); ☎ 668 0866; www.rds.ie
Dublin's traditional funfair (from 26 December to 9 January) features all kinds of stomach-turning rides and arcade games, as well as hundreds of thousands of light bulbs and millions of reasons why the kids needn't be cooped up indoors.

COSTS & MONEY

The decline of rental costs and the price of food, coupled with the fall in value of the euro against the US dollar, means that Dublin is no longer the prohibitively expensive city it was even a couple of years ago. According to Mercer (the folks who do those cost-of-living indices), Dublin fell from 16th to 25th on the World's Most Expensive Cities list…in less than six months. It now ranks comfortably behind Paris, London and Rome on the list topped by Tokyo.

Accommodation will be your biggest expense, but the fall in prices has been most dramatic in the cost of a hotel room. A room in the city's best hotels can be had for around €200 and a bunk in a hostel dorm will go for as little as €13. In between is a broad range – from an adequate-if-anodyne room in a bog-standard business chain to a beautifully appointed room in a Georgian townhouse,

both of which can be yours for the night for between €80 and €100. If you're willing to endure a little bit of taxi trauma or the tolerance test of public transport, hotels on the north side of the city or in the salubrious suburbs south of the Grand Canal will give you far more bang for your buck. See the Sleeping chapter (p210) for more details.

A major bugbear with value-conscious Dubliners has long been restaurant prices, but even there things have improved, with many restaurants cutting the average price of their main courses by 30% in an effort to stay busy: these days, you can eat pretty well for less than €25. If you're looking to spend no more than €10 on lunch, you'd better like sandwiches. Lunch and early-bird specials – those three-course things that inevitably only ever include the menu's less inviting choices – are ubiquitous and a good way to save a few euro.

So, between a place to crash and daily sustenance, you should factor in anything between €50 (at the truly budget end of the scale) and, well, the sky's limit (OK, let's say €250) daily. Anything less than that and you're performing miracles; anything more and we want *you* to take *us* on holiday.

But Dublin is about a hell of a lot more than sleeping and eating – let's not forget the all-important nights out. The price of a pint hovers around the €5 mark (up to €5.50 in Temple Bar), so you can calculate how drunk you can actually afford to get from there. And if you're really popular, there's the round system to contend with – whereby you take turns buying a round of drinks for the group. But that roughly works out even in the end, unless of course you're only in for

HOW MUCH?
Admission to a big-name club on a Friday €15
CD €14.99
City-centre bus ticket up to €2
Cup of coffee €3
Irish Times €1.80
Petrol per litre €1.34
Pint of Guinness Temple Bar/city/suburbs €5.50/€4.80/€4
Theatre ticket €13-25
Three-course meal with wine/beer from €35
Ticket to a Gaelic match €25-45

one or two and your 10 new friends are all looking thirsty.

If you want to give your wallet a rest, you can also have a great time in Dublin without your plastic going into meltdown. Parks are all free, as are the National Gallery (p82), National Museum of Ireland (Archaeology; p80), National Museum of Ireland (Natural History; p83), Dublin City Gallery – The Hugh Lane (p104) and pretty much all of the city's other gallery spaces – not to mention our favourite collection of all: the Chester Beatty Library (p72). Cinemas all have an early-bird price for shows up to 2pm of about €6, while there's absolutely no charge for strolling along the beach in Killiney (p230), climbing Howth Head (p227) or enjoying the entertainment on Grafton St!

INTERNET RESOURCES

BalconyTV (www.balconytv.com) Interviews and music from a balcony in central Dublin.

Beaut.ie (www.beaut.ie) A superb blog ostensibly about beauty tips but really a great commentary on the Irish and their wants.

Daft.ie (www.daft.ie) If you're looking to rent in Dublin, this is the place to look.

Discover Ireland (www.discoverireland.ie) Official website of Discover Ireland, the public face of the Irish Tourist Board.

Dublin City Council (www.dublincity.ie) Dublin Corporation's own website has a great link to live traffic cams.

Dublin Tourism (www.visitdublin.com) Official website of Dublin Tourism.

Entertainment.ie (www.entertainment.ie) One-stop shop for reviews and all kinds of listings, from comedy to films.

Nialler9 (www.nialler9.com) Best website and blog for music in the city, with reviews and listings.

Nixers.com (www.nixers.ie) A good place to check if you're looking for casual work over summer.

Overheard in Dublin (www.overheardindublin.com) Proof that the general public are better than any scriptwriter.

State Magazine (www.state.ie) Music news, reviews and gig listings.

Totally Dublin (www.totallydublin.ie) Music news, reviews and gig listings for the capital.

SUSTAINABLE DUBLIN

Dublin ain't that green, but it's trying. Its saving grace, at least in terms of reducing its carbon footprint, has been the global downturn, which has seen production drop across a range of industries.

For most Dubliners, however, carbon credits are less of a factor than financial credit, especially of the huge mortgage and massive debt kind. The bottom may have fallen out of the automobile market (new car sales fell 60% from 2008 to 2010), but they're more concerned with repayments on the one they have rather than congratulating themselves on reducing the total number of cars on the road.

What will get a Dubliner going, though, is the queue, which has done more than any Al Gore movie to remind Dubliners that life needs to get a little more sustainable. Fewer cars on the road also means reduced traffic jams; fewer foreign holidays means shorter lines at the airport when you do get the chance to travel – in short, when eco-responsibility is presented as restoring a sense of sanity, most Dubs react positively.

This is largely how they reacted in 2004 when the government passed a total smoking ban in the workplace – which also meant the pub, the restaurant and anywhere else they gather to socialise. They also responded well to the introduction of a 15c levy on plastic bags, which was raised to 22c in 2007 and resulted in a 90% reduction in use – in 2010 there was talk of doubling the tax to 44c, however, it that's probably a step too far for most people.

The best resource in town is Cultivate (☎ 674 5773; www.cultivate.ie; The Greenhouse, St Andrew's St), Ireland's only sustainability focused living and learning centre. It has an eco-shop and lots of information stands, and hosts workshops and classes on everything from composting to green building.

ECOCABS

A clean and green solution to public transport in the city centre is to take an Ecocab (Map p70; www.ecocabs.ie; ⏰ 10am-7pm Mar-Dec), basically modern-looking rickshaws. They can carry up to two passengers and are free of charge for short distances within the city centre – although a gratuity for your hard-pedalling driver is always appreciated. Pick one up at the top of Grafton St, by the St Stephen's Green Shopping Centre.

FLY LESS

The grounding of Irish (and European) flights throughout 2010 as a result of the Icelandic ash cloud forced locals and visitors alike to re-examine their over-dependence on airline travel, particularly for an island nation. The obvious solution is to rediscover the boat: there are numerous boat services to Dublin from Britain and often some return fares don't cost that much more than one-way tickets, not to mention the plethora of special offers designed to challenge the cheap flight hegemony. Boats arrive in Dublin Port or Dun Laoghaire; for details, see p242.

STAY LONGER

An extended visit to Dublin – as opposed to the rush-in, rush-out limitations of city-break travel – is preferable because it allows for 'slow travel', the kind of exploratory travel that allows you to take your time and get to know a place without needing to rush. And it's the only way to get to know Dubliners properly!

OFFSETTING

Paying someone else to offset your greenhouse gas emissions isn't exactly the perfect solution to the major issue of global warming, but it is a step in the right direction. The most popular offsetting program involves tree-planting, but there are other schemes such as methane collection and combustion. The Carbon Shop (www.carbonshop.ie) can help you calculate your emissions and work out how to offset them.

HISTORY

More than just about any other city we know, Dublin wears its history on its sleeve. Dubliners themselves are highly passionate scholars of their own history – and we mean their *own* history. Perhaps because it continues to have such a strong bearing on modern life, it's near impossible for any two Irish people to agree on the details of any one historical episode.

However, they'll instantly unite against an outsider's version, and there are great contradictions between Irish and English historical accounts of events that took place here. Take Oliver Cromwell for example. An Irish text would describe him as an English parliamentarian who raped, pillaged and plundered his way through Ireland – a complete and utter bastard. If you picked up an English history book on the other hand you might learn that Cromwell defeated the Royalists in the English Civil War and apparently used to holiday in Ireland.

On your travels, you will surely hear different spins on the same subjects, and bear in mind that *everybody* has a bias – some are just cleverer at hiding it than others. See if you can spot ours.

THE RECENT PAST

The public at large only got wind of it in October 2008, just after the collapse of Lehman Brothers and the onset of the global financial crisis. But within a matter of days it was all Dubliners could talk about: the dramatic bursting of the property bubble that had kept the economy artificially afloat and Dubliners living the high life for the last five years. A city that had become so comfortable with conspicuous consumption suddenly had to adjust to a new reality, and many Dubliners who had bought houses during the boom were now sitting in a ticking time bomb of negative equity. Needless to say, the city is mightily pissed off at politicians, bankers and other commentators who encouraged them to borrow, spend and fritter because, hey, that's what'll make the economy grow! Want to watch a Dubliner lose their temper? Ask them about bankers and the government.

The future remains uncertain. 'Looking for the green shoots of recovery' was the hackneyed catchphrase of 2010, as Dublin looked to economic forces they can't predict or readily understand to restore a semblance of comfort to a city that got pretty used to easy street over the last decade. In the meantime, the 'brain drain' that was such a feature of life in the city before the boom has once again began bleeding Dublin of some of its brightest young minds – experts have predicted that 100,000 young people will have emigrated in 2010–11, the majority of them from or around Dublin.

But Dubliners are guardedly optimistic, especially those of a certain vintage, who recognise that everything happens in cycles. They can't take as many holidays, or explore the menus of as many restaurants, and that '06 car will have to do for another few years more, but so long as they have a job to go to and interest rates don't make their mortgage prohibitively expensive, they've something to get up for in the morning and blow off steam about in the pub of a weekend evening.

10,000–8000 BC	AD 431–432	917
Human beings arrive in Ireland during the mesolithic era, originally crossing a land bridge between Scotland and Ireland and later the sea in hide-covered boats.	Pope Celestine I sends Bishop Palladius to Ireland to minister to those 'already believing in Christ'; St Patrick arrives the following year to continue the mission.	Plundering Vikings take a break from attacking monasteries, raping and pillaging to establish a new settlement at the mouth of the harbour and call it 'Dyfflin', which soon becomes a centre of economic power. They begin making alliances with some Irish kings.

FROM THE BEGINNING
Early Footprints & Celtic Highways

Stone Age farmers who arrived in Ireland between 10,000 and 8000 BC provided the country's genetic stock and lay the foundations of its agricultural economy. During the following Bronze

FROM BOOM TO BUST

In a few short months between 2008–09, Gross National Product (GNP) fell by 17%, the swiftest and deepest contraction by a Western economy since the Great Depression. The collapse was both shocking and traumatic: yes, the global economic crisis was the catalyst, but Ireland was especially susceptible to the downturn because for the previous five years, its economy got high on the fumes of a boom that was, in essence, little more than hot air.

The bubble was created by a construction boom, which saw investment in housing as a percentage of GNP rise from around 6% in 1996 to almost 15% in 2006 as the Irish got into the business of selling houses to one another. This was a practice made easy by the banks, who were lending money to literally anybody that wanted it because they were availing of the vast amounts of cheap credit generated by the out-of-control derivatives market. The problem was an international one, but while other Western economies also saw a rapid rise in bank lending, Irish lending was twice the Western average – almost 200% of GDP, with a massive chunk of that to dangerously over-exposed property developers. These were staggering numbers, everyone agreed, but they were also unsustainable, but it seemed *nobody* wanted to hear that.

The Irish property market got its first major warning in 2007, when demand for residential housing finally began to recede in the face of high prices and over-saturation, but it wasn't until the end of 2008 – after Lehmann Brothers and the other giants of finance went to the wall – that the credit lines shrivelled up and the banks' massive exposure to the developers threw the whole economy into turmoil.

A bank bailout in October 2008 stopped the banking system from collapsing; the government's solution to this economic tsunami has been to create the National Asset Management Authority (NAMA), basically a government-owned 'bad bank'. NAMA has bought all of the nonperforming property loans held by the six main Irish banks at a discount of 47% on the original book value of the loans. The aim is that by assuming all of this bad debt, it will free up the banks' own loan books and allow them to start lending again and thus stimulate the stagnant economy. Once the economy is back in business, NAMA will then collect on the loans from the original debtors at market value, which supporters argue will be roughly what it was when the loans were taken out in the first place.

Critics of NAMA – and there have been many – argue that property values will never reach the inflated values of the early part of the millennium, thereby leaving NAMA – and by extension, the taxpayer – with the burden of these toxic loans and a repayment schedule that will take generations to pay off. Most of these bad loans were held by Anglo-Irish Bank, an institution that dealt almost exclusively with property developers; Anglo and its former CEO, Sean Fitzpatrick, have become the personification of all that is wrong with the Irish economy, and are easy hate figures for a frustrated city that, for the most part, doesn't understand the ins and outs of NAMA but are painfully aware that in the end it'll cost them money they can ill-afford. In 2010, NAMA and all its convoluted theories was the main topic of debate among Dubliners, so it pays to inform yourself of at least the basics!

What of the future? It's impossible to get economists to agree, but very few are overly optimistic, at least for the foreseeable future. Still, in mid-2010, the Economic and Social Research Institute (ESRI) in Dublin predicted that there would be a 2.8% rise in GDP in 2011 (following a drop of 0.5% in 2010) and unemployment numbers, which had topped 15% in 2010 (during the boom it was 3.5%), wouldn't increase so propitiously. It is undeniable that Ireland is in an economic mess. The Nobel Prize–winning economist Paul Krugman reckons that it'll take the country up to 10 years to get out of this economic hole. The Celtic Tiger is truly dead: what now, pussycat?

988	1169	1170
High King Mael Seachlainn II leads the initial Irish conquest of Dyfflin, giving the settlement its modern name in Irish – Baile Átha Cliath, meaning 'Town at the Hurdle Ford'.	Henry II's Welsh and Norman barons quickly capture Waterford and Wexford with the help of Dermot MacMurrough (King of Leinster). Although no one knew it at the time, this was the beginning of an 750-year occupation of Ireland by Britain.	Strongbow captures Dublin and then takes Aoife, MacMurrough's daughter, as his wife before being crowned King of Leinster. The marriage is the subject of a famous painting by Daniel Maclise that can be viewed in the National Gallery (p82).

Age, in addition to discovering and crafting metals to stock the future National Museum, they also found time to refine their farming techniques and raise livestock.

Iron Age warriors from Eastern Europe, who were known as the Celts, arrived in the country around 500 BC and divided Ireland into provinces and myriad districts ruled by chieftains. Their society was ruled by Brehon Law, the tenets of which still form the basis of Ireland's ethical code today. Roads connecting these provinces converged at a ford over the River Liffey called Átha Cliath (Ford of the Hurdles) and the settlement that grew up at this junction during the 9th century was to give Dublin its Irish name, Baile Átha Cliath (Town of the Hurdle Ford).

The Coming of Christianity

St Patrick founded the See of Dublin sometime in the mid-5th century and went about the business of conversion in present-day Wicklow and Malahide, before laying hands on Leoghaire, the King of Ireland, using water from a well next to St Patrick's Cathedral. Or so the story goes. Irrespective of the details, Patrick and his monk buddies were successful because they managed to fuse the strong tradition of druidism and pagan ritual with the new Christian teaching, which created an exciting hybrid known as Celtic, or Insular, Christianity.

Compared to new hot spots like Clonmacnois in County Offaly and Glendalough in County Wicklow, Dublin was a rural backwater and didn't really figure in the Golden Age, when Irish Christian scholars excelled in the study of Latin and Greek learning and Christian theology. They studied in the monasteries that were, in essence, Europe's most important universities, producing brilliant students, magnificent illuminated books such as the *Book of Kells* (now housed in Trinity College, p66) ornate jewellery and the many carved stone crosses that dot the island 'of saints and scholars'.

The nature of Christianity in Ireland was one of marked independence from Rome, especially in the areas of monastic rule and penitential practice, which emphasised private confession to a priest followed by penances levied by the priest in reparation – which is the spirit and letter of the practice of confession that exists to this day. The Irish were also exporting these teachings abroad, setting up monasteries across Europe, such as the ones in Luxeuil in France and Bobbio in Italy, both founded by St Columbanus (AD 543–615).

The Vikings

Raids by marauding Vikings had been a fact of Irish life for quite some time, before a group of them decided to take some R & R from their hell-raising and build a harbour (or *longphort*, in Irish) on the banks of the Liffey in 837. Although a Celtic army forced them out some 65 years later, they returned in 917 with a massive fleet, established a stronghold (or *dun*) by the black pool at Wood Quay (Map p91), just behind Christ Church Cathedral, and dug their heels in. They went back to plundering the countryside but also laid down guidelines on plot sizes and town boundaries for their town of 'Dyflinn', which became the most prominent trading centre in the Viking world. But their good times came to an end in 1014 when an alliance of Irish clans, which were led by Brian Ború, decisively whipped them at the Battle of Clontarf, forever breaking the Scandinavian grip on the eastern seaboard. However, rather than abandoning the place in defeat, the Vikings enjoyed Dublin so much that they decided to stay there and integrate.

1172	1350–1530	1534
King Henry II of England invades Ireland, using the 1155 Bull Laudabiliter issued to him by Pope Adrian IV to claim sovereignty over the island, and forces the Cambro-Norman warlords and some of the Gaelic Irish kings to accept him as their overlord.	The Anglo-Norman barons establish power bases independent of the English crown. Over the following two centuries, English control gradually extends to an area around Dublin known as 'the Pale'.	'Silken' Thomas Fitzgerald, son of the reigning Earl of Kildare, storms Dublin and its English garrisons. The rebellion is squashed, and Thomas and his followers are subsequently executed.

Strongbow & The Normans

When the Anglo-Normans arrived in 1169, led by Richard de Clare (better known as Strongbow), they were so taken with the place that they decided to stay. They took Dublin the following year, and essentially kept it for the following 750 years. Strongbow inherited the kingship of the province of Leinster – of which modern Dublin is capital – and made himself at home. The English king, Henry II, soon sent his own army over to keep an eye on Strongbow and his consorts who, he reckoned, were becoming 'more Irish than the Irish themselves'.

The Anglo-Normans set about reconstructing and fortifying the captured city. In 1172 construction began on Christ Church Cathedral (p96), and 20 years later work began on St Patrick's Cathedral (p93), a few hundred metres to the south. Dublin soon became a pilgrimage city, particularly because it housed the *bacall Íosa* (staff of Jesus; St Patrick's legendary crozier reputedly given to him on a Mediterranean island on his way from Rome to Ireland).

Henry II's son, King John, commissioned the construction of Dublin Castle (p76) in 1204 '…for the safe custody of our treasure…and the defence of the city'. As capital of the English 'colony' in Ireland, Dublin expanded. Trade was organised and craft guilds developed, although membership was limited to those of 'English name and blood'.

For all their might, the Anglo-Normans' dominance was limited to a walled area surrounding what today is loosely Greater Dublin, and was then called 'the Pale'. Beyond the Pale – a phrase that entered the English language to mean 'beyond convention' – Ireland remained unbowed and unconquered.

As Dublin grew bigger so did its problems, and over the next few centuries misery seemed to pile upon mishap. In 1317 Ireland's worst famine of the Middle Ages killed off thousands and reduced some to cannibalism. In 1348 the country was decimated by the Black Death, the devastating recurrence of which over the following century indicates the terrible squalor of medieval Dublin.

In the 15th century, the English extended their influence beyond the Pale by cleverly throwing their weight behind the dominant Irish lords. The atmosphere was becoming markedly cosier as the Anglo-Norman occupiers began to follow previous invaders by integrating into Irish culture. For more on Viking and medieval Dublin see Dvblinia (p97).

The Tudors & the Protestant Ascendancy

Irish actor Jonathan Rhys Meyers might be TV's most popular Henry VIII, but the real King Hank (1491–1547) was not especially fond of the Irish. When he ascended to the throne in 1509 he decreed absolute royal power over Ireland, thereby tethering the unfettered power of the lords. When in 1534 the most powerful of Leinster's Anglo-Normans, 'Silken' Thomas Fitzgerald, renounced his allegiance to the king, Henry came at him ferociously: within a year Fitzgerald was dead and all his lands confiscated. Henry ordered the surrender of all lands to the English Crown and, three years later, after his spat with Rome, he dissolved all the monasteries and all Church lands passed to the newly constituted Anglican Church. Dublin was declared an Anglican City and relics such as the *bacall Íosa* were destroyed.

Elizabeth I (1533–1603) took over the throne in 1558 and took the same conquering attitude to the Irish as her father. The Crown met with most resistance from the province of Ulster, which became the last outpost of the Irish chiefs. The Irish fought doggedly under the lead of Hugh O'Neill, the Earl of Tyrone, but were defeated in 1603. O'Neill achieved a Pyrrhic victory

1592	1640s–1682	1680
Trinity College is founded on the grounds of a former monastery just outside the city walls, on the basis of a charter granted by Elizabeth I to 'stop Ireland being infected by popery'.	Dublin's resurgence begins as the city's population grows from 10,000 in the mid-1640s to nearly 60,000 in 1682.	The architectural style known as Anglo-Dutch results in the construction of notable buildings such as the Royal Hospital, Kilmainham (p98), now the Irish Museum of Modern Art.

of sorts, refusing to surrender until Elizabeth had died. The chiefs fled the country in what came to be known as the Flight of the Earls. This defeat sounded the death knell for Gaelic Ireland and the country was set for total Anglicisation.

After Elizabeth's reign, the country was colonised through plantation. Loyal Protestants from England and Scotland were awarded the rich agricultural, confiscated lands of Ulster, which sowed the seeds of the bitter divisions that blight the province to this day. Unlike previous invaders, the Tudors never integrated.

Although most of the Irish were now disenfranchised and reduced to a state of near misery, Dublin prospered as the bulwark of English domination and became a bastion of Protestantism. A chasm developed between the 'English' city and the 'Irish' countryside, where there was continuing unrest and growing resentment. After winning the English Civil War, the battle-happy Oliver Cromwell came to Ireland to personally reassert English control and, while Protestant Dublin was left untouched (save the use of St Patrick's Cathedral as a stable for English horses), his troops behaved mercilessly up and down the eastern coast.

Georgian Dublin & The Golden Age

Following the Restoration of 1660 and the coronation of Charles II (1630–85), Dublin embarked upon a century of unparalleled development and essentially waved two fingers at the rest of Ireland, which was being brought to its grubby Catholic knees. In 1690 the rest of Ireland backed the losing side once more when it took up arms for the Catholic king of England, James II (1633–1701), who was ultimately defeated by the Protestant William of Orange at the Battle of the Boyne, not far from Dublin, in 1690.

William's victory ushered in the punitive Penal Code, which stripped Catholics of most basic rights in a single, sweeping legislative blow. Again, however, the country's misfortune proved the capital's gain as the city was flooded with landless refugees willing to work for a pittance. The end of the century also saw an influx of Huguenot weavers, who settled in Dublin after fleeing anti-Protestant legislation in France and established a successful cloth industry that helped fuel the city's growth.

With plenty of cash to go around and an eagerness to live in a city that reflected their new-found wealth, the Protestant nobility overhauled Dublin during the reigns of the four Georges (1714–1830). Speculators bought up swathes of land and commissioned substantial projects of urban renewal, including the creation of new streets, the laying out of city parks and the construction of magnificent new buildings and residences (see p49).

It was impossible to build in the heart of the medieval city, so the nouveau riche moved north across the river, creating a new Dublin of stately squares surrounded by fine Georgian mansions. The elegantly made-over Dublin became the second city in the British Empire and the fifth largest in Europe.

Dublin's teeming, mostly Catholic, slums soon spread north in pursuit of the rich, who turned back south to grand new homes around Merrion Sq, St Stephen's Green and Fitzwilliam Sq. In 1745, when James Fitzgerald, the Earl of Kildare, started construction of Leinster House, his magnificent mansion south of the Liffey, he was mocked for his foolish move into the wilds. 'Where I go society will follow', he confidently predicted, and he was soon proved right; today Leinster House is used as the seat of Irish parliament and is in modern Dublin's centre.

1695	1757	1759
Penal laws – aka the 'popery code' – prohibit Catholics from owning a horse (a military tactic), marrying outside their religion and, most importantly, from buying or inheriting property; within 100 years Catholics will own only 5% of Irish land.	The Wide Street Commission is set up to design new civic spaces and the framework of a modern city: new parks are laid out, streets widened and new public buildings commissioned, rendering Dublin a magnificent example of Georgian town planning.	Arthur Guinness buys a disused brewery on a plot of land opposite St James's Gate, once part of the city's western defences. Initially he brews only ale, but in the 1770s turns his expertise to a new beer called porter.

Dublin Declines, Catholicism Rises

Constant migration from the countryside into Dublin meant that, by the end of the 18th century, the capital had a Catholic majority. Influenced by the principles of the 1789 French Revolution, many influential Irish figures began to instigate revolt against English rule. Rebellion was in the air at the turn of the century, starting with the abortive French invasion encouraged and led by Dubliner Wolfe Tone and the United Irishmen in 1798, and the idealistic insurgence led by Robert Emmet (1778–1803) in 1803.

It was only a matter of time before Dublin's bubble burst, and the pin came in the form of the 1801 Act of Union, which dissolved the Irish parliament and reintroduced direct rule from Westminster. Many of the upper classes fled to London, the dramatic growth that had characterised Dublin in the previous century came to an almost immediate halt, and the city fell into a steady decline.

While Dublin was licking its wounds, a Kerry lawyer by the name of Daniel O'Connell (1775–1847) launched his campaign to recover basic rights for Catholics, achieving much with the Catholic Emancipation Act of 1829. The 'Liberator', as he came to be known, became the first Catholic lord mayor of Dublin in 1841.

Ireland Starves

Rural Ireland had become overwhelmingly dependent on the easily grown potato. When it was hit by potato blight in 1845, it was the beginning of the country's greatest disaster. The crops failed dismally for the next three years; 1847, the third consecutive year, was apocalyptic and has been remembered through the ages as 'Black 47'. The human cost was cataclysmic: up to one million people died from disease and starvation, while more again fled the country, preferring to take their chances on 'coffin ships' riddled with disease than remain in their God-forsaken homeland. The damage was compounded by the laissez-faire attitude of the British government and the landlords who continued to extract money and export food *out* of the country, while incarcerating the poor in workhouses and prisons for defaulting on their rents.

As Britain continued to rule with an iron fist, opposition to its rule hardened. The famine, the deaths and the mass exodus changed the social and cultural structure of Ireland profoundly and left a scar on the Irish psyche that cannot be overestimated.

Although Dublin escaped the worst effects of the famine, its streets and squares became overcrowded with desperate migrants. Wealthier citizens began moving southwards to the more salubrious suburbs along the coast, made accessible by Ireland's first railway line, which was built in 1834 to connect the city and Kingstown (present-day Dun Laoghaire). The flight from the city continued for the next 70 years and many of the fine Georgian residences became slum dwellings. By 1910 it was reckoned that 20,000 Dublin families each occupied a single room. Booze had long been a source of solace for Dubliners but alcohol abuse became a huge social problem.

The Blossoming of National Pride

Early-20th-century Dublin was staunchly divided along sectarian lines and, although Catholics were still partly second-class citizens, a burgeoning Catholic middle class provided the impetus for Ireland's march towards independence.

1801	1845–51	1905
The Act of Union unites Ireland politically with Britain. The Irish Parliament votes itself out of existence following an intensive campaign of bribery. Dublin's role as 'second city of the Empire' comes to a swift end.	A mould called phytophthora ravages the potato harvest. The Great Famine is the single greatest catastrophe in Irish history, with the deaths of up to one million people, and the emigration of up to two million others.	Journalist Arthur Griffiths founds a new movement whose aim is independence under a dual monarchy, similar to that of the Austro-Hungarian empire. Making a case for national self-reliance, he names the movement Sinn Féin, meaning 'ourselves alone'.

It was the dashing figure of Protestant landlord Charles Stewart Parnell (1846–91), from County Wicklow, that first harnessed the broad public support for Home Rule. Elected to Westminster in 1875, the 'Uncrowned King of Ireland' campaigned tirelessly for land reform and a Dublin parliament.

He appeared to have an ally in the British prime minister, William Gladstone, who lightened the burden on tenants by passing Land Acts enabling them to buy property. He also agreed on Ireland's need for some form of self-government, although British opposition was galvanised following the 1882 murder of two high-ranking English officials in Phoenix Park by an obscure revolutionary group called the 'Invincibles'. Gladstone tried to pass the Home Rule bill three times between 1886 and 1895 but it was defeated in the House of Lords each time (after which the Lords' ability to kill a bill was limited to three times).

Parnell himself suffered a swift fall from grace after it was made public that he had been having an affair with a married woman, Kitty O'Shea. Castigated by the Church and the morally indignant, he was ditched as leader of his own Irish Parliamentary Party. He fought unstintingly to regain his reputation but died of pneumonia within two years of the scandal. Dublin seemed to forgive him and turned out in droves for his funeral at Glasnevin Cemetery.

In the twilight of the 19th century there was a move to preserve all things Irish. The Gaelic Athletic Association (GAA) was set up in 1884 to promote Irish sports while Douglas Hyde and Eoin McNeill formed the Gaelic League in 1893 to encourage Irish arts and language. The success of the Gaelic League paved the way for the Celtic Revival Movement, spearheaded by WB Yeats and Lady Gregory, who founded the Abbey Theatre in 1904.

The Struggle for Independence

Irish culture was thriving at the start of the 20th century but the country was still in Westminster's headlock, and peaceful efforts to free itself from British rule were thwarted at every juncture. Dublin had the worst slums in Europe, and the emergence of militant trade unionism introduced a socialist agenda to the struggle for self-determination.

In 1905 Arthur Griffith (1871–1922) founded a new political movement called Sinn Féin ('Ourselves Alone'), which sought to achieve Home Rule through passive resistance rather than political lobbying. It urged the Irish to withhold taxes and its MPs to form an Irish government in Dublin.

Meanwhile, trade union leaders Jim Larkin and James Connolly agitated against low wages and corporate greed. This culminated in the Great Lockout of 1913, which was marked by state-sponsored violence and the establishment of the Irish Citizen Army (ICA) by Connolly to defend the striking workers. Things were heating up in Dublin.

In 1914 Westminster passed a Home Rule bill, but suspended its implementation for the duration of WWI. Bowing to pressure from the Protestant-dominated north where 140,000 members of the newly formed Ulster Volunteer Force (UVF) swore to resist any efforts to weaken British rule, the bill made provisions for the partition of Ireland. In response, nationalists in the south established the Irish Volunteer Force (IVF) but when WWI broke out, the majority of them enlisted in the British Army thinking they would return to an independent Ireland.

Some 180,000 Irish volunteers fought, including many committed nationalists who thought they would help Ireland in the long run by aiding Britain now. By the end of the Great War, almost 50,000 Irish citizens had died.

1916	1919–21	1921–22
The Easter Rising: dedicated Republicans take the GPO in Dublin and announce the formation of an Irish Republic. After less than a week of fighting, the rebels surrender to the superior British forces and are summarily executed.	The Irish War of Independence begins in January 1919. Two years (and 1400 casualties) later, the war ends in a truce on 11 July 1921, leading to peace talks.	The Anglo-Irish Treaty is signed on 6 December. It gives 26 counties of Ireland independence and six Ulster counties the choice of opting out. The Irish Free State is founded in 1922.

It is doubtful that the leaders of the Rising thought they could achieve anything more than a symbolic victory. One of its ringleaders, the poet and passionate patriot Pádraig Pearse, was convinced of the need for 'blood sacrifice'. During his oration at the funeral of another Irish rebel, O'Donovan Rossa, he said, 'Life springs from death, and from the graves of patriotic men and women spring living nations'. Pearse was a visionary with his head in the clouds, not a military man, and the ragtag brigade that turned up for the Rising couldn't have had much of an idea of what he was banging on about. Each of the signatories of the Proclamation, however, would have known that by putting their name to that document they were virtually condemning themselves to certain death when the insurrection failed.

The 1916 Easter Rising

The more radical factions within Sinn Féin, the IVF and the ICA saw Britain's difficulty as Ireland's opportunity, and planned to rise up against the Crown on Easter Sunday, 1916. In typical fashion, the rhetoric of the rebellion was far superior to the planning.

When the head of the IVF, Eoin McNeill, got wind of the plans, he published an advertisement in the newspaper cancelling the planned 'manoeuvres'. The leaders rescheduled the revolution for the following day but word never spread beyond the capital, where a motley band of about a thousand rebels assembled and seized strategic buildings. The main garrison was the General Post Office (GPO; see p107), outside which the poet and school teacher Pádraig Pearse (see the boxed text, left) read out the Proclamation of the Republic.

The British Army didn't take the insurgence seriously at first but after a few soldiers were killed, they sent a gunboat down the Liffey to rain shells on the rebels. After six days of fighting the city centre was ravaged and the death toll stood at 300 civilians, 130 British troops (many of whom were Irish) and 60 rebels.

The rebels, prompted by Pearse's fear of further civilian casualties, surrendered and were arrested. Crowds gathered to mock and jeer them as they were led away. Initially, Dubliners resented them for the damage they had caused in their futile rising. Then, in a cruel and monumental miscalculation, Britain executed all the leaders at Kilmainham Gaol.

Among those shot was 18-year-old Willie Pearse whose main crime was being the brother of Pádraig. James Connolly, the hero of the working man, was severely injured during the Rising and then detained at the military hospital in Dublin Castle. At dawn on 12 May, he was taken by ambulance to Kilmainham Gaol, carried on a stretcher into the prison yard, strapped into a chair and executed by firing squad. This was too much for Dublin to bear; the British had made a fatal mistake and passive sympathy for the rebels turned to passionate support.

The War of Independence

In the 1918 general election, the radical Sinn Féin won three-quarters of the Irish seats. Its members thumbed their noses to Westminster, declared independence and, in May 1919, established the first Dáil Éireann (Irish Assembly) in Dublin's Mansion House. The assembly was led by Éamon de Valera, who had been spared the firing squad in 1916 because of his US birth (killing him would have been a public-relations disaster). This was effectively a declaration of war.

Mindful that they could never match the British on the battlefield, Sinn Féin's military wing – made up of Irish Volunteers now renamed the Irish Republican Army (IRA) – began attacking

1948	1969	1972
Fine Gael, in coalition with the new Republican Clann na Poblachta, wins the 1948 general election and declares the Free State to be a republic at last. Ireland leaves the British Commonwealth (1949), and the South cut its links to the North.	Marches in Derry by the Northern Ireland Civil Rights Association (NICRA) are disrupted by Loyalist attacks and heavy-handed police action, culminating in the 'Battle of the Bogside' (12–14 August). It marks the beginning of the 'Troubles'.	On Bloody Sunday, 30 January, 13 civilians are killed by British troops in Derry. Westminster suspends the Stormont government and introduces direct rule; a crowd of 20,000 protest outside the British Embassy in Dublin, which is burnt to the ground.

WOMEN OF THE REVOLUTION

The 1916 Proclamation was a radical document for its day, and called for equal rights between men and women (Britain only gave women full suffrage in 1928). Two key reasons for this were Countess Markievicz (1868–1927) and Maud Gonne (1865–1953), two English women who inspired a generation of revolutionaries. A committed Republican and socialist, Countess Markievicz was a military leader of the 1916 Easter Rising and went on to become a minister in the first government. Before independence she'd been the first woman ever elected to the British Parliament, although as a member of Sinn Féin (who didn't recognise British governance in Ireland), she never took her seat. Maud Gonne, also a staunch Republican, is perhaps better known as WB Yeats' gorgeous muse (and desperately unrequited love).

arms dumps and barracks in guerrilla strikes. The British countered by strengthening the Royal Irish Constabulary (RIC) and introducing a brutal, unforgiving auxiliary force made up of returning WWI servicemen known as the Black and Tans (after the colour of their uniforms).

They met their match in Michael Collins, the IRA's commander and a master of guerrilla warfare. Although the British knew his name, Collins masterfully concealed his identity and throughout the war was able to freewheel around the city on his bicycle like he didn't have a care in the world.

On 10 November 1920, Collins learned that 14 undercover British intelligence operatives known as the 'Cairo Gang' had just arrived in Dublin. The following morning, he had his own crack squad ('the Apostles') assassinate each one of them as they lay in their beds.

Furious and unrestrained, the British retaliated that afternoon by opening fire on the crowd at a hurling match at Croke Park. Ten spectators and the captain of the Tipperary hurling team, Michael Hogan, were killed (the main stand at Croke Park is named after Hogan). 'Bloody Sunday', as it became known, served to quash any moral doubts over the often brutal tactics adopted by the IRA.

The fighting was worst in the province of Munster, particularly west Cork and other rural areas, where the legendary 'flying columns' achieved notable success with their hit-and-run tactics. Dublin was comparatively calm although ambushes and street shootings were frequent, and the heavy military presence raised tensions. In May 1921, Irish rebels struck a blow against the British civil service when they burned down the Custom House. Although obviously a military act, tens of thousands of hesitant Dublin taxpayers rejoiced at the burning of the tax records.

The struggle reached a stalemate and, as foreign pressure was brought to bear on British Prime Minister Lloyd George to resolve the issue one way or the other, a truce was signed on 11 July 1921. Unknown to the British government, the IRA had been on the verge of collapse.

Civil War

The terms of – and the circumstances surrounding – the Treaty that ended the War of Independence make up the single most divisive episode in Irish politics, one that still breeds prejudice, inflames passions and shapes the political landscape of the whole island.

De Valera sent a reluctant Michael Collins over to London to head the party, a move that made little sense considering Collins' inexperience and the loss of his most valuable asset, his anonymity. Some believe that de Valera knew that only limited independence was on the table and wanted to disassociate himself from it.

1974	1988	1990s
A series of simultaneous bombings in Monaghan and Dublin on 17 May leave 33 dead and 300 injured, the biggest loss of life in any single day in the history of the Troubles.	Dublin celebrates its millennium, even though the town was established long before 988.	Thanks to low corporate tax, decades of investment in domestic higher education, transfer payments from the EU and a low-cost labour market, the 'Celtic Tiger' booms, transforming Ireland from one of Europe's poorer countries into one of its wealthiest.

After months of argument and facing the threat of, in the words of Lloyd George, an 'immediate and terrible war', Collins and the Irish team signed the Anglo-Irish Treaty on 6 December 1921. Instead of establishing the Irish Republic for which the IRA had fought, it created an Irish Free State, effectively a British dominion, in which members of the newly constituted parliament would have to swear allegiance to the British Crown before they could participate in government. Perhaps even worse than this blow to national pride was the fact that it paved the way for the partitioning of Ireland. Although Collins was dissatisfied with the deal, he hoped it would be the 'first real step' in the journey towards an Irish republic. Nevertheless, he also foresaw trouble and remarked prophetically that 'I've just signed my own death warrant'.

De Valera vehemently opposed the Treaty and the two erstwhile comrades were pitted against one another into pro-Treaty and anti-Treaty camps. Although the Dáil narrowly ratified the Treaty and the electorate accepted it by a large majority, Ireland slid into civil war during June 1922. It began when anti-Treaty IRA forces occupied Dublin's Four Courts (see p108) and were shelled by pro-Treaty forces, led by Collins himself. Ironically, the capital suffered far more during the Civil War than it had during the War of Independence of just a year earlier.

One of the many tragedies of the Civil War was the assassination of Collins by anti-Treaty forces in his home county of Cork on 22 August. Many more deaths followed with the Dáil introduction of a mandatory death sentence for any IRA member caught in possession of a gun. Robert Erskine Childers – whose yacht, the *Asgard,* had brought arms for the Republican cause to Howth in 1914 – was executed for possessing a revolver given to him by Collins. After 11 months and about 3000 deaths (including 77 state executions), de Valera ordered the anti-Treaty IRA to drop their arms.

The Irish Republic

Ireland finally entered a phase of peace. Without an armed struggle to pursue – at least not one pursued by the majority – the IRA became a marginalised force in independent Ireland and Sinn Féin fell apart. In 1926, de Valera created a new party, Fianna Fáil ('Soldiers of Destiny'), which has dominated Irish politics ever since.

Over the following decades, Fianna Fáil gradually eliminated most of the clauses of the Treaty with which it had disagreed (including the oath). In 1932, a freshly painted Dublin hosted the 31st Eucharistic Congress, which drew visitors from around the world. The Catholic Church began to wield disproportionate control over the affairs of the state; contraception was made illegal in the 1930s and the age of consent was raised from 16 to 17.

In 1936, when the IRA refused to disarm, de Valera had it banned. The following year the Civil War–tainted moniker Free State was dropped in favour of Eire as the country's official name in a rewrite of the constitution.

Although Ireland remained neutral during WWII – as a way of pushing its independence – Dublin's North Strand was hit by a 227kg German bomb on 31 May 1941, killing more than 30 and injuring 90.

Despite having done much of the groundwork, Fianna Fáil lost out to its rivals Fine Gael, descendants of the original pro-Treaty Free State government, on declaring the 26 counties a republic in 1949.

2007	2008	2009
On 28 July the IRA issues a statement formally ending its campaign of violence and orders all of its units to dump arms and to assist 'the development of purely political and democratic programs through exclusively peaceful means'.	The global financial crisis triggers the collapse of the Irish banking system and the property boom; Ireland's economy goes into financial freefall as unemployment goes up and investment shrivels to nothing.	The long-awaited publication of the Murphy Report on clerical sex abuse within the Dublin diocese reveals a vast network of secrecy and cover-up of widespread crimes of abuse by serving priests.

top picks

BOOKS ON DUBLIN HISTORY

- A Short History of Dublin (2000) Pat Boran
- Cities of the Imagination: Dublin (2007) Siobhán Kilfeather
- Dublin – A Celebration (2000) Pat Liddy
- Dublin: A Cultural & Literary History (2005) Siobhán Kilfeather
- Encyclopaedia of Dublin (2005) Douglas Bennett

The Stroll to Modernisation

Sean Lemass succeeded de Valera as taoiseach (prime minister) in 1959 and set about fixing the Irish economy, which he did so effectively that the rate of emigration soon halved. While neighbouring London was swinging in the '60s, Dublin was definitely swaying. Youngsters from rural communities poured into the expanding city and it seemed like the good times were never going to end. But, almost inevitably, the economy slid back into recession.

On the 50th anniversary of the 1916 Easter Rising, Nelson's Pillar on O'Connell St was partially blown up by the IRA and crowds cheered as the remainder was removed the following week. Republicanism was still prevalent and a new round of the 'Troubles' were about to flair up in the North. Dublin was hardly touched by the sectarian tensions that would pull Northern Ireland asunder over the next three decades, although 25 people died after three Loyalist car bombs exploded in the city in 1974.

Ireland joined the European Economic Community (EEC), a forerunner to the European Union (EU), in 1973 and got a significant leg-up from the organisation's coffers over the following decades. Pope John Paul II popped over for a few days in 1979 and more than one million people flocked to Phoenix Park to hear him say Mass.

Political instability and an international recession forced the country deeper into the doldrums in the early 1980s and high emigration returned. But arguably the two greatest factors holding Ireland back at this stage were the stranglehold of the ultraconservative Catholic Church and a government that was increasingly seen as corrupt – in 1979 Taoiseach Charles Haughey famously urged the country to 'tighten its belt' in the face of recession, while he himself was taking money from business interests and his party's own coffers to fund his extravagant lifestyle.

The Roar of the Tiger

European aid was to prove instrumental in kick-starting the Irish economy in the early 1990s. Huge sums of money were invested in education and physical infrastructure, while the renewal of Lemass' industrial policy of incentivising foreign investment through tax breaks and the provision of subsidies made Ireland very attractive to high-tech businesses looking for a door into EU markets. In less than a decade Ireland went from being one of the poorest countries in Europe to one of the wealthiest: unemployment fell from 18% to 3.5%, total exports quadrupled, the average industrial wage somersaulted to the top of the European league and GNP rose between 5% to 15% every year from 1991 to 2006. In a 1994 report for finance house Morgan Stanley, analyst Kevin Gardiner coined the term 'Celtic Tiger' to describe this unparalleled level of growth and the name (eventually) stuck, becoming a byword for economic prosperity.

Coupled with Ireland's economic growth was a steady social shift away from the Catholic Church's overwhelmingly conservative influence that had been felt virtually everywhere, not least in the state's schools and hospitals and over every aspect of social policy. From the 1980s onwards, steady campaigning resulted in new laws protecting gay rights, access to contraception and a successful referendum on divorce.

The dramatic decline in the influence of the Church over the last two decades is primarily the result of global trends and greater prosperity in Ireland. But the terrible revelations of widespread abuse of children by parish priests, and the untidy efforts of the Church authorities to sweep the truth under the carpet – including the shuffling of guilty priests from parish to parish – have provoked a seething rage among many Dubliners at the Church's gross insensitivity to the care of their flock. Many older believers feel an acute sense of betrayal that has led them to question a lifetime's devotion to their local parishes. A belated apology on the part of Church authorities has assuaged some, but is considered far too little, far too late by many others.

One group to buck this trend is the largely Catholic Polish community in Dublin, which has increased dramatically in recent years and continues to keep the faith, as do large numbers of the African community, although they tend to affiliate with smaller Reformist churches like the Baptists.

ARTS

Dublin has always operated an enormous cultural surplus, filling the world's artistic coffers with far greater wealth than should ever have been expected from so small a city. There's hardly been any let-up in the last couple of centuries and the city is still racing further and further into the black. Even by Ireland's standards, the capital is especially creative these days, with more poetry readings, book launches, live gigs, contemporary dance shows, operas, plays, films, comedy acts and club nights than you could shake a decent listings guide at, while Dubliners continue to regale the world with books, films and albums.

LITERATURE

Dubliners know a thing or two about the written word. No other city of comparable size can claim four Nobel Prize winners for literature, but the city's impact on the English-reading world extends far beyond the fab four of Shaw, Yeats, Beckett and Heaney…one name folks: James Joyce.

Before Dublin was even a glint in a Viking's eye, Ireland was the land of saints and scholars, thanks to the monastic universities that sprang up around the country to foster the spread of Christianity and the education of Europe's privileged elite (the nearest to Dublin was Glendalough). But for our purposes, we need to fast-forward 1000 years to the 18th century and the glory days of Georgian Dublin, when the Irish and English languages began to cross-fertilise. Experimenting with English, using turns of phrase and expressions translated directly from Gaeilge, and combining these with a uniquely Irish perspective on life, Irish writers have dazzled and delighted readers for centuries. British theatre critic Kenneth Tynan summed it up thus: 'The English hoard words like misers: the Irish spend them like sailors.'

Dublin has as many would-be sailors as Hollywood has frustrated waitresses, and it often seems like a bottomless well of creativity. The section given over to Irish writers is often the largest and busiest in any local bookstore, reflecting not only a rich literary tradition and thriving contemporary scene, but also an appreciative, knowledgeable and hungry local audience that attends readings and poetry recitals like rock fans at a gig.

Indeed, Dublin has produced so many writers, and has been written about so much, that you could easily plan a Dublin literary holiday. *A Literary Guide to Dublin,* by Vivien Igoe, includes detailed route maps, a guide to cemeteries and an eight-page section on literary and historical pubs. A Norman Jeffares' *Irish Writers: From Swift to Heaney* also has detailed and accessible summaries of writers and their work.

See p128 for our Literary Dublin walking tour.

Old Literary Dublin

Modern Irish literature begins with Jonathan Swift (1667–1745), the master satirist, social commentator and dean of St Patrick's Cathedral. He was the greatest Dublin writer of the early Georgian period and is most famous for *Gulliver's Travels,* a savage social satire that has morphed into a children's favourite. He was an 'earnest and dedicated champion of liberty', as he insisted on writing in his own epitaph.

NOT SO TAXING TIMES

Although Dublin is as proud as punch of its literary credentials, and is willing to flaunt its genius at every opportunity, the awkward truth is that most of the city's greatest writers – including Wilde, Beckett and Joyce – got the hell out of the place after suffering censorship or receiving no support. Since the 1970s, to ensure that Ireland doesn't endure this embarrassment again and to maintain the creative output, the Irish government has provided tax exemptions for all artists who choose to live in Ireland, from musicians through to authors. Creative folk have flocked to these shores ever since, although of course it's for the people, the kinship and the earthiness of the place that they come, not the tax breaks.

He was followed by Oliver Goldsmith (1728–74), author of *The Vicar of Wakefield,* and Thomas Moore (1779–1852), whose poems formed the repertoire of generations of Irish tenors. Dublin-born Oscar Wilde (1854–1900) is renowned for his legendary wit, immense talent and striking sensitivity (also see Theatre, p41). Bram Stoker (1847–1912) created the most famous Gothic ghouls of them all, and his novel *Dracula* remains one of the world's most popular books. The name of the count may have come from the Irish *droch fhola* (bad blood).

Playwright and essayist George Bernard Shaw (1856–1950), author of *Pygmalion* (which was later turned into *My Fair Lady*), hailed from Synge St near the Grand Canal, while James Joyce (1882–1941), the city's most famous son and one of the greatest writers of all time, was born not far away in Rathgar.

William Butler (WB) Yeats (1865–1939) is best remembered as a poet, though he also wrote plays and spearheaded the late-19th-century Irish Literary Revival, which culminated in the founding of the Abbey Theatre in 1904. *Sailing to Byzantium* and *Easter 1916* are two of his finest poems – the latter, about the Easter Rising, ends with the famous line 'A terrible beauty is born'. His poetry is mostly tied up with his sense of Irish heroism, esoteric mysticism and the unrequited love he had for Maud Gonne.

Oliver St John Gogarty (1878–1957) is said to have borne a lifelong grudge against his one-time friend James Joyce because of his appearance as Buck Mulligan in the latter's *Ulysses.* He was a character in his own right and his views are presented in his memoirs *As I Was Going Down Sackville Street* (1937). He had a mean streak though, and took exception to a throwaway remark written by Patrick Kavanagh (1904–67) alluding to him having a mistress; he successfully sued the poet, whom he described as 'that Monaghan boy'.

Kavanagh, from farming stock in Monaghan, walked to Dublin (a very long way) in 1934 and made the capital his home. His later poetry explored Ireland's city versus country dynamic. He was fond of the Grand Canal, along the banks of which he is commemorated, with 'just a canal-bank seat for the passer-by', as he had wished.

You can't imagine the brooding Samuel Beckett (1906–89) hanging around in this company and, while his greatest literary contributions were as a dramatist in self-imposed exile (also see Theatre, p41), he did write a collection of short stories in Dublin, *More Pricks Than Kicks* (1934), about an eccentric local character. The book so irked the new Free State government that it was banned, no doubt hastening Beckett's permanent move to Paris.

One-time civil servant Brian O'Nolan (1911–66), also known as Flann O'Brien and Myles na Gopaleen, was a celebrated comic writer and career drinker. He wrote several books, most notably *At Swim-Two-Birds* (1939) and *The Third Policeman* (1940), but was most fondly remembered for the newspaper columns he penned for nearly three decades before his death.

He was eclipsed – at least in the drinking stakes – by novelist, playwright, journalist and quintessential Dublin hell-raiser, Brendan Behan (1923–64), who led a short and frantic life. In 1953, Behan began work as a columnist with the now-defunct *Irish Press,* and over the next decade wrote about his beloved Dublin, using wonderful, earthy satire and a keen sense of political commentary that set him apart from other journalists. A collection of his newspaper columns was published under the title *Hold Your Hour and Have Another.*

The Contemporary Scene

'I love James Joyce. Never read him, but he's a true genius.' And while this is certainly true of Dublin's greatest literary son, most Dubliners feel more or less the same about the other literary giants of yesteryear. Ask them for their favourite contemporary authors, though, and you'd kick off a knowledgeable debate peppered with dozens of worthy names.

The best known of them is undoubtedly Roddy Doyle (1958–), whose mega-successful Barrytown quartet – The Commitments, The Snapper, The Van and Paddy Clarke, Ha Ha Ha – have all been made into films. He's gone serious of late, addressing the problems of alcoholism and abuse in novels like *The Woman*

DUBLIN'S NOBEL LAUREATES

- George Bernard Shaw (1925)
- William Butler Yeats (1938)
- Samuel Beckett (1969)
- Seamus Heaney (1995; born in Derry but lives in Dublin)

JAMES JOYCE

Uppermost among Dublin writers is James Joyce, author of *Ulysses*, the greatest book of the 20th century – although we've yet to meet five people who've actually finished it. Still, Dubliners are immensely proud of the writer once castigated as a literary pornographer by locals and luminaries alike – even George Bernard Shaw dismissed him as vulgar. Joyce was so unappreciated that he left the city, never to reside in it again, though he continued to live here through his imagination and literature.

Born in Rathgar in 1882, the young Joyce had three short stories published in an Irish farmers' magazine under the pen name Stephen Dedalus in 1904. The same year he fled town with the love of his life, Nora Barnacle (when James' father heard her name he commented that she would surely stick to him). He spent most of the next 10 years in Trieste, now part of Italy, where he wrote prolifically but struggled to get published. His career was further hampered by recurrent eye problems and he had 25 operations for glaucoma, cataracts and other conditions.

The first major prose he finally had published was *Dubliners* (1914), a collection of short stories set in the city, including the three stories he had written in Ireland. Publishers began to take notice and his autobiographical *A Portrait of the Artist as a Young Man* (1916) followed. In 1918 the US magazine *Little Review* started to publish extracts from *Ulysses* but notoriety was already pursuing his epic work and the censors prevented publication of further episodes after 1920.

Passing through Paris on a rare visit to Dublin, he was persuaded by Ezra Pound to stay a while in the French capital, and later said he 'came to Paris for a week and stayed 20 years'. It was a good move for the struggling writer for, in 1922, he met Sylvia Beach of the Paris bookshop Shakespeare & Co, who finally managed to put *Ulysses* (1922) into print. The publicity of its earlier censorship ensured instant success.

Buoyed by the success of the inventive *Ulysses*, Joyce went for broke with *Finnegans Wake* (1939), 'set' in the dreamscape of a Dublin publican. Perhaps not one to read at the airport, the book is a daunting and often obscure tome about eternal recurrence. It is even more complex than *Ulysses* and took the author 17 years to write.

In 1940 WWII drove the Joyce family back to Zürich, where the author died the following year.

Ulysses

Ulysses is the ultimate chronicle of the city in which, Joyce once said, he intended to 'give a picture of Dublin so complete that if the city suddenly one day disappeared from the earth it could be reconstructed out of my book'. It is set here on 16 June 1904 – the day of Joyce's first date with Nora Barnacle – and follows its characters as their journeys around town parallel the voyage of Homer's *Odyssey*.

The experimental literary style makes it difficult to read, but there's much for even the slightly bemused reader to relish. It ends with Molly Bloom's famous stream of consciousness discourse, a chapter of eight huge, unpunctuated paragraphs. Because of its sexual explicitness, the book was banned in the US and the UK until 1933 and 1937, respectively.

In testament to the book's enduring relevance and extraordinary innovation, it has inspired writers of every generation since. Joyce admirers from around the world descend on Dublin every year on 16 June to celebrate Bloomsday and retrace the steps of its central character, Leopold Bloom. It is a slightly gimmicky and touristy phenomenon that appeals almost exclusively to Joyce fanatics and tourists, but it's plenty of fun and a great way to lay the groundwork for actually reading the book.

Who Walked into Doors (1997) and its sequel, *Paula Spencer* (2006); and nonfiction with *Rory & Ita* (2002), basically an interview with his parents. Most recently, he's turned to social and political history with a new trilogy, beginning with *A Star Called Henry* (2000), the story of an IRA hitman called Henry Smart; followed by *Oh, Play That Thing!* (2004) and *The Dead Republic* (2010), both of which follow Henry on his adventures in the United States.

Sebastian Barry (1955–) started his career as a poet with *The Water Colorist* (1983), became famous as a playwright but achieved his greatest success as a novelist: he was shortlisted for the Man Booker Prize twice, in 2005 for his WWI drama *A Long Way Down* and the absolutely compelling *The Secret Scripture* (2008), about a 100-year-old inmate of a mental hospital who decides to write an autobiography. It was the Costa Book of the Year in 2008 and won the prestigious James Tait Black Memorial Prize in 2009.

Anne Enright (1962–) nabbed the Booker for *The Gathering* (2007), a Zeitgeist tale of alcoholism and abuse – she described it as 'the intellectual equivalent of a Hollywood weepie'. Another Booker Prize winner is heavyweight John Banville (1945–), who won it for The Sea (2009); we recommend either *The Book of Evidence* (1989) or the masterful roman-á-clef *The Untouchable* (1998), based loosely on the secret-agent life of art historian Anthony Blunt. Banville's precise and often cold prose divides critics, who consider him either the English language's greatest living stylist or an unreadable intellectual; if you're of the latter inclination then you should check out his immensely enjoyable (and highly readable) crime novels, written under the pseudonym of Benjamin Black: *Christine Falls* (2006), *The Silver Swan* (2007), *The Lemur* (2008) and *Elegy for April* (2010).

Another big hitter is Wexford-born but Dublin-based Colm Tóibín (1955–), who spent four years looking for a publisher for his first novel *The South* (1990) but has gone on to become a hugely successful novelist and scholar – *The Master* (2004), about Henry James, won the Los Angeles Times Novel of the Year award, while his latest novel, the Booker-nominated *Brooklyn* (2009), was Costa Book of the Year for 2010. Of the host of younger writers making names for themselves, we recommend the work of Claire Kilroy (1973–), whose three novels – *All Summer* (2003), *Tenderwire* (2006) and *All the Names Have Been Changed* (2009) have established her as a genuine talent.

RECOMMENDED READING

All the Names Have Been Changed (2009; Claire Kilroy) Claire Kilroy's third novel, about the travails of being a university student in the late 1980s, is an accurate depiction of Dublin before the boom of the 1990s.

Amongst Women (1990; John McGahern) Focuses on a rough old Republican whose story is told through his three daughters. It's essentially a study of the faults and comforts of humanity and an exploration of family ties, told by an exceptionally skilled author who combines a gentle tone with an unfailing eye for the human condition.

At Swim-Two-Birds (1939; Flann O'Brien) By the late satirical columnist and regarded by many as the great Dublin novel. It's funny and absurd, and uses inventive wordplay in telling the story within a story of a student novelist.

At Swim, Two Boys (2001; Jamie O'Neill) A beautifully crafted masterpiece that has drawn comparisons to Joyce and Beckett for its language and characterisation. Essentially it's a coming-of-age tale of gay youth set against the backdrop of revolutionary Dublin c 1916. It's ambitious, absorbing and absolutely brilliant.

The Book of Evidence (1989; John Banville) Written by the former literary editor of the *Irish Times*, this consists of the prison memoir of Freddie Montgomery, on trial for the brutal murder of a female servant. It's a terrific and elaborate piece of literary, philosophical and political fiction.

Dubliners (1914; James Joyce) In our humble opinion, one of the most perfectly written collections of short stories ever; 15 poignant and powerful tales of Dubliners and the moments that define their lives. Even if you never visit, read this book.

The Gathering (2007; Anne Enright) Enright won the Booker Prize for this chilling portrayal of a family torn apart by the secrets of its past. It's particularly poignant given the recent revelations of clerical sexual abuse.

The Ginger Man (1955; JP Donleavy) A high-energy foray around Dublin from the perspective of an Irish-American scoundrel. It received the Catholic Church's 'seal of approval' by being banned in Ireland for many years.

The Informer (1925; Liam O'Flaherty) The classic book about the divided sympathies that plagued Ireland during its independence struggle and the ensuing Civil War. Set in the Dublin underworld, this enthralling revolutionary drama was successfully brought to the big screen by the legendary John Ford.

My Left Foot (1954; Christy Brown) The story of the author's life growing up with cerebral palsy, which he overcame to become an accomplished painter and writer. This autobiography was later expanded into the novel *Down all the Days* (1970), which formed the basis of the acclaimed film *My Left Foot*.

New Dubliners (2005; edited by Oona Frawley) The likes of Maeve Binchy, Dermot Bolger, Roddy Doyle, Colum McCann and Joseph O'Connor lend their respective talents to creating short stories about modern-day Dublin.

The Speckled People (2003; Hugo Hamilton) A brilliant – and pertinent to today's immigrants – novel-memoir of the author's German-Irish upbringing in 1950s Dublin; a boy tells of a family's homesickness for a culture to call their own.

Star of the Sea (2004; Joseph O'Connor) A brilliant and racy tale of a 19th-century Atlantic crossing on a so-called 'coffin' ship, so-named because they were transporting Irish emigrants fleeing the ravages of the Potato Famine for America.

Tatty (2003; Christine Dwyer Hickey) A beautiful and brutal portrayal of an alcoholic Dublin family and its slow and terrible disintegration as seen through the eyes of a child.

LIVING POET'S SOCIETY

Seamus Heaney (1939–) was born in Derry but now lives mostly in Dublin. He is the bard of all Ireland and evokes the spirit and character of the country in his poetry. He won the Nobel Prize for Literature in 1995, and the humble wordsmith compared all the attention to someone mentioning sex in front of their mammy. *Opened Ground – Poems 1966–1996* (1998) is our favourite of his books.

Dubliner Paul Durcan (1944–) is one of the most reliable chroniclers of changing Dublin. He won the prestigious Whitbread Prize for Poetry in 1990 for *'Daddy, Daddy'* and is a funny, engaging, tender and savage writer. Poet, playwright and Kerryman Brendan Kennelly (1936–) is an immensely popular character around town. He lectures at Trinity College and writes a unique brand of poetry that is marked by its playfulness, as well as historical and intellectual impact. Eavan Boland (1944–) is a prolific and much-admired writer, best known for her poetry, who combines Irish politics with outspoken feminism; *In a Time of Violence* (1995) and *The Lost Land* (1998) are two of her most celebrated collections.

If you're interested in finding out more about poetry in Ireland in general, visit the website of the excellent Poetry Ireland (www.poetryireland.ie), which showcases the work of new and established poets.

Like some of their famous antecedents, some Irish novelists have gone abroad to write and find success. Joseph O'Neill (1964–) won the PEN/Faulkner Award for fiction for his post-9/11 novel *Netherland* (2009), while Dublin-born Colum McCann (1965–), who also tackled 9/11 but in a far more allegorical fashion, picked up the National Book Award for *Let the Great World Spin* (2009).

Authors hate the label and publishers profess to disregard it, but chick lit is big business, and few have mastered it as well as the Irish. Doyenne of them all is Maeve Binchy (1940–) whose mastery of the style has seen her outsell most of the literary greats – her latest in a long line of bestsellers is *Heart and Soul* (2008). Hot on her heels is Marion Keyes (1963–), author of 11 bestsellers that tackle themes like alcoholism and mental health, issues that Keyes has battled with herself. Her latest book is *The Brightest Star in the Sky* (2009). Former agony aunt Cathy Kelly has written 13 novels, each more successful than the last – in 2010 she published two, *The Perfect Holiday* and *Homecoming*. And there's just no ignoring Cecelia Ahern (1981), daughter of former taoiseach Bertie and author of the staggeringly successful *PS, I Love You* (2004), which was made into a terrible film starring Hilary Swank. She's followed it up with six similarly saccharine books since and still found time to produce *Samantha Who?* (since cancelled) for the US network ABC.

If you want more substance to your reading, Nuala O'Faolain (1940–2008), former opinion columnist for the *Irish Times*, 'accidentally' wrote an autobiography when a small publisher asked her to write an introduction to a collection of her columns. Her irreverent, humorous and touching prose struck a chord with readers and the essay was re-published as *Are You Somebody?* (1996), followed by *Almost There – the Onward Journey of a Dublin Woman* (2003), both of which became international bestsellers.

MUSIC

Dublin's literary tradition may have the intellectuals nodding sagely, but it's the city's musical credentials that has the rest of us bopping, for it's no cliché to say that music is as intrinsic to the local lifestyle as a good night out. Feelings are all right, Dubs will tell you, but don't you dare express them outside a song. Which goes some way towards explaining the city's love affair with the singer-songwriter, the guy or gal with a guitar who unpeels the layers of their heart through the tortured choruses of song. But even if the slovenly sentiment of the miserable minstrel doesn't draw you in, there's plenty else that will: rock gigs, DJ nights and traditional sessions take place in venues throughout the city every night of the week and, if someone isn't actually making the music, you can be sure there's a fancy stereo filling in the background so that you hear something else besides the sound of your own voice. Oh, for an occasional bit of *whist* (silence): does every new bar have to test our eardrums? Even the streets – well, OK, Grafton St – are alive with the sounds of music, and you can hardly get around without stubbing your toe on the next international superstar busking their way to a record contract. One thing's for certain, you'll have the music of Dublin ringing in your ears long after your gig here is done.

BACKGROUND ARTS

LUKE KELLY: THE ORIGINAL DUBLINER

With a halo of wiry ginger hair and a voice like hardened honey, Luke Kelly (1940–84) was perhaps the greatest Irish folk singer of the 20th century, a performer who used his voice in the manner of the American blues singers he admired so much, to express the anguish of being 'lonely and afraid in a world they never made' (to quote AE Housman). He was a founder member of The Dubliners along with Ronnie Drew (1934–2008), Barney McKenna (1939–) and Ciaran Burke (1935–88), but he treated Dublin's most famous folk group as more of a temporary cooperative enterprise. He shared the singing duties with Drew, lending his distinctive voice to classic drinking ditties like 'Dirty Old Town' and rousing rebel songs like 'A Nation Once Again', but it was his mastery of the more reflective ballad that made him peerless. His rendition of 'Raglan Road', from a poem by Patrick Kavanagh which the poet himself insisted he sing, is the most beautiful song about Dublin we've ever heard; but it is his version of Phil Coulter's 'Scorn Not His Simplicity' that grants him his place among the immortals. Coulter wrote the song following the birth of a son with Down syndrome and even though it became one of Luke's best-loved songs, he had such respect for it that he rarely sang it at the Dubliners' boisterous gigs.
Recommended listening: *Luke Kelly: The Collection*.

Traditional & Folk

Dublin's not the best place in Ireland to savour a traditional session although, thanks to the tourist demand, it's a lot better than it was 10 years ago. There are some lively sessions in pubs throughout the city, and some of them are as good as you'll hear anywhere in the country.

Irish music has retained a vibrancy not found in other traditional European forms, which have lost out to the overbearing influence of pop music. This is probably because, although Irish music has retained many of its traditional aspects, it has itself influenced many forms of music, most notably US country and western – a fusion of Mississippi Delta blues and Irish traditional tunes that, combined with other influences like Gospel, is at the root of rock and roll. Other reasons for its current success include the willingness of its exponents to update the way it's played (in ensembles rather than the customary *céilidh* – communal dance – bands), the habit of pub sessions (introduced by returning migrants) and the economic good times that encouraged the Irish to celebrate their culture rather than trying to replicate international trends. And then, of course, there's *Riverdance,* which made Irish dancing sexy and became a worldwide phenomenon, despite the fact that most aficionados of traditional music are seriously underwhelmed by its musical worth. Good stage show, crap music.

If you want to hear musical skill that will both tear out your heart and restore your faith in humanity, go no further than the fiddle-playing of Tommy Peoples on *The Quiet Glen* (1998), the beauty of Paddy Keenan's uillean pipes on his eponymous 1975 album, or the stunning guitar playing of Andy Irvine on albums like *Compendium: The Best of Patrick Street* (2000).

The most famous traditional band – arguably the original 'band' – is The Chieftains, formed in 1963 and still going strong after four decades. The most loved band in the capital, although more folksy than traditional, is the Dubliners, fronted by the distinctive gravel voice and grey beard of Ronnie Drew, whose photograph should appear above the word Dublin whenever it's printed. Luke Kelly (1940–84) was the most talented and beloved member of the band and his solo version of 'Scorn Not His Simplicity' is one of the saddest, most beautiful songs ever recorded. Another band whose career has been stitched into the fabric of Dublin life is the Fureys, comprising four brothers originally from the travelling community (no, not like the Wilburys) along with guitarist Davey Arthur. And if it's rousing renditions of Irish rebel songs you're after, you can't go past the Wolfe Tones. Ireland is packed with traditional talent and we strongly recommend that you spend some time in a specialised traditional shop like Claddagh Records (p143).

top picks

TRADITIONAL PLAYLIST

- *Compendium: The Best of Patrick Street* (2000) Patrick Street
- *Old Hag You Have Killed Me* (1976) The Bothy Band
- *Paddy Keenan* (1975) Paddy Keenan
- *The Chieftains 6: Bonaparte's Retreat* (1976) The Chieftains
- *The Quiet Glen* (1998) Tommy Peoples

Since the 1970s, various bands have tried to blend traditional music with more progressive genres with mixed success. The first band to pull it off was Moving Hearts, led by Christy Moore, who went on to become the greatest Irish folk musician ever.

While traditional music continues to be popular in its own right both in Ireland and abroad, it also continues to provide the base for successful new genres. Think of ambient music with a slightly mystical tinge and invariably Enya will come to mind, while a wonderful product of contemporary Ireland has been the Afro-Celt Foundation, which fuses African rhythms and electronic beats with traditional Irish sounds to great effect.

Popular Music

Dublin may rely on the rest of the country to buck up its traditional rep, but no such help is required with rock music, save maybe the huge and overwhelming influence of London, which has inspired, attracted, rejected and made many a Dublin rock band.

BACKGROUND ARTS

Fuelled by the pop explosion and the 1960s London scene, Dublin bands began to believe that they had a future beyond the stages of their local dance hall. The most important of these was Thin Lizzy, formed in 1969 and led by the simply fantastic Phil Lynott (see the boxed text, p195); they finally got their breakthrough with *Jailbreak* (1975). Their finest hour, literally, was *Live & Dangerous* (1978), one of the greatest live albums ever recorded. Thin Lizzy's music aged better than its charismatic and hard-living lead singer, whose life and creativity were blighted by drug use and physical deterioration – he died in 1986.

During the punk explosion of the mid-1970s, Bob 'for fuck's sake' Geldof and the Boomtown Rats carried the mantle for Dublin, strutting their way to centre stage with hit singles 'Rat Trap' and 'I Don't Like Mondays'. By the time the band had begun to wane, Geldof had moved onto more important matters and for the last 20 years he has been mixing moral outrage and annoying condescension in his lecture to the world on the terrible crises that afflict Africa. To be fair, without him we would never have had Live Aid, Live 8 or those Make Poverty History wristbands.

And then, in 1976, a supernova was born in North Dublin. The world and her sister have an opinion about U2 and, especially, their shy, un-opinionated lead singer Bono, but U2 have not only eclipsed virtually every other band save the Rolling Stones for mega-stardom and longevity, but have come to represent Dublin on the international stage in a way that nobody – including James Joyce and Guinness – have done before. If we had to pick just one album, it would be the simply magnificent *The Joshua Tree* (1987), although *Achtung Baby* (1991) is quite something too. Their musical output of late has dipped, as inevitably it would with a band whose members are comfortably middle-aged: their last album, *No Line on the Horizon* (2009), was released to very mixed reviews.

U2's success cast a long shadow over the city's musical scene in the 1980s – despite the valiant and wonderful efforts of Sinéad O'Connor to bask in her own sunlight and the singular genius of My Bloody Valentine, who were the true pioneers of the shoegazer alt-rock movement of the late 1980s (1991's *Loveless* is one of Dublin's greatest musical moments) – but their global megastardom and the explosion of dance music in the 1990s lessened their day-to-day relevance to Dublin. U2 became yet another example of the city producing artistic genius for the world to savour and for Dubliners, in their own, inimitable begrudgery, to shrug their shoulders and give out about Bono being a pretentious arsehole.

The late 1990s saw a thriving economy, and the feel-good vibes of a city anaesthetised by pleasure was hardly a healthy breeding ground for great rock. Enter the too-horrible-for-words phenomenon of the boy band, masterfully manipulated by impresario Louis Walsh, who created Boyzone, Ronan Keating and Westlife, and got very rich in the process. And that's enough type wasted on them.

Infinitely more memorable – although not necessarily for the biggest participants – was the emergence of the dance music scene, a five-year party fuelled by ecstasy, bottled water and the pounding beat of techno as played by a host of top-class local DJs and a constant stream of (overpaid) international superstars. The latter don't play much anymore, but you can still hear the likes of Billy Scurry, Liam Dollard and Johnny Moy in club nights around the city (see p186).

The Contemporary Scene

As the DJ recedes out of the limelight, live music is back – although many would argue with great irritation that it never went away. Still, the live music scene in Dublin is perhaps more rich and varied than ever, which may come as a surprise given the DIY spirit that is the new reality of the music industry: most bands are unsigned (and if they are, it is to microlabels that provide little more than a platform for a record release), they record their music locally and are obliged to use social networking and the internet to spread their respective musical gospel. All of which is a boon to creativity and hard work, as bands are free to pursue whatever sound they want but have to gig constantly so as to have enough to eat!

There are far more bands on the scene than we have room to mention here, but some of the more interesting ones include indie-electronica outfit Codes, whose debut *Trees Dream in Algebra* (2009) earned them lots of critical kudos; Dark Room Notes, an electro-synthpop band whose album *We Love You Dark Matter* (2009) is slightly reminiscent of Joy Division or New Order; and the Duckworth-Lewis Method, the brainchild of Divine Comedy frontman Neil Hannon and Dubliner Thomas Walsh – their eponymous album, released just days before the 2009 Ashes series, is a 'concept' album of 12 songs 'about the beautiful and silly world of cricket'.

Dubliners like their sensitive souls, and there's no shortage of the feelings-out-front singer-songwriter. The established crop include Paddy Casey, Damien Rice and the excellent Fionn Regan (his single 'Be Good or Be Gone' was a big hit and featured on *Grey's Anatomy*), while Belfast-born Duke Special followed up on the success of *Songs from the Deep Forest* (2007) with two albums in quick succession: *Orchestral Manoeuvres in Belfast* and *I Never Thought This Day Would Come* (both 2008). Oh, and don't forget a certain Glen Hansard, whose band The Frames was a fixture on the scene for nearly two decades but he only achieved international fame

---

BELIEVE THE HYPE

In 1976, Larry Mullen pinned a note on the noticeboard of Mt Temple Comprehensive School in 1976 looking for fellow students to join his new band. Six lads agreed to join, but within a few days two had dropped out, leaving Larry on drums, Adam Clayton on bass and two members of a surrealist street gang called Lipton Village, Paul Hewson and Dave Evans (known to their friends as Bono and The Edge) on vocals and guitar respectively. The Edge's older brother Dik was the fifth member, and also played guitar.

At first, Larry had suggested they be called The Larry Mullen Project, but they quickly ditched that name in favour of Feedback, which lasted until March 1977, when they became The Hype. Dik was in college, and wasn't quite on the same wavelength as the other four, so he finally left the band in March 1978, when they made their final name change, settling on U2 after considering five others.

Until then, the band had mostly played covers – badly. In fact, their musical ability wasn't at all clear, but then they decided to stop murdering other people's songs and started writing their own. On St Patrick's Day 1978 they won a talent competition in Limerick, which allowed them to record their first demo. By September of the following year they had a new manager (Paul McGuinness) and their first single release, U2 3, featuring three original songs: 'Out of Control', 'Stories for Boys' and 'Boy/Girl'.

On the strength of that and their subsequent single, 'Another Day' (February 1980), Island Records, which had hitherto largely specialised in reggae records, agreed to sign them in March 1980. Their debut album *Boy* came out in September of that year to largely positive reviews, but nobody (save perhaps the band themselves?) could have imagined that 30 years later they would still be going strong as one of the world's most successful rock bands, with 12 studio albums and 145 million record sales to their name.

---

when he (and co-singer Markéta Irglová) won the Oscar for Best Song in 2008 for 'Falling Slowly' from the movie *Once*; their success resulted in a new band, The Swell Season, whose album *Strict Joy* (2009) has been well received.

Other names to look out for are Julie Feeney (her second album *Pages* from 2009 is stunning) Cathy Davey (2007's *Tales of Silversleeve* is worth a listen), and Lisa Hannigan, who played for a number of years with Damien Rice before heading out on her own with the superb *Sea Saw* (2009). We're also big fans of the Nick Cave–like Adrian Crowley – *Season of the Sparks* (2009) and *Long Distance Swimmer* (2007) are recommended (the latter won Ireland's most prestigious musical award, the Choice Music Prize, in 2009) – and Villagers, the most hotly tipped act of 2010.

top picks

DUBLIN SONGS

- I Don't Like Mondays (1979) Boomtown Rats
- Lay Me Down (2001) The Frames
- One (1990) U2
- Raglan Road (1972) Luke Kelly & the Dubliners
- Still in Love With You (1978) Thin Lizzy

THEATRE

Dubliners have a unique affinity with theatre; it seems to course through their veins. Perhaps this explains why dramatists Oliver Goldsmith, Oscar Wilde and George Bernard Shaw conquered the theatre world in London even before there was such an entity as Irish drama. While Dublin has a long association with the stage – the first theatre was founded here in 1637 – it wasn't until the late-19th-century Celtic Revival Movement and the establishment of the Abbey Theatre that Irish drama really took off.

Perhaps the first renowned Dublin playwright was Oliver Goldsmith (1730–74) who enjoyed much success with *The Good Natur'd Man* (1768) and *She Stoops to Conquer* (1773) before his early death. Language enthusiasts might like to know that another Dublin-born London favourite, Richard Brinsley Sheridan (1751–1816), gave us the word 'malapropism' after the misguided character Mrs Malaprop from his play *The Rivals* (1775).

The infinitely quotable Oscar Wilde (1854–1900) left Dublin for London after studying at Trinity and caused a sensation with his uproarious, challenging plays such as *The Importance of Being Earnest* (1895) and *An Ideal Husband* (1895). However, his most important and vigorous work is *The Ballad of Reading Gaol* (1898), which he wrote while serving a prison sentence for being a progressive homosexual in a backward society. Wilde paid a heavy toll for the harsh prison conditions and the ignorance of Victorian society, dying bankrupt not long after his release.

Fellow Trinity alumnus John Millington Synge (1871–1909) was one of the first to create headlines at Dublin's Abbey Theatre, established in 1904 by WB Yeats and Lady Gregory to stage Irish productions and stimulate the local scene. In stark contrast to Wilde, Synge's plays focused on the Irish peasantry, whose wonderful language, bawdy witticisms and eloquent invective he transposed into his plays. His honest portrayal of the brutality of rural life in his most famous drama, *The Playboy of the Western World* (1907), resulted in rioting when it first opened at the Abbey. Sadly for Irish drama, Synge died of Hodgkin's disease within two years, aged just 38.

Sean O'Casey (1880–1964), from the working-class north inner city, didn't even become a full-time writer until his 40s but made up for the slow start with a brilliant burst in which he wrote the powerful trilogy on patriotism and life in Dublin's slums, *Shadow of a Gunman* (1923), *Juno and the Paycock* (1924) and *The Plough and the Stars* (1926). The last also caused riots in the Abbey Theatre when it was first staged and it's a wonder WB Yeats and co could afford the insurance to carry on.

Brendan Behan (1923–64) was another immensely talented Dublin playwright whose creative fire was quenched much too early. A die-hard Republican, he shot to prominence with his autobiographical accounts of his time in prison in Dublin and England, in the play *The Quare Fellow* (1954) and the tale *Borstal Boy* (1958). His masterpiece was *The Hostage* (1958), a devastatingly satirical play about an English soldier being ransomed by the IRA. He struggled to cope with the fame his talent brought, and his alcoholism – and the image of celebrity hell-raiser that he tried to live up to – delivered his early demise.

It hardly seems possible that he could have shared the same era as Dublin-born Samuel Beckett (1906–89). Beckett spent most of his adult life in Paris and wrote much of his work in French, but is still thought of as an Irish playwright, perhaps because it was as much his rejection of Irish culture that drove him as a longing for anything else. His greatest works are associated with the bleakness and self-examination that occurred in continental Europe following WWII, from which he himself spent a good time on the run. Many consider his *Waiting for Godot* (1953) to be the modernist theatrical masterpiece. Beckett got the nod from the Nobel committee in 1969 and literary Dublin got another feather in its well-plumed cap.

The Contemporary Scene

Irish theatre is still sincerely and refreshingly self-absorbed, which means it offers visitors a direct short cut into the heart of Irish culture – at least in theory. After a mid-century descent into the doldrums – when lack of funds and resources, coupled with a tired theatrical vision, missed an important artistic opportunity to offer an insight into a sick and stagnant society – the theatre bounced back in the early 1990s, thanks largely to a reinvigorated establishment and a host of new companies geed up by the boundless possibilities of the new economy. Inspired by the ground-breaking work being explored in other countries, Irish companies began their own forays into experimentation, creating a buzz of activity not seen on the city's stages since the days of Yeats and Lady Gregory.

Yet a buoyant economy has had a negative effect too: rising property prices and the developers' bottom line has meant that no new stages have opened up in the city centre, forcing companies onto the streets – literally. Open-air performances are an increasing part of the theatrical landscape. So are the purpose-built performance centres in the suburbs, which are themselves a wonderful addition to the local cultural landscape but hardly speak loudly of a city committed to its theatrical identity. Basically, Dublin wants its theatres, but it wants them out of the way of the ongoing development of every inch of centre space.

Under pressure to justify itself as a going concern, Dublin theatres have subconsciously turned more and more towards the fizz bang wallop of spectacle, often at the expense of quality. Some of the most successful plays of recent years seem obsessed with re-creating the high-paced neurotic energy of the action thriller on the stage, as though the audience isn't patient enough to be engrossed by the slow build-up usually associated with theatrical drama. The introduction of more noise, more guns and sharp dialogue out of an American pulp novel might keep the audience laughing on the edge of their seats, but it doesn't make for lasting, quality theatre.

Theatre's tattered flag is still kept flying, however, by the efforts of some excellent writers and companies. Brian Friel and Tom Murphy are the country's leading established playwrights; neither is from Dublin although most of their work premieres here, often in the Gate Theatre. Rough Magic, one of the most successful independent companies of recent years, specialises in bringing new works to Ireland and new Irish writers to the stage, so the future may be very bright indeed for a bunch of new writers like Michael Collins, John Comiskey, Oonagh Kearney, Gina Moxley and Arthur Riordan. The present is also pretty shiny for the likes of Enda Walsh, author of *Disco Pigs* (1996; made into a film starring Cillian Murphy in 2001) – he's written 11 plays since then, the most recent of which is *The Man in the Moon* (2009). Mark O'Rowe, who presented an electrifying picture of gangland Dublin in his award-winning *Howie the Rookie* (1999) and followed it with *Made in China* (2001) and *Crestfall* (2003), is one of the very hot names in the contemporary scene, and he too has made the move into film writing, co-scripting *Intermission* (2003); his latest play, *Terminus* (2007), was very well received. Conor McPherson cemented his reputation as a dramatist with a series of plays that explores dysfunctional relationships and the importance of traditional folklore, like *The Weir* (1997) and *The Seafarer* (2006).

The really exciting period for Dublin theatre is festival time, usually late September/early October. The main Dublin Theatre Festival attracts some worthy plays, but the superb fringe festival is also worth attending: it runs just before the bigger event and features some of the best work you'll see all year. For more information, see the boxed text, p198.

CINEMA & TV

Cinema

Ireland's film making tradition is pretty poor, largely because the British cinema industry has drained much of its talent and creative energies, and also because the Irish government

RECOMMENDED VIEWING

A Man of No Importance (1994; Suri Krishnamma) Stars the brilliant Albert Finney as a repressed bus conductor trying to come to terms with his own homosexuality in 1960s Dublin while at the same time staging an amateur production of Oscar Wilde's *Salome*. Melancholy and beautiful, it feels like a poem.

About Adam (2000; Gerry Stembridge) Set in contemporary Dublin, a watchable tale that focuses on one man's ability to woo three sisters by appealing to what each woman wants in a man (apparently, sometimes more than a Dublin accent). It features local actor Stuart Townsend and US sensation Kate Hudson.

Adam and Paul (2004; Lenny Abrahamson) Mark O'Hallorahan and Tom Murphy put in compelling and convincing performances as two junkies from the inner-city projects desperate for a fix. It's funny, pithy and occasionally silly, but a great debut for Abrahamson nonetheless.

The Dead (1987; John Huston) Based on a short story from James Joyce's *Dubliners, The Dead* focuses on a dinner party in Dublin at the end of the 19th century and specifically the thoughts of one of the party goers. A difficult task for Huston in his last film, and he pulls it off with aplomb.

Dead Bodies (2003; Robert Quinn) A dark and stylish thriller set in contemporary Dublin against the backdrop of a general election. It's a terrific debut from the first-time director and features serial Irish bad guy Gerard McSorley among a terrific cast.

I Went Down (1997; Paddy Breathnach) A quirky comedy caper with two characters borrowed from Quentin Tarantino's rogues gallery, which works particularly well with the Irish humour and sensibility. It stars one of our favourite actors, Brendan Gleeson, and is Ireland's all-time highest grossing film.

Inside I'm Dancing (2004; Damien O'Donnell) One of our favourite Irish films of the last decade is an uplifting yarn about a young man with cerebral palsy (played by Steven Robertson) whose institutionalised life is transformed by the arrival of the fast-talking, rebellious and fatally ill Rory (James McAvoy). Brenda Fricker is excellent as the formidable Eileen, a Nurse Ratchett–type character.

The Magdalene Sisters (2002; Peter Mullan) A confronting and uncompromising film based on the true story of four young 'sinners' who were sent to one of the infamous Magdalene asylums in Dublin in the 1960s, where they suffered abuse by the nuns who ran the place (instances of inhumanity still being investigated by the state). It's as moving as it is bleak.

Michael Collins (1996; Neil Jordan) This biopic of the man who delivered Irish independence and was assassinated during the 1922 civil war is an epic tale and a great film with pride and passion. The only downside is Jordan's shameful revision of history, specifically his portrayal of Éamon de Valera as a weak and pathetic collaborator in Collins' murder.

My Left Foot (1989; Jim Sheridan) The best film made in and about Dublin in modern history. Based on the life story of Christy Brown, an Irish writer/artist with cerebral palsy, this stirring and triumphant film is made by the astonishing performance of Daniel Day-Lewis, who didn't leave his character on set for the duration of the shoot, even forcing crew to carry him around.

The Secret of Kells (2009; Tomm Moore) A marvellous animated feature film set in the 9th century, this film tells the story of the young monk Brendan, who serves as apprentice to master illustrator Aidan, who is working on the *Book of Kells*. It was nominated for an Oscar in 2010 but lost to *Up*.

The Snapper (1993; Stephen Frears) A made-for-TV movie about how a Dublin family copes when their daughter gets 'up the pole' and won't tell anyone who the father is. Our choice of the Barrytown trilogy, which also includes *The Commitments* and *The Van*. Full of slang and pathos, it is Dublin to the core and absolutely brilliant. Colm Meaney is outstanding as the father.

When Brendan Met Trudy (2001; Kieron Walsh) A likable, light-hearted romance based in Dublin that apes scenes from old movies (there's a clue in the title) to add an extra layer for anyone who feels stiffed by the superficiality of a feel-good flick.

pleaded poverty any time a film maker came looking for some development cash. To be fair, the last decade has seen a change in the attitude of the government, but, still, what has long been true is that the country has contributed more than its fair share of glorious moments to the silver screen, as well as a disproportionate number of the film world's most prominent stars.

Hot on the heels of such luminaries as Gabriel Byrne *(Miller's Crossing, The Usual Suspects* and, most recently, the excellent TV series *In Treatment)*, Stephen Rea *(The Crying Game, The End of the Affair)*, the Oscar-winning Liam Neeson (for *Schindler's List*), Daniel Day-Lewis and Brenda Fricker (both for *My Left Foot)*, are the late-arriving but always excellent Brendan Gleeson, who has had supporting roles in literally dozen of films, the very handsome Cillian Murphy *(Breakfast on Pluto, The Wind That Shakes the Barley)* and the reformed bad-boy Brando wannabe himself, Colin Farrell, whose work has been, well, less than…anybody see *Alexander*? Hot on his heels is Jonathan Rhys Meyers, whose most notable work to date is his Henry VIII on the TV hit *The Tudors*, but has also been seen in Woody Allen's *Match Point* (2005) and 2009's *From Paris With Love*. Other stars on the rise are teenagers Sarah Bolger *(In America, The Tudors)* and the impossibly talented Saoirse Ronan *(Atonement, The Lovely Bones)*, who is being talked up as the next Cate Blanchett.

Ireland has worked hard to cast off that ridiculous 'Oirland' identity so beloved of Hollywood's plastic paddies – watch *The Quiet Man* (1952) and you'll get the picture – but the local film industry is under huge pressure to come up with the goods, and in film, the 'goods' means a commercial success. Exit the creative space to make really insightful films about a host of Irish subjects, enter the themed film designed to make a commercial splash in Britain and the US. Favourite themes include Mad 'n' Quirky – *The Butcher Boy* (1997) and *Disco Pigs* (2001); Smart-arse Gangsters – *I Went Down* (1997) and *Intermission* (2003); and Cutsy Formulaic Love Story – *When Brendan Met Trudy* (2001). Never mind the Irish Welles or Fellini, where's the local equivalent of Loach, Leigh or Winterbottom?

The film board may wince and then point us in the direction of Neil Jordan and Jim Sheridan. Jim Sheridan has reeled off a series of well-made hits, including *The Field* (1989), *In the Name of the Father* (1993) and *The Boxer* (1997), but his most recent films have seen him forsake Irish themes in favour of more mainstream American stories: *Get Rich or Die Tryin'* (2005), the semi-autobiographical story of Curtis '50 Cent' Jackson, and *Brothers* (2009), which is about a returning vet of the war in Afghanistan.

Neil Jordan has never been pigeon-holed as a director, and has thrilled us with a diverse selection of films that began with the excellent *Angel* (1982), continued with the weird and wonderful *The Company of Wolves* (1983), the just brilliant *Mona Lisa* (1986) and *The Crying Game* (1992), the blockbuster biopic *Michael Collins* (1996), the already mentioned *Butcher Boy* and, more recently, *The End of the Affair* (1999) and the vastly underrated *The Good Thief* (2002). In 2009 he brought us the fantasy-drama *Ondine,* starring Colin Farrell as an Irish fisherman who discovers a beautiful and mysterious woman in his fishing net.

New directors include the impossibly young but well connected Kristen Sheridan, daughter of Jim and director of *Disco Pigs* and *August Rush* (2007). John Crowley followed up *Intermission* with the excellent *Is Anybody There?* (2008), starring Michael Caine. Lenny Abrahamson is another big talent – *Adam & Paul* (2004), a portrayal of two Dublin junkies and their quixotic quest for a fix, and *Garage* (2007), a tragicomedy set in a gas station, are both wonderful. And let us not forget John Carney, former bass player with The Frames who turned Hollywood heads in 2006 with the awfully lovely *Once*, a tale of love between busker and young immigrant that picked up an Oscar for Best Song ('Falling Slowly') as performed by the two lead actors, Glen Hansard and Markéta Irglová. Carney has followed it up with *Zonad* (2009), a weird comedy about an alcoholic who bamboozles a small town by pretending to be from outer space.

OSCAR COLLEGE

At the 2010 Oscars, Irish interest was represented by four nominations, all graduates of the excellent animation course at the unheralded Ballyfermot College of Further Education. Darragh O'Donnell and Nicky Phelan produced the short animated film *Granny O'Grimm's Sleeping Beauty;* Tomm Moore directed *The Secret of Kells,* nominated in the animated feature category; and Richard Baneham was part of the New Zealand–based Weta Digital team that created the special effects for Avatar. When the gongs were handed out, only Richard Baneham was a winner, but the presence of the others on the nominations list *(The Secret of Kells* had to fight it out with *Coraline, The Princess & the Frog, Fantastic Mr Fox* and the eventual winner, *Up)* is a fine tribute to the college, which has for years operated in the shadows of more 'prestigious' programs at other third-level institutions in the capital. We're guessing that enrolments for 2011 have increased dramatically!

TV

Irish TV is small fry; it always has been. It lacks the funding and audience available to behemoths like the BBC or the US networks. But – and this is a huge but – compared to that of most other European countries it is actually good. Critics lambast it for being parochial and conservative, but most Irish are pretty pleased that their national station hasn't gone down the road of endless variety shows featuring semi-clad wannabe starlets and really crap humour.

Instead, RTE plods along with a homemade drama, a farming program or a series exploring the importance of faith in the modern world. Ireland is a small country with a culture in flux, and while RTE may not be leading the charge into the world of tomorrow it is careful not to throw the baby out with the bathwater. Hold on a minute, say the critics, what about the Angelus? Turn on the TV at 6pm (or the radio at noon or 6pm) and you will hear Ireland's very own call to prayer, 18 sombre hits of a church bell. The Angelus has been broadcast every day since radio and TV began in Ireland. It is undoubtedly out of step with the fast-paced change overcoming Irish society, but what's so wrong with stopping for a minute to ponder something deeper than the price of petrol or whether the light blue goes well with the off-white?

RTE's strength is in its news and current affairs programming – it's thorough, insightful and often hard-hitting. Programs like *The Frontline* (Mondays, RTE1) and *Prime Time* (Thursday, RTE1) are as good as, or better than, anything you'll see elsewhere in the world; the reporting treats the audience like mature responsible adults who don't need issues dumbed down or simplified.

Where RTE falls way short is in drama. Its most popular program is the long-running soap *Fair City*, which depicts working-class life in Dublin and is known locally as 'Fairly Shitty'. The national broadcaster is also home to the world's longest-running chat show, the *Late Late Show* (Friday 9.30pm), which began in 1962 and is still going under the guidance of Ryan Tubridy. If you're watching it during your visit to Dublin you've made a mistake in planning your Friday night.

All of the main British TV stations – excluding Channel 5 – are available via cable, but Dublin homes are increasingly giving in to the lure of the digibox. The main players are UPC Ireland and the behemoth that is Rupert Murdoch's Sky, who have a proportionally bigger share of the Irish market than they do the British one.

The following are the four main Irish channels:

RTE 1 Ireland's main station, with a pretty standard mix of programs, from news, current affairs and sports programs to variety shows, soap operas and movies.

RTE 2 The second state-controlled channel generally has lighter programs aimed at younger audiences.

TG4 Irish-language station with the most diverse and challenging output, combining great movies (in English) with an interesting selection of dramas and documentaries *as gaeilge* (but with English subtitles).

TV3 A lightweight programming philosophy, with second-string US fluff to complement its diet of reality TV shows and celebrity nonsense – although its *Nightly News with Vincent Browne* is an intelligent barometer of the day's affairs.

PAINTING & VISUAL ARTS

Although they started off brilliantly – think of the gold and bronze works in the National Museum and the *Book of Kells* – Irish artists never really delivered on their early promise, and in recent decades, the country has been more famous for its art heists than artists. Russborough House in County Wicklow has been robbed four times since 1974, with Vermeer, Goya and Gainsborough all among the targets.

Beyond one Impressionist who settled and died in Dublin, Jack B Yeats, and the Surrealist Francis Bacon, who wanted nothing to do with the city after he left it aged 16, Dublin has

top picks

GALLERIES

- National Gallery (p82)
- Dublin City Gallery – The Hugh Lane (p104)
- RHA Gallagher Gallery (p85)
- Douglas Hyde Gallery at Trinity College (p70)
- Temple Bar Gallery & Studios (p88)

BACKGROUND ARTS

contributed little to the world of art. Or perhaps it just seems little compared to its other artistic endeavours.

But even this apparent cultural fallibility has been revised in recent years with 20th-century Irish art more than tripling in value since 1990. While it was probably underrated beforehand, this revaluation no doubt has more to do with the wealth of Irish collectors, their rediscovery of indigenous art and their hunger for a piece of heritage.

The National Gallery (p82) has an extensive Irish School collection, much of it chronicling the personages and pursuits of the Anglo-Irish aristocracy. Garrett Murphy (1680–1716) and James Latham (1696–1747) were respected portrait painters of their day. Nathaniel Hone (1831–1917), an important 19th-century landscape artist, was born in Ireland and returned to Dublin after a lengthy stint working in France.

Roderic O'Conor (1861–1940) was the first Irish painter to make a splash. He was dubbed the Irish Van Gogh because he grasped the Dutch genius's revolution and matched his vibrant, exuberant and extraordinary strokes. He too was drawn to France, but never returned to his homeland. Dublin-born William Orpen (1878–1931) became well known for his depictions of Irish life – his *Portrait of Gardenia St George with Riding Crop* (1912) once held the distinction of being the most expensive Irish painting ever sold at auction, fetching £1.8 million. That was until 2005, when he was posthumously beaten into second place by *The Bridge at Grez* (1883) by Belfast-born John Lavery (1856–1941), which sold for £2.18 million.

The most original and famous of the Irish painters was Jack B Yeats (1871–1957), the first Impressionist painter from the British Isles. Like his big brother, poet WB, Jack was a champion of the Celtic Revival Movement. He mastered a range of painting techniques but is best known for setting down thick and broad strokes of pigment in a bold and gutsy spin on Impressionism. This style provided a self-confident art form for the newly independent Ireland, created after the formation of the Irish Free State in 1922. The characters he drew were often strong, isolated and solitary – and every stroke seems to reveal his deep love for all things Irish. The National Gallery has a specific gallery devoted to his work, and a visit here should be one of the highlights of your trip to Dublin. Among our favourites are *The Liffey Swim* (1923), *Returning to the Shore* (1948) and *The Singing Horseman* (1949).

Most modern Irish artists turned their backs on the nationalism that so defined the work of Yeats. The abstract painters Mainie Jellett (1896–1943) and Evie Hone (1894–1955) are considered two of the greatest innovators of modern Irish art. The self-taught Louis le Brocquy

FRANCIS BACON

Dubliners like to tell you that Francis Bacon, the foremost British painter of his generation, was actually Irish, although it's a pretty tenuous claim to call him one of their own.

Born in Dublin – of English parentage – in 1909, Bacon was thrown out of home at the age of 16 when his parents discovered he was actively homosexual. In the great Irish artistic tradition, Bacon split as soon as he could and turned his back on his narrow-minded birthplace forever, pointedly denying his roots thereafter. He flitted about Berlin and Paris before settling in London in 1928, where he developed his distinctive, distorted, violent and utterly captivating style.

Critics dismissed him as a warped caricaturist, and it is true that his best-known works are distortions of other painters' creations – Velázquez' *Portrait of Innocent X* became Bacon's most celebrated series *The Screaming Popes* (1949–55) – but there is no denying his extraordinary ability to paint isolation, pain and suffering, major themes of post-WWII iconography and of homosexuality in repressed times.

His notoriously debauched lifestyle was nearly as well publicised as his genius. Although remarkably productive, he destroyed many of his canvases and relatively little of his work survives. Precious little is on display in Dublin – no doubt the way he would have wanted it – although the Hugh Lane Gallery (p104) did acquire the contents of the London studio where Bacon worked for three decades until his death in 1992. It has been faithfully reconstructed here in perhaps the most oddly compelling art exhibit in Dublin.

THE LAST SUPPER

One of our favourite works of art is John Byrne's *Last Supper* (2004), on public display along a wall in the Quartier Bloom, by Caffé Cagliostro. This visually striking piece is a reinterpretation of Da Vinci's masterpiece – with a contemporary Irish twist. In an effort to reflect the changing face and growing cultural mix of Irish society, Byrne has cast two women: an East African and, in the role of Jesus, a Sikh studying at Trinity College.

(1916–) is one of the foremost Irish painters of the 20th century and, while his works aren't necessarily innovative (they borrow heavily from Picasso, Manet and others), they are unique in their Irishness. He is most famous for his depictions of the travelling community in the 1940s in a series known as the *Tinker Paintings*.

Today Dublin is at the forefront of a new Irish artistic revolution that has seen a fundamental transformation in the infrastructure and culture of visual arts. There is now a thriving network of part-funded and fully commercial galleries in the city, and a buoyant, dynamic local scene. Local artists to look out for include the Corkonian Dorothy Cross, whose work is exhibited in both the Irish Museum of Modern Art (p98) and the Dublin City Gallery (p102); video artist James Coleman; Shane Cullen, who carved the 11,500 words of the 1998 Anglo-Irish Good Friday Agreement in his vast sculptural work *The Agreement* (2002); and Grace Weir, whose multimedia work is both beautiful and challenging. Other artists to watch out for include Nick Miller, New York–based Sean Scully and Fionnuala Ní Chíosain.

Experimental photographer Clare Langan's work has gained international recognition with her trademark ethereal images of elemental landscapes.

COMEDY

The Irish are renowned for being funny, which is hardly surprising considering that this is a nation that has regularly dealt with its difficulties and crippled emotions with the greatest defence mechanism of them all: humour. Self-deprecating but always brilliantly observed wit is a strong suit of the great Irish comic; crap, I-drank-so-much-last-night-I-complimented-my-mother-in-law jokes are the choice of every other halfwit who thinks being Irish automatically entitles them to a sense of humour. Sadly, there are far too many of the latter.

The former are fewer in number and, mostly, living in England, as Ireland is sadly too small to support their talents. Of the recent greats, our highly subjective list of the capital's comedy talents include the greatest storyteller of them all, Dave Allen, who sadly left us in 2005; the pioneering stand-up of Sean Hughes; and the greatest Irish satirist of the modern age, Dermot Morgan, who followed his brilliant political radio sketch show *Scrap Saturday* with his unforgettable role as *Father Ted*.

The contemporary crop includes Dylan Moran and his one-time school classmate Tommy Tiernan, who have both gone on to great international success. Deirdre O'Kane has been making audiences laugh for years, while Maeve Higgins is another in a new brood of comics worth paying the admission price to see. Irish-American Des Bishop, PJ Gallagher and Jason Byrne, who has sold more tickets at the Edinburgh Festival in recent years than any other comedian, are all popular names, while David McSavage has finally earned the kudos his talent deserves when he was given his own TV show, *The Savage Eye*, which takes few prisoners in poking fun at Irish politicians, personalities and mores (and earning McSavage the kind of opprobrium that fuels his material). Our favourite comedian of them all, however, is unquestionably Dara O'Briain, Ireland's very own Jerry Seinfeld and now a mainstay of British TV comedy panel shows like *Have I Got News For You*.

DANCE

There's good and bad news. Yes, *Riverdance* and its various mutations like *Lord of the* (Tight) *Pants* are still going strong, stomping their way around the world, but the *good* news is that you're far less likely to be bombarded with the hand-by-the-sides phenomenon in Dublin than just about anywhere else in the world. Now don't get us wrong. We've got nothing against the sexing up of Irish dancing – there's nowt wrong with a little quick-step pizzazz – but *Riverdance* and its spin-offs are the dancing equivalent of boy bands. Take a bite, have a chew and move on.

Broadway hits and multiple international touring companies are a far cry from the dusty halls of rural Ireland where the tradition of Irish dancing was preserved on life support throughout the last century. Formerly the dancing was only performed at *céilidhs* and accompanied by traditional bands with musicians in green waistcoats. The etiquette was rigidly strict, fun was discouraged, and it seemed like most of the dancers were there under duress rather than to celebrate a tradition that has been around in some form since at least the 16th century. But not any more. Since *Riverdance*, the roots of Irish dancing have been given a good soaking and the tradition is blossoming once again. While still true to the jigs and reels of its past, the dancing has evolved into something more tribal, vital and – we can still hardly believe it – sexy.

Up until fairly recently, Irish dancing was virtually the only dancing in Ireland, although this is no longer the case: Dublin has become a destination for touring companies, while city venues are putting on their own shows and local companies creating their own.

ARCHITECTURE

Dublin raced into the third millennium with most of its finest architecture intact and with a rate of development not seen since the height of its Georgian heyday, when the city was regarded as one of the finest in Europe. Most of the public architecture to rise out of the booming town has generated a wonderful sense of energy and adventure about renaissance Dublin. Of course some mistakes have been made in the mad recent rush to build, but Dubliners have learned from them and are more architecturally savvy these days. They demand higher standards of design for their most deserving city and local authorities haven't let them down.

Although there's been a lull in activity in the last couple of years, it's a good opportunity for planners to take stock and refocus on the old problems, such as housing and transport.

MEDIEVAL DUBLIN

For architectural evidence of the pre-Norman settlers you will have to look further afield than the capital, which has been rebuilt far too many times, often in spite of the wealth of historical residue below ground. Treatment of the remains of Viking Dublin found at Wood Quay during the laying of the foundations for two massive modern buildings for the Dublin Corporation was one of the biggest crimes against culture and heritage perpetrated by the Irish State (see the boxed text, p50). Dublin's tangled history has left very few survivors, even from Norman days, and what is left is either fragmentary or has been heavily reconstructed. The imposing Dublin Castle (Map p68) – or the complex of buildings that are known as Dublin Castle – bears little resemblance to the fortress that was erected by the Anglo-Normans at the beginning of the 13th century and more to the neoclassical style of the 17th century. However, there are some fascinating glimpses of the lower reaches of the original, which you can visit on a tour.

Although the 12th-century cathedrals of Christ Church (Map p91) and St Patrick's (Map p91) were heavily rebuilt in Victorian times, there are some original features, including the crypt in Christ Church, which has a 12th-century Romanesque door. The older of the two St Audoen's Churches (Map p91) dates from 1190 and it too has a few Norman odds and ends, including a late-12th-century doorway.

ANGLO-DUTCH PERIOD

After the restoration of Charles II in 1660, Dublin embarked upon almost a century and a half of unparalleled growth as the city raced to become the second most important in the British empire. The grandest example of 17th-century architecture, and indeed Dublin's first classical building, is the hugely impressive Royal Hospital Kilmainham (1680; Map p91), which was designed by William Robinson as a home for invalid soldiers. Comprising a vast, cobbled courtyard in the centre of a quadrangular building with arcades, it was given a stunning makeover in the 1980s and now houses the Irish Museum of Modern Art (IMMA).

Similar in stature – and now also in shape, size and function – the Royal Barracks (Collins Barracks; 1701; Map p102) was built by Thomas Burgh as the first purpose-designed military barracks in Europe. The awesome square could accommodate six regiments, and the barracks was the oldest to remain in use until the National Museum commandeered the premises to stock its decorative arts.

Robinson moved from the mammoth to the miniature when he built the enchanting Marsh's Library (1701; Map p91), which was the first public library in Ireland and has remained virtually untouched.

GEORGIAN DUBLIN

Dublin's architectural apogee can roughly be placed in the period spanning the rule of the four English Georges, between the accession of George I in 1714 and the death of George IV in 1830. The greatest influence on the shape of modern Dublin throughout this period was the Wide Street Commissioners, appointed in 1757 and responsible for designing civic spaces and the framework of the modern city. Their efforts were complemented by Dublin's Anglo-Irish Protestant gentry who, flush with unprecedented wealth, dedicated themselves wholeheartedly towards improving their city.

Their inspiration was the work of the Italian architect Andrea Palladio (1508–80), who revived the symmetry and harmony of classical architecture. When the Palladian style reached these shores in the 1720s, the architects of the time tweaked it and introduced a number of, let's call them, 'refinements'. Most obvious were the elegant brick exteriors and decorative touches, such as coloured doors, fanlights and ironwork, which broke the sometimes austere uniformity of the fashion. Consequently, Dublin came to be known for its 'Georgian style'.

The architect credited with the introduction of this style to Dublin's cityscape was Sir Edward Lovett Pearce (1699–1733), who first arrived in Dublin in 1725 and turned heads with the building of Parliament House (Bank of Ireland; 1728–39; Map p70). It was the first two-chamber debating house in the world and the main chamber, the House of Commons, is topped by a massive pantheon-style dome.

Pearce also created the blueprint for the city's Georgian townhouses, the most distinguishing architectural feature of Dublin. The local version typically consists of four storeys, including the basement, with symmetrically arranged windows and an imposing, often brightly painted front door. Granite steps lead up to the door, which is often further embellished with a delicate leaded fanlight. The most celebrated examples are on the south side of the city, particularly around Merrion and Fitzwilliam Sqs (Map p80), but the north side also has some magnificent streets, including North Great George's and Henrietta Sts (Map p102). The latter features two of Pearce's originals (at Nos 9 and 10) and is still Dublin's most unified Georgian street. Mountjoy Sq (Map p102), the most elegant address in 18th-century Dublin, is currently being renewed after a century of neglect.

German architect Richard Cassels (Richard Castle; 1690–1751) hit town in 1728. While his most impressive country houses are outside Dublin, he did design Nos 85 and 86 St Stephen's Green (1738), which were combined in the 19th century and renamed Newman House (Map p68), and No 80 (1736), which was later joined with No 81 to create Iveagh House, now the Department of Foreign Affairs; you can visit the peaceful gardens (Map p68) there still. The Rotunda Hospital (1748; Map p102), which closes off the top of O'Connell St, is also one of Cassels' works. As splendid as these buildings are, it seems he was only warming up for Leinster House (1745–48; Map p80), the magnificent country residence built on what was then the countryside, now the centre of government.

GEORGIAN PLASTERERS

The handsome exteriors of Dublin's finest Georgian houses are often matched by superbly crafted plasterwork within. The fine work of Michael Stapleton (1770–1803) can be seen in Trinity College (Map p67), Ely House (Map p80) near St Stephen's Green, and Belvedere House (p102) in north Dublin. The LaFranchini brothers, Paolo (1693–1770) and Filippo (1702–79), are responsible for the outstanding decoration in Newman House on St Stephen's Green (Map p68). But perhaps Dublin's most famous plastered surfaces are in the chapel at the heart of the Rotunda Hospital (Map p102). Although hospitals are never the most pleasant places to visit, it's worth it for the German stuccodore, Bartholomew Cramillion's fantastic rococo plasterwork.

49

SAMPLING SAM STEPHENSON

One of the architects who designed the Electrical Supply Board (ESB) offices that broke up Dublin's 'Georgian Mile' – and a name synonymous with the 'rape of the city' in the 1970s and '80s – was Sam Stephenson. To be fair, he owes much of his notoriety to being in the right place (*in* with the government) at the wrong time (a government that happened to be more than a little dodgy). His two most infamous buildings are the Central Bank of Ireland (1975; Map p87) and the Dublin Civic Offices (Phase I, 1976; Map p91) at Wood Quay, neither of which he was allowed to complete for various reasons.

The Central Bank of Ireland is a bold geometric presence towering over today's Temple Bar. Although innovatively designed, its brutal bulkiness was controversially at odds with the low-rise old city it occupied. Furthermore, the building was left incomplete because brazen project managers exceeded the height limit and the roof had to be removed.

Even more vilified were the Dublin Civic Offices he designed for Wood Quay. His original plan was for four squat towers descending towards the river and linked by a glass atrium but, not long after construction began, the remains of the Viking city were discovered, and so began several years of hurried excavations, court cases and much palaver. The corporation eventually went ahead with its plans – the archaeological treasure was sealed and the bunkers built – but bottled out halfway through and, compounding the damage, only completed half the plan. In the mid-1990s an extension was added to the original building, which proved popular among the public and critics alike. It's certainly easier on the eye, although we think it looks a bit like a camel.

Dublin's boom attracted such notable architects as the Swedish-born Sir William Chambers (1723–96), who designed some of Dublin's most impressive buildings, though he never actually bothered to visit the city. It was the north side of the Liffey that benefited most from Chambers' genius: the chaste and elegant Charlemont House (Hugh Lane Gallery; 1763; Map p102) lords over Parnell Sq, while the Casino at Marino (1755–79; Off Map p125) is his most stunning and bewitching work.

Across the river, Chambers designed the Examination Hall (1779–91) and the Chapel (1798), which flank the elegant 18th-century quadrangle of Trinity College (Map p67), known as Parliament Sq. However, Trinity College's most magnificent feature, the old Library Building, with its breathtaking Long Room (1712; Map p67), had already been designed by Thomas Burgh.

It was towards the end of the 18th century that Dublin's developers really kicked into gear, when the power and confidence of the Anglo-Irish Ascendancy seemed boundless. Of several great architects of the time, James Gandon (1743–1823) stood out, and he built two of Dublin's most enduring and elegant neoclassical landmarks, Custom House (1781–91; Map p115) and the Four Courts (1786–1802; Map p102). They were both built on the quays to afford plenty of space in which to admire them.

Gandon's greatest rival was Thomas Cooley (1740–84), who died too young to reach his full potential. His greatest building, the Royal Exchange (City Hall; 1779; p68), was butchered to provide office space in the mid-19th century, but returned to its breathtaking splendour in a stunning 2000 restoration.

REGENCY & VICTORIAN

There is precious little 19th-century Dublin architecture, which is a reflection of the city's sharp decline during the period. Francis Johnston (1760–1829) was unfortunate to miss out on the boom, which ended with the Act of Union in 1801. His most famous building is the General Post Office (GPO; 1814; Map p102) on O'Connell St, although he's also well known for something he didn't do. When Parliament House was sold in 1803, on the proviso that it could never again be used for political assembly, Johnston was hired to adapt the building and he managed to surreptitiously maintain the architectural integrity of the House of Lords, a piece of history which you can now tour (Map p70). Cheers, Frank.

A rare Victorian highlight is the stunning series of curvilinear glasshouses in the National Botanic Gardens (Map p125), which were designed mid-century by the Dublin iron-master Richard Turner (1798–1881) and restored in 1995.

After Catholic Emancipation in 1829, there was a wave of church building, and later the two great Protestant cathedrals of Christ Church (Map p91) and St Patrick's (Map p91) were reconstructed. In a space between two Georgian houses on St Stephen's Green, Cardinal Newman commissioned his professor of fine arts at Newman University, John Hungerford Pollen (1820–1902), to create the splendidly ornate and incongruous Newman University Church (1856; Map p70), which was done in a Byzantine style simply because the cardinal was none too keen on the Gothic that was all the rage at the time.

Most public funds from the mid-18th to late 20th century were spent on providing sanitation and housing, and for the most part Dublin's architecture and infrastructure deteriorated. Perhaps a reflection on where priorities lay during this time, one of the best examples of high-Victorian architecture – and the one we've seen most of – is the magnificent Stag's Head pub (1895; Map p70) on Dame Ct, which has a dazzling interior of panelling, arcading, mirrors and stained glass.

MODERN ARCHITECTURE

The beginning of the 20th century was more about destroying notable buildings than erecting them; the GPO, Custom House and Four Courts all became collateral damage in Ireland's rocky road to independence.

As an exception, one of Dublin's most majestic constructions, and the last great British building here, the Royal College of Science (1904–22, p84) was actually completed after independence. It was massively and lavishly refurbished in the late 1980s to become the government buildings, and was dubbed 'Taj MaHaughey' after the controversial taoiseach of the time.

The Dublin Airport terminal (1940; Map p225) was built by a consortium of architects and comprises a curved, art deco building that embraces incoming passengers. But it wasn't until the bus station, Busáras (1953; Map p102), that modernity really began to express itself in Dublin – amid howls of protest from a population unimpressed with its expense and stark appearance. It was designed by the influential Michael Scott, and is noteworthy for its pioneering glass facades and wave canopy roof. Locals still love it and loathe it in equal measure, but you have to admire its vigour and personality. A major revamp, mostly internal, was completed in 2004.

NIAMH KIERNAN, ARCHITECT

Until recently, Dublin's development was being conducted at a pace unknown since Georgian times, and not surprisingly the city's future appearance is of major concern to most people, not least the capital's very own architects. Niamh Kiernan understands the concerns of the critics who feel that the developers are exclusively about turning a profit rather than doing what is best for the city's long-term future.

'Development has two major problems. It has been so incredibly fast that transport development has lagged seriously behind land-use development; and large sites in the city are often developed at the expense of the nature and the grain of the traditional urban block.'

But it isn't all development gloom. 'Developers and planners have become increasingly aware of the merits of the traditional European planning model of "living over the shop", using the grain, scale and nature of the urban block to instigate development. Some of the most successful urban development schemes using this model have been Quartier Bloom, Clarion Quay in the International Financial Services Centre (IFSC) and the apartments along Cow's Lane in Temple Bar, where walking along these "inhabited" pedestrian routes is both interesting and a pleasure.'

We asked Niamh for her top five buildings or spaces in town:

- Berkeley Library (Map p67) I often try to walk through the internal courtyards of Trinity College: in wet weather there is an amazing light that bounces off the cobblestones, and this superb building by Paul Koralek is a timeless piece of architecture. I love the texture of the boarded concrete and the considered attention that the architects have given to detail.
- George's St Arcade (Map p70) They speak for themselves really. These are a collection of beautifully busy, richly decorated market buildings that have retained a wonderful sense of character and liveliness that is hard to equal elsewhere in the city.
- Utility Building (Off Map p125) This wonderful, award-winning building on Vernon Ave in Clontarf by Tom de Paor stops me in my tracks every time I pass it. The diamond-shaped green copper cladding is so eye-catching.
- Printworks (Map p87) I love the depth of the building facade of this building in Temple Bar, designed by Group 91/Derek Tynan. It is a lovely element to the building as often we think of facades as two-dimensional elements only.
- Wooden Building (Map p87) The materiality of this building by De Blacam and Meaghar is wonderful. It is a very soft and interesting building set among the grey limestones and granites. It looks as though the entire timber facade wants to fold down to the ground.

DESIGNS ON DUBLIN

Archéire (www.irish-architecture.com) is a comprehensive website covering all things to do with Irish architecture and design. If you want something in book form, look no further than Christine Casey's superb *The Buildings of Ireland: Dublin* (2005; Yale University Press), which goes through the city literally street by street.

The tallest most denigrated structure – for now, at least – is the shamefully shabby Liberty Hall (1965; Map p102) on the quays; *this* is probably why the city has dragged its heels on skyscrapers. Paul Koralek's bold and brazen Berkeley Library (1967; Map p67), in the grounds of Trinity College, is the most interesting construct to come out of 1960s Dublin.

The poorly regulated building boom of succeeding decades paid no attention to the country's architectural heritage and destroyed more than it created. There were no noble causes to blame this time around, just sheer stupidity. The most notorious case of cultural vandalism occurred in 1970 when the state-owned Electricity Supply Board (ESB) demolished 16 Georgian houses on Lower Fitzwilliam St to build its headquarters, breaking a unique, mile-long Georgian streetscape. Adding insult to injury, after just 30-odd years, the company is in the process of selling the building and shifting out to the suburbs.

The 1980s were a miserable time to be in Dublin; the city was in the jaws of a depression and seemed to be disintegrating into 100 shades of grey. The Temple Bar area was being left to waste away and, according to Frank McDonald, environment correspondent of the *Irish Times,* there wasn't a single private apartment available for sale in the centre of Dublin. In 2004 there were some 15,000 apartments and the city is *still* one of the lowest density capitals in Europe, although there is currently a commitment to more high-density housing such as sky-rises and larger apartment blocks.

BOOM TOWN

Ireland's explosive growth during the 1990s was mostly focused on its capital, where the tower cranes punched the sky triumphantly. The first major development was the (now) unspectacular International Financial Services Centre (IFSC; Map p115), built around the turn of the 21st century. It's big, it sparkles, but it's not that impressive.

More successful developments around Dublin include the Waterways Visitor Centre (1994; Map p115), which is colloquially known as the 'box in the docks' because the steel-framed, white-panelled structure appears to float. The Millennium Wing (2001) of the National Gallery (p82) is a superb example of civic architecture and has a compelling, sculpted Portland-stone facade and a tall, light-filled atrium.

Another terrific civic development is the Boardwalk (2001; Map p102), a 650m promenade along the Liffey, which complements the new bridges, makes a feature of the river, and provides a pleasant, occasionally even sunny, stroll away from the noise and traffic fumes of the northern quays.

Entire areas were earmarked for redevelopment, creating different centres around the city. The previously dilapidated Smithfield market area now has a snazzy plaza (2000) surrounded by a collection of shiny new buildings, one of which is home to the superb Lighthouse Cinema (Map p102). Flanking the square are a series of lofty lighting masts topped by gas braziers, which evoke a sense of the area's medieval past.

The most impressive makeover has occurred in the Docklands (Map p115), which has been transformed from quasi-wasteland to a fine example of contemporary urban design. Old buildings have been refurbished, including the CHQ building at Spencer Dock (Map p115), the last surviving warehouse of the Docklands, but it's the new buildings that really catch the eye. On the north side, the impressive, tube-shaped National Convention Centre (Map p115), designed by Kevin Roche, is slated to open at the end of 2010. On the south side of the river, most of the action is centred on the new Grand Canal Square: the magnificent new Grand Canal Theatre (Map p115), designed by Daniel Libeskind, is breathtaking.

Just south of the Docklands in the southern suburb of Donnybrook, the new 50,000-seat Aviva Stadium (Map p122) – formerly the Lansdowne Rd Stadium – opened in 2010 to plenty of praise. Designed by Populous in tandem with famous Dublin firm Scott Tallon Walker, it's curvilinear-shaped stand, enclosing all four sides of the ground, is just gorgeous: hopefully the Irish rugby and football teams who will share the ground can do it justice and keep winning games.

At last, all of the work on O'Connell St (Map p102) has borne some fruit. Although not quite completed – the upper end of the street is still under wraps – the pavements are cleaner and wider, a pedestrianised plaza beneath the Spire (Map p102) has given Spanish students and junkies a whole new spot to hang out, and traffic has been severely limited up and down the thoroughfare. Now if they could just get rid of those poxy fast-food joints…

Some of the most impressive works of recent times have been the superb restorations and redevelopments of wonderful buildings, such as the Royal Hospital Kilmainham (Map p91), Collins Barracks (p102), City Hall (Map p68) and Dublin Castle (Map p68).

In 2001 the Guinness brewery also commissioned a spectacular refit of its original Fermentation House (1904), reputedly the first steel-framed, multistorey building in the British Isles – an undertaking that some years ago would instead have seen the building torn down but for the prohibitive costs of demolition. It now houses the Guinness Storehouse (Map p91), which is designed around a pint-shaped atrium and topped with the circular, glass-panelled Gravity Bar, from where you have awesome panoramic views of the city – best viewed through the bottom of your complimentary pint.

The economic meltdown has probably come at a good time for Dublin to take a breather, and for Dubliners to have another long, hard look at how their city is shaping up. Architectural integrity is a watchword these days, but only time will tell how well aesthetics and the needs of the burgeoning city are reconciled.

ENVIRONMENT & PLANNING

Though it doesn't suffer the air pollution that chokes some other European capitals, James Joyce's 'dear, dirty Dublin' does have its fair share of environmental concerns. Chief among these is the woeful traffic congestion and urban sprawl that has emerged in the last decade – in fact, you can combine the two because it's the car-oriented sprawl into the countryside that is concerning planners most these days.

THE LAND

Dublin used to spread conveniently around the arc of Dublin Bay, but these days, largely due to Dubliners fleeing the exorbitant house prices, the city is all over the place and the commuter belt has well and truly spilled over into neighbouring counties, which are poorly equipped to cope. Ireland is one of the most car-dependent societies in the world and the vast majority of these commuters drive in and out of the city daily.

GREEN DUBLIN

The government coalition that's been in power since 2007 may include the Green Party (then again, they may all be gone by the time you read this), but their desire to sit at the big table meant that much of their agenda was left at the door. It's not that Dubliners are especially indifferent to the needs of the environment – the Green Party's success at the polls (they did particularly well in south Dublin) suggests otherwise – but history has a way of making even the best intentions go awry: it's hard to tell a city that got wealthy a wet week ago after pissing potless for centuries that they *shouldn't* buy an SUV or go on four foreign holidays a year. The construction boom of the last decade was supported by virtually everyone, even though it resulted in the sacrifice of much of the green belt that surrounded the city centre, and the resultant stress on the city's inadequate road system created a major traffic crisis, with most of the city's arteries choked with pollution-emitting cars during most daylight hours. It was all in the name of progress. In 2007 Ireland's carbon footprint was 5.0 global hectares per person – more than double the global average – meaning that the country had to pay a total of 3.6 million tonnes of carbon credits per year.

Enter the economic collapse of 2008–09. All of a sudden, production has dropped across a range of industries and the Environmental Protection Agency has altered its forecast, estimating that the country would now be liable for about half the amount of carbon credits it had been previously – between 1.3 and 1.8m tonnes. Such improvements notwithstanding, Ireland will still struggle to meet its obligations under the Kyoto Protocol, and the EU's own binding targets, which are scheduled to be met by 2020.

Real progress has been achieved in the key area of recycling. By the end of 2010, local authorities planned to have 12 full-scale recycling centres in the Greater Dublin area as well as in excess of 450 bring banks spread across the city (although most of these are small and don't allow residents to dump all of their glassware, for instance, in one go). Other initiatives include the introduction of a brown bin collection for organic waste.

One real plus has been the hi-tech waste-water treatment centre that opened in 2003 and has already improved the water quality in Dublin Bay. However, Dublin residents are still perplexed as to why their tap water, once as drinkable and tasty as any sporting a fancy French label, still tastes like a metallic mixture.

Check out the Sustainable Dublin section (p20) for how green policies and issues affect you.

URBAN PLANNING & DEVELOPMENT

In 2006, at the height of the construction boom, the European Environment Agency was using Dublin as a worst-case scenario of urban planning. Indifferent planning strategies determined by venality and greed rather than the better interests of the city resulted in irresponsible re-zoning policies and an unchecked urban sprawl that has strained the city's resources and infrastructure to near breaking point.

Despite the welcome introduction of the Luas light-rail system, public transport is woefully inadequate, resulting in tens of thousands of daily commuters using a road system that was not built to handle that kind of traffic – even the newish M50 ring road (completed in 2005) has needed upgrading, by means of the addition of extra lanes. The Dublin Port Tunnel, built between the port and the M1 motorway close to Dublin Airport in order to move heavy-goods vehicles away from the city centre, has been very successful, but the resultant day-time ban on five-axle HGVs along the quays isn't always enforced.

GOVERNMENT & POLITICS

The Irish political system is a parliamentary democracy, and virtually all national political sway rests with the government, comprised of a cabinet of 14 all-powerful ministers. Whatever the government decides is approved by the parliament, which is dominated by the government. An appointed 'whip' ensures that everyone in the ruling party toes the party line when it comes to voting.

Irish politics, and society at large, is largely homogenous, and voters are mostly influenced by local issues and personalities rather than ideologies or national policies. You can hardly see light between the positions of the major parties and it's not unusual for supposedly left- and right-leaning parties to cosy up together to form government. The current taoiseach (prime minister) and tanaiste (deputy prime minister) are Brian Cowen and Mary Coughlan, who are both members of Fianna Fáil; Fianna Fáil is the majority party in its current coalition with the Green Party, which is led by John Gormley, currently Minister for the Environment, Heritage & Local Government.

IN TERMS OF IRISH POLITICS

An tUachtarán (awn *uk*-ta-rawn) – president

Dáil (dawl) – Lower House

Oireachtas na Éireann (ow-rawk*tus* na *hair*-in) – Irish parliament

Seanad (shan-ad) - Upper House

Tanaiste (*taw*-nashta) – deputy prime minister

Taoiseach (*tea*-shok) – prime minister

Teachta Dalai (tee-ochta dawl-*lee*) – deputies, members of parliament; also known as TDs

The Republic's electoral system is proportional representation, where voters mark the candidates in order of preference. Elections must take place at least once every five years. In May 2007, the centre-right Fianna Fáil, led by the then-Taoiseach Bertie Ahern, won handsomely for the third time, but by the following year Ahern had resigned as a result of a scandal around his personal finances; he handed the baton of power over to his deputy, the then–Minister of Finance, Cowen.

With a solid voter base of around 40% of the electorate, Fianna Fáil has traditionally been Ireland's best-supported party since it first came to power in 1932. However, its fortunes have tanked dramatically in the wake of the economic collapse, sparked by the global economic crisis of late 2008. In mid-2010, support for the party hovered at around 22% – the lowest in its history – and most commentators agree that it would be a miracle if they were to hold on to power following the next general election, likely to be held sometime in 2011. Its junior partner in government, the Green Party, hovers around the 3% popularity mark, due to a common perception that its eagerness for power saw it ditch too much of

top picks

BLOGS

Some of the best and most fearless – not to mention funniest – reporting is done by bloggers, the best of which reveal what is *really* going on in this city.

- Blurred Keys (http://blurredkeys.com) A superb blog that focuses on the media and how it covers current affairs – a watchdog for the watchdogs.
- Dublin Blog (www.dublinblog.ie) A great forum for all kinds of debate, from student housing to the weather.
- Dublin Opinion (www.dublinopinion.com) A marvellous group blog with incisive commentary on all matters affecting the capital.
- Irish Election (www.irishelection.com) The best political blog, featuring comprehensive analysis of all the major issues.
- Twenty Major (http://twentymajor.net) An award-winning blog regularly considered the best in the country for its in-your-face, hilarious commentary.

its agenda and that it has failed to take Fianna Fáil to task for the widespread corruption and venality that occurred under Fianna Fáil's stewardship.

The party waiting to assume power is Fine Gael, traditional antagonists of Fianna Fáil as they are both direct descendants, respectively, of the anti-Treaty and pro-Treaty sides in the Civil War. Fine Gael, who, despite the disastrous showing of its rivals, struggles to muster support beyond 32% of the electorate, is led by Enda Kenny. In third place, and vying for an important role in the next government, is centre-left Labour, led by Eamon Gilmore, which is favoured by around 25% of the electorate. Labour's popularity is in part due to its longstanding opposition to the irresponsible smash-and-grab policies that made a mess out of the economy in the first place.

Sinn Féin, the political wing of the now-decommissioned IRA, promotes itself as the party for all the disenfranchised and currently has four TDs (members of parliament) – each of its TDs donates two-thirds of their parliamentary salary (€100,191) to the party.

The constitutional head of state is the president (An tUachtarán), elected by popular vote for a seven-year term. While this position has little real power, the largely apolitical (at least in an Irish party sense) Mary Robinson wielded considerable informal influence over social policies when she was elected in 1990. She was succeeded by the more low-key, although equally ballsy, Mary McAleese, a Belfast-born Catholic nationalist who was re-elected unopposed in 2004.

At local level, Dublin is mainly governed by two elected bodies: Dublin City Council and Dublin County Council. The city version used to be known as Dublin Corporation (the Corpo), a name synonymous with inefficiency and incompetence, but the new incarnation is a progressive and admired local government. Each year, it elects a Lord Mayor who shifts into the Mansion House, speaks out on matters to do with the city and is lucky if half of Dublin knows his or her name by the time they have to hand back the chains.

MEDIA

Five national dailies, six national Sundays, stacks of Irish editions of British publications, hundreds of magazines, more than a dozen radio stations, four terrestrial TV stations and more digital channels than you could shake the remote control at…media may be in crisis everywhere else in the world, but they're doing *relatively* well in Dublin – mostly because Dubliners have always been avid consumers of the word, both printed and uttered.

The dominant local player is Independent News & Media, owned by Ireland's primo businessman, Tony O'Reilly. Its newspapers – the *Irish Independent, Sunday Independent* and *Evening Herald* – are by far the biggest sellers in each market. See p251 for details of Dublin-based newspapers and magazines.

The massive overspill of British media, particularly in relation to the saturated Sunday market, is the biggest challenge facing the Irish media. Rupert Murdoch's News Corporation recognised the importance of the Irish market early, established an office in Dublin and set about an assault of the newspaper racks with its main titles, the *Irish Sun, News of the World* and *Sunday Times*.

Magazine publishing blossomed during the boom, and while the economic slowdown has seen the disappearance of glossy monthlies devoted to niche subjects like horse dressage and flower arranging, the craving for celebrity tittle-tattle means that a host of devoted English magazines and their Irish counterparts is here to stay.

There are four terrestrial TV channels in Ireland (see p45). Arguably the best thing about the state broadcaster, RTE, is its news programming and its sports coverage, particularly of Gaelic games. Meanwhile, Dublin's gone digital and the two big players are the home-grown UPC and the behemoth that is Sky, which continues to make solid progress in bringing the multichannel revolution into Dublin homes.

The state of local radio is very healthy. There is a huge choice incorporating talk radio, current affairs, pirate stations, progressive music channels and lots of commercial dross. If you want to take the pulse of the city, check out the housewives' favourite, talk-show host Joe Duffy on *Liveline* (RTE 1, 88.5FM; from 1.45pm Monday to Friday), the favourite place for Ireland to have a moan. If you like sport, listen no further than *Off the Ball* (Newstalk 106–108, 7pm to 10pm Monday to Friday).

LANGUAGE

Although Gaeilge (Irish) is the official language – and all official documents, street signs and official titles are either in Gaeilge or bilingual – it's only spoken in isolated pockets of rural Ireland known as Gaeltacht areas.

While all Dubliners must learn it at school, the teaching of Gaeilge has traditionally been thoroughly academic and unimaginative, leading most kids to resent it as a waste of time. Ask Dubliners if they can speak Irish and nine out of 10 of them will probably reply, 'ahhh cupla focal' (literally 'a couple of words') and they generally mean it. It's a pity that the treatment of Irish in schools has been so heavy-handed because many adults say they regret not having a greater grasp of it. A new curriculum has been in place for the last few years that aims to redress this shortcoming by cutting the hours devoted to the subject, and making the lessons more fun, practical and celebratory.

DUBLIN SLANG

Dubliners are like the mad scientists of linguistics, and have an enormous lexicon of slang words from which to choose. For example, there is said to be more than 50 alternative words for 'penis', while it's quite possible they have more words to describe 'drunkenness' than the Eskimos have for 'snow'. Here are just a few doozies:

banjaxed – broken down

chiseller – a young child

couldn't be arsed – couldn't be bothered

fair play/fucks to you – well done

header – mentally unstable person

I will in me bollix – I won't

jax – toilet

make a bags of something – mess it up

me belly tinks me trote's been cut – I'm rather hungry

rag order – bad condition

ride – have sex with

scarlet (*scarl*eh) – blushing

shite – rubbish

shorts – spirits

slagging – teasing

trow a wobbler – have a temper tantrum

work away – go ahead, after you

yer man – that guy

yer one – that girl

yer wha'? – excuse me?!?

yoke – inserted to describe a noun when the actual word has slipped the speaker's mind

Here are a few useful phrases *os gaeilge* (in Irish) to help you impress the locals:

Fool.	ohm-a-*dawn*	*Amadáin.*
Hi.	dee-a gwit	*Dia dhuit.*
How are you?	kunas aw *taw* two	*Conas a tá tú?*
I don't like Big Brother.	*knee* moh lum Big Brother	*Ní maith liom Big Brother.*
I'm good.	thawm go*moh*	*Táim go maith.*
I'm never ever drinking again.	knee ohl-*hee* mey gu *brawkh* u-*reesh*	*Ní ólfaidh mé go brách arís.*
Kiss my arse.	*pogue* ma hone	*Póg ma thóin.*
My name is Amanda.	iss *misha* Amanda	*Is mise Amanda.*
One hundred thousand welcomes.	kade meela fallcha	*Céad míle fáilte.*
Shut your mouth.	doon daw klob	*Dún do chlab.*
Thanks.	gur rev moh ag*ut*	*Go raibh maith agat.*
What is your name?	cawd iss an*im* dit	*Cad is ainm duit?*
Your health/Cheers.	*slawn*-cha	*Sláinte.*

BACKGROUND LANGUAGE

While most Dubliners overlooked Gaeilge, their command of English and their inventive use of vocabulary is second to none. Huge numbers of foreign-language students, particularly from continental Europe, flock to the city for study because the average Dubliner's elocution is so clear. When travelling in Italy or Spain, it's gas (funny) to hear locals speaking English with Dublin accents. Dubliners love the sound of their own voices and they are genuinely interested in the way words sound as much as in their meaning. They're generally very articulate, confident orators, and like nothing more than a good debate (preferably over a pint).

Dublin accents – there are several – have all the traits of the typical Irish brogue, including softened, shortened vowels, hardened consonants and discarded 'h's in the 'th' sound (as in the old 't'irty t'ree and a t'ird' joke). The average, or neutral, Dublin accent is possibly one of the most eloquent and easily understandable in the English-speaking world while the extremes are barely comprehensible at all. The 'real Dublin' accent is clipped, drawn out and slack-jawed. It discards consonants disdainfully, particularly the letter 't' (all right becomes origh) and is peppered with so many instances of 'feck', 'jaysus' and 'yer wha'?' that you think the speaker might be dumbstruck without them.

Yet this Dublin accent is infinitely preferable to the plummy accent of affluent southsiders, who contort and squeeze vowels at will. Formerly known as the Dublin 4 accent, this diction has since come to be known as the 'DART accent' (or 'dort' as its speakers would pronounce it) because it has spread out south along the coastal railway line.

The spread of this pseudo-received accent is so alarming that Frank McNally of the *Irish Times* has suggested the only way to eradicate the DART accent would be to make it compulsory in schools – it damn nearly worked for Gaeilge!

NEIGHBOURHOODS

top picks

- **Chester Beatty Library** (p72) A stunning collection of books and objets d'art.
- **Trinity College** (p66) Ireland's foremost university and most beautiful campus.
- **Dublin City Gallery – The Hugh Lane** (p104) Modern art at its finest, including Francis Bacon's studio.
- **Kilmainham Gaol** (p97) Irish history in all its bloody gore and horror.
- **Irish Museum of Modern Art** (IMMA; p98) The country's foremost collection of contemporary art.
- **Marsh's Library** (p95) Ireland's oldest library is a well-kept secret wonder.
- **St Patrick's Cathedral** (p93) Elegance, piety and a tempestuous history.
- **Old Jameson Distillery** (p105) The nuts and bolts of Irish whiskey, plus a taster.

NEIGHBOURHOODS

Dublin may be bulging round its ever-expanding edges, but the city centre – defined by the bits within the two canals that create an almost perfect ring around it – remains very compact, lending it the atmosphere of a busy provincial town rather than an alienating metropolis. Not that you can't get confused around here though: the geographic area of Dublin's city centre may be small, but it's a somewhat haphazard mix of medieval street arrangements and 18th-century town planning, which sought to make some sense of the spider's web of streets and alleys that spread their way outwards from both sides of the river.

'the city centre...remains very compact, lending it the atmosphere of a busy provincial town rather than an alienating metropolis'

The River Liffey – that pea-brown stretch of barely moving water that bisects the city into neat halves – serves as the handiest way of determining your whereabouts: you're either north or south of it, presented simply as north side and south side. The river also serves as the traditional social divide of Dublin: working class and poor north of the Liffey, posh and wealthy south of it. Spend enough time in Dublin and you'll hear the jokes.

Although most of the city centre has been given the gentrification once-over, the south side remains the most salubrious part of the city and will probably be the focus of most of your visit here. At the heart of it all is the pedestrianised shopping feast that is Grafton St, bookended by the beautiful expanses of the Elizabethan Trinity College to the north and Georgian St Stephen's Green to the south; as pretty a city square as you're likely to see anywhere in Europe. This is where you'll find the bulk of the city's main attractions, the best bars and much of the nightlife.

To the east, the equally elegant Merrion Sq is the heart of the Georgian city and the nexus of Irish political power – the front entrance of the houses of parliament and the office of the taoiseach (prime minister) look over the square, as do two of the city's most impressive museums.

To the west, past the oldest bits of the city (the medieval Liberties) and the two Norman cathedrals, is the world-famous Guinness factory and museum, as well as Kilmainham Gaol and the Irish Museum of Modern Art, two outstanding attractions that should be a part of every itinerary.

North of the river, the graceful avenue that is O'Connell St introduces visitors to what many Dubliners believe is the 'real' Dublin, where salt-of-the-earth locals traditionally suspicious of their south side counterparts are now mixing it with whole new communities of non-nationals, creating genuinely multicultural neighbourhoods where old-style fish-and-fowl vendors of the Molly Malone variety and entrepreneurs from Nigeria, Korea, Poland and elsewhere are all looking to make a buck.

To the east, straddling both sides of the river, is the Docklands area, where the new office blocks and eye-catching modern architecture are the most conspicuous example of the sky-high ambitions of the Celtic Tiger. West of O'Connell St is the old market section of Smithfield, which has a couple of interesting night-time distractions, and beyond it, the pride of all Dubliners, Phoenix Park – the city's gigantic green lung, which is twice the size of New York's Central Park.

Beyond the canals – the Royal to the north, the Grand to the south – are the suburbs, where you'll find a handful of interesting attractions, including a botanic garden, a superb sports museum and some lovely little seaside villages that privileged Dubliners expensively call 'home'.

East Wall

Irishtown

Sandymount

Ballsbridge

Marino

North Wall

Docklands

Ringsend

Beggar's Bush

BEYOND THE GRAND CANAL
(p121)

Donnybrook

Drumcondra

DOCKLANDS
(p114)

BEYOND THE ROYAL CANAL
(p124)

MERRION SQUARE & AROUND
(p79)

Ranelagh

Philsboro

Trinity College

TEMPLE BAR
(p86)

Grafton Street

GRAFTON STREET & AROUND
(p66)

NORTH OF THE LIFFEY
(p101)

The Liberties

Smithfield

Dolphin's Barn

Harold's Cross

Cabra

KILMAINHAM & THE LIBERTIES
(p90)

PHOENIX PARK
(p118)

Islandbridge

Kilmainham

Inchicore

Goldenbridge

1 km

0.6 miles

ITINERARY BUILDER

Dublin is small, but it's not that small, so you'll need to plan your days somewhat, lest you end up lost with sore feet and shopping bags that are just getting heavier. The south central neighbourhoods all run into one another, but the north side is an expanse that runs the width of the city itself. The two neighbourhoods beyond the canals are best reached by public transport or taxi.

AREA	ACTIVITIES Sights	Eating
Grafton Street & Around	Trinity College (p66) Chester Beatty Library (p72) St Stephen's Green (p73)	L'Gueuleton (p155) Green Nineteen (p158) Bottega Toffoli (p158)
Merrion Square & Around	National Gallery (p82) National Museum of Ireland – Natural History (p83) National Museum of Ireland – Archaeology (p80)	L'Ecrivain (p160) Chez Max (p161) Restaurant Patrick Guilbaud (p160)
Temple Bar	Gallery of Photography (p88) Temple Bar Gallery (p88) Ark Children's Cultural Centre (p88)	Gruel (p163) Eden (p161) Mermaid Café (p161)
Kilmainham & the Liberties	Kilmainham Gaol (p97) Irish Museum of Modern Art (p98) Guinness Storehouse (p90)	Leo Burdock's (p163)
North of the Liffey & Phoenix Park	Dublin City Gallery – The Hugh Lane (p104) National Museum of Ireland – Decorative Arts & History (p106) Phoenix Park (p118)	Chapter One (p164) Winding Stair (p164)
Docklands	Custom House (p114) Jeanie Johnston (p116)	Herbstreet (p166)
Beyond the Grand Canal	National Print Museum (p121)	La Peniche (p167) Jo'Burger (p168)
Beyond the Royal Canal	Croke Park & GAA Museum (p124) National Botanic Gardens (p126) Casino at Marino (p126)	

HOW TO USE THIS TABLE

The table below allows you to plan a day's worth of activities in any area of the city. Simply select which area you wish to explore, and then mix and match from the corresponding listings to build your day. The first item in each cell represents a well-known highlight of the area, while the other items are more off-the-beaten-track gems.

Drinking	Shopping	Nightlife, Arts & Activities
Anseo (p174) Bar With No Name (p173) Kehoe's (p176)	Costume (p139) Smock (p140) Avoca Handweavers (p138)	Tripod (p189 & p195) National Concert Hall (p193)
Hartigan's (p177) Doheny & Nesbitt's (p177) James Toner's (p177)		Sugar Club (p195)
Porterhouse Brewing Company (p178) Purty Kitchen (p179)	Urban Outfitters (p143) Gutter Bookshop (p143)	Irish Film Institute (p179) Button Factory (p188 & p194)
Fallon's (p180)	Oxfam Home (p144) Fleury Antiques (p144)	Vicar Street (p195)
Pantibar (p181) Dice Bar (p180) Sin É (p181)	Winding Stair (p144)	Abbey Theatre (p197) Gate Theatre (p198) Cobblestone (p196)
La Cuvée @ Eno Wine Bar (p182)		Grand Canal Theatre (p193)
Kiely's (p183)	Havana (p146)	Civic Theatre (p198) Marlay Park (p194)
Gravediggers (p183)		Croke Park (p206)

DUBLIN

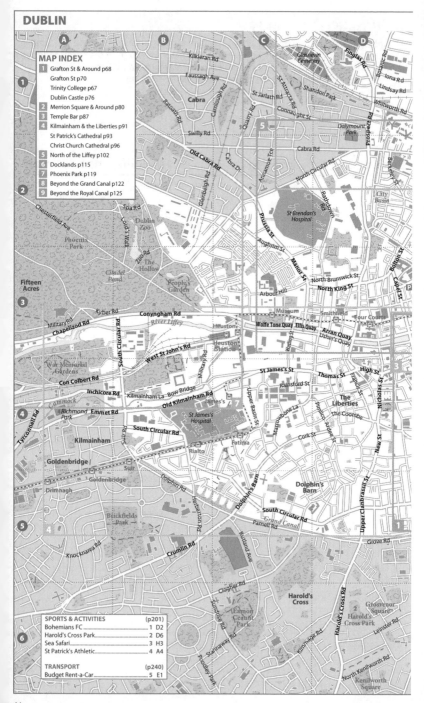

MAP INDEX
1 Grafton St & Around p68
  Grafton St p70
  Trinity College p67
  Dublin Castle p76
2 Merrion Square & Around p80
3 Temple Bar p87
4 Kilmainham & the Liberties p91
  St Patrick's Cathedral p93
  Christ Church Cathedral p96
5 North of the Liffey p102
6 Docklands p115
7 Phoenix Park p119
8 Beyond the Grand Canal p122
9 Beyond the Royal Canal p125

SPORTS & ACTIVITIES	(p201)	
Bohemians FC	1	D2
Harold's Cross Park	2	D6
Sea Safari	3	H3
St Patrick's Athletic	4	A4
TRANSPORT	(p240)	
Budget Rent-a-Car	5	E1

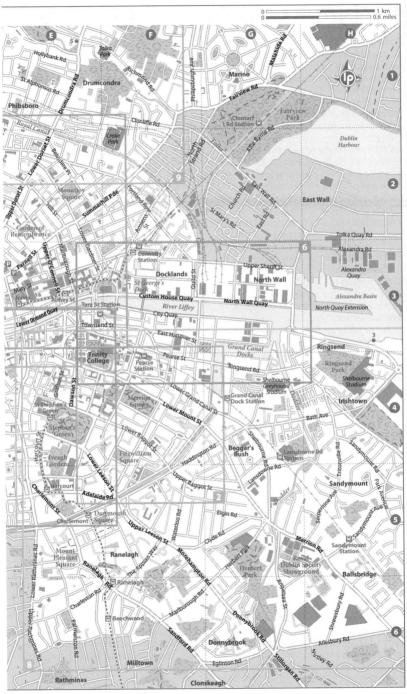

GRAFTON STREET & AROUND

Drinking p172; Eating p152; Shopping p137; Sleeping p212

Less neighbourhood and more pulsating heart of the city, the swathe of supremely elegant streets and landscaped green spaces that fill out the area around Grafton St, directly south of the river, is what most visitors and not an insignificant number of Dubliners are talking about when they refer to the 'city centre'. Bordered to the north by Temple Bar, to the west by the medieval boundaries of the Liberties, to the south by the meandering Grand Canal, and to the east by the green edge of St Stephen's Green, this compact district is the focus of most visits to the city.

Running roughly through the middle of it is pedestrianised Grafton St, lined with four-storey Georgian buildings that are home to a mix of familiar international stores and chichi local retailers. The jewel in the retail crown remains Brown Thomas (p138), the swankiest department store in town. Its window displays in December are as important to a Dubliner's idea of Christmas as an old man with a white beard.

Named after the 17th-century Duke of Grafton, who owned much of these parts, Grafton St proper starts from the area known as College Green, directly in front of the elegant facades of Elizabethan Trinity College (Map p70) and the Bank of Ireland (Map p70; built to house Ireland's first parliament). An unremarkable statue of Molly Malone (Map p70) leads us, bosoms first, to the pedestrianised street that is Grafton St.

The street has been a fashionable precinct for more than 200 years but only really took off in 1982 when the cars were driven out and the pedestrians paraded in on a newly cobbled surface, ushering in the era of the Grafton St amble. Along its length an assortment of street performers set the mood, providing the soundtrack for a memorable stroll. On any given day, you can listen to a guitarist knock out some electrifying bluegrass, applaud young conservatory students putting Mozart through his paces, or stare down a silver-skinned mime and see who moves first. You will.

But to really get the most of the neighbourhood, you'll need to get off Grafton St and into the warren of narrow lanes and streets to the west of it – here you'll find a great mix of funky shops and boutiques, some of our favourite eateries and a handful of the best bars in the city.

Just south of Grafton St is the centrepiece of Georgian Dublin, St Stephen's Green, beautifully landscaped and dotted with statuary that provides a veritable who's who of Irish history.

Thankfully, Dublin's compact size doesn't mean you have to stay here to have it all at your doorstep, but if you do, you *absolutely* must be aware that most of the lodgings are among the priciest in town.

All cross-city buses make their way to – or through, at least – this part of the city; the Luas Green Line has its terminus at the south end of Grafton St, on the west side of St Stephen's Green (see Map p68).

TRINITY COLLEGE Map p67

☎ 896 1000; www.tcd.ie; admission free; ◷ 8am-10pm; ▣ all city centre

Don your gown and dust off that tome on elocution, for this calm and cordial retreat from the bustle of contemporary Dublin is not just Ireland's most prestigious university (and the home of the blockbuster hit that is the *Book of Kells*) but a throwback to those far-off days when a university education was the preserve of a very small elite who spoke passionately of the importance of philosophy and the need for empire. Today's alumni are an altogether different bunch, but Trinity still *looks* the part, and on a summer's evening, when the crowds thin and the chatter subsides, there are few more delightful places in the world to be.

A great way to see Trinity's grounds is on a walking tour (☎ 896 1827; admission €5, incl Book of Kells €10; ◷ tours every 40min 10.15am-3.40pm Mon-Sat, 10.15am-3pm Sun mid-May–Sep), which depart from the College Green entrance.

The college was established by Elizabeth I in 1592 on land confiscated from an Augustinian priory in an effort to stop the brain drain of young Protestant Dubliners, who were skipping across to continental Europe for an education and were becoming 'infected with popery'. With bigotry as a base, Trinity went on to become one of Europe's most outstanding universities, producing a host of notable graduates – how about Jonathan Swift, Oscar Wilde and Samuel Beckett at the same alumni dinner?

It remained completely Protestant until 1793, but even when the university relented and began to admit Catholics, the Church forbade it; until 1970, any Catholic who enrolled here could consider themselves excommunicated. Although hardly the bastion of British Protestantism that it once was – most of its 15,000 students are Catholic – it is still a popular choice for British students. Women were first admitted to the college in 1903, earlier than at most British universities.

The 16-hectare site is now in the centre of the city, but when founded, it was described as being 'near Dublin' and was bordered on two sides by the estuary of the Liffey. Nothing now remains of the original Elizabethan college, which was replaced in the Georgian building frenzy of the 18th century. The elegant Regent House entrance on College Green was built between 1752 and 1759, and is guarded by statues of the writer Oliver Goldsmith (1730–74) and the orator Edmund Burke (1729–97). The railings outside the entrance are a popular meeting spot.

Through the entrance, past the Students Union, are Front Sq and Parliament Sq, the

latter dominated by the 30m-high Campanile, designed by Edward Lanyon and erected from 1852 to 1853 on what was believed to be the centre of the monastery that preceded the college. Students who pass beneath it when the bells toll will fail their exams, according to superstition. To the north of the Campanile is a statue of George Salmon, the college provost from 1886 to 1904, who fought bitterly to keep women out of the college. He carried out his threat to permit them in 'over his dead body' by dropping dead when the worst happened. To the south of the Campanile is a statue of historian WEH Lecky (1838–1903).

TRINITY COLLEGE

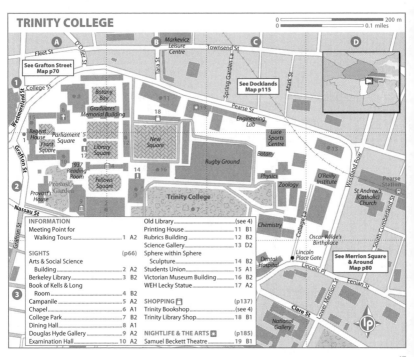

INFORMATION		Old Library .... (see 4)
Meeting Point for		Printing House 11 B1
Walking Tours 1 A2		Rubrics Building 12 B2
		Science Gallery 13 D2
SIGHTS	(p66)	Sphere within Sphere
Arts & Social Science		Sculpture 14 B2
Building 2 A2		Students Union 15 A1
Berkeley Library 3 B2		Victorian Museum Building 16 B2
Book of Kells & Long		WEH Lecky Statue 17 A2
Room 4 B2		
Campanile 5 A2		SHOPPING 🛍 (p137)
Chapel 6 A1		Trinity Bookshop .... (see 4)
College Park 7 B2		Trinity Library Shop 18 B1
Dining Hall 8 A1		
Douglas Hyde Gallery 9 A2		NIGHTLIFE & THE ARTS ✚ (p185)
Examination Hall 10 A2		Samuel Beckett Theatre 19 B1

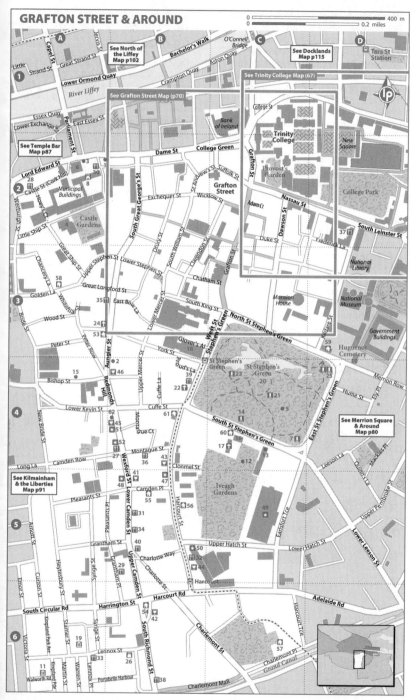

GRAFTON STREET & AROUND

GRAFTON STREET & AROUND

INFORMATION
City Pharmacy.................................1 A2
Department of Foreign
  Affairs....................................(see 13)
National Map Centre 2 B4
Sandeman's New Dublin
  Tour...3 A2

SIGHTS   (p66)
Chester Beatty Library...................4 A2
Children's Playground 5 C4
City Hall.......................................6 A2
Countess Markievicz Bust.............7 C4
Dublin Castle................................8 A2
Famine Victims Memorial.............9 D4
Huguenot Cemetery....................10 D4
Irish-Jewish Museum...................11 A6
Iveagh Gardens...........................12 C4
Iveagh House
  (Department of Foreign
  Affairs).....................................13 C4
James Joyce Bust.........................14 C4
National Archives.........................15 A4
Newman House............................16 C4
Newman University
  Church.....................................17 C4
Royal College of Surgeons..........18 B3
Shaw Birthplace..........................19 A6
St Stephen's Green.....................20 C4
Three Fates Statue.....................21 C4
Unitarian Church.........................22 B4

WB Yeats Statue.........................23 C4
Whitefriars Street
  Carmelite Church.....................24 A3
Wolfe Tone Monument................25 D4

SHOPPING   (p137)
Bretzel Bakery............................26 B6
Toejam Carboot Sale.................(see 42)

EATING   (p152)
Bobo's.......................................27 B4
Bottega Toffoli...........................28 A2
Cake Shop..................................29 B5
Chez Max....................................30 A2
Green Nineteen..........................31 B5
Harcourt St Food Market............32 B5
Lennox Café Bistro.....................33 A6
Listons.......................................34 B5
Milk & Honey.............................35 A3
Milk Bar.....................................36 B4
Pig's Ear....................................37 D2
Seagrass....................................38 B6
Shanahan's on the Green...........39 B4
Silk Road Café..........................(see 4)
Zaytoon.....................................40 B5

DRINKING   (p172)
Anseo..41 B5
Bernard Shaw............................42 B6
Dicey Reilly's.............................43 B4
Horseshoe Bar.........................(see 59)

Odeon..44 B5
Solas..45 B4
Swan..46 B4
Village......................................(see 51)
Whelan's..................................(see 52)

NIGHTLIFE & THE ARTS   (p185)
Copper Face Jack's.....................47 B5
Crawdaddy................................(see 50)
Crypt Arts Centre.......................(see 8)
Devitt's.......................................48 B5
Krystle.....................................(see 43)
National Concert Hall 49 C5
Pod...(see 50)
Tripod...50 B5
Village..51 B4
Whelan's....................................52 B4

SLEEPING   (p212)
Avalon House..............................53 A3
Camden Court Hotel....................54 B6
Frankies Guesthouse 55 B5
Harrington Hall...........................56 B5
Hilton...57 C6
Radisson Blu Royal Hotel 58 A3
Shelbourne.................................59 D3
Staunton's on the Green.............60 C4
Stephen's Green Hotel................61 B4

TRANSPORT   (p240)
MacDonald Cycles.......................62 B4

North of Parliament Sq is the Chapel
(☎ 896 1260; admission free), designed by William Chambers and completed in 1799.
It has some fine plasterwork by Michael
Stapleton, Ionic columns and painted glass
windows, and has been open to all denominations since 1972. It's only accessible
by organised tour. Next is the Dining Hall,
originally built by Richard Cassels in the
mid-18th century. The great architect must
have had an off day because the vault collapsed twice and the entire structure was
dismantled 15 years later. The replacement
was completed in 1761, but extensively
restored after a fire in 1984.

On the grassy expanse of Library Sq is
a 1969 sculpture by British sculptor Henry
Moore (1898–1986), and two large Oregon
maples. On the north side is the 1892
Graduates' Memorial Building, and an area
known as Botany Bay.

On the far east of the square, the redbrick Rubrics Building dates from around 1690,
making it the oldest building in the college.
It was extensively altered in an 1894 restoration, and then underwent serious structural
modification in the 1970s. Behind this is
New Sq, featuring the highly ornate Victorian

Museum Building (☎ 608 1477; admission free), which
houses a geological museum. It's open by
prior arrangement only. The Doric-fronted
Printing House, on the other side of the square,
was also designed by Richard Cassels.

If you are following the less studious-
looking throng, however, you'll find yourself magnetically drawn south of Library Sq
to the Old Library (☎ 896 2320; East Pavilion, Library
Colonnades; adult/student/child €8/7/free; ⓨ 9.30am-
5pm Mon-Sat year-round, noon-4.30pm Sun Oct-Apr,
9.30am-4.30pm Sun May-Sep), home to Trinity's
prize possession and biggest crowd-puller,
the astonishingly beautiful Book of Kells (see
the boxed text, p72).

Upstairs from the star attraction is the
highlight of Thomas Burgh's building, the
magnificent 65m Long Room with its barrel-
vaulted ceiling. It's lined with shelves
containing 200,000 of the library's oldest
books and manuscripts, along with busts of
eminent scholars, a 14th-century harp and
an original copy of the Proclamation of the
Irish Republic, read out by Pádraig Pearse
at the beginning of the 1916 Easter Rising.
Despite Ireland's independence, the 1801
Library Act entitles Trinity College Library
to a free copy of every book published in

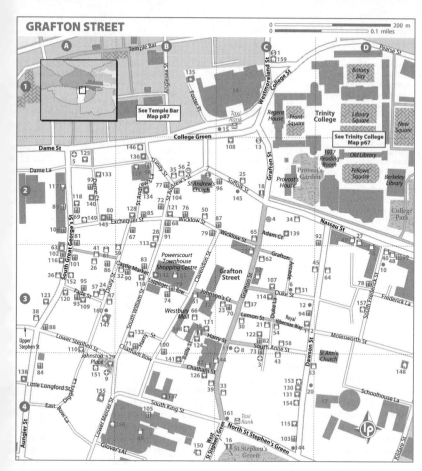

GRAFTON STREET

See Temple Bar Map p87

See Trinity College Map p67

Britain. Housing this bounty requires nearly 1km of extra shelving every year and the collection amounts to about five million titles, which are stored at various facilities around town.

In Fellows' Sq is the brutalist and brilliant Berkeley Library, designed by Paul Koralek in 1967 and once hailed by the Architectural Association of Ireland as the best example of modern architecture in the country. It's fronted by Arnaldo Pomodoro's sculpture *Sphere Within Sphere* (1982–83). George Berkeley (1685–1753), the distinguished Irish philosopher, studied at Trinity when he was only 15 years old. His influence spread to North America, where Berkeley (California) and its university are named after him.

West of the library, the Arts & Social Science Building is home to another Trin-

ity treat, the Douglas Hyde Gallery (☎ 608 1116; www.douglashydegallery.com; Arts & Social Sciences Bldg, Trinity College; admission free; ☺ 11am-6pm Mon-Wed & Fri, 11am-7pm Thu, 11am-4.45pm Sat). This is one of the country's leading contemporary galleries, and hosts regularly rotating shows presenting the works of top-class Irish and international artists across a wide range of media. It's worth checking out; you can also access it via the campus entrance on Nassau St.

On the way back towards the main entrance, past the Reading Room, is the late-18th-century Palladian Examination Hall, which closely resembles the chapel opposite because it too was the work of William Chambers, and also features plasterwork by Michael Stapleton. It contains an oak chandelier rescued from the Irish parliament (now the Bank of Ireland – see p75).

GRAFTON STREET

INFORMATION
1916 Rebellion Walking Tour...(see 121)
Allied Irish Bank 1 C1
An Post 2 B2
Anne's Lane Dental Centre 3 C4
Bank of Ireland .... (see 14)
Central Internet Café 4 C2
Dame House Dental Surgery........... 5 A2
Dublin Footsteps Walking Tour.(see 70)
Dublin Literary Pub Crawl 6 C3
Dublin Tourism Centre 7 B2
Grafton Medical Practice 8 C3
Mercer Medical Centre 9 A4
Meridian Tour Guides...................... 10 D3
O'Connell's Late Night
    Pharmacy 11 C3
Reed Recruitment Agency 12 C3
Thomas Cook 13 C2

SIGHTS   (p66)
Bank of Ireland 14 C1
College Green 15 C1
Fusiliers' Arch. 16 C4
Mansion House 17 D4
Molly Malone Statue........................ 18 C2
Phil Lynott Statue 19 B3
Powerscourt Townhouse
    Shopping Centre ....(see 55)
Royal Irish Academy........................ 20 C4

SHOPPING   (p137)
Alias Tom 21 C3
Angles 22 B3
Appleby 23 C3
Asia Market 24 A3
Avoca Handweavers 25 C2
Barry Doyle Design Jewellers....... 26 A3
Blarney Woollen Mills...................... 27 D2
Blue Eriu 28 B2
Bow Boutique ....(see 55)
Brown Thomas 29 C3
BT2 .... 30 C3
Cathach Books 31 C3
Circus Store & Gallery ....(see 55)
Costume 32 B3
Crafts Council Gallery ....(see 55)
Decent Cigar Emporium 33 C4
Design Centre ....(see 55)
Designyard 34 C2
Dublin Camera Exchange............. 35 B2
Dublin Camera Exchange 36 A3
Dubray Books 37 C3
Dunnes Home 38 A3
Dunnes Stores 39 B4
Fallon & Byrne ....(see 80)
Genealogy Bookshop........................ 40 D3
George's St Arcade 41 A3
Great Outdoors 42 B4
H Danker 43 C4
Harlequin ....(see 90)
HMV 44 C4
Hodges Figgis 45 D3
House of Names 46 D3
Jenny Vander 47 A3
Kilkenny Shop 48 D3
Knobs & Knockers 49 D2
Louis Copeland 50 B2
Magill's 51 B3
Marks & Spencer 52 C3
Murder Ink 53 C4
Optica... 54 C3

Powerscourt Townhouse Shopping
    Centre 55 B3
Rhinestones 56 B2
Road Records 57 A3
Sheridan's Cheesemongers............ 58 C3
Smock 59 B3
St Stephen's Green Shopping
    Centre 60 B4
Stokes Books...................................... 61 A3
Tommy Hilfiger 62 C3
Walton's 63 A3
Waterstone's 64 D3
Weir & Son's 65 C2
Westbury Mall 66 B3

EATING   (p152)
Avoca ....(see 25)
Balzac ....(see 154)
Blazing Salads 67 B2
Brown's Bar....................................(see 29)
Butler's Chocolate Café 68 B2
Café Bardeli 69 A2
Café Bardeli/Bewley's..................... 70 C3
Café Mao 71 B3
Cedar Tree 72 B2
Chilli Club 73 C3
Coppinger Row.................................. 74 B3
Coppinger Row Market.................... 75 B3
Cornucopia 76 B2
Cultivate 77 B2
Dunne & Crescenzi........................... 78 D3
El Bahia 79 B2
Fallon & Byrne 80 A2
Fresh ....(see 55)
Good World 81 A2
Gourmet Burger Kitchen 82 C3
Gourmet Burger Kitchen 83 B3
Govinda's 84 A4
Green Hen 85 B2
Honest to Goodness 86 A3
Imperial Chinese Restaurant......... 87 C2
Jaipur 88 A3
Juice 89 A2
La Maison 90 B3
Lemon 91 B2
Lemon 92 D2
L'Gueuleton.. 93 A3
Marco Pierre White Steakhouse &
    Grill 94 C3
Market Bar 95 A3
Nude 96 C2
Odessa 97 A2
Pichet 98 B2
Pig's Ear 99 D3
Saba 100 B3
Simon's Place 101 A3
Sixty6 .... 102 A3
Thornton's ....(see 150)
Tiger Becs ....(see 131)
Town Bar & Grill 103 C4
Trocadero 104 B2
Wagamama 105 B4
Yamamori... 106 A2

DRINKING   (p172)
Bailey... 107 C3
Bank 108 C2
Bar With No Name 109 A3
Bia Bar 110 A3
Bruxelles 111 B3
Café en Seine 112 C3

Dakota.. 113 B2
Davy Byrne's 114 C3
Dawson Lounge................................ 115 C4
Dragon 116 A3
George 117 A2
Globe 118 A2
Grogan's Castle Lounge.......... 119 B3
Hogan's.. 120 A3
International Bar 121 B2
Kehoe's.. 122 C3
Long Hall 123 A3
Market Bar ....(see 95)
McDaid's 124 B3
Mercantile... 125 A2
Neary's... 126 B4
No 4 Dame Lane.............................. 127 B2
Old Stand 128 B2
Peter's Pub.. 129 A4
Pygmalion ....(see 55)
Ron Black's.. 130 C4
SamSara 131 C4
South William 132 B3
Stag's Head 133 A2

NIGHTLIFE & THE
ARTS   (p185)
Andrew's Lane Theatre 134 B2
Bank of Ireland Arts Centre....135 B1
Banker's 136 B2
Bewley's Café Theatre............(see 70)
Gaiety Theatre 137 B4
Globe ....(see 118)
HMV ....(see 44)
Hogans ....(see 120)
International Bar ....(see 121)
JJ Smyth's 138 A4
Lillie's Bordello................................ 139 C2
Rí Rá 140 A2
Sheehan's.. 141 B4
Spy/Wax 142 B3
Ticketmaster ....(see 60)
Ukiyo 143 A2

SPORTS & ACTIVITIES   (p201)
Elvery's 144 C4
Elvery's 145 C2
Mandala Day Spa ....(see 154)

SLEEPING   (p212)
Abbott & Matthews Letting &
    Management 146 B2
Brooks Hotel 147 A3
Buswell's Hotel 148 D4
Central Hotel 149 A2
Fitzwilliam Hotel............................. 150 B4
Grafton Capital Hotel.................... 151 A4
Grafton Guesthouse....................... 152 A3
Home Locators 153 C4
La Stampa Hotel.............................. 154 C4
Mercer Court Campus
    Accommodation 155 A4
Mercer Hotel 156 A4
Trinity Lodge 157 D3
Westbury Hotel 158 B3
Westin Dublin 159 C1

TRANSPORT   (p240)
Automobile Association of
    Ireland 160 A3
Ecocabs Pick-Up 161 C4

THE PAGE OF KELLS

More than half a million yearly visitors queue up to see Trinity's top show-stopper, the world-famous *Book of Kells*. This illuminated manuscript, dating from around AD 800 and thus one of the oldest books in the world, was probably produced by monks at St Colmcille's Monastery on the remote island of Iona, off the western coast of Scotland. It contains the four gospels of the New Testament, written in Latin, as well as prefaces, summaries and other text. If it were merely words, the *Book of Kells* would simply be a very old book – it's the extensive and amazingly complex illustrations (the illuminations) that make it so wonderful. The superbly decorated opening initials are only part of the story, for the book has smaller illustrations between the lines.

Repeated looting by marauding Vikings forced the monks to flee to the temporary safety of Kells, County Meath, in Ireland in AD 806, along with their masterpiece. It was stolen in 1007, then rediscovered three months later buried underground. Some time before the dissolution of the monastery, the *cumdach* (metal shrine) was lost, possibly taken by looting Vikings who wouldn't have valued the text itself. About 30 of the beginning and ending folios (double-page spreads) are also missing. It was brought to the college for safekeeping in 1654. The 680-page (340-folio) book was rebound in four calfskin volumes in 1953.

And here the problems begin. Of the 680 pages, only two are on display – one showing an illumination, the other showing text – hence the 'page of Kells' moniker. No getting around that one, though: you can hardly expect the right to thumb through a priceless treasure at random. No, the real problem is its immense popularity, which makes viewing it a rather unsatisfactory pleasure. Punters are herded through the specially constructed viewing room at near lightning pace, making for a quick-look-and-move-along kind of experience.

To really appreciate the book, you can get your own reproduction copy for a mere €22,000. Failing that, the library bookshop stocks a plethora of souvenirs and other memorabilia, including Otto Simm's excellent *Exploring the Book of Kells* (€12.95), a thorough guide with attractive colour plates, and a popular DVD showing all 680 pages for €31.95.

Towards the eastern end of the complex, College Park is a lovely place to lounge around on a sunny day and occasionally you'll catch a game of cricket, a bizarre sight in Ireland. Keep in mind that Lincoln Place Gate is located in the southeast corner of the grounds, providing a handy shortcut to Merrion Sq (p79).

Although part of the campus, you'll have to walk along Pearse St to get into Trinity's newest attraction, the Science Gallery (☎ 896 4091; http://sciencegallery.com; Naughton Institute, Pearse St; admission free; ☒ exhibitions usually noon-6pm Tue-Sun, cafe 8am-8pm Tue-Fri, noon-6pm Sat & Sun). Since opening in 2008, it has proven immensely popular with everyone for its refreshingly lively and informative exploration of the relationship between science, art and the world we live in. In 2010, exhibits touched on a range of fascinating topics including the science of desire and an exploration of the relationship between music and the human body. The ground-floor Flux Café, bathed in floor-to-ceiling light, is a pretty good spot to take a load off.

CHESTER BEATTY LIBRARY Map p68

☎ 407 0750; www.cbl.ie; Dublin Castle, Cork Hill; admission free; ☒ 10am-5pm Mon-Fri, 11am-5pm Sat, 1-5pm Sun, closed Mon Oct-Apr, free tours 1pm Wed, 3pm & 4pm Sun; ☒ 50, 51B, 77, 78A or 123 from city centre

Book of Kells, shmells...the world-famous Chester Beatty Library, housed in the Clock Tower at the back of Dublin Castle, is not just Ireland's best small museum, but one of the best you'll find anywhere in Europe. This extraordinary collection, so lovingly and expertly gathered by New York mining magnate Alfred Chester Beatty (1875–1968) – a man of exceedingly good taste – is breathtakingly beautiful and virtually guaranteed to impress. How's that for a build-up?

An avid traveller and collector, Beatty was fascinated by different cultures and amassed more than 20,000 manuscripts, rare books, miniature paintings, clay tablets, costumes and any other objets d'art that caught his fancy and could tell him something about the world. Fortunately for Dublin, he also happened to take quite a shine to the city and made it his adopted home. In return, the Irish made him their first honorary citizen in 1957.

The collection is spread over two levels. On the ground floor you'll find the Art of the Book, a compact but stunning collection of artworks from the Western, Islamic and East Asian worlds. Highlights include the finest collection of Chinese jade books in the world and illuminated European texts featuring exquisite calligraphy that stand up in comparison with the *Book of Kells*. Audiovisual displays explain the process of bookbinding, paper-making and printing.

The 2nd floor is home to Sacred Traditions, a wonderful exploration of the world's major religions through decorative and religious art, enlightening text and a cool cultural-pastiche video at the entrance. The collection of Korans dating from the 9th to the 19th centuries (the library has more than 270 of them) is considered by experts to be the best example of illuminated Islamic texts in the world. There are also outstanding examples of ancient papyri, including renowned Egyptian love poems from the 12th century, and some of the earliest illuminated gospels in the world, dating from around AD 200. The collection is rounded off with some exquisite scrolls and artwork from China, Japan, Tibet and Southeast Asia, including the two-volume Japanese *Chogonka Scroll,* painted in the 17th century by Kano Sansetu.

As if all of this wasn't enough for one visit, the library also hosts temporary exhibits that are usually too good to be missed. Not only are the contents of the museum outstanding, but the layout, design and location are also unparalleled, from the marvellous Silk Road Café (see p157) and gift shop, to the Zen rooftop terrace and the beautiful landscaped garden out the front. These features alone would make this an absolute Dublin must-do.

ST STEPHEN'S GREEN Map p68
admission free; ⊙ 8am-dusk Mon-Sun; 🚌 all city centre; 🚊 St Stephen's Green
As you watch the assorted groups of friends, lovers and individuals escaping the confines of the office, splaying themselves across the nine elegantly landscaped hectares of St Stephen's Green and looking to catch a few rays of precious sun, consider that those same hectares once formed a common for public whippings, burnings and hanging. These days, the harshest treatment you'll get at Dublin's favourite lunchtime escape is the warden chucking you off the green for playing football or Frisbee.

The buildings around the square date mainly from the mid-18th century, when the green was landscaped and became the centrepiece of Georgian Dublin. The northern side was known as the Beaux Walk and it's still one of Dublin's most esteemed stretches, home to Dublin's original society hotel, the Shelbourne (p212). Nearby is the tiny Huguenot Cemetery (Map p68), established in 1693 by French Protestant refugees.

Railings and locked gates were erected in 1814 when an annual fee of one guinea was charged to use the green. This private use continued until 1877 when Sir Arthur Edward Guinness pushed an act through parliament opening the green to the public once again. He also financed the central park's gardens and ponds, which date from 1880.

The main entrance to the green today is beneath Fusiliers' Arch (Map p70), at the top of Grafton St. Modelled to look like a smaller version of the Arch of Titus in Rome, the arch commemorates the 212 soldiers of the Royal Dublin Fusiliers who were killed fighting for the British in the Boer War (1899–1902).

Across the road from the western side of the green is the 1863 Unitarian Church (Map p68; ☎ 478 0638; www.unitarianchurchdublin.org; 112 St Stephen's Green West; admission free; ⊙ 12.30-2.30pm Mon-Fri, services 11am Sun) and the early-19th-century Royal College of Surgeons (Map p68), which has one of the finest facades on St Stephen's Green. During the 1916 Easter Rising, the building was occupied by rebel forces led by Countess Markievicz (1868–1927; see the boxed text, p30). The columns are scarred from the bullet holes.

Among the statues and memorials dotting the green, there's one of the Countess in the southeast corner. Since it was Guinness money that created the park you see today, it's only right that Sir Arthur should be present, and there's an 1892 statue of him on the western side of the park. Just north of here, outside the railings, is a statue of Irish patriot Robert Emmet (1778–1803), who was born across the road where numbers 124 and 125 stand; his actual birthplace has been demolished. The statue was placed here in 1966 and is a replica of an Emmet statue in Washington, DC. There is also a bust of poet James Clarence Mangan (1803–49) and a curious 1967 statue of WB Yeats by Henry Moore. The centre of the park has a garden for the blind, complete with signs in Braille and plants that can be handled. There is also a statue of the Three Fates, presented to Dublin in 1956 by West

Germany in gratitude for Irish aid after WWII. In the corner closest to the Shelbourne Hotel is a monument to Wolfe Tone, the leader of the abortive 1798 invasion; the vertical slabs serving as a backdrop to Wolfe Tone's statue have been dubbed 'Tonehenge'. At this entrance is a memorial to all those who died in the Famine.

On the eastern side of the green is a children's playground and to the south there's a fine old bandstand, erected to celebrate Queen Victoria's jubilee in 1887. Musical performances often take place here in summer. Near the bandstand is a bust of James Joyce, facing Newman House (below), part of University College Dublin (UCD), where Joyce was once a student. On the same side as Newman House is Iveagh House (Map p68). Originally designed by Richard Cassels in 1730 as two separate houses, they were bought by Benjamin Guinness in 1862 and combined to create the family's city residence. After independence the house was donated to the Irish State and is now home to the Department of Foreign Affairs.

Of the many illustrious streets fanning from the green, the elegant Georgian Harcourt St has the most notable addresses. Edward Carson was born at No 4 in 1854. As the architect of Northern Irish unionism, he was never going to be the most popular figure in Dublin but he did himself no favours acting as the prosecuting attorney during Oscar Wilde's trial for homosexuality. George Bernard Shaw lived at No 61.

NEWMAN HOUSE Map p68

☎ 716 7422; 85-86 St Stephen's Green; 🚌 10, 11, 13, 14 or 15A from city centre; 🚇 St Stephen's Green

Cardinal Newman established the Catholic University of Ireland here in 1865. To see one of the finest examples of Georgian architecture currently open to the public, you'll need to take one of the guided tours (adult/concession €6/5), which leave at noon, 2pm, 3pm and 4pm Tuesday to Friday from June to August (the house isn't open to general admission). The school provided education to the likes of James Joyce, Pádraig Pearse and Éamon de Valera, who would otherwise have had to submit to the Protestant hegemony of Trinity College if they wanted to receive higher education in Ireland. Newman House is still part of the college, which later decamped to the suburb of Belfield and changed its name to University College Dublin.

The house comprises two exquisitely restored townhouses; number 85, the granite-faced original, was designed by Richard Cassels in 1738 for parliamentarian Hugh Montgomery, who sold it to Richard Chapel Whaley, MP, in 1765. Whaley wanted a grander home, so he commissioned another house next door at number 86.

Aside from Cassels' wonderful design, the highlight of the building is the plasterwork, perhaps the finest in the city. For No 85, the artists were the Italian stuccodores Paolo and Filipo LaFranchini, whose work is best appreciated in the wonderfully detailed Apollo Room on the ground floor. The plasterwork in No 86 was done by Robert West, but it is not quite up to the high standard of next door.

When the newly founded, Jesuit-run Catholic University of Ireland took possession of the house in 1865, alterations were made to some of the more graphic plasterwork, supplying the nude figures with 'modesty vests'.

During Whaley's residency, the house developed certain notoriety, largely due to the activities of his son, Buck, a notorious gambler and hell-raiser who once walked all the way to Jerusalem for a bet and somehow connived to have himself elected to parliament at the tender age of 17. During the university's tenure, however, the residents were a far more temperate lot. The Jesuit priest and wonderful poet Gerard Manley Hopkins lived here during his time as professor of classics, from 1884 until his death in 1889. Hopkins' bedroom is preserved as it would have been during his residence, as is the classroom where the young James Joyce studied while obtaining his Bachelor of Arts degree between 1899 and 1902.

NEWMAN UNIVERSITY CHURCH Map p68

☎ 478 0616; www.universitychurch.ie; 83 St Stephen's Green; admission free; ⏰ 8am-6pm; 🚌 10, 11, 13, 14 or 15A; 🚆 St Stephen's Green
Next to Newman House, this neo-Byzantine charmer was built in the mid-18th century (Cardinal Newman didn't care too much for the Gothic style of the day). Its richly decorated interior was mocked at first but has since become the preferred surroundings for Dublin's most fashionable weddings.

BANK OF IRELAND Map p70

☎ 671 1488; College Green; ⏰ 10am-4pm Mon-Fri, 10am-5pm Thu; 🚌 all city centre
Facing Trinity College across College Green, this sweeping Palladian pile was built to house the Irish parliament and was the first purpose-built Parliament House in the world. The original building, the central colonnaded section that distinguishes the present-day structure, was designed by Sir Edward Lovett Pearce in the first half of the 18th century.

When the parliament voted itself out of existence through the 1801 Act of Union, the building was sold under the condition that the interior would be altered to prevent it ever again being used as a debating chamber. It was a spiteful strike at Irish parliamentary aspirations, but while the central House of Commons was remodelled and offers little hint of its former role, the smaller House of Lords (admission free) chamber survived and is much more interesting (see p50). It has Irish oak woodwork, a mahogany longcase parliament clock and a late-18th-century Dublin crystal chandelier. The tapestries date from the 1730s and depict the Siege of Derry (1689) and the Battle of the Boyne (1690), the two Protestant victories over Catholic Ireland. In the niches are busts of George III, George IV, Lord Nelson and the Duke of Wellington. There are tours of the House of Lords (10.30am, 11.30am and 1.45pm Tuesday), by Dublin historian and author Éamon MacThomás, which include a talk as much about Ireland and life in general as the building itself.

Also part of the complex, and reached via the sedate Foster Place, is the Bank of Ireland Arts Centre (p192), which hosts a variety of cultural events, including classical concerts and regular free lunchtime recitals and poetry readings. It also screens an eight-minute film about banking and Irish history, called the Story of Banking (☎ 671 2261; adult/concession €2/1.50; ⏰ screenings hourly 10am-3pm Tue-Fri). An exhibition features a 10kg silver-gilt mace that was made for the House of Commons – it was retained by the Speaker of the House when the parliament was dissolved, and in later years it was sold by the Speaker's descendants and was bought back from Christies in London by the Bank of Ireland in 1937.

COLLEGE GREEN STATUARY

The imposing grey sculptures adorning College Green (Map p70) – that area between the Bank of Ireland and Trinity College that has nary a blade of grass left – are monuments to two of Ireland's most notable patriots. In front of the bank is Henry Grattan (1746–1820), a distinguished parliamentary orator, while nearby is a modern memorial to the patriot Thomas Davis (1814–45). Where College St meets Pearse St, another traffic island is topped by a 1986 sculpted copy of the *Steyne* (the Viking word for 'stone'), which was erected on the riverbank in the 9th century to stop ships from grounding and removed in 1720.

DUBLIN CASTLE Map p76

☎ 677 7129; www.dublincastle.ie; Cork Hill; adult/
concession €4.50/3.50; ⏱ 10am-4.45pm Mon-Fri,
2-4.45pm Sat & Sun; ➄ 50, 54, 56A, 77 or 77A from
city centre

If you're looking for a medieval castle
straight out of central casting you'll be
disappointed; the stronghold of British
power here for 700 years is principally an
18th-century creation that is more hotchpotch palace than turreted castle. Only the
Record Tower survives from the original
Anglo-Norman fortress built in the early
13th century. It was subject to a siege by
'Silken' Thomas Fitzgerald in 1534, virtually
destroyed by a fire in 1684 and provided
the setting for some momentous scenes
during Ireland's battle for independence. It
was officially handed over to Michael Collins on behalf of the Irish Free State in 1922,
when the British viceroy is reported to have
rebuked Collins on being seven minutes
late. Collins replied, 'We've been waiting
700 years, you can wait seven minutes.' The
castle is now used by the Irish government
for meetings and functions, and can only
be visited on a guided tour of the State
Apartments and excavations of the former
Powder Tower.

As you walk in to the grounds from the
main Dame St entrance, there's a good example of the evolution of Irish architecture.
On your left is the Victorian Chapel Royal (occasionally part of the Dublin Castle tours),
decorated with more than 90 heads of
various Irish personages and saints carved
out of Tullamore limestone. The interior is
wildly exuberant, with fan vaulting alongside quadripartite vaulting, wooden galleries, stained glass and lots of lively-looking
sculpted angels. Beside this is the Norman
Record Tower, which has 5m-thick walls and
now houses the Garda Museum (☎ 668 9998;
admission free), which follows the history of
the Irish police force. It doesn't have all that
much worth protecting, but the views are
fab (ring the bell for entry). On your right is
the Georgian Treasury Building, the oldest office block in Dublin, and behind you, yikes,
is the uglier-than-sin Revenue Commissioners
Building of 1960.

Heading away from that eyesore, you
ascend to the Upper Yard. On your right is
a Figure of Justice with her back turned to
the city, an appropriate symbol for British
justice, reckoned Dubliners. Next to it is the
18th-century Bedford Tower, from which the
Irish Crown Jewels were stolen in 1907 and
never recovered. Opposite is the entrance
to the tours.

The 45-minute guided tours (departing every 20 to 30 minutes, depending on
numbers) are pretty dry, seemingly pitched
at tourists more likely to ooh and aah over
period furniture than historical anecdotes,
but they're included in the entry fee. You
get to visit the State Apartments, many of
which are decorated in dubious taste. There
are beautiful chandeliers (ooh!), plush Irish
carpets (aah!), splendid rococo ceilings, a
Van Dyck portrait and the throne of King
George V. You also get to see St Patrick's
Hall, where Irish presidents are inaugurated
and foreign dignitaries toasted, and the

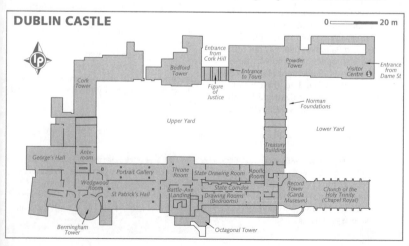

DUBLIN CASTLE

0 ▭▬▬ 20 m

Entrance
from
Cork Hill

Powder
Tower

Visitor
Centre ℹ

Entrance
from
Dame St

Bedford
Tower

Entrance
to Tours

Cork
Tower

Figure
of
Justice

Norman
Foundations

Upper Yard

Lower Yard

Treasury
Building

George's Hall

Ante-
room

Portrait Gallery

Throne
Room

State Drawing Room

Apollo
Room

Wedgwood
Room

St Patrick's Hall

Battle-Axe
Landing

State Corridor

Drawing Rooms
(Bedrooms)

Record
Tower
(Garda
Museum)

Church of the
Holy Trinity
(Chapel Royal)

Bermingham
Tower

Octagonal Tower

room in which the wounded James Connolly was tied to a chair while convalescing after the 1916 Easter Rising – brought back to health to be executed by firing squad.

The highlight is a visit to the subterranean excavations of the old castle, discovered by accident in 1986. They include foundations built by the Vikings (whose long-lasting mortar was made of ox blood, eggshells and horse hair), the hand-polished exterior of the castle walls that prevented attackers from climbing them, the steps leading down to the moat and the trickle of the historic River Poddle, which once filled the moat on its way to join the Liffey.

CITY HALL Map p68
☎ 672 2204; www.dublincity.ie; Cork Hill; admission free, exhibition adult/concession €4/2; ⏲ 10am-5.15pm Mon-Sat, 11am-5pm Sun; ▣ 50, 50A, 54, 56A, 77, 77A, 123 or 150 from city centre

One of the architectural triumphs of the Dublin boom was the magnificent restoration of City Hall, originally built by Thomas Cooley as the Royal Exchange between 1769 and 1779, and botched in the mid-19th century when it became the offices of the local government. Thankfully, a more recent restoration has restored it to its gleaming Georgian best. The rotunda and its ambulatory form a breathtaking interior, bathed in natural light from enormous windows to the east. A vast marble statue of former mayor and Catholic emancipator Daniel O'Connell stands here as a reminder of the building's links with Irish nationalism (the funerals of both Charles Stewart Parnell and Michael Collins were held here). Dublin City Council still meets here on the first Monday of the month, gathering to discuss the city's business in the Council Chamber, which was the original building's coffee room.

There was a sordid precursor to City Hall in the shape of the Lucas Coffee House and the adjoining Eagle Tavern, in which the notorious Hellfire Club was founded by Richard Parsons, Earl of Rosse, in 1735. Although the city abounded with gentlemen's clubs, this particular one gained a reputation for messing about in the arenas of sex and Satan, two topics that were guaranteed to fire the lurid imaginings of the city's gossipmongers.

The striking vaulted basement hosts a multimedia exhibition The Story of the Capital, which traces the history of the city from its

earliest beginnings to its rosy future – with ne'er a mention of sex, Satan or sex with Satan. There's more info here than even the most nostalgic expat could take in, and exhibits are a little text-heavy, but it's all slickly presented and the audiovisual displays are informative and easy to absorb.

POWERSCOURT TOWNHOUSE SHOPPING CENTRE Map p70
☎ 679 4144; 59 South William St; ▣ all city centre

This elegant Richard Cassels–designed townhouse was built between 1771 and 1774, and boasts some fine plasterwork by Michael Stapleton among its features. These days it struts its stuff as Dublin's most stylish shopping centre as well as one of the more pleasant spots to get a bite of lunch. See p142 for more.

SHAW BIRTHPLACE Map p68
☎ 475 0854; 33 Synge St; adult/child/student €6/4/5; ⏲ 10am-1pm & 2-5pm Mon-Sat, from 11am Sun Easter-Oct; ▣ 16, 19 or 122 from Trinity College

Close to the Grand Canal, the birthplace of playwright George Bernard Shaw is now a restored Victorian home that is interesting even to nonliterary buffs because it provides an insight into the domestic life of the 19th century's middle classes. Shaw's mother held musical evenings in the drawing room, and it is likely that her son's store of fabulous characters was inspired by those who attended.

IRISH-JEWISH MUSEUM Map p68
☎ 453 1797; 4 Walworth Rd; admission free; ⏲ 11am-3.30pm Tue, Thu & Sun May-Sep, 10.30am-2.30pm Sun Oct-Apr; ▣ 16, 19 or 122 from Trinity College

Housed in an old synagogue, this museum recounts the history and cultural heritage of Ireland's small but prolific Jewish community. It was opened in 1985 by the Belfast-born, then-Israeli president, Chaim Herzog. The various memorabilia includes photographs, paintings, certificates, books and other artefacts.

IVEAGH GARDENS Map p68

8.15am-6pm Mon-Sat, 10am-6pm Sun May-Sep, 8.15am-dusk Oct-Apr; Harcourt

These beautiful gardens may not have the sculpted elegance of the other city parks, but they never get too crowded and the warden won't bark at you if you walk on the grass. They were designed by Ninian Niven in 1863 as the private grounds of Iveagh House, and include a rustic grotto, cascade, fountain, maze and rosarium. Enter the gardens from Clonmel St, off Harcourt St.

MANSION HOUSE Map p70

Dawson St; all city centre; St Stephen's Green

Built in 1710 by Joshua Dawson – after whom the street is named – this has been the official residence of Dublin's mayor since 1715, and was the site of the 1919 Declaration of Independence and the meeting of the first parliament. The building's original brick Queen Anne style has all but disappeared behind a stucco facade added in the Victorian era.

ROYAL IRISH ACADEMY Map p70

676 2570; www.ria.ie; 19 Dawson St; admission free; 10am-5.30pm Mon-Thu, 10am-5pm Fri; all city centre; St Stephen's Green

Next door to Mansion House is the seat of Ireland's pre-eminent society of letters, whose 18th-century library houses many important documents, including a collection of ancient manuscripts such as the *Book of Dun Cow;* the *Cathach of St Columba;* and the entire collection of 19th-century poet Thomas Moore (1779–1852).

WHITEFRIARS STREET CARMELITE CHURCH Map p68

475 8821; 56 Aungier St; admission free; 8am-6.30pm Mon & Wed-Fri, 8am-9.30pm Tue, 8am-7pm Sat, 8am-7.30pm Sun; 16, 19, 19A, 83 or 122 from Trinity College

If you find yourself mulling over the timing of a certain proposal – or know someone who needs some prompting – walk through the automated glass doors of this church and head for the remains of none other than St Valentine, donated by Pope Gregory XVI in 1835. The Carmelites returned to this site in 1827, when they re-established their former church, which had been seized by Henry VIII in the 16th century. In the northeastern corner is a 16th-century Flemish oak statue of the Virgin and Child, believed to be the only wooden statue in Ireland to have escaped the Reformation unscathed.

Drinking p177; Eating p159; Sleeping p215

Genteel, sophisticated and elegant, the exquisite Georgian architecture spread around handsome Merrion Sq is a near-perfect mix of imposing public buildings, museums, and private offices and residences. It is round these parts that much of moneyed Dublin works and plays, amid the neoclassical beauties thrown up during Dublin's 18th-century prime. When James Fitzgerald, the Earl of Kildare, built his mansion south of the Liffey, he was mocked for his foolhardy move into the wilds. But Jimmy Fitz had a nose for real estate: 'Where I go society will follow,' he confidently predicted and he was soon proved right. Today, Leinster House is used as the Irish parliament and is in the epicentre of Georgian Dublin.

The area around Kildare St is the administrative core of the country as well as a repository for its treasures, housed in places like the National Museum (Archaeology), National Gallery and National Museum (Natural History). The most celebrated emblems of the time are the magnificent Merrion and Fitzwilliam Sqs, surrounded by buildings that still retain their period features. This was the original stomping ground of Ireland's Protestant ascendancy, and the many plaques on the buildings remind us that it was behind these brightly coloured doors that the likes of Oscar Wilde and William Butler Yeats hung their hats.

top picks

MERRION SQUARE & AROUND

- Merrion Square (left), an oasis of calm steeped in Irish history.
- The collection at the National Gallery (p82).
- The antiquated National Museum of Ireland – Natural History (p83), which will captivate young and old.
- National Museum of Ireland – Archaeology (p80), full of fascinating treasures.

The streets running off these squares house the offices of some of the country's most important businesses. When there's even a hint of sunshine, workers pour out into the various parks, or follow the lead of poet Patrick Kavanagh and lounge along the banks of the Grand Canal. When they clock off, these same workers head to the wonderfully atmospheric and historical pubs of Baggot St and Merrion Row for a couple of scoops of chips and some unwinding banter. There are also plenty of smart restaurants, including several of Dublin's best.

Most cross-city buses will get you here (or near enough); the most convenient DART stop is Pearse St, with the station entrance on Westland Row.

MERRION SQUARE Map p80

admission free; dawn-dusk; 🚌 7, 7A, 10, 11, 13 or 172 from city centre

St Stephen's Green may win the popularity contest, but elegant Merrion Sq snubs its nose at such easy praise and remains the most prestigious of Dublin's squares. Its well-kept lawns and beautifully tended flower beds are flanked on three sides by gorgeous Georgian houses with colourful doors, peacock fanlights, ornate door knockers and, occasionally, foot-scrapers, used to remove mud from shoes before venturing indoors. The square, laid out in 1762, is bordered on its remaining side by the National Gallery (p82) and Leinster House (p83) – all of which, apparently, isn't enough for some. One former resident, WB Yeats (1865–1939), was less than impressed and described the architecture as 'grey 18th

century'; there's just no pleasing some people.

Despite the air of affluent calm, life around here hasn't always been a well-pruned bed of roses. During the Famine, the lawns of the square teemed with destitute rural refugees who lived off the soup kitchen organised here. The British Embassy was at 39 Merrion Sq East until 1972, when it was burnt out in protest against the killing of 13 civilians on Bloody Sunday in Derry.

Damage to fine Dublin buildings hasn't always been the prerogative of vandals, terrorists or protesters. East Merrion Sq once continued into Lower Fitzwilliam St in the longest unbroken series of Georgian houses in Europe. Despite this, in 1961 the Electricity Supply Board (ESB) knocked down 26 of them to build an office block

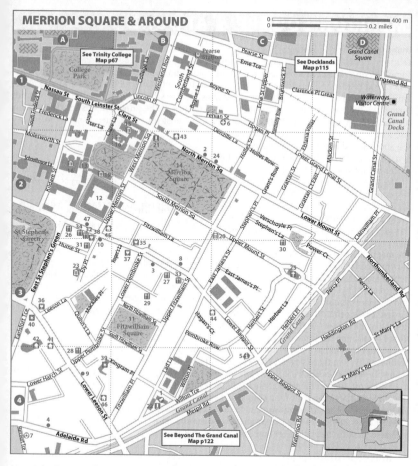

(see p84) – just another in a long list of crimes against architectural aesthetics that plagued the city in the latter half of the 20th century. The Royal Institute of the Architects of Ireland (☎ 676 1703; www.riai.ie; 8 North Merrion Sq; admission free; ☽ 9am-5pm Mon-Fri) is rather more respectful of its Georgian address and hosts regular exhibitions.

NATIONAL MUSEUM OF IRELAND – ARCHAEOLOGY Map p80

☎ 677 7444; www.museum.ie; Kildare St; admission free; ☽ 10am-5pm Tue-Sat, 2-5pm Sun; ☐ 7, 7A, 10, 11, 13 or 172 from city centre

The mother of Irish museums and the country's most important cultural institution was established in 1977 as the primary repository of the nation's archaeological treasures. The collection is so big, however, that it has

expanded beyond the walls of this superb purpose-built building next to the Irish parliament into three other separate museums – the stuffed beasts of the natural history branch (p83), the decorative arts and history section at Collins Barracks (p106) and a country life museum in County Mayo, on Ireland's west coast. They're all fascinating, but the star attractions are all here, mixed up in Europe's finest collection of Bronze- and Iron-Age gold artefacts, the most complete collection of medieval Celtic metalwork in the world, fascinating prehistoric and Viking artefacts, and a few interesting items relating to Ireland's fight for independence. If you don't mind groups, the themed guided tours (€1.50; ☽ 11am, 12.30pm, 2pm & 3pm Tue-Sat, 2pm & 3pm Sun) will help you wade through the myriad exhibits.

MERRION SQUARE & AROUND

INFORMATION
Australian Embassy 1 B4
Brightwater Selection 2 B2
Canadian Embassy........................(see 1)
Careers Register.................................3 B3
Department of Enterprise,
  Trade & Employment....................4 A4
Dublin Tourism ....(see 5)
Fáilte Ireland 5 C4
Gallagher & Associates....................6 C1
Garda Station....................................7 A4
Global Partnerships..........................8 B3
Rape Crisis Centre 9 A4

SIGHTS   (p79)
Ely House..10 A3
Fitzwilliam Square...........................11 B3
Government Buildings 12 A2
Leinster House – Irish
  Parliament 13 A2
Merrion Square 14 B2
Millennium Wing National
  Gallery...15 B1
National Gallery 16 B2

National Library &
  Genealogical Office....................17 A2
National Museum of Ireland –
  Archaeology.................................18 A2
National Museum of Ireland –
  Natural History 19 A2
Number Twenty-nine 20 C2
Oscar Wilde Statue 21 B2
Patrick Kavanagh Statue................22 B4
Royal Hibernian Academy
  (RHA) Gallagher Gallery.............23 A3
Royal Institute of the
  Architects of Ireland (RIA)..........24 C2
St Stephen's 'Pepper Canister
  Church'..25 C3

EATING   (p159)
Bang Café..26 A2
Chez Max 27 B3
Dax...28 A4
Diep le Shaker 29 B3
Dobbins...30 C3
Ely..31 A3
Govinda's..32 A2

L'Ecrivain...33 B3
Restaurant Patrick Guilbaud.......(see 45)
Unicorn 34 A2

DRINKING   (p177)
Doheny & Nesbitt's 35 B3
Hartigan's...36 A3
James Toner's...................................37 B3
O'Donoghue's..................................38 A2

NIGHTLIFE & THE ARTS   (p185)
Focus Theatre 39 A4
Sugar Club 40 A3

SLEEPING   (p215)
Clarion Stephen's Hall....................41 A3
Conrad Dublin International.......... 42 A3
Davenport Hotel 43 B2
Latchfords 44 C3
Merrion 45 A2
Number 31 ....46 A4

TRANSPORT   (p240)
Irish Ferries......................................47 A2

The Treasury is perhaps the most famous part of the collection, and its centrepieces are Ireland's two most famous crafted artefacts, the Ardagh Chalice and the Tara Brooch. The 12th-century Ardagh Chalice is made of gold, silver, bronze, brass, copper and lead; it measures 17.8cm high and 24.2cm in diameter and, put simply, is the finest example of Celtic art ever found. The equally renowned Tara Brooch was crafted around AD 700, primarily in white bronze, but with traces of gold, silver, glass, copper, enamel and wire beading, and was used as a clasp for a cloak. It was discovered on a beach in Bettystown, County Meath, in 1850, but later came into the hands of an art dealer who named it after the hill of Tara, the historic seat of the ancient high kings. It doesn't have quite the same ring to it, but it was the Bettystown Brooch that sparked a revival of interest in Celtic jewellery that hasn't let up to this day. There are many other pieces that testify to Ireland's history as the land of saints and scholars.

Virtually all of the treasures are named after the location in which they were found. It's interesting to note that most of them were discovered not by archaeologists' trowels but by bemused farmers out ploughing their fields, cutting peat or, in the case of the Ardagh Chalice, digging for spuds.

Elsewhere in the Treasury is the exhibition Ór-Ireland's Gold, featuring stunning jewellery and decorative objects created by Celtic artisans in the Bronze and Iron Ages. Among them are the Broighter Hoard, which includes a 1st-century-BC large gold collar, unsurpassed anywhere in Europe, and an extraordinarily delicate gold boat. There's also the wonderful Loughnasade bronze war trumpet, which dates from the 1st century BC. It is 1.86m long and made of sheets of bronze, riveted together, with an intricately designed disc at the mouth. It produces a sound similar to the Australian didgeridoo, though you'll have to take our word for it. Running alongside the wall is a 15m log boat, which was dropped into the water to soften, abandoned and then pulled out 4000 years later, almost perfectly preserved in the peat bog.

On the same level is the Road to Independence exhibition, which features the army coat worn by Michael Collins on the day he was assassinated (there's still mud on the sleeve). In the same case is the cap purportedly also worn by Collins on that fateful day, complete with a bullet hole in its side – somehow, however, we think if the authorities had any confidence in this claim, the exhibit wouldn't be on the floor of the cabinet without even a note.

If you can cope with any more history, upstairs are Medieval Ireland 1150–1550, Viking Age Ireland – which features exhibits from the excavations at Wood Quay, the area between Christ Church Cathedral and the river – and our own favourite, the aptly named Clothes from Bogs in Ireland, a collection of 16th- and

17th-century woollen garments recovered from the bog. Enthralling stuff!

NATIONAL GALLERY Map p80

☎ 661 5133; www.nationalgallery.ie; West Merrion Sq; admission free; ☉ 9.30am-5.30pm Mon-Wed, Fri & Sat, 9.30am-8.30pm Thu, noon-5.30pm Sun, free tours 2pm Sat, 1pm & 2pm Sun; 🚌 7, 7A, 10, 11, 13 or 172 from city centre

A stunning Caravaggio and a whole room full of Ireland's pre-eminent artist, Jack B Yeats, are just a couple of stand-out highlights from this fine collection, amassed by the State since 1854. Its original collection of 125 paintings has grown, mainly through bequests, to over 13,000 artworks, including oils, watercolours, sketches, prints and sculptures.

The building itself was designed by Francis Fowke (1823–65), whose architectural credits also include London's Victoria & Albert Museum. On the lawn in front of the main entrance is a statue of the Irish railways magnate William Dargan, who organised the 1853 Dublin Industrial Exhibition on this spot; the profits from the exhibition were used to found the gallery. Next to him is George Bernard Shaw, another great benefactor of the gallery.

The entire building comprises 54 galleries; works are divided by history, school, geography and theme. There are four wings: the original Dargan Wing, the Milltown Wing (1899–1903), the Beit Wing

(1964–68) and the Millennium Wing (2002). The new section – also accessible via a second entrance on Clare St – provides two floors of galleries for visiting exhibitions, a centre for the study of Irish art and a multimedia room that lets you track down any painting in the gallery.

The collection spans works from the 14th to the 20th centuries and includes all the major continental schools. Obviously there is an emphasis on Irish art, and among the works to look out for are William Orpen's Sunlight, Roderic O'Conor's Reclining Nude and Young Breton Girl, and Paul Henry's The Potato Diggers. But the highlight, and one you should definitely take time to explore, is the Yeats Room, devoted to and containing more than 30 paintings by Jack B Yeats, a uniquely Irish impressionist and arguably the country's greatest artist (see p46). Some of his finest moments are The Liffey Swim, Men of Destiny and Above the Fair.

The absolute star exhibit from a pupil of the European schools is Caravaggio's sublime The Taking of Christ, in which the troubled Italian genius attempts to light the scene figuratively and metaphorically (the artist himself is portrayed holding the lantern on the far right). The masterpiece lay undiscovered for more than 60 years in a Jesuit house in nearby Leeson St, and was found accidentally by the chief curator of the gallery, Sergio Benedetti, in 1992. Fra Angelico, Titian and Tintoretto are all in this neighbourhood. Facing Caravaggio, way down the opposite end of the gallery, is A Genovese Boy Standing on a Terrace by Van Dyck. Old Dutch and Flemish masters line up in between, but all defer to Vermeer's Lady Writing a Letter, which is lucky to be here at all, having been stolen by Dublin gangster Martin Cahill in 1992, as featured in the film The General.

The French section contains Jules Breton's famous 19th-century The Gleaners, along with works by Monet, Degas, Pisarro and Delacroix, while Spain chips in with an unusually scruffy *Still Life with Mandolin* by Picasso, as well as paintings by El Greco and Goya, and an early Velázquez. There is a small British collection with works by Reynolds, Hogarth and Gainsborough (*The Cottage Girl* is especially beautiful). One of the most popular exhibitions occurs only in January, when the gallery hosts its annual display of watercolours by Joseph Turner. The 35 works in the collection are best viewed at this time due to the particular quality of the winter light.

NATIONAL MUSEUM OF IRELAND – NATURAL HISTORY Map p80

☎ 677 7444; www.museum.ie; Merrion St; admission free; 🕑 10am-5pm Tue-Sat, 2-5pm Sun; 🚌 7, 7A, 10, 11, 13 or 172 from city centre

Dusty, weird and utterly compelling, this window into Victorian times has barely changed since Scottish explorer Dr David Livingstone opened it in 1857 – before disappearing off into the African jungle for a meeting with Henry Stanley. Which was perfectly fine until July 2007 when a large section of the original stone staircase collapsed, injuring 10 people and forcing the closure of one of the city's most beloved museums for a major restoration. It reopened in 2010, once again allowing us in to explore its (slightly less) creaking interior crammed with some two million stuffed animals, skeletons and other specimens from around the world, ranging from West African apes to pickled insects in jars. Some are freestanding, others behind glass, but everywhere you turn the animals of the 'dead zoo' are still and staring.

Compared to the multimedia, interactive this and that of virtually every modern museum, this is a beautifully preserved example of Victorian charm and scientific wonderment. It is usually full of fascinated kids, but it's the adults who seem to make the most noise as they ricochet like pinballs between displays. The Irish Room on the ground floor is filled with mammals, sea creatures, birds and butterflies all found in Ireland at some point, including the skeletons of three 10,000-year-old Irish elk that greet you as you enter. The World Animals Collection, spread across three levels, has the skeleton of a 20m-long fin whale found beached in County Sligo as its centrepiece. Evolutionists will love the line-up of orang-utan, chimpanzee, gorilla and human skeletons on the 1st floor. A new addition is the Discovery Zone, where visitors can do some first-hand exploring of their own, handling taxidermy and opening drawers. Other notables include the extinct Australian marsupial the Tasmanian tiger (mislabelled as a Tasmanian wolf), a giant panda from China, and several African and Asian rhinoceros. The wonderful Blaschka Collection comprises finely detailed glass models of marine creatures whose zoological accuracy is incomparable.

THE MUSEUM BUS

Dublin Bus 172 is known as the 'museum bus', as it links all three sections of the National Museum on a circular route (which is particularly handy for getting across the river to Collins Barracks; p106). You can catch it outside any of the three.

LEINSTER HOUSE – IRISH PARLIAMENT Map p80

☎ 618 3000; www.oireachtas.ie; Kildare St; 🚌 7, 7A, 10, 11, 13 or 172 from city centre

All the big decisions are made – or rubber-stamped – at Oireachtas na Éireann (Irish Parliament). It was built by Richard Cassels in the Palladian style between 1745 and 1748, and was considered the forerunner of the Georgian fashion that became the norm for Dublin's finer residences. Its Kildare St facade looks like a townhouse (which inspired Irish architect James Hoban's designs for the US White House), whereas the Merrion Sq frontage was made to resemble a country mansion.

The first government of the Irish Free State moved in from 1922, and both the Dáil (lower house) and Seanad (senate) still meet here to discuss the affairs of the nation and gossip at the exclusive members bar. The 60-member Seanad meets for fairly low-key sessions in the north-wing saloon, while there are usually more sparks and tantrums when the 166-member Dáil bangs heads in a less-interesting room, formerly a lecture theatre, which was added to the original building in 1897. Parliament sits for 90 days a year. You get an entry ticket to the lower- or upper-house observation galleries (🕑 2.30-8.30pm Tue, 10.30am-8.30pm Wed, 10.30am-5.30pm Thu Nov-May) from the Kildare St entrance on production of photo identification. Free, pre-arranged guided tours (☎ 618 3271; 10.30am, 11.30am, 2.30pm & 3.30pm Mon-Fri) are available when parliament is in session.

The obelisk in front of the building is dedicated to Arthur Griffith, Michael Collins and Kevin O'Higgins, the architects of independent Ireland.

NUMBER TWENTY-NINE Map p80

☎ 702 6165; www.esb.ie/numbertwentynine; 29 Lwr Fitzwilliam St; adult/child/student €6/free/3; ⏲ 10am-5pm Tue-Sat, noon-5pm Sun, closed 2 weeks at Christmas; 🚌 6, 7, 10 or 45 from city centre

In an effort to atone at least partly for its sins against Dublin's Georgian heritage – it broke up Europe's most perfect Georgian row to build its headquarters – the ESB restored this home to give an impression of genteel family life at the beginning of the 18th century. From rat-traps in the kitchen basement to handmade wallpaper and Georgian cabinets, the attention to detail is impressive, but the regular tours (dependent on numbers) are disappointingly dry.

GOVERNMENT BUILDINGS Map p80

☎ 662 4888, ticket office ☎ 661 5133; www.taoiseach.gov.ie; Upper Merrion St; 🚌 7, 7A, 10, 11 or 13 from city centre

This gleaming Edwardian pile was the last building (almost) completed by the British before they were booted out; it opened as the Royal College of Science in 1911. When the college vacated in 1989, Taoiseach Charlie Haughey and his government moved in and spent a fortune refurbishing the complex. Among Haughey's needs, apparently, was a private lift from his office that went up to a rooftop helipad and down to a limo in the basement.

Free 40-minute guided tours (⏲ 10.30am-3.30pm Sat only, tickets from National Gallery ticket office; p82) take you through the taoiseach's office, the Cabinet Room, the ceremonial staircase with a stunning stained-glass window – designed by Evie Hone (1894–1955) for the 1939 New York Trade Fair – and many fine examples of modern Irish arts and crafts.

Directly across the road from here, and now part of the Merrion Hotel, 24 Upper Merrion St is thought to be the birthplace of Arthur Wellesley (1769–1852), the first Duke of Wellington, who downplayed his Irish origins and once said 'being born in a stable does not make one a horse'. It is also possible that the cheeky bugger was born in Trim, County Meath.

FITZWILLIAM SQUARE Map p80

⏲ closed to public; 🚌 10, 11, 13B or 46A from city centre

South of Merrion Sq, the smallest and the last of Dublin's great Georgian squares was completed in 1825. It's also the only one where the central garden is still the private domain of the square's residents. William Dargan (1799–1867), the railway pioneer and founder of the National Gallery, lived at No 2, and the artist Jack B Yeats (1871–1957) lived at No 18. Look out for the attractive 18th- and 19th-century metal coal-hole covers. The square is now a cen-

TRACING YOUR ANCESTORS

Go on, you're dying to see if you've got a bit of Irish in you, and maybe tracking down your roots is the main reason for your visit. It will have made things much easier if you did some preliminary research in your home country – particularly finding out the precise date and point of entry of your ancestors – but you might still be able to plot your family tree even if you're acting on impulse.

The Genealogy Advisory Service (p85) will advise you on how to trace your ancestry, which is a good way to begin your research if you have no other experience. For information on commercial agencies that will do the research for you, contact the Association of Professional Genealogists in Ireland (APGI; www.apgi.ie; c/o the Genealogy Advisory Service, Kildare St). The Births, Deaths & Marriages Register (Map 115; ☎ 671 1863; www.birthsdeathsmarriages.ie; Joyce House, East Lombard St; ⏲ 9.30am-12.30pm & 2.15-4.30pm Mon-Fri) and the files of the National Library and the National Archives (Map p68; ☎ 407 2300; www.nationalarchives.ie; Bishop St, Dublin 8; ⏲ 10am-5pm Mon-Fri) are all potential sources of genealogical information.

There are also lots of books on the subject, with *Irish Roots Guide*, by Tony McCarthy, serving as a useful introduction. Other publications include *Tracing Your Irish Roots* by Christine Kineally and *Tracing Your Irish Ancestors: A Comprehensive Guide* by John Grenham. All these, and other items of genealogical concern, can be obtained from the Genealogy Bookshop (Map p70; 3 Nassau St).

tre for the medical profession by day and a notorious beat for prostitutes at night.

ROYAL HIBERNIAN ACADEMY (RHA) GALLAGHER GALLERY Map p80

☎ 661 2558; www.royalhibernianacademy.ie; 15 Ely Pl; admission free; 🕑 11am-5pm Mon-Wed, Fri & Sat, 11am-9pm Thu, 2-5pm Sun; 🚌 10, 11, 13B or 51X from city centre

This large, well-lit gallery at the end of a serene Georgian street has a grand name to fit its exalted reputation as one of the most prestigious exhibition spaces for modern and contemporary art in Ireland. Indeed, if your name is affixed to any of the works on ever-changing display you must be doing something right in the artistic world, especially as the gallery has worked hard to shrug off its reputation for having conservative tastes and these days plays host to an increasingly challenging array of work. The big event is the RHA Annual Exhibition, held in May, which shows the work of those artists deemed worthy enough by the selection committee, made up of members of the academy (easily identified amid the huge throng that attends the opening by the scholars' gowns). The show is a mix of technically proficient artists, Sunday painters and the odd outstanding talent.

NATIONAL LIBRARY & GENEALOGICAL OFFICE Map p80

☎ 603 0200; www.nli.ie; Kildare St; admission free; 🕑 9.30am-9pm Mon-Wed, 9.30am-5pm Thu & Fri, 9.30am-1pm Sat; 🚌 all city centre

Next door to the Kildare St entrance of Leinster House, the suitably sedate National Library was built from 1884 to 1890, at the same time and to a similar design as the National Museum, by Sir Thomas Newenham Deane. Its extensive collection has many valuable early manuscripts, first editions, maps and other items of interest. Parts of the library are open to the public, including the domed reading room where Stephen Dedalus expounded his views on Shakespeare in *Ulysses*. For those prints that are worth a thousand words, you'll have to head down to Temple Bar to the National Photographic Archive (p89) extension of the library.

There's a Genealogy Advisory Service (🕑 9.30am-5pm Mon-Fri, 9.30am-1pm Sat) on the 2nd floor, where you can obtain free information on how best to trace your Irish roots (see the boxed text, p84).

ST STEPHEN'S 'PEPPER CANISTER' CHURCH Map p80

☎ 288 0663; www.peppercanister.ie; Upper Mount St; admission free; 🚌 10, 11, 13B or 51X from city centre

Built in 1825 in Greek Revival style and commonly known as the 'pepper canister' on account of its appearance, St Stephen's is one of Dublin's most attractive and distinctive churches, and looks particularly fetching at twilight when its exterior lights have just come on. It occasionally hosts classical concerts, but don't go out of your way to see the interior. It's only open during services, usually held at 11am Sunday and 11.30am Wednesday, with an extra one at 11am Friday July and August.

Drinking p178; Eating p161; Shopping p143; Sleeping p216

For nearly two decades it has been the city's party district, packed with brash bars and pubs standing cheek by jowl with restaurants, cutesy boutiques, funky shops…and more bars. It has been the destination of choice for legions of revellers in themed T-shirts and reveal-all outfits who land in Dublin on a Friday and drink their body weight and more, before returning home on Sunday sick, sore and swearing that this was the best weekend they'll never remember.

Temple Bar has thrived on this kind of business, even if for years the critics (including this guidebook) have slammed it as being a sham version of the Cultural Quarter promised to the city. In the early 1990s, developers salvaged the maze of cobbled streets slotted between Dame St and the river, running roughly from Trinity College to the shadow of Christ Church Cathedral.

Yet the struggle between bohemia and bacchanalia is real enough. If you visit during the day or on the quieter weekday nights, Temple Bar's Left Bank credentials don't seem so out of place. You can browse for vintage clothes, get your nipples pierced and nibble on Mongolian barbecue. You can buy organic food, pick up the latest musical releases and buy books on every conceivable subject. You can check out the latest art installations, watch an outdoor movie or join in a pulsating drum circle.

Come the weekend evenings, though, it's a different story. Alcopop- and lager-fuelled

top picks

TEMPLE BAR

- A summertime outdoor film (p191) in Meeting House Sq.
- The always excellent exhibits at the Gallery of Photography (p88).
- Radical fashions and oddball knick-knacks at the weekend Cow's Lane Designer Mart (p145).
- Dropping the kids off at the Ark Children's Cultural Centre (p88), where their inner performer may be awakened.

mayhem ensues, as the streets are full of stag parties from the northeast of England begging a group of girls on a hen's weekend to get their kit off for the lads – or the same hens daring the same lads to show them what they're made of. By closing time (usually around 2am), the district is awash with staggering drunks doing their level best to justify the nickname 'Temple Barf'. Thankfully, most of them don't have far to go to sleep it off, although most of the area's hotels are so cramped and noisy that a night out on the booze isn't necessarily a guarantee for a good night's sleep.

It's not an altogether different picture from the early 18th century, when the cobbled streets and lanes were first laid out on land acquired by William Temple (1554–1628) sometime after Henry VIII dissolved the monasteries in 1537, including the Augustinian friary that had stood here for nearly 500 years. Once the monks had gone, the publicans and the prostitutes stepped in, and for a century or so thereafter it had a pretty disreputable reputation. Within a few years, however, trade businesses and small craft shops began springing up, lending the area a commercial character of a more acceptable flavour. On Parliament St, which runs down to the quays from Dublin Castle (p76), the Sunlight Chambers (Map p87; named after a brand of soap) has a beautiful frieze showing the Lever Brothers' view of the world and soap: men make clothes dirty, women wash them.

Like so much of inner-city Dublin, Temple Bar languished in dereliction for most of the 20th century. In the 1960s, the government earmarked the area as the perfect spot to build a gigantic bus depot. While it went about the slow business of acquiring the remaining properties, many of the condemned buildings were leased on short-term contracts to artists, artisans and community groups. By the early 1990s, Dublin had its very own artistic quarter.

Then, just as the Celtic Tiger began to growl, the developers set about cementing Temple Bar's new-found identity: the rundown streets and buildings were revitalised, derelict buildings demolished and new squares built. Among the cultural gems of the quarter are the progressive Project Arts Centre (p199), Temple Bar Gallery & Studios (p88) and the Irish Film Institute (IFI; p191). The Millennium Bridge opens up a fetching vista of Eustace St, while Crown Alley and the atmospheric Merchant's Arch open splendidly onto the Ha'penny Bridge.

As Temple Bar is right in the heart of the city, all cross-city buses will deposit you by the cobbled, largely pedestrianised streets, making access – and escape – that bit easier.

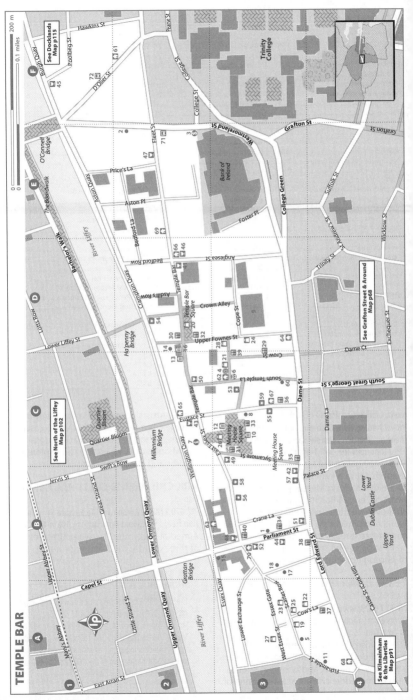

TEMPLE BAR

See Docklands Map p115

See North of the Liffey Map p102

See Grafton Street & Around Map p68

See Kilmainham & the Liberties Map p91

Trinity College

Bank of Ireland

Quartier Bloom

Dublin Castle

0   200 m
0   0.1 miles

TEMPLE BAR

INFORMATION
BeLonG To 1 B3
Dublin Musical Pub Crawl ....(see 46)
Dublin Rock 'n' Roll Bus Tour.......... 2 E2
First Rate... 3 E2
Internet Exchange.................................. 4 C3
National Lesbian & Gay
 Federation.. 5 A3
Talk Shop... 6 C3
Temple Bar Information
 Centre 7 C2

SIGHTS (p86)
Ark Children's Cultural Centre 8 C3
Central Bank.. 9 D3
Gallery of Photography.................10 C3
Handel's Hotel (Site of Neal's
 Music Hall)...11 A4
National Photographic
 Archives...12 C3
Original Print Gallery.......................13 C2
Printworks..14 D2
Sunlight Chambers...........................15 B3
Temple Bar Gallery & Studios.......16 D2
Wooden Building 17 B3
Wooden Building 18 B3

SHOPPING (p143)
5 Scarlett Row......................................19 A3
Book Fair...20 D2
Claddagh Records............................21 C3
Cow's Lane Designer Mart.............22 A3
Cow's Lane Designer Mart (St
 Michael's & St John's
 Banquet Hall)....................................23 A3
Flip..24 D3
Gutter Bookshop...............................25 A3

Meeting House Square
 Market 26 C3
Smock 27 A3
Urban Outfitters 28 D3

EATING (p161)
Ar Vicoletto...29 D3
Chameleon...30 D2
Eden 31 C3
Gourmet Burger
 Kitchen 32 D2
Il Baccaro...33 C3
Larder..34 B3
Mermaid Café.....................................35 C3
Monty's of Kathmandu...................36 C3
Queen of Tarts...................................37 A4
Queen of Tarts...................................38 B3
Tante Zoé's...39 C3
Tea Rooms ....(see 63)
Zaytoon..40 B3

DRINKING (p178)
Auld Dubliner.....................................41 D2
Brogan's 42 B3
Fitzsimons 43 C2
Front Lounge.......................................44 B3
Messrs Maguire..................................45 F1
Octagon Bar..................................(see 63)
Oliver St John Gogarty....................46 D2
Palace Bar...47 E2
Porterhouse Brewing
 Company...48 B3
Purty Kitchen......................................49 C3
Sycamore Club.............................(see 49)
Temple Bar...50 C2
Thomas Read's....................................51 B3
Turk's Head 52 B3

NIGHTLIFE & THE ARTS ☆ (p185)
Ark Children's Cultural
 Centre..(see 8)
Button Factory....................................53 C3
Ha'penny Bridge Inn........................54 D2
Irish Film Institute............................55 C3
New Theatre 56 B3
Olympia Theatre 57 B3
Project Arts Centre 58 B3
Think Tank..59 C3

SPORTS & ACTIVITIES (p201)
Melt 60 C3

SLEEPING (p216)
Ashfield House 61 F2
Barnacles Temple Bar
 House 62 C3
Clarence Hotel....................................63 B2
Dublin Citi Hotel 64 D3
Eliza Lodge..65 C2
Gogarty's Temple Bar
 Hostel..66 D2
Irish Landmark Trust........................67 C3
Kinlay House.......................................68 A4
Morgan Hotel......................................69 E2
Oliver St John Gogarty's
 Penthouse Apartments............(see 66)
Paramount Hotel 70 B3

TRANSPORT (p240)
Nitelink bus stop................................71 E2
Nitelink bus stop................................72 F1

GALLERY OF PHOTOGRAPHY Map p87

☎ 671 4654; www.irish-photography.com;
Meeting House Sq, Temple Bar; admission free;
⏲ 11am-6pm Tue-Sat, 1-6pm Sun

This small gallery devoted to the photograph is set in a light and airy three-level space overlooking Meeting House Sq in the heart of Temple Bar. It features a constantly changing menu of local and international work, and while it's a little too small to be considered a really good gallery, the downstairs shop is well stocked with all manner of photographic tomes and manuals.

TEMPLE BAR GALLERY & STUDIOS
Map p87

☎ 671 0073; www.templebargallery.com; 5
Temple Bar; admission free; ⏲ 10am-6pm Tue-Sat,
to 7pm Thu

This multistoried gallery showcases the works of dozens of up-and-coming Irish artists at any one time, and is a great spot to see cutting-edge Irish art across a range of

media. Artists' studios are also part of the complex, but these are off-limits to casual visitors, although the gallery runs occasional open days when you can explore the studios and chat to the artists.

ARK CHILDREN'S CULTURAL CENTRE
Map p87

☎ 670 7788; www.ark.ie; 11a Eustace St; admission free; ⏲ 9.30am-4pm Tue-Fri, 10am-4pm Sat

Aimed at youngsters between the ages of three and 14, the Ark is enormously

READ ALL ABOUT IT

The Temple Bar Information Centre (Map p87; ☎ 677 2255; www.templebar.ie; 12 East Essex St; ⏲ 9am-5.30pm Mon-Fri) publishes a guide to Temple Bar's attractions and restaurants, available from its office or in businesses around Temple Bar. The website also has details of the excellent Diversions Festival (p17) and other events.

popular – and perpetually booked out. The centre runs activities aimed at stimulating children's interests in science, the environment and the arts, and has an open-air stage for summer events.

NATIONAL PHOTOGRAPHIC ARCHIVES Map p87

☎ 671 0073; www.nli.ie; Meeting House Sq, Temple Bar; admission free; ☺ 11am-6pm Mon-Sat, 2-6pm Sun

What should be a wonderful resource putting a face on all facets of Irish history is actually a sadly disappointing archive of photographs taken from the 19th century onwards. Its visitor-friendly catalogue is computer accessible and the eager staff are always willing to help with queries, but the available material is not nearly as extensive as we'd hoped.

ORIGINAL PRINT GALLERY Map p87

☎ 677 3657; www.originalprint.ie; Black Church Studio, 4 Temple Bar; admission free; ☺ 10.30am-5.30pm Mon-Sat, 2-5pm Sun

This gallery specialises in original, limited-edition prints, including etchings, lithographs and silk-screens, mostly by Irish artists.

KILMAINHAM & THE LIBERTIES

Drinking p180; Eating p163; Shopping p144

West of most of the action, Dublin's most traditional neighbourhoods are a little light on entertainment but they are home to three of the city's superstar sights, including the city's number one attraction – the high cathedral of all things related to the black gold.

Coming from the heart of the city centre, you'll first stumble into the Liberties, so-called because in medieval times, when Dublin was but a mere twinkle in a developer's eye, this sprawling area outside the city walls was self-governing and free of many of the tithes and taxes of Dublin proper.

That the two major cathedrals of Christ Church and St Patrick's were built here is testament to its medieval importance. In some ways it became the engine room for Dublin's growth, a centre of industry, into which migrants flocked looking for employment. Around 10,000 Huguenot refugees from France flooded into the area from the mid-17th century, introducing silk and linen weaving, which transformed the place and had a profound effect on the city as a whole. The Liberties prospered, standards of living increased and a fierce community pride emerged.

top picks

IT'S FREE

- Chester Beatty Library (p72)
- National Museum – Archaeology (p80) &
  National Museum – Decorative Arts & History
  (p106)
- National Gallery (p82)
- National Museum – Natural History (p83)
- Glasnevin Cemetery tour (p125)

The boom busted when Britain imposed high levies on Irish produce from the late 18th century and Irish manufacturers lost out to cheaper imports. Tens of thousands of weavers were put out of work, gangs went about attacking people wearing foreign fabrics and the Liberties descended into squalor.

The Liberties has never really recovered and is still one of the inner city's most deprived areas, racked by unemployment and drug abuse. Yet it retains the passionate pride of a community that has been knitted together over many centuries, and many Dubliners are increasingly looking nostalgically towards the area as an example of their city 'in the rare auld times'.

Their nostalgia is usually expressed over a few pints, and the western border of the Liberties is where you'll find the source of their favourite nectar, the Guinness brewery at St James's Gate, where an old storehouse has been converted into the city's most visited museum (thanks in part to the promise of the best Guinness on the planet at the end of the visit). Further west again, just as the Liffey becomes more of a pastoral river in the riverside burg of Kilmainham, you'll come across the country's greatest modern art museum and Kilmainham Gaol, which has played a key role in the tormented history of a country's slow struggle to gain its freedom. Both are well worth the westward trek (which can be made easier by bus). This is strictly day-trip territory – there's almost nothing in the way of accommodation and decent eating options.

GUINNESS STOREHOUSE & ST JAMES'S GATE BREWERY Map p91

☎ 408 4800; www.guinness-storehouse.com; St James's Gate; admission €15/11, under 6 yr free, discounts apply for online bookings; ☷ 9.30am–5pm Sep-Jun, 9.30am–7pm Jul-Aug; ☐ 51B, 78A or 123 from city centre; ☐ St James's

More than any beer produced anywhere in the world, Guinness has transcended its own brand and is not just the best-known symbol of the city but a substance with near spiritual qualities, according to its legions of devotees the world over. The mythology of Guinness is remarkably

durable: it doesn't travel well; its distinctive flavour comes from Liffey water; it is good for you – not to mention the generally held belief that you will never understand the Irish until you develop a taste for the black stuff. All absolutely true, of course, so it should be no surprise that the Guinness Storehouse, in the heart of the St James's Gate Brewery, is the city's most visited tourist attraction, an all-singing, all-dancing extravaganza that combines sophisticated exhibits, spectacular design and a thick, creamy head of marketing hype.

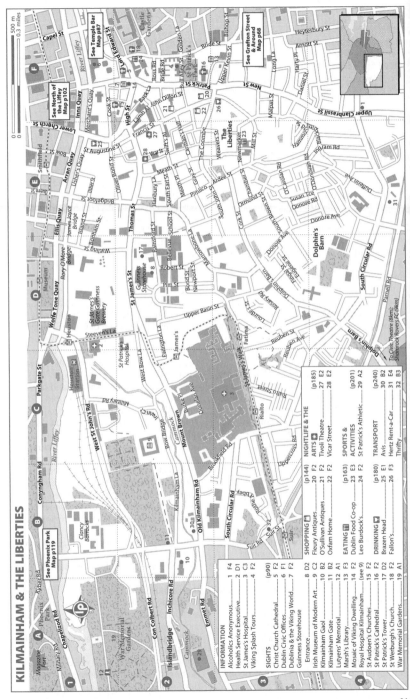

KILMAINHAM & THE LIBERTIES

See Phoenix Park Map p119

See North of the Liffey Map p102

See Temple Bar Map p87

See Grafton Street & Around Map p68

INFORMATION	
Alcoholics Anonymous............	1 F4
Health Service Executive........	2 D1
St James's Hospital................	3 C3
Viking Splash Tours................	4 F2

SIGHTS	(p90)
Christ Church Cathedral.........	5 F2
Dublin Civic Offices...............	6 F1
Dublinia & the Viking World....	7 F2
Guinness Storehouse	
Entrance............................	8 D2
Irish Museum of Modern Art....	9 C2
Kilmainham Gaol...................	10 B2
Kilmainham Gate...................	11 B2
Lutyens' Memorial................	12 A1
Marsh's Library.....................	13 F3
Mosaic of Viking Dwelling......	14 F2
Royal Hospital Kilmainham.....	(see 9)
St Audoen's Churches............	15 F2
St Patrick's Cathedral............	16 F2
St Patrick's Tower..................	17 D2
St Werburgh's Church............	18 F2
War Memorial Gardens...........	19 A1

SHOPPING	(p144)
Fleury Antiques....................	20 F2
O'Sullivan Antiques..............	21 F2
Oxfam Home........................	22 F2

EATING	(p163)
Dublin Food Co-op...............	23 E3
Leo Burdock's......................	24 F2

DRINKING	(p180)
Brazen Head........................	25 E1
Fallon's..............................	26 F3

NIGHTLIFE & THE	
ARTS	(p185)
Tivoli Theatre......................	27 F2
Vicar Street.........................	28 E2

SPORTS &	
ACTIVITIES	(p201)
St Patrick's Athletic..............	29 A2

TRANSPORT	(p240)
Avis..................................	30 B2
Hertz Rent-a-Car.................	31 E4
Thrifty..............................	32 B3

500 m
0.3 miles

To get here, head westwards beyond Christ Church, and you'll end up in the area known as the Liberties, home of the historic 26-hectare St James's Gate Brewery, which stretches along St James's St and down to the Liffey. On your way you'll pass No 1 Thomas St, where Arthur Guinness used to live, across the road from the 40m-tall St Patrick's Tower (Map p91), built around 1757 and the tallest surviving windmill tower outside the Netherlands.

When Arthur started brewing in Dublin in 1759, he couldn't have had any idea that his name would become synonymous with Dublin around the world. Or could he? Showing extraordinary foresight, he had just signed a lease for a small disused brewery under the terms that he would pay just £45 annually for the next 9000 years, with the additional condition that he'd never have to pay for the water used.

In the 1770s, while other Dublin brewers fretted about the popularity of a new English beer known as porter – which was first created when a London brewer accidentally burnt his hops – Arthur started making his own version. By 1799 he decided to concentrate all his efforts on this single brew. He died four years later, aged 83, but the foundations for world domination were already in place.

At one time a Grand Canal tributary was cut into the brewery to enable special Guinness barges to carry consignments out onto the Irish canal system or to the Dublin port. When the brewery extensions reached the Liffey in 1872, the fleet of Guinness barges became a familiar sight. Pretty soon Guinness was being exported as far afield as Africa and the West Indies. As the barges chugged their way along the Liffey towards the port, boys used to lean over the wall and shout 'bring us back a parrot'. Dubliners still say the same thing to each other when they're going off on holiday.

The company was once the city's biggest employer – in the 1930s up to 5000 people made their living at the brewery. Today, however, the brewery is no longer the prominent employer it once was; a gradual shift to greater automatisation has reduced the workforce to around 450.

One link with the past that hasn't been broken is the yeast used to make Guinness, essentially the same living organism that has been used since 1770. Another vital ingredient is a hop by the name of fuggles, which used to be grown exclusively around Dublin but is now imported from Britain, the US and Australia (everyone take a bow).

The brewery is far more than just a place where beer is manufactured. It is an intrinsic part of Dublin's history and a key element of the city's identity. Accordingly, the quasi-mythical stature of Guinness is the central theme of the brewery's museum, the Guinness Storehouse, which opened in 2000 and is the only part of the brewery open to visitors.

While inevitably overpriced and overhyped, this paean to the black gold is done exceptionally well. It occupies the old Fermentation House, built in 1904. As it's a listed building the designers could only adapt and add to the structure without taking anything away. The result is a stunning central atrium that rises seven storeys and takes the shape of a pint of Guinness. The head is represented by the glassed Gravity Bar, which provides panoramic views of Dublin to savour with your complimentary pint.

Before you race up to the top, however, you might want to check out the museum for which you've paid so handsomely. Actually, it's designed as more of an 'experience' than a museum. It has nearly four acres of floor space, featuring a dazzling array of audiovisual, interactive exhibits that cover most aspects of the brewery's story and explain the brewing process in overwhelming detail.

On the ground floor, a copy of Arthur Guinness' original lease lies embedded beneath a pane of glass in the floor.

Wandering up through the various exhibits, including 70-odd years of advertising, you can't help feeling that the now wholly foreign-owned company has hijacked the mythology Dubliners attached to the drink, and it has all become more about marketing and manipulation than mingling and magic.

The climax, of course, comes when you emerge onto the circular Gravity Bar for your complimentary Guinness. It may well be the most technically perfect pint of Guinness you'll ever have – and the views are breathtaking – but if you're like us, you'll probably be more excited about getting back down to earth and having a pint with some real Dubliners.

ST PATRICK'S CATHEDRAL Map p91

☎ 475 4817; www.stpatrickscathedral.ie; St Patrick's Close; adult/senior & student/child €5.50/4.50/free; ◷ 9am-5.30pm Mar-Oct, 9am-5pm Mon-Sat, 9am-3pm Sun Nov-Feb; ◻ 50, 50A or 56A from Aston Quay or 54 or 54A from Burgh Quay

Situated on the very spot that St Paddy himself supposedly rolled up his sleeves and dunked the heathen Irish into a well

and thereby gave them a fair to middling shot at salvation, this is one of Dublin's earliest Christian sites and a most hallowed chunk of real estate. Although a church has stood here since the 5th century, this building dates from the turn of the 12th century and has been altered several times, most notably in 1864 when it was saved from ruin and, some might say, overenthusiastically restored. The interior is as calm and soothing as the exterior is sombre, and it's crammed with interesting curios, monuments and memorials. The picturesque St Patrick's Park, adjoining, was a crowded slum until it was cleared in the early 20th century.

It's likely that St Patrick's was intended to replace Christ Church as the city's cathedral but the older church's stubborn refusal to be usurped resulted in the two cathedrals being virtually a stone's throw from one another. Separated only by the city walls (with St Patrick's outside), each possessed the rights of cathedral of the diocese. While St Pat's isn't as photogenic as its neighbour (it doesn't get the clicks, if you like), it probably one-ups its sexier-looking rival in historical terms.

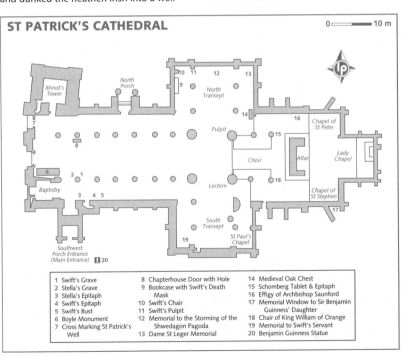

ST PATRICK'S CATHEDRAL

0 — 10 m

1 Swift's Grave	8 Chapterhouse Door with Hole
2 Stella's Grave	9 Bookcase with Swift's Death
3 Stella's Epitaph	Mask
4 Swift's Epitaph	10 Swift's Chair
5 Swift's Bust	11 Swift's Pulpit
6 Boyle Monument	12 Memorial to the Storming of the
7 Cross Marking St Patrick's	Shwedagon Pagoda
Well	13 Dame St Leger Memorial

14 Medieval Oak Chest
15 Schomberg Tablet & Epitaph
16 Effigy of Archbishop Saunford
17 Memorial Window to Sir Benjamin
Guinness' Daughter
18 Chair of King William of Orange
19 Memorial to Swift's Servant
20 Benjamin Guinness Statue

It was built on unstable ground, with the subterranean River Poddle flowing beneath its foundations, and, because of the high water table, it does not have a crypt. The cathedral had been built twice by 1254 but succumbed to a series of natural disasters over the following century. Its spire was taken out in a 1316 storm, while the original tower and part of the nave were destroyed by fire in 1362 and rebuilt immediately after.

Its troubles were to be more than structural, however. Following Henry VIII's 16th-century hissy fit and the dissolution of the monasteries, St Patrick's was ordered to hand over all of its estates, revenues and possessions. The chapter (bureaucratic head of the church) was imprisoned until they 'agreed' to the handover, the cathedral's privileges were revoked and it was demoted to the rank of parish church. It was not restored to its previous position until 1560.

Further indignity arrived with Cromwell in 1649, when the nave was used as a stable for his horses. In 1666 the Lady Chapel was given to the newly arrived Huguenots and became known as the French Church of St Patrick. It remained in Huguenot hands until 1816. The northern transept was known as the parish church of St Nicholas Without (meaning outside the city), essentially dividing the cathedral into two distinct churches.

Such confusion led to the building falling into disrepair as the influence of the deanery and chapter – previously charged with the church's maintenance – waned. Although the church's most famous dean, Jonathan Swift (author of *Gulliver's Travels,* who served here from 1713 to 1745), did his utmost to preserve the integrity of the building, by the end of the 18th century it was close to collapse. It was just standing when the benevolent Guinness family stepped in to begin massive restoration in 1864.

Fittingly, the first Guinness to show an interest in preserving the church, Benjamin, is commemorated with a statue at the main entrance to the cathedral. Immediately inside to your left is the oldest part of the building, the baptistry, which was probably the entrance to the original building. It contains the original 12th-century floor tiles and medieval stone font, which is still in use. Inside the cathedral proper, you come almost immediately to the graves of Jonathan Swift and his long-term companion Esther Johnson, better known as Stella. The Latin epitaphs are both written by Swift, and assorted Swift memorabilia lies all over the cathedral, including a pulpit and a death mask.

Beginning clockwise around the cathedral, you can't miss the huge Boyle Monument, erected in 1632 by Richard Boyle, Earl of Cork. It stood briefly beside the altar until, in 1633, Dublin's viceroy, Thomas Wentworth, Earl of Strafford, had it shifted from its prominent position because he felt he shouldn't have to kneel to a Corkman. Boyle took his revenge in later years by orchestrating Wentworth's impeachment and execution. A figure in a niche at the bottom left of the monument is the earl's son Robert who went on to become a noted scientist and discovered Boyle's Law, which sets out the relationship between the pressure and the volume of a gas.

In the opposite corner, there is a cross on a stone slab that once marked the position of St Patrick's original well, where the patron saint of Ireland rolled up his sleeves and got to baptising the natives.

Towards the north transept is displayed a door that has become a symbol of peace and reconciliation since it helped resolve a scrap between the earls of Kildare and Ormond in 1492. After a feud, supporters of the squabbling nobles ended up in a pitched battle inside the cathedral, during which Ormond's nephew – one

EVENSONG AT THE CATHEDRALS

In a rare coming together, the choirs of St Patrick's Cathedral and Christ Church Cathedral both participated in the first-ever performance of Handel's *Messiah* in nearby Fishamble St in 1742, conducted by the great composer himself. Both houses of worship carry on their proud choral traditions, and visits to the cathedrals during evensong will provide enchanting and atmospheric memories. The choir performs evensong in St Patrick's at 5.45pm Monday to Friday (not on Wednesday in July and August), while the Christ Church choir competes at 5.30pm on Sunday, 6pm on Wednesday and Thursday, and 5pm Saturday. If you're going to be in Dublin around Christmas, do not miss the carols at St Patrick's; call ahead for the hard-to-get tickets on ☎ 453 9472.

Black James – barricaded himself into the chapterhouse. Kildare, having taken a deep breath and calmed down, cut a hole in the door between them and stuck his arm through it to either shake his opponent's hand, or lose a limb in his attempt to smooth things over. Luckily for him, James chose mediation over amputation and took his hand. The term 'to chance your arm' entered the English lexicon, the door, complete with hole, was preserved for posterity and everyone lived happily ever after – except Black James, who was murdered by Kildare's son-in-law four years later.

The north transept contains various military memorials to Royal Irish Regiments, while the northern choir aisle has a tablet marking the grave of the Duke of Schomberg, a prominent casualty of the Battle of the Boyne in 1690. Swift provided the duke's epitaph, caustically noting on it that the duke's own relatives couldn't be bothered to provide a suitable memorial. On the opposite side of the choir is a chair that was used by William of Orange when he came to the cathedral to give thanks to God for his victory over the Catholic James II during the same battle.

Passing through the south transept, which was once the chapterhouse where the Earl of Kildare chanced his arm, you'll see magnificent stained-glass windows above the funerary monuments. The south aisle is lined with memorials to prominent 20th-century Irish Protestants, including Erskine Childers, who was president of Ireland from 1973 to 1974, and whose father was executed by the Free State during the Civil War. The son never spoke of the struggle for Irish independence because, on the eve of his death, his father made him promise never to do anything that might promote bitterness among the Irish people.

On your way around the church, you will also take in the four sections of the permanent exhibition, Living Stones, which explores the cathedral's history and the contribution it has made to the culture of Dublin.

MARSH'S LIBRARY Map p91

☎ 454 3511; www.marshlibrary.ie; St Patrick's Close; adult/child/student €2.50/free/1.50; ⊙ 10am-1pm & 2-5pm Mon & Wed-Fri, 10.30am-1pm Sat; 🚌 50, 50A or 56A from Aston Quay, or 54 or 54A from Burgh Quay

It mightn't have the immediate appeal of a brewery or a big old church, but this magnificently preserved scholars' library, virtually unchanged in three centuries, is one of Dublin's most beautiful open secrets, and an absolute highlight of any visit. Few think to scale its ancient stairs to see its beautiful, dark oak bookcases, each topped with elaborately carved and gilded gables, and crammed with books. Here you can savour the atmosphere of three centuries of learning, slow into synch with the tick-tocking of the 19th-century grandfather clock, listen to the squeaky boards and record the scent of leather and learning. It's amazing how many people visit St Patrick's Cathedral next door and overlook this gem – they're mad, they don't deserve a holiday.

Founded in 1701 by Archbishop Narcissus Marsh (1638–1713) and opened in 1707, the library was designed by Sir William Robinson, the man also responsible for the Royal Hospital Kilmainham (p98). It's the oldest public library in the country, and contains 25,000 books dating from the 16th to the early 18th century, as well as maps, manuscripts (including one in Latin dating back to 1400) and a collection of incunabula (books printed before 1500). In its one nod to the 21st century, the library's current 'keeper', Dr Muriel McCarthy, is the first woman to hold the post.

Apart from theological books and bibles in dozens of languages, there are tomes on medicine, law, travel, literature, science, navigation, music and mathematics. One of the oldest and finest books is a volume of Cicero's Letters to His Friends, printed in Milan in 1472. The most important of the four main collections is the 10,000-strong library of Edward Stillingfleet, bishop of Worcester.

Most of Marsh's own extensive collection is also here, and there are various items that used to belong to Jonathan Swift (dean of St Patrick's Cathedral), including his copy of History of the Great Rebellion. His margin notes include a number of comments vilifying Scots, of whom he seemed to have a low opinion. He also held a low opinion of Archbishop Marsh, whom he blamed for holding him back in the church. When Swift died in 1745, he was buried in St Patrick's Cathedral, near his former enemy.

Like the rest of the library, the three alcoves, in which scholars were once locked to peruse rare volumes, have remained virtually unchanged for three centuries. Don't worry though: the skull in the furthest one doesn't belong to some poor forgotten scholar, it's a cast of the head of Stella, Swift's other half. The library's also home to Delmas Conservation Bindery, which repairs and restores rare old books, and makes an appearance in Joyce's *Ulysses*.

CHRIST CHURCH CATHEDRAL Map p91

Church of the Holy Trinity; ☎ 677 8099; www. cccdub.ie; Christ Church Pl; adult/senior/student €6/4/3; ⏲ 9.45am-4.15pm Mon-Sat, 12.30-2.30pm Sun Sep-May, 9.45am-6.15pm Mon-Tue & Fri, to 4.15pm Wed-Thu & Sat, 12.30-2.30pm & 4.30-6.15pm Sun Jun–mid-Jul, 9.45am-6.15pm Mon-Fri, to 4.15pm Sat, 12.30-2.30pm & 4.30-6.15pm Sun mid-Jul–Aug; 🚌 50, 50A or 56A from Aston Quay or 54 or 54A from Burgh Quay

Its hilltop location and eye-catching flying buttresses make this the most photogenic by far of Dublin's three cathedrals as well as one of the capital's most recognisable symbols.

A wooden church was first erected here by Dunán, the first bishop of Dublin, and Sitric, the Viking king, around 1030, at the southern edge of Dublin's Viking settlement. In 1163, however, the secular clergy was replaced by a group of Augustinian monks installed by the patron saint of Dublin, Archbishop Laurence O'Toole. Six years later, Strongbow's Normans blew into town and got themselves into the church-building business, arranging with O'Toole (and his successor John Cumin)

for the construction of a new stone cathedral that would symbolise Anglo-Norman glory. The new cathedral opened its doors late in the 12th century, by which time Strongbow, O'Toole and Cumin were long dead.

Above ground, the north wall, the transepts and the western part of the choir are almost all that remain from the original. It has been restored several times over the centuries and, despite its apparent uniformity, is a hotchpotch of different styles, ranging from Romanesque to English Gothic.

Until the disestablishment of the Church of Ireland in 1869, senior representatives of the Crown all swore their allegiance here. The church's fortunes, however, were not guaranteed. By the turn of the 18th century its popularity waned along with the district as the upper echelons of Dublin society fled north, where they attended a new favourite, St Mary's Abbey. Through much of its history, Christ Church vied for supremacy with nearby St Patrick's Cathedral, but both fell on hard times in the 18th and 19th centuries. Christ Church was virtually derelict – the nave had been used as a market and the crypt had earlier housed taverns – by the time restoration took place. Whiskey distiller Henry Roe donated the equivalent of €30 million to save the church, which was substantially rebuilt from 1871 to 1878. Ironically, both of the great Church of Ireland cathedrals are essentially outsiders in a Catholic nation today, dependent on tourist donations for their very survival.

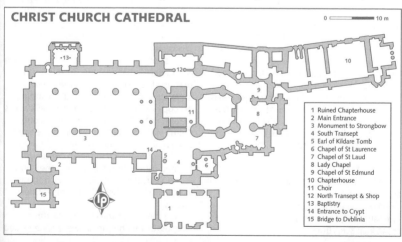

CHRIST CHURCH CATHEDRAL

0 ▭▭▭ 10 m

1 Ruined Chapterhouse
2 Main Entrance
3 Monument to Strongbow
4 South Transept
5 Earl of Kildare Tomb
6 Chapel of St Laurence
7 Chapel of St Laud
8 Lady Chapel
9 Chapel of St Edmund
10 Chapterhouse
11 Choir
12 North Transept & Shop
13 Baptistry
14 Entrance to Crypt
15 Bridge to Dvblinia

From its inception, Christ Church was the State Church of Ireland, and when Henry VIII dissolved the monasteries in the 16th century, the Augustinian priory that managed the church was replaced with a new Anglican clergy, which still runs the church today.

From the southeastern entrance to the churchyard you walk past ruins of the chapterhouse, which dates from 1230. The main entrance to the cathedral is at the southwestern corner and as you enter you face the ancient northern wall. This survived the collapse of its southern counterpart but has also suffered from subsiding foundations (much of the church was built on a peat bog) and, from its eastern end, it leans visibly.

The southern aisle has a monument to the legendary Strongbow. The armoured figure on the tomb is unlikely to be of Strongbow (it's more probably the Earl of Drogheda), but his internal organs may have been buried here. A popular legend relates an especially visceral version of the daddy-didn't-love-me tale: the half-figure beside the tomb is supposed to be Strongbow's son, who was cut in two by his loving father when his bravery in battle was suspect – an act that surely would have saved the kid a fortune in therapist's bills.

The southern transept contains the superb baroque tomb of the 19th earl of Kildare, who died in 1734. His grandson, Lord Edward Fitzgerald, was a member of the United Irishmen and died in the abortive 1798 Rising. The entrance to the Chapel of St Laurence is off the south transept and contains two effigies, one of them reputed to be of either Strongbow's wife or sister.

An entrance by the south transept descends to the unusually large arched crypt, which dates back to the original Viking church. Curiosities in the crypt include a glass display-case housing a mummified cat in the act of chasing a mummified mouse, frozen midpursuit inside an organ pipe in the 1860s. Also on display are the stocks from the old 'liberty' of Christ Church, used when church authorities meted out civil punishments to wrongdoers. The Treasury exhibit includes rare coins, the Stuart coat of arms and gold given to the church by William of Orange after the Battle of the Boyne. From the main entrance, a bridge, part of the 1871–78 restoration, leads to Dvblinia.

VIKING TRACES

Temple Bar's western boundary is marked by Fishamble St, Dublin's oldest street, which dates back to Viking times. Brass symbols in the pavement direct you towards a mosaic, just southwest of the overpass between Christ Church Cathedral and Dvblinia, laid out to show the ground plan of the sort of Viking dwelling excavated here in the early 1980s.

DVBLINIA & THE VIKING WORLD Map p91

☎ 679 4611; www.dublinia.ie; adult/student/child €6/5/3.50; ☾ 10am-5pm Apr-Sep, 11am-4pm Mon-Sat & 10am-4.30pm Sun Oct-Mar; ☒ 50, 50A or 56A from Aston Quay or 54 or 54A from Burgh Quay
A must for the kids, the old Synod Hall, added to Christ Church Cathedral during its late-19th-century restoration, is home to the seemingly perennial Dvblinia, a lively and kitschy attempt to bring medieval Dublin to life. Models, streetscapes and somewhat old-fashioned interactive displays do a fairly decent job of it, at least for kids. The model of a medieval quayside and a cobbler's shop are both excellent, as is the scale model of the medieval city. Up one floor is Viking World, which has a large selection of objects recovered from Wood Quay, the world's largest Viking archaeological site. Interactive exhibits tell the story of Dublin's 9th- and 10th-century Scandinavian invaders, but the real treat is exploring life aboard the recreated longboat. Finally, you can climb neighbouring St Michael's Tower and peek through its grubby windows for views over the city to the Dublin hills. There is also a pleasant cafe and the inevitable souvenir shop. Your ticket gets you into Christ Church Cathedral free, via the link bridge.

KILMAINHAM GAOL Map p91

☎ 453 5984; www.heritageireland.com; Inchicore Rd; adult/student/child €6/2/2; ☾ 9.30am-5pm Apr-Oct, 9.30am-4pm Mon-Sat, 10am-4pm Sun Nov-Mar; ☒ 23, 51, 51A, 78 or 79 from Aston Quay
If you have *any* interest in Irish history, especially the juicy bits about resistance to English rule, you will be shaken and stirred by a visit to this infamous prison. It was the stage for many of the most tragic and heroic episodes in Ireland's recent past, and the list of its inmates reads like a who's who of Irish nationalism. Solid and sombre,

its walls absorbed the barbarism of British occupation and recount them in whispers to visitors.

It took four years to build, and the prison opened – or rather closed – its doors in 1796, when the first reluctant guests were led in. The Irish were locked up for all sorts of misdemeanours, some more serious than others. A six-year-old boy spent a month here in 1839 because his father couldn't pay his train fare, and during the Famine it was crammed with the destitute who had been imprisoned for stealing food and begging. But it is most famous for incarcerating 120 years of Irish nationalists, from Robert Emmet in 1803 to Éamon de Valera in 1923. All of Ireland's botched uprisings ended with the leaders' confinement here, usually before their execution.

It was the treatment of the leaders of the 1916 Easter Rising that most deeply etched the gaol into the Irish consciousness (also see p29). Fourteen of the rebel commanders were executed in the exercise yard, including James Connolly who was so badly injured at the time of his execution that he was strapped to a chair at the opposite end of the yard, just inside the gate. The places where they were shot are marked by two simple black crosses. The executions turned an apathetic nation on a course towards violent rebellion.

The gaol's final function was as a prison for the newly formed Irish Free State, an irony best summed up with the story of Ernie O'Malley, who managed to escape from the gaol when incarcerated by the British but was locked up again by his erstwhile comrades during the Civil War. This chapter is somewhat played down on the tour, and even the passing comment that Kilmainham's final prisoner was the future president, Éamon de Valera, doesn't reveal that he had been imprisoned by his fellow Irish citizens. The gaol was finally decommissioned in 1924.

Visits are by guided tour and start with a stirring audiovisual introduction, screened in the former chapel where 1916 leader Joseph Plunkett was wed to his beloved just 10 minutes before his execution. The lively, thought-provoking (but too crowded) tour takes you through the old and new wings of the prison, where you can see former cells of famous inmates, read graffiti on the walls and immerse yourself in the atmosphere of the execution yards.

Incongruously sitting outside in the yard is the *Asgard,* the ship that successfully ran the British blockade to deliver arms to nationalist forces in 1914. It belonged to, and was skippered by, Erskine Childers, father of the future president of Ireland. He was executed by Michael Collins' Free State army in 1922 for carrying a revolver, which had been a gift from Collins himself. There is also an outstanding museum dedicated to Irish nationalism and prison life. On a lighter, more musical note, *real* U2 fans will be chuffed to recognise the prison as the setting for the video to their 1982 single 'A Celebration'; now that's a slice of history. Buffs of the other kind of history should allow at least half a day for a visit.

ROYAL HOSPITAL KILMAINHAM & IRISH MUSEUM OF MODERN ART
Map p91

IMMA; ☎ 612 9900; www.imma.ie; Military Rd; admission free; ⊗ 10am-5.30pm Tue-Sat, noon-5.30pm Sun; ⊜ 24, 79 or 90 from Aston Quay; ⊠ Heuston

IMMA is the country's foremost gallery for contemporary Irish art, although it takes second billing to the majestic building in which it is housed. The Royal Hospital Kilmainham was built between 1680 and 1684 as a retirement home for veteran soldiers, a function it fulfilled until 1928, after which it was left to languish for half a century before being saved in a 1980s restoration.

The inspiration for the design came from James Butler, duke of Ormonde and Charles II's viceroy, who had been so impressed by Les Invalides on a trip to Paris that he commissioned William Robinson to knock up a Dublin version. What the architect designed was Dublin's finest 17th-century building and the highpoint of the Anglo-Dutch style of the day. It consists of an unbroken range enclosing a vast, peaceful courtyard with arcaded walks. A chapel in the centre of the northern flank has an elegant clock tower and spire. This was the first truly classical building in Dublin and marked the beginning of the Georgian boom. Christopher Wren began building London's Chelsea Royal Hospital two years after work commenced here.

The spectacularly restored hospital was unveiled in 1984, on the 300th anniversary of its construction. The next year it received the prestigious Europa Nostra award for 'distinguished contribution to the conservation of Europe's architectural heritage'. There are free guided tours of the museum's exhibits at 2.30pm on Wednesday, Friday and Sunday throughout the year, but we strongly recommend the free, seasonal heritage itinerary 50-minute tour (ⓨ hourly 11am-4pm Tue-Sat, 1-4pm Sun Jun-Sep) run by the Office of Public Works. It shows off some of the building's treasures, including the Banqueting Hall, with 22 specially commissioned portraits, and the stunning baroque chapel, with papier-mâché ceilings and a set of exquisite Queen Anne gates. Also worth seeing are the fully restored formal gardens.

In 1991 it became home to IMMA and the best of modern and contemporary Irish art. The blend of old and new works wonderfully, and you'll find contemporary Irish artists such as Louis Le Brocquy, Sean Scully, Barry Flanagan, Kathy Prendergrass and Dorothy Cross featured here, as is a film installation by Neil Jordan. The permanent exhibition also features paintings from heavy-hitters Pablo Picasso and Joan Miró, and is topped up by regular temporary exhibitions. There's a good cafe and bookshop on the grounds.

KILMAINHAM GATE Map p91

🚌 23, 51, 51A, 78 or 79 from Aston Quay

The Kilmainham Gate was designed by Francis Johnston (1760–1829) in 1812 and originally stood at the Watling St junction with Victoria Quay, near the Guinness brewery, where it was known as the Richmond Tower. It was moved to its current position opposite the prison in 1846 as it obstructed the increasingly heavy traffic to the new Kingsbridge Station (now Heuston Station), which opened in 1844.

ST AUDOEN'S CHURCHES Map p91

☎ 677 0088; Cornmarket, High St; admission free; ⓨ 9.30am-4.45pm Jun-Sep; 🚌 50, 50A or 56A from Aston Quay or 54 or 54A from Burgh Quay

It was only right that the newly arrived Normans would name a church after their patron saint Audoen (the 7th-century bishop of Rouen, aka Ouen), but they didn't quite figure on two virtually adjacent churches bearing his name, just west of Christ Church Cathedral. The more interesting of the two is the Church of Ireland, the only

medieval parish church in the city that's still in use. It was built between 1181 and 1212, although a 9th-century burial slab in the porch suggests that it was built on top of an even older church. Its tower and door date from the 12th century and the aisle from the 15th century, but the church today is mainly a product of a 19th-century restoration.

As part of the tour you can explore the ruins as well as the present church, which has funerary monuments that were beheaded by Cromwell's purists. Through the heavily moulded Romanesque Norman door you can also touch the 9th-century 'lucky stone' that was believed to bring good luck to business.

St Anne's Chapel, the visitor centre, houses a number of tombstones of leading members of Dublin society from the 16th to the 18th centuries. At the top of the chapel is the tower, which holds the three oldest bells in Ireland, dating from 1423. Although the church's exhibits are hardly spectacular, the building itself is beautiful and a genuine slice of medieval Dublin.

The church is entered from the south off High St through St Audoen's Arch, which was built in 1240 and is the only surviving reminder of the city gates. The adjoining park is pretty but attracts many unsavoury characters, particularly at night.

Joined onto the Protestant church is the newer, bigger, 19th-century Catholic St Audoen's, an expansive church in which Father 'Flash' Kavanagh used to read Mass at high speed so that his large congregation could head off to more absorbing Sunday pursuits, such as football matches. In 2006 it was handed over to the Polish chaplaincy and is now the main church for Dublin's substantial Polish community.

ST WERBURGH'S CHURCH Map p91

☎ 478 3710; Werburgh St; ⓨ services 1st & 3rd Sunday of the month at 11am, call for access at other times; 🚌 50, 50A or 56A from Aston Quay or 54 or 54A from Burgh Quay

Lying west of Dublin Castle, St Werburgh's Church stands upon ancient foundations (probably from the 12th century), but was rebuilt several times during the 17th and 18th centuries. The church's tall spire was dismantled after Robert Emmet's rising in 1803, for fear that future rebels might use it as a vantage point for snipers. Interred in the vault is Lord Edward Fitzgerald, who turned against Britain, joined the United Irishmen and was a leader of the 1798 Rising. In what was a frequent theme of Irish uprisings, compatriots gave him away and his death resulted from the wounds he received when captured. Coincidentally, Major Henry Sirr, the man who captured him, is buried out in the graveyard. On the porch you will notice two fire pumps that date from the time when Dublin's fire department was composed of church volunteers. The interior is rather more cheerful than the exterior, although the church is rarely used today. Phone, or see the caretaker at 8 Castle St, to see inside. Donations are welcome.

WAR MEMORIAL GARDENS Map p91

☎ 677 0236; www.heritageireland.ie; South Circular Rd, Islandbridge; admission free; � 8am-twilight Mon-Fri, from 10am Sat & Sun; 🚌 25, 25A, 26, 68 or 69 from city centre; 🚆 Heuston

Hardly anyone ever ventures this far west, but they're missing a lovely bit of landscaping in the shape of the War Memorial Gardens, by our reckoning as pleasant a patch of greenery as any you'll find in the heart of the Georgian centre. Designed by Sir Edwin Lutyens, the memorial commemorates the 49,400 Irish soldiers who died during WWI – their names are inscribed in the two huge granite bookrooms that stand at one end. A beautiful spot and a bit of history to boot.

NORTH OF THE LIFFEY

Drinking p180; Eating p163; Shopping p144; Sleeping p218

What does a northsider use for protection? A bus shelter. Boom boom. Northsider/southsider jokes are a permanent fixture of the city's canon of humour, mostly because they highlight the perceived gap between the city's two halves, with the north side generally coming off second-best in all things save social ills and – as northsiders will happily tell you – true Dublin character. What does a southsider use for protection? Personality.

As gritty as the south side is glitzy, the north side is not just where Dubliners are at their most authentic, but where the great multicultural experiment is having its greatest success. A stroll through the street market on Moore St, once the epitome of auld Dublin, will reveal a weather-beaten street trader intoning 'five bananas for a euro' while young Koreans hawk phonecards from their shop hatches. On Parnell St, Nigerian teenagers rustle through beaded curtains into African salons for hair extensions while upstairs, their parents belt out gospel hymns in makeshift churches. Next door, Russians leave the supermarket laden with tinned caviar and *prianik* cookies.

This is the new Dublin, and it is slotting in comfortably alongside the older version of the north city centre, which radiates away from the grand dame of Dublin thoroughfares, the imperially wide O'Connell St. This famous street has played host to key episodes of Dublin's – and the nation's – history, none more so than the 1916 Easter Rising, when the proclamation announcing Ireland's independence was read out to a slightly bemused crowd from the steps of the General Post Office before the British Army pounded the building and its occupants into submission.

O'Connell St became Dublin's main street in 1794, when O'Connell Bridge was built and the city's axis shifted east. The north side was the residential area of choice at the start of the Georgian period, but when the hoi polloi got too close, the aristocracy doubled back over the Liffey and settled the new areas surrounding Leinster House. The Georgian squares named after Parnell and Mountjoy fell into rapid decline and were partly converted into slum dwellings. Although they've been largely neglected, they nevertheless display a certain dishevelled charm and are gradually being restored. O'Connell St leads north to the large Parnell Sq, which is flanked by museums, other public buildings and some fine, if a little rundown, Georgian residences.

West of O'Connell St along the refurbished river quays is the small but sterling Quartier Bloom, a little slice of Italy in the heart of the city. Further along is the cobbled neighbourhood of Smithfield, a *quartier* of office blocks and residential apartments that was up-and-coming for so many years that many now say it has been-and-gone. Not quite.

Built around a main square that was synonymous with markets since the 17th century, the fruit-and-veg and horse markets were hurriedly moved along because, frankly, a horse trader sealing the deal with spit in your hand wasn't quite the aesthetic the developers had in mind. The 400,000-odd antique cobblestones that saw their fair share of horse manure over the decades were carefully removed, hand-cleaned and relaid alongside new granite slabs, giving the whole square a look that got an enthusiastic thumbs-up from pretty much everyone – except, we're guessing, the traditional traders themselves. Still, not all tradition has been lost: there are still a couple of sensational pubs to hear music in, an old whiskey distillery draws them in by the thousands and, further west, the magnificent 18th-century Collins Barracks is home to one section of the National Museum of Ireland. Even the newest additions have a nostalgic feel about them: the snazzy new art-house cinema (see p191) is the contemporary reincarnation of an old Dublin favourite, albeit in a brand new location just off Smithfield Plaza.

If you're looking to base yourself on the north side, chances are you'll find yourself bedding down on or around B&B Row – Gardiner St, east of O'Connell St. This street has long been the preferred spot for those happy to trade luxury for an affordable bed, but even here the standards have improved substantially over the last decade or so, especially at the southern end of the street. You can still manage to find some bargain-basement options at Gardiner St's northern end, but note that that part of the 'hood gets a little iffy after dark, so they're not highly recommended.

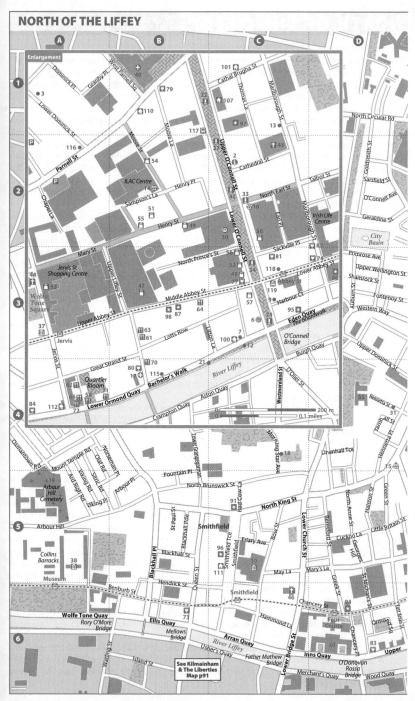

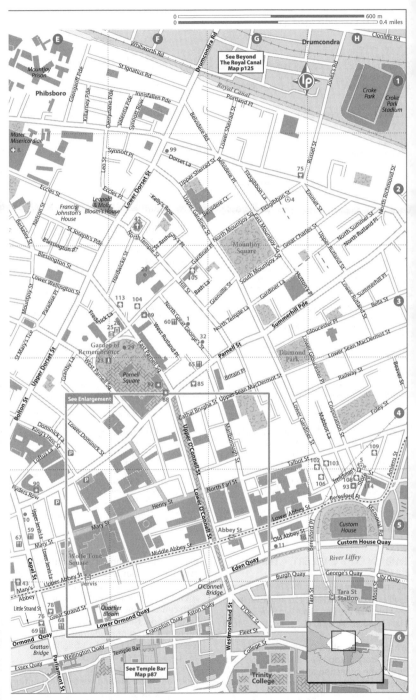

0 ——————————— 600 m
0 ——————————— 0.4 miles

E Mountjoy Prison
Phibsboro
Whitworth Rd
St Ignatius Rd
Innisfallen Pde
F
Drumcondra Rd
See Beyond The Royal Canal Map p125
G Drumcondra
H Clonliffe Rd

Royal Canal
Portland Pl
Croke Park
Croke Park Stadium
1

Mater Misericordiae
Eccles St
Synnott Pl
Leo St
Dorset La
99
Upper Sherrard St
Belvidere Rd
Lower Sherrard St
Belvidere Pl
Fitzgibbon St
Fitzgibbon St
4
75
North Richmond St
2

Francis Johnston's House
Leopold & Molly Bloom's House
Eccles Pl
Kelly's Row
St Joseph's Pde
Blessington St
Blessington Pl
Lower Wellington St
Mountjoy St
Paradise Pl
St Mary's Tce
North Temple St
North Anthony's Pde
Hardwicke St
Gardiner St
North Great George's St
Hill St
Bath La
Grenville St
North Temple La
North Mountjoy Sq
East Mountjoy Sq
South Mountjoy Sq
Mountjoy Square
Gardiner La
Hutton La
Great Charles St
Upper Rutland St
North Summer St
North Rutland Pl
Lower Rutland St
Lower Summerhill Pl
Summerhill Pde
Bella St
3

43
Frederick La
113 104
26
25
89
60
1
32
105
29
Garden of Remembrance
23
Parnell Square
92
85
88
West Parnell Sq
East Parnell Sq
West Rutland Pl
Parnell St
65
Britain Pl
Cathal Brugha St
Upper Sean MacDermot St
Lower Sean MacDermot St
Railway St
Gloucester Pl
Gloucester La
Lower Gloucester Pl
Matbot La
Diamond Park
Foley St
Corporation St
Beaver St
4

Bolton St
Upper Dorset St
Dominick La
King's Inns La
Loftus La
Lower Dominick St
Upper O'Connell St
Marlborough St
Lower Gardiner St
Talbot St
102 103
106
109
5
Amiens St
Friendly St
108
93
4
5

Ryders Row
90
Upper Jervis La
10
59
67
Mary St
Lower Jervis La
Capel St
Henry St
North Earl St
Lower O'Connell St
Abbey St
Lower Abbey St
Old Abbey St
11
Beresford Pl
Custom House
Custom House Quay
River Liffey
Tara St
Beresford Pl
5

43
Mary's Abbey
Upper Abbey St
Jervis
Little Strand St
78
76
68
69
Ormond Quay
Grattan Bridge
Essex Quay
Parliament St
Wolfe Tone Square
Mary St
Middle Abbey St
O'Connell Bridge
Quartier Bloom
Lower Ormond Quay
Wellington Quay
Temple Bar
See Temple Bar Map p87
Eden Quay
Burgh Quay
George's Quay
City Quay
O'Connell Bridge
Crampton Quay
Aston Quay
Westmoreland St
D'Olier St
Fleet St
College St
Trinity College
Tara St Station
6

103

INFORMATION
Access Service 1 F3
City Sightseeing .... (see 2)
Dublin Bus .... (see 117)
Dublin Tourism 2 C2
Executive Nannies.................................. 3 A1
Garda Station.. 4 G2
Garda Station.. 5 H4
General Post Office (GPO) .... (see 30)
Global Internet Café 6 C3
Grayline Dublin Tour............................ 7 C3
James Joyce Walking Tour.......... (see 32)
Mater Misericordiae Hospital 8 E2
O'Connell's Late Night Pharmacy . 9 C3
Outhouse 10 E5
Planet Recruitment 11 G5
River Liffey Cruises............................. 12 C3
Samaritans.. 13 C1
Talk is Cheap 14 B2
Talk is Cheap 15 D4
Talk Shop.. 16 C2
Well Woman Centre 17 B4
Women's Emergency Hostel 18 C4

SIGHTS (p101)
Arbour Hill Cemetery...................... 19 A5
Belvedere House 20 F3
Boardwalk... 21 B4
Charles Stewart Parnell Statue 22 B1
Children of Lir Monument............. 23 E4
Daniel O'Connell Statue.................. 24 C3
Dublin City Gallery – The Hugh
    Lane... 25 F3
Dublin Writers Museum.................. 26 F3
Father Theobald Mathew Statue 27 C2
Four Courts... 28 D6
Garden of Remembrance 29 F3
General Post Office (GPO) 30 C2
Henrietta St 31 D4
James Joyce Cultural Centre 32 F3
James Joyce Statue............................ 33 C2
Jim Larkin Statue 34 C3
King's Inns 35 D4
Liberty Hall 36 G5
National Leprechaun Museum 37 A3
National Museum – Decorative
    Arts & History.............................. 38 A5
Old Jameson Distillery..................... 39 C5
Rotunda Hospital 40 B1
Royal Barracks .... (see 38)
Spire.. 41 C2
St George's Church 42 F2

St Mary's Abbey.................................. 43 E6
St Mary's Church................................. 44 A3
St Mary's Pro-Cathedral 45 C2
St Michan's Church............................ 46 C6

SHOPPING (p144)
Arnott's.. 47 B3
Clark's... 48 C3
Clark's... 49 B2
Clery's & Co 50 C2
Debenhams 51 B2
Eason's.. 52 C3
Jervis Centre 53 A3
Moore Street Market......................... 54 B2
Penney's... 55 B2
Penney's... 56 C3
Schuh 57 C3
Walton's.. (see 113)
Winding Stair .... (see 71)

EATING (p163)
Bar Italia.. 58 A4
Bon Ga 59 E5
Chapter One .... (see 26)
Cobalt Café & Gallery....................... 60 F3
Coffee Society 61 B3
Dublin City Gallery - The Hugh
    Lane.. (see 25)
Enoteca Delle Langhe 62 A4
Epicurean Food Hall.......................... 63 B3
Govinda's... 64 B3
Halo .... (see 112)
Kimchi/The Hop House 65 F4
La Taverna di Bacco........................... 66 A4
Melody.. 67 E5
Panem.. 68 E6
Soup Dragon 69 E6
Taste of Emilia 70 B4
Winding Stair 71 A4
Yamamori Sushi.................................. 72 A4

DRINKING (p180)
Dice Bar.. 73 B6
Flowing Tide 74 D3
Gill's 75 G2
Morrison Bar .... (see 112)
Nealon's.. 76 E6
Oval 77 C3
Pantibar.. 78 E6
Patrick Conway's 79 B1
Pravda... 80 B4
Sackville Lounge 81 C3

Sean O'Casey's.................................... 82 D2
Sin É... 83 D6
Tea Garden 84 A4
Welcome Inn 85 F4

NIGHTLIFE & THE ARTS (p185)
Abbey Theatre 86 D3
Academy... 87 B3
Ambassador Theatre 88 F4
Belvedere 89 F3
Cineworld Multiplex 90 E5
Cobblestone.. 91 C5
Gate Theatre 92 F4
Good Bits 93 H5
Hughes' Bar.. 94 D6
Laughter Lounge 95 C3
Lighthouse Cinema 96 C5
Peacock Theatre............................ (see 86)
Savoy 97 C1
Twisted Pepper 98 B3

SPORTS & ACTIVITIES (p201)
GAA Ticket Office 99 F2

SLEEPING (p218)
Abbey Court Hostel 100 C3
Academy Hotel.................................. 101 C1
Anchor Guesthouse......................... 102 H4
Brown's Hotel...................................... 103 H4
Castle Hotel 104 F3
Clifden Guesthouse 105 F3
Globetrotters Tourist Hostel...... 106 C6
Gresham Hotel.................................... 107 C1
Isaac's Hostel 108 H5
Jacob's Inn 109 H4
Jury's Inn Parnell St 110 B1
Maldron Hotel Smithfield 111 C5
Morrison Hotel................................... 112 A4
Townhouse.................................... (see 106)
Walton's Hotel 113 F3

TRANSPORT (p240)
Busáras.. 114 H5
Cyclelogical 115 B4
Cycleways.. 116 A2
Dublin Bus Office............................. 117 B1
Rail Travel Centre (Iarnród
    Éireann) 118 C3
Taxi Rank 119 C3

DUBLIN CITY GALLERY – THE HUGH LANE Map p102

Municipal Gallery of Ireland; ☎ 874 1903; www.
hughlane.ie; 22 North Parnell Sq; admission free;
🕙 10am-6pm Tue-Thu, 10am-5pm Fri & Sat,
11am-5pm Sun; 🚌 3, 10, 11, 13, 16, 19 or 22 from
city centre

Whatever reputation Dublin may have as
a repository of top-class art is in large part
due to the collection at this magnificent
gallery, which is not only home to works by

some of the supernovas in the impressionist firmament, but where you'll find one of
the most singular exhibitions to be seen
anywhere: the *actual* studio of one of the
20th century's most famous artists, Francis
Bacon. And if that wasn't art to keep you
interested, a recent modernist extension
has seen the addition of 13 bright galleries spread across three floors of the old
National Ballroom to show work from the
1950s onwards. Oh, and we should mention

that the gallery has resided in the simply stunning Charlemont House since 1933, which was designed by Georgian superstar architect William Chambers in 1763.

The gallery owes its 1908 origins to one Hugh Lane, whose failure to get any funding from an uninterested government and other commercial interests prompted WB Yeats to really have a go at the authorities and mercenary materialism in one of his most vitriolic poems, *September 1913*. Yeats was very annoyed, and while his disgust with those who 'fumble in a greasy till/ and add the halfpence to the pence' was certainly justified, we wonder if his ire had anything to do with the fact that the very, very rich Lane was the nephew of Lady Gregory, Yeats' own patron?

Poor old Hugh Lane didn't get to enjoy his wealth or his art collection for too much longer, however, as he was a passenger on the ill-fated *Lusitania* and died in 1915 (see the boxed text, below). There followed a bitter wrangle over Lane's bequest, between the gallery he founded and the National Gallery in London. The collection was eventually split in a complicated 1959 settlement that sees some of the paintings moving back and forth. The conditions of the exchanges are in the midst of a convoluted negotiation, but for the time being the gallery has Manet's *Eva Gonzales,* Pissarro's *Printemps,* Berthe Morisot's *Jour d'Eté* and the most important painting of the entire collection (and one of our favourites of all time), Renoir's *Les Parapluies*.

Impressionist masterpieces notwithstanding, the gallery's most popular exhibit is the Francis Bacon Studio, which was painstakingly moved, in all its shambolic mess, from 7 Reece Mews, South Kensington, London, where the Dublin-born artist (1909–92)

lived for 31 years. The display features some 80,000 items madly strewn about the place, including slashed canvases, the last painting he was working on, tables piled with materials, walls daubed with colour samples, portraits with heads cut out, favourite bits of furniture and many assorted piles of crap. It's a teasing and tantalising, riveting and ridiculous masterpiece that provides the viewer – peering in at the chaos through thick Perspex – no real sense of the artist himself. Far more revealing is the 10-minute profile of him with Melvyn Bragg and the immensely sad photographs of Bacon's immaculately tidy bachelor pad, which suggest a deep, personal loneliness.

You can round off a (hopefully) satisfying visit with lunch in the superb cafe (p165) in the basement of the new extension, before making a stop in the well-stocked gift shop.

OLD JAMESON DISTILLERY Map p102

☎ 807 2355; www.jameson.ie; Bow St; adult/child/student €13.50/8/10; ☉ tours every 35min 9am-5.30pm; 🚌 67, 67A, 68, 69, 79 or 134 from city centre; 🚇 Smithfield

Smithfield's biggest draw is devoted to *uisce beatha* (*ish*-kuh ba-ha, 'the water of life'). The whowhatnow? It's whiskey, the essential Irish spirit, which doesn't quite bestow life, but, if drunk enough, will undoubtedly take it away. Here, in the original home of one of its most famous and renowned distillers, you can get an excellent introduction to the history and culture of this most potent of drinks. Serious fans might be put off by the slickness of the tour and museum, which shepherds visitors through a compulsory tour of the re-created factory and into the ubiquitous gift shop.

The museum occupies a section of the old distillery, which kept the capital in

HUGH LANE

It's hardly surprising that wealthy Sir Hugh Lane (1875–1915) was miffed by the Irish and decided to bequeath his paintings to some other nation, as he was treated with less respect than he felt he deserved in his own land. Born in County Cork, he began to work in London art galleries from 1893, and five years later set up his own gallery in Dublin. He had a connoisseur's eye and a good nose for the directions of the market, which enabled him to build up a superb and valuable collection, particularly strong in impressionists.

Unfortunately for Ireland, neither his talents nor his collection were much appreciated, and in exasperation he turned his attention to opportunities in London and South Africa. Irish rejection led him to rewrite his will and bequeath some of the finest works in his collection to the National Gallery in London. Later he relented and added a rider to his will leaving the collection to Dublin but failed to have it witnessed, thus causing a long legal squabble over which gallery had rightful ownership. He was just 40 years old when he went down with the ill-fated *Lusitania* in 1915, after it was torpedoed by a German U-boat off the southern coast of Ireland.

If you're listening to folk legends the Dubliners, you might come across a singalong ditty called 'Monto (Take Her Up to Monto)', which is a playful reference to what was once Dublin's most notorious red-light district and the favoured destination of off-duty soldiers looking for a little night-time action. The name comes from Mountgomery St, which was just east of O'Connell St and where the light shone reddest. James Joyce lost his virginity here (as did many others) within spitting distance of the city's Catholic cathedral. A couple of years after independence the new, ultra-Catholic authorities decided to take action and closed all of the brothels. Catholic girls from the Legion of Mary marched through the streets attaching holy pictures to the doors of former dens of disrepute, and Mountgomery St, whose name was synonymous with pleasures of the flesh, was renamed the suitably chaste Cathedral St.

whiskey from 1780 to 1971 (after which the remaining distillers moved to a new ultramodern distillery in Middleton, County Cork). The museum can only be visited on guided tours, which run every 35 minutes. They start with a short film and then, with the aid of models and exhibitions, explain everything you ever wanted to know about Irish whiskey, from its fascinating history to how it's made and why it differs from Scotch – ex-footballer (and Scot) Ally McCoist once joked that the Irish thought of everything, including putting an 'e' in whiskey. At the end of the tour you'll be invited into the Jameson Bar for a dram of complimentary whiskey. Stay alert and make sure to volunteer for the tasting tour, where you get to sample whiskeys from all around the world and train your palate to identify and appreciate the differences between each.

At the end of the tour, you're deposited in the shop, which was kinda the whole point of the tour in the first place you might reckon. If you do want to bring a bottle or two home, make sure you buy one that you can't get in your local. There are some 100 brands of Irish whiskey (not all sold here) but only three – Jameson, Bushmills and Tullamore Dew – are widely available. Our tip is Red Breast, pure pot still, the way all Irish whiskey used to be made, although the swashbuckling Power's is numero uno in Ireland and difficult to get elsewhere. You can also get a rare distillery reserve with your name printed on the label – kind of tacky, but neat, the way we like our whiskey.

There's also a good cafe and restaurant on the premises.

NATIONAL MUSEUM OF IRELAND – DECORATIVE ARTS & HISTORY Map p102

☎ 677 7444; www.museum.ie; Benburb St; admission free; ☻ 10am-5pm Tue-Sat, 2-5pm

Sun; 🚌 25, 25A, 66, 67 or 90 from city centre; 🚇 Museum

No wonder the British army were so reluctant to pull out of Ireland, when they were occupying this magnificent space, the oldest army barracks in Europe. The building – the museum bit can wait – was completed in 1704 according to the design of Thomas Burgh, whose CV also includes the Old Library (p69) in Trinity College and St Michan's Church (p110). Its central square held six entire regiments and is a truly awesome space, surrounded by arcaded colonnades and blocks linked by walking bridges. Following the handover to the new Irish government in 1922, the barracks was renamed to honour Michael Collins, a hero of the struggle for independence, who was killed that year in the Civil War; to this day most Dubliners refer to the museum as the Collins Barracks.

Any city would be hard-pressed to come up with a museum to match these surroundings, and the decorative arts don't exactly get the heart pumping. That said, the museum has done an exceptional job of presenting an impressive, if hardly remarkable, collection, featuring fashion, furniture, weaponry, folk life, silver, ceramics and glassware. Some of the best pieces are gathered in the Curator's Choice exhibition, which is a collection of 25 objects hand-picked by different curators, and displayed alongside an account of why they were chosen.

The exhibitions are designed to offer a bird's-eye view of Ireland's social, economic and military history over the last millennium. It's a big ask – too big, say its critics – but well-designed displays, interactive multimedia and a dizzying array of disparate artefacts make for an interesting and valiant effort. On the 1st floor is the museum's Irish silver collection, one of the largest collections of silver in the world; on the 2nd floor you'll find Irish period furniture and scientific instruments, while the 3rd floor has simple and sturdy Irish country furniture. Modern-furniture-and-design lovers will enjoy the exhibition on iconic Irish designer Eileen Gray (1878–1976), one of the museum's highlights. One of the most influential designers of the 20th century, Gray's life and work are documented in the exhibit, which shows examples of her most famous pieces. The fascinating Way We Wore exhibit displays Irish clothing and jewellery from the past 250 years. An intriguing socio-cultural study, it highlights the symbolism jewellery and clothing had in bestowing messages of mourning, love and identity.

A new exhibition chronicling Ireland's 1916 Easter Rising is on the ground floor. Visceral memorabilia, such as first-hand accounts of the violence of the Black & Tans and post-Rising hunger strikes, the handwritten death certificates of the republican prisoners and their postcards from Holloway prison, bring to life this poignant period of Irish history.

GENERAL POST OFFICE (GPO)
Map p102
☎ 705 7000; www.anpost.ie; O'Connell St; ⏰ 8am-8pm Mon-Sat; 🚌 all city centre; 🚇 Abbey St

Imagine trying to post a letter at the country's main post office, only for a bunch of armed and most serious men interrupting your chore by declaring an Irish republic from the doorways before barricading themselves inside in anticipation of a week-long bombardment by the British Army. On Easter Monday 1916, the leaders of the Rising made the GPO their operational HQ, thus ensuring that this huge neoclassical building (designed by Francis Johnston in 1818) would become the focal point for all kinds of protests, parades and remembrances of the struggle for Irish independence.

It's not as if the GPO didn't earn it either: along with much of Lower O'Connell St, the building was left a smouldering wreck (now that's going postal!). You can still see pockmarks and bullet holes in the huge pillars supporting the Ionic portico, which spans the five central bays and is topped by three statues representing Fidelity, Hibernia and Mercury. The damage was so bad that it didn't reopen until 1929. For more on the Easter Rising, see p29.

In the spacious and light-filled interior there's a beautiful bronze statue, the *Death of Cuchulainn* (1935), depicting the legendary hero of Ulster, whose spirit was evoked in the poetry of Pádraig Pearse. He was an awesome warrior slain at the age of 27 after being tricked into an unfair fight. Even as he lay dead, nobody dared approach the body for fear of attack and it wasn't until ravens landed on him that they were convinced he was dead. The statue is dedicated to those who died in the Rising. Also inside is a series of communist nobleworker-style paintings depicting scenes from the Easter Rising. There are also lots of people going about the everyday business of buying stamps and posting letters. Finally, among all the flags hanging in here, notice that the Union Jack is hung behind the counter and out of reach? It had to be moved there because people kept setting it alight.

NATIONAL LEPRECHAUN MUSEUM
Map p102
☎ 873 3899; www.leprechaunmuseum.ie; Twilfit House, Jervis St; adult/child & student €10/7; ⏰ 9.30am-6.30pm Mon-Sat, from 10.30am Sun; 🚌 all city centre; 🚇 Jervis

Nobody believes in them, so a museum dedicated to the diminutive folk of Irish myth can't be anything other than an exercise in low-end tourism, right? It seems 'National Folklore Museum' didn't test well with potential visitors, but that would have been a case of misdirection, because this new museum offers little more than an introductory glimpse at the leprechaun story, from the (largely American) image of a gold-burying, good-luck-bringing Lucky

WHERE NOW THE ABBEY?

As of 2010, the future of the Abbey (see p197) – Ireland's national theatre – was uncertain. There has long been a desire to move it to a purpose-built facility – for a few years the money was on somewhere in the Docklands – but the financial crisis put paid to any plan to build a new theatre and so alternatives were looked at. The most interesting of them was Senator David Norris' (of the James Joyce Cultural Centre, see p108) proposition that it be moved to the GPO in time for the centenary of the Easter Rising. Will it happen? We have until 2016 to find out.

O'CONNELL STREET STATUARY

Although overshadowed by the Spire, O'Connell St is lined with statues of Irish history's good and great (see Map p102). The big daddy of them all is the 'Liberator' himself, Daniel O'Connell (1775–1847), completed in 1880, whose massive bronze bulk soars high above the street at the bridge end. The four winged figures at his feet represent O'Connell's supposed virtues: patriotism, courage, fidelity and eloquence. Dubs began to refer to the street as O'Connell St soon after the monument was erected, but its name was only officially changed after independence.

Heading away from the river, past a monument to William Smith O'Brien (1803–64), leader of the Young Irelanders, is a statue that easily rivals O'Connell's for drama: just outside the GPO is the spread-armed figure of trade-union leader Jim Larkin (1876–1947). His big moment came when he helped organise the general strike in 1913 – the pose catches him in full flow, urging workers to rise up for their rights. We're with you, comrade.

Next up and difficult to miss is the Spire (p110), but just below it, on pedestrianised North Earl St, is the detached figure of James Joyce, looking on the fast and shiny version of 21st-century O'Connell St with a bemused air. Dubs have lovingly dubbed him the 'prick with the stick' and we're sure Joyce would have loved the vulgar rhyme.

Further on is the statue of Father Theobald Mathew (1790–1856), the 'apostle of temperance'. There can't have been a tougher gig in Ireland, but he led a spirited campaign against 'the demon drink' in the 1840s and converted hundreds of thousands to teetotalism.

The top of the street is completed by the imposing statue of Charles Stewart Parnell (1846–91), the 'uncrowned king of Ireland', who was an advocate of Home Rule and became a political victim of Irish intolerance. Despite his fall from grace, it's Parnell who gets the most imposing monument.

Charms–type figure to the creature associated with the mythical Tuatha dé Danann people that preceded the Celts. There's the optical illusion tunnel (which makes you appear smaller to those at the other end), the room full of oversized furniture, the wishing wells and, invariably, the pot of gold; all of which is strictly for kids, who will no doubt enjoy the magical storytelling element of it all as their parents issue a patient sigh. But if Walt Disney himself went on a leprechaun hunt when visiting Ireland during the filming of *Darby O'Gill and the Little People* in 1948, what the hell do we know?

FOUR COURTS Map p102

☎ 872 5555; Inns Quay; admission free; 🚌 25, 25A, 66, 67, 90 or 134 from city centre; 🚇 Four Courts

Impossible to miss if you're up this end of town, James Gandon's (1743–1823) masterpiece is a mammoth complex stretching 130m along Inns Quay. Construction on the Four Courts began in 1786, soon engulfing the Public Offices (built a short time previously at the western end of the same site), and continued until 1802. By then it included a Corinthian-columned central block connected to flanking wings with enclosed quadrangles. The ensemble is topped by a diverse collection of statuary. The original four courts – Exchequer, Common Pleas, King's Bench and Chancery – branch off the central rotunda.

The Four Courts played a brief role in the 1916 Easter Rising without suffering damage, but it wasn't so lucky during the Civil War. When anti-Treaty forces seized the building and refused to leave, Free State forces led by Michael Collins shelled it from across the river. As the occupiers retreated, the building was set on fire and many irreplaceable early records were burned. These were the opening salvos in the Irish Civil War. The building wasn't restored until 1932.

Visitors are allowed to wander through, but not to enter the courts or other restricted areas. In the lobby of the central rotunda you'll see bewigged barristers conferring and police officers handcuffed to their charges waiting to enter court.

JAMES JOYCE CULTURAL CENTRE Map p104

☎ 878 8547; www.jamesjoyce.ie; 35 North Great George's St; adult/child/student €5/free/4; 🕙 10am-5pm Tue-Sat; 🚌 3, 10, 11, 13, 16, 16A, 19, 19A or 22 from city centre

Denis Maginni, the exuberant, flamboyant dance instructor and 'confirmed bachelor' immortalised by James Joyce in *Ulysses*, taught the finer points of dance out of this beautifully restored Georgian house, now a centre devoted to promoting and preserving the Joycean heritage. Although Jimmy probably never set foot in the house, he lived in the 'hood for a time, went to a local school and lost his virginity a stone's throw away in what was once Europe's largest red-light district. We couldn't imagine a more fitting location for the centre.

The centre owes its existence to the sterling efforts of Senator David Norris, a charismatic Joycean scholar and gay-rights activist who bought the house in 1982 and oversaw its restoration and conversion into the centre that it is today.

What it is today is more of a study centre than a museum, although there are a handful of exhibits that will pique the interest of a Joyce enthusiast. These include some of the furniture from Joyce's Paris apartment, which was rescued from falling into German hands in 1940 by Joyce's friend Paul Léon; a life-size re-creation of a typical Edwardian bedroom (not Joyce's, but one similar to what James and Nora would have used); and the original door of 7 Eccles St, the home of Leopold and Molly Bloom in *Ulysses,* which was demolished in real life to make way for a private hospital.

It's not much, but the absence of period stuff is more than made up for by the superb interactive displays, which include three short documentary films on various aspects of Joyce's life and work, and – the highlight of the whole place – computers that allow you to explore the content of *Ulysses* episode by episode and trace Joyce's life year by year. It's enough to demolish the myth that Joyce's works are an impenetrable mystery and render him as he should be to the contemporary reader: a writer of enormous talent who sought to challenge and entertain his audience with his breathtaking wit and use of language.

While here, you can also admire the fine plastered ceilings, some of which are restored originals while others are meticulous reproductions of Michael Stapleton's designs. Senator Norris fought a long,

unrewarding battle for the preservation of Georgian Dublin, and it's wonderful to see others have followed his example – the street has been given a much-needed face-lift and now boasts some of the finest Georgian doorways and fanlights in the city.

For information on James Joyce–related walking tours departing from the centre, see p253.

DUBLIN WRITERS MUSEUM Map p104
☎ 872 2077; www.writersmuseum.com; 18 North Parnell Sq; adult/child/student €7.50/4.70/6.30; ☷ 10am-5pm Mon-Sat Sep-May, to 6pm Jun-Aug, 11am-5pm Sun year-round; 🚍 3, 10, 11, 13, 16, 19 or 22 from city centre

Memorabilia aplenty and lots of literary ephemera line the walls and display cabinets of this elegant museum devoted to preserving the city's rich literary tradition. Although the busts and portraits of the greats in the gallery upstairs are worth more than a cursory peek, the real draw are the ground-floor displays, which include Samuel Beckett's phone (with a button for excluding incoming calls, of course), a letter from the 'tenement aristocrat' Brendan Behan to his brother, and a first edition of Bram Stoker's *Dracula*. However, the museum's decision to omit living writers limits its appeal, in our opinion; the exhibits stop in 1970 and no account at all is given to contemporary writers, who would arguably be more popular with today's readers. We can't help thinking that a city with such a rich heritage of great writers deserves a more thorough and fitting tribute. Admission includes taped guides in English and other languages, which have the annoying habit of repeating quotes with actor's voices.

The building, comprising two 18th-century houses, is worth exploring on its

DA NORT'SOYID & THE SOUTHSYDE

It is commonly assumed that the south side is totally posh and the north side a derelict slum – it makes the jokes easier to make and the prejudices easier to maintain. But the truth is a little more complex. The 'south side' generally refers to Dublin 4 and the fancy suburbs immediately west and south – conveniently ignoring the traditionally working-class neighbourhoods in southwestern Dublin like Bluebell and Tallaght. North Dublin is huge, but the north side tag is usually applied to the inner suburbs, where incomes are lower, accents are more pronouncedly Dublin and – most recently – the influx of foreign nationals is more in evidence. All Dubliners are familiar with the posh twit stereotype born and raised on the south side, but there's another kind of Dubliner, usually from the middle-class districts of northern Dublin, who affects a salt-of-the-earth accent while talking about the 'gee-gees' and says things like 'tis far from sushi we was rared' while tucking into a *maki* roll.

own. Dublin stuccodore Michael Stapleton decorated the upstairs gallery. The Gorham Library next door is worth a peek and there's also a calming Zen garden. The museum cafe is a pleasant place to linger, while the basement restaurant, Chapter One (p164), is one of the city's best.

While the museum focuses on the dearly departed, the Irish Writers Centre (☎ 872 1302; 19 North Parnell Sq) next door provides a meeting and working place for their living successors.

SPIRE Map p102

🚇 all city centre; 🚆 Abbey St

For 50 years, the traditional meeting place in the city centre for young lovers, friends or out-of-towners requiring a distinctive landmark was Clery's clock, the timepiece hanging from O'Connell St's most famous department store. Nowadays – and surely the ultimate mark of success – it's metal Spire that soars over the city, erected in 2001 as the standout example of the program of urban regeneration that has slowly transformed O'Connell St over the last 10 years.

The brainchild of London-based architect Ian Ritchie, it is apparently the highest sculpture in the world, but much like the Parisian reaction to the construction of the Eiffel Tower, Dubliners are divided as to its aesthetic value. Whatever its aesthetics, it's an impressive bit of architectural engineering: from a base of only 3m in diameter, it soars more than 120m into the sky and tapers into a 15cm-wide beam of light and, for no reason other than the fact that it's tall and shiny, we think it does the trick rather nicely. Which doesn't stop Dubliners making fun of it, of course: among other names, we like 'the erection in the intersection', the 'stiletto in the ghetto', and the altogether brilliant 'eyeful tower'.

ST MICHAN'S CHURCH Map p102

☎ 872 4154; Lower Church St; adult/child/student €4/2/3.50; 🕐 10am-12.45pm & 2-4.45pm Mon-Fri, 10am-12.45pm Sat May-Oct, 12.30-3.30pm Mon-Fri Nov-Apr; 🚇 134 from city centre; 🚆 Four Courts

Macabre remains are the main attraction at this church, which was founded by the Danes in 1096 and named after one of their saints. The oldest architectural feature is the 15th-century battlement tower; otherwise the church was rebuilt in the

late 17th century, considerably restored in the early 19th century and again after the Civil War.

The interior of the church, which feels more like a courtroom, is worth a quick look as you wait for your guide. It contains an organ from 1724, which Handel may have played for the first-ever performance of his *Messiah*. The organ case is distinguished by the fine oak carving of 17 entwined musical instruments on its front. A skull on the floor on one side of the altar is said to represent Oliver Cromwell. On the opposite side is the Stool of Repentance, where 'open and notoriously naughty livers' did public penance.

The tours of the underground vaults are the real draw, however. The bodies within are aged between 400 and 800 years, and have been preserved by a combination of methane gas coming from rotting vegetation beneath the church, the magnesium limestone of the masonry (which absorbs moisture from the air), and the perfectly constant temperature. The corpses have been exposed because the coffins in the vaults were stacked on top of one another and some toppled over and opened when the wood rotted. Among the 'attractions' is an 800-year-old Norman crusader who was so tall that his feet were lopped off so he could fit in a coffin. The guide sounds like he's been delivering the same, albeit fascinating, spiel for too long, but you'll definitely be glad you're not alone down there.

ARBOUR HILL CEMETERY Map p102

🕐 821 3021; www.heritageireland.ie; Arbour Hill; admission free; 🕐 8am-4pm Mon-Fri, 11am-4pm Sat, 9.30am-4pm Sun; 🚇 25, 25A, 37, 38, 39, 66, 67, 90 or 134 from city centre; 🚆 Museum

Just north of Collins Barracks, this small cemetery is the final resting place of all 14 of the executed leaders of the 1916 Easter Rising (see p29). The burial ground is plain, with the 14 names inscribed in stone. Beside the graves is a cenotaph bearing the Easter Proclamation, a focal point for official and national commemorations. The front of the cemetery incongruously, but poignantly, contains the graves of British personnel killed in the War of Independence. Here, in the oldest part of the cemetery, as the gravestones toppled, they were lined up against the boundary walls where they still stand solemnly today.

HENRIETTA STREET Map p102

🚌 25, 25A, 37, 38, 39, 66, 67, 90 or 134 from city centre; 🚇 Four Courts

Henrietta St dates from the 1720s and was the first project of Dublin's pre-eminent Georgian developer, Luke Gardiner. It was designed as an enclave of prestigious addresses (Gardiner himself lived at No 10), and remained one of Dublin's most fashionable streets until the Act of Union (1801). It's looking a little forlorn these days after spending much of the 20th century as tenement housing, where up to 70 tenants were crammed into each four-storey house. Some of the residences are in disrepair, yet it's still a wonderful insight into the evolution of Georgian residential architecture, and features mansions of varying size and style.

KING'S INNS Map p102

☎ 874 4840; www.kingsinns.ie; Henrietta St; 🚌 25, 25A, 66, 67, 90 or 134 from city centre, 🚇 Four Courts

Home to Dublin's legal profession, King's Inns occupies a classical building on Constitution Hill, which was built by James Gandon between 1795 and 1817, with Francis Johnston chipping in with the cupola. In 1541, when Henry VIII staked his claim to be King of Ireland as well as England, the country's lawyers took the title the Honourable Society of King's Inns and moved into a Dominican monastery on the site of the modern-day Four Courts. When that building was erected they relocated here, where Irish barristers are still trained. It's only open to members and their guests.

GARDEN OF REMEMBRANCE Map p102

☎ 874 3074; Parnell Sq; ⏰ 8.30am-6pm Apr-Sep, 9.30am-4pm Oct-Mar; 🚌 3, 10, 11, 13, 16, 19 or 22 from city centre

This rather austere little park was opened by President Éamon de Valera in 1966 for the 50th anniversary of the Easter Rising. It is still known to some Dubs as the 'Garden of Mature Recollection', mocking the linguistic gymnastics employed by former favourite for president Brian Lenihan, who was caught out lying in a minor political scandal and used the phrase to try and wiggle his way out of it.

The most interesting feature in the garden is a bronze statue of the Children of Lir by Oisín Kelly; according to Irish legend

the children were turned into swans by their wicked stepmother. It was probably intended to evoke the famous lines penned by WB Yeats in his poem *Easter 1916*: 'All changed, changed utterly/A terrible beauty is born.'

BELVEDERE HOUSE Map p102

6 Great Denmark St; 🚌 3, 10, 11, 13, 16, 19 or 22 from city centre

Great Denmark St runs northeast towards Mountjoy Sq and passes the 18th-century Belvedere House at No 6. This has been used as the Jesuit Belvedere College since 1841, and one James Joyce studied here between 1893 and 1898, describing it later in *A Portrait of the Artist as a Young Man*. The building is renowned for its magnificent plasterwork by the master stuccodore Michael Stapleton and for its fireplaces by the Venetian artisan Bossi, but the only chance you'll get to admire these features is if you enrol for a class at this secondary school as the building is closed to the public. The plasterwork isn't *that* special.

ROTUNDA HOSPITAL Map p102

☎ 873 0700; Parnell Sq; ⏰ visiting hours 6-8pm; 🚌 3, 10, 11, 13, 16, 19 or 22 from city centre

Irish public hospitals aren't usually attractions, by any stretch of the imagination, but this one makes for an interesting walk-by or an unofficial wander inside if you're interested in Victorian plasterwork. It was the first maternity hospital in the British Isles – and once the world's largest – and was established by Dr Bartholomew Mosse in 1748, at a time when the burgeoning urban population was enduring shocking infant mortality rates.

It shares its basic design with Leinster House (p83) because the architect of both, Richard Cassels, used the same floor plan to economise. He added a three-storey tower, which Mosse intended to use for fundraising purposes (charging visitors an entry fee). He also laid out pleasure gardens, which were fashionable among Dublin's high society for a time, and built the Rotunda Assembly Hall to raise money. The hall is now occupied by the Ambassador Theatre, and the Supper Rooms house the Gate Theatre (p198).

Inside, the public rooms and staircases give some idea of how beautiful the hospital once was, and they lead to one of Dublin's largely hidden gems, the sumptuous

Rotunda Chapel, built in 1758, and featuring superb coloured plasterwork by German stuccodore Bartholomew Cramillion. The Italian artist Giovanni Battista Capriani was supposed to supplement the work but his paintings were never installed, which is probably just as well because you can't imagine how this little space would have looked with even more decoration. If you intend visiting, you have to bear in mind that this is still a functioning hospital and you must be very quiet when coming to see the chapel. It's not terribly well sign-posted inside and is often locked outside visiting hours (although if you ask kindly or look like you're in desperate need of a prayer, somebody will let you in).

ST MARY'S ABBEY Map p102

☎ 833 1618; www.heritageireland.ie; Meeting House Lane; 🚌 11, 16 or 41 from city centre

Where now the glories of Babylon? All that remains of what was once Ireland's wealthiest and most powerful monastery is the chapterhouse, so forgotten that most Dubliners are unaware of its existence. In its medieval day, this Cistercian abbey ran the show when it came to Irish church politics, although its reputation with the authorities was somewhat sullied when it became a favourite meeting place for rebels against the crown. On 11 June 1534, 'Silken' Thomas Fitzgerald, the most important of Leinster's Anglo-Norman lords, entered the chapterhouse and flung his Sword of State on the ground in front of the awaiting King's Council – a ceremonial two-fingered salute to King Henry VIII and his authority. Visitors today are slightly less dramatic, but they can enjoy a small exhibition and view a model of what the abbey looked like in the good old days. From May to September, tours can be booked through the Casino at Marino (p127).

ST MARY'S CHURCH Map p102

Mary St; 🚌 11, 16 or 41 from city centre

Designed by William Robinson in 1697, this is the most important church to survive from that period (although it's no longer in use and is closed to the public). John Wesley, founder of Methodism, delivered his first Irish sermon here in 1747 and it was the preferred church of Dublin's 18th-century social elite. Many famous Dubliners were baptised in its font, and Arthur Guinness was married here in 1793.

ST MARY'S PRO-CATHEDRAL Map p102

☎ 874 5441; Marlborough St; admission free; ⏱ 8am-6.30pm; 🚌 3, 10, 11, 13, 16, 19 or 22 from city centre

Dublin's most important Catholic church is not quite the showcase you'd expect. It's in the wrong place for starters. This large neoclassical building, constructed from 1816 to 1825, was supposed to be on O'Connell St where the GPO now stands, but the local Protestant community – who pretty much ran the show back then – went nuts about the idea of it having such a prominent position. So it was built in a much less conspicuous side street, away from the main thoroughfare and smack in the middle of Monto, where purveyors of the world's oldest profession plied their trade (see the boxed text, p106). In fact, it's so cramped for space around here that you'd hardly notice the church's six Doric columns, which were modelled on the Temple of Theseus in Athens, much less be able to admire them. The interior is fairly functional, and its few highlights include a carved altar by Peter Turnerelli and the alto relief representation of the Ascension by John Smyth. The best time to visit is 11am on Sunday when the Latin Mass is sung by the Palestrina Choir, with whom Ireland's most celebrated tenor, John McCormack, began his career in 1904.

The design of the church is shrouded in some mystery. In 1814 John Sweetman won a competition held to find the best design for the church, a competition that had actually been organised by his brother William. It's not certain whether John actually designed the building, since he was living in Paris at the time and may have bought the plans from the French architect Auguste Gauthier, who designed the similar Notre Dame de Lorette in northern France. The only clue as to the church's architect is in the ledger, which lists the builder as 'Mr P'.

Finally, a word about the term 'pro' in the title. It implies, roughly, that it is an 'unofficial cathedral'. More accurately it was built as a sort of interim cathedral to be replaced when sufficient funds were available. Church leaders never actually got around to it, leaving the capital of this most Catholic of countries with two incredible-but-under-used Protestant cathedrals and one fairly ordinary Catholic one. Irony one, piety nil.

ST GEORGE'S CHURCH Map p102

Hardwicke Pl; 🚌 11, 16 or 41 from city centre

If you're on the north side, the steeple of this deconsecrated church may catch your eye. The church was built by Francis Johnston from 1802 in Greek Ionic style, and the 60m-high steeple was modelled on that of St Martin-in-the-Fields in London. Although this was one of Johnston's finest works, and the Duke of Wellington was married here, the church has been sorely neglected – probably because it's Church of Ireland and not Roman Catholic, it has to be said. The bells that Leopold Bloom heard in *that* book were removed, the ornate pulpit was carved up and used to decorate the pub Thomas Read's (p179), and the spire is in danger of crumbling, which has resulted in it being sheathed in scaffolding pending a patch-up job. The church is not open to the public.

DOCKLANDS

Drinking p182; Eating p166; Shopping p146; Sleeping p220

It's a cardinal rule of any program of urban development: if your city is at the mouth of the sea, you cannot modernise without giving the docklands a revamp. And so it was with Dublin; the eastern banks north and south of the Liffey have been given a major makeover and now sport an impressive array of contemporary office blocks, fancy apartments and snazzy public buildings.

The engine behind the development was the Dublin Docklands Development Authority (DDDA), who took a 'sky's the limit' approach to developing an area that had been the site of some of the city's most downtrodden slums as far back as the early years of the 19th century. And while it's hardly surprising that a port area wouldn't be especially salubrious, the docklands' descent into dereliction began with the construction of one of the city's most impressive Georgian buildings, the Custom House (below), in 1791. Before then, the streets on the northern banks were lined with fine Georgian mansions, but their residents soon abandoned the area when the streets along the North Wall became clogged with livestock being marched to and from customs pens, their 'issue' being used to run a busy fertiliser plant in the vicinity. It also didn't help that until the end of WWI much of the city's sewage was dumped into the eastern end of the river. After WWII, the demise of the Liffey as a major trading conduit added abandonment to dereliction, leaving the docklands to languish until the end of the 1990s.

The DDDA's plans were very ambitious. At the heart of it all is the new 10,000-sq-metre Grand Canal Square, designed by American landscape architect Martha Schwartz. Flanking its southeastern side is the magnificent Grand Canal Theatre, designed by Daniel Libeskind and opened in March 2010. Stretching across the square from its entrance is a red 'carpet' – a series of red, resin-glass angled sticks that glow – and a green one – made up of polygon-shaped planters filled with marshlike vegetation.

On the north banks of the Liffey, the standout buildings are the snazzy new National Convention Centre, designed by Kevin Roche, and the newly refurbished O2 (formerly the Point Depot), the city's premier indoor arena for gigs (see p195).

And there was meant to be more, but the economic crash of 2008–09 put paid to some other big projects, including the long-expected U2 Tower and a gigantic sculpture by Antony Gormley, as well as a raft of new bars and restaurants. Revelations of gross financial improprieties by the DDDA have soured the taste of the project in the eyes of many Dubliners, but there's little doubt that 'Canary Dwarf' has enough going on to keep you entertained and sustained.

CUSTOM HOUSE Map p115

☎ 888 2538; Visitor Centre, Custom House Quay; admission €1.30; ⏰ 10am-12.30pm & 2-5pm Mon-Fri, 2-5pm Sat & Sun, closed Mon, Tue & Sat Nov–mid-Mar; 🚌 all city centre

Georgian genius James Gandon (1743–1823) announced his arrival on the Dublin scene with this magnificent building (1781–91), constructed just past Eden Quay at a wide stretch in the River Liffey. When it was being built, angry city merchants and dockers from the original Custom House further upriver in Temple Bar were so menacing that Gandon often came to work wielding a broadsword. He was supported by the era's foremost property developer, Luke Gardiner, who saw the new Custom House as a major part of his scheme to shift the axis of the city eastwards from medieval Capel St to what was then Gardiner's Mall (now O'Connell St).

It's a colossal, neoclassical pile that stretches for 114m along the River Liffey.

It can only be taken in and admired from the south side of the river, although its fine detail deserves closer inspection. Arcades, each with seven arches, join the centre to the end pavilions and the columns along the front have harps carved in their capitals. Motifs alluding to transport and

WORTH THE TRIP: POOLBEG LIGHTHOUSE

One of the city's most rewarding walks is a stroll along the South Wall to the Poolbeg Lighthouse (that red tower visible in the middle of Dublin Bay). To get there, you'll have to make your own way from Ringsend (which is reachable by buses 1, 2 or 3 from the city centre), past the power station to the start of the wall (it's about 1km). It's not an especially long walk – about 800m or so – but it will give you a stunning view of the bay and the city behind you, a view best enjoyed just before sunset.

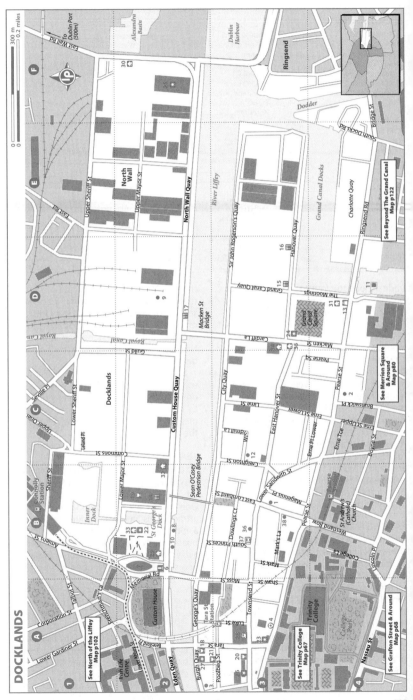

DOCKLANDS

300 m
0.2 miles

To Dublin Port (500m)
East Wall Rd

Alexandra Basin

Dublin Harbour

Ringsend

Dodder

South Docks Rd

Bridge St

North Wall

Upper Sheriff St

Upper Mayor St

North Wall Quay

River Liffey

Grand Canal Docks

Charlotte Quay

Ringsend Rd

See Beyond The Grand Canal
Map p122

Sir John Rogerson's Quay

Hanover Quay

Grand Canal Quay

The Moorings

East Rd

Royal Canal

Guild St

Docklands

Lower Sheriff St

Seville Pl

Upper Oriel St

Connolly Station

Sheriff St

Macken St Bridge

Cardiff La

Grand Canal Square

Macken St

Pearse Sq

See Merrion Square & Around
Map p80

Custom House Quay

Commons St

Leland Pl

Lower Mayor St

St George's Dock

Inner Dock

City Quay

Lime St

Creighton St

Windmill La

East Hanover St

Erne St Lower

Erne St Upper

Pearse St

Brunswick Pl

Erne Tce

Boyne St

Sean O'Casey Pedestrian Bridge

East Lombard St

Lower Sandwith St

Magennis Pl

Fenian St

Westland Row

St Andrew's (Catholic) Church

College La

Lincoln Pl

See North of the Liffey
Map p102

Talbot St

Corporation St

Lower Gardiner St

Amiens St

Memorial Rd

Custom House

George's Quay

Tara St Station

Townsend St

Moss St

Shaw St

Mark St

Price's St

South Princes St

Dowlings Ct

Gloucester St

Burgh Quay

Eden Quay

Irish Life Centre

Butterfield Pl

Store St

Poolbeg St

Luke St

Tara St

College St

Nassau St

Trinity College

College Park

See Trinity College
Map p67

See Grafton Street & Around
Map p68

115

DOCKLANDS

INFORMATION
Births, Deaths &
  Marriages Register....................... 1 B3
Drugs Advisory &
  Treatment Centre 2 C4
Garda National
  Immigration Bureau...................... 3 A2
Garda Station................................... 4 A3

SIGHTS   (p114)
CHQ Building.............................(see 14)
Custom House................................. 5 A2
Famine Memorial 6 B2
International
  Financial Services
  Centre... 7 B2
Jeanie Johnston.............................. 8 B2
National Convention
  Centre... 9 D2
Sea Safari Ticket
  Office...10 B2
Waterways Visitor
  Centre..11 D4
Windmill Lane
  Studios...12 C3

SHOPPING 🛍   (p146)
Tower Craft Design
  Centre...13 D4

EATING 🍴   (p166)
Ely CHQ Bar &
  Brasserie 14 B2
Ely HQ 15 D3
Herbstreet 16 D3
Quay 16 ....17 D2

DRINKING 🍷   (p182)
Kennedy's..18 A2
La Cuvee @ Eno Wine
  Bar..19 B2
Long Stone......................................20 A3
Mulligan's.......................................21 A2

NIGHTLIFE & THE ARTS ⭐   (p185)
Abbey Theatre
  (under
  construction)..............................22 B2
Fireworks 23 A3
Grand Canal Theatre......................24 D3
O2...25 F2

Screen..26 A3
White Horse Inn 27 A2

SPORTS & ACTIVITIES 🏊   (p201)
Markievicz Leisure
  Centre..28 A3

SLEEPING 🛏   (p220)
Clarion Hotel IFSC..........................29 B2
Gibson Hotel 30 F2
Home from Home
  Apartments 31 D4
Jurys Custom House
  Inn 32 B2
Jurys Custom House
  Quay 33 B2
Maldron Hotel
  Cardiff Lane..................................34 D3
Quality Hotel..................................35 D3

TRANSPORT   (p240)
Avis Rent-a-Car...............................36 B3
Bus Stop for Bus 44
  to Powerscourt.............................37 B3
Thrifty Car Rental...........................38 B3

trade include the four rooftop statues of Neptune, Mercury, Plenty and Industry, destroyed when the building was gutted in a five-day fire during the independence struggle in 1921, but replaced in 1991. The interior was extensively redesigned after 1921 and again in the 1980s. Below the frieze are heads representing the gods of Ireland's 13 principal rivers, and the sole female head, above the main door, represents the River Liffey. The cattle heads honour Dublin's beef trade, and the statues behind the building represent Africa, America, Asia and Europe. The building is topped by a copper dome with four clocks and, above that, a 5m-high statue of Hope.

Beneath the dome, the Visitor Centre features a small museum on Gandon and the history of the building.

FAMINE MEMORIAL Map p115
Custom House Quay; 🚌 all city centre
One of Dublin's most thought-provoking examples of public art is the remarkable set of life-sized bronze figures (1997) by Rowan Gillespie on the quay just east of the Custom House known simply as 'Famine'. They were designed to commemorate the many thousands forced to emigrate in order to escape the ravages of the Famine (1845–51): their haunted, harrowed look testifies to a journey that was both hazardous and unwelcome. The location of the sculptures is also telling, for it was from this very point

that in 1846 one of the first 'coffin ships' (as they quickly came to be called; see below) set sail for the United States. Steerage fare on the *Perseverence* was £3 and 210 passengers made that first journey, landing in New York on 18 May 1846, with all passengers and crew intact.

In June 2007, a second series of Famine sculptures by Rowan Gillespie was unveiled on the quayside in Toronto's Ireland Park by Irish president Mary McAleese to commemorate the arrival of Famine refugees in the New World.

JEANIE JOHNSTON Map p115
☎ 066 712 9999; www.docklands.ie; Custom House Quay; adult/child €5/3; ☽ 10.30am-5pm Sat & Sun Oct-Apr; 🚌 all city centre
One of the city's most original tourist attractions is an exact, working replica of a 19th-century coffin ship, as the sailing boats that transported starving emigrants away from Ireland during the Famine were gruesomely known. The good news is that

---

THINGS YOU DIDN'T KNOW ABOUT DUBLIN

The restored CHQ building on Spencer Dock (Map p115) is the last surviving warehouse of the Docklands. In 1856, the warehouse hosted 4000 veterans of the Crimean War for a fine feast.

the *Jeanie Johnston*, a three-masted barque originally built in Québec in 1847, made 16 transatlantic voyages, carrying more than 2500 people, and never suffered a single death. A small on-board museum details the harrowing plight of a typical journey, which usually took around 47 days. The ship also operates as a Sail Training vessel, with journeys taking place from May to September. If you are visiting during these times, check the website for details of when it will be in dock.

WATERWAYS VISITOR CENTRE Map p115
☎ 677 7510; www.waterwaysireland.org; Grand Canal Quay; ⊠ Grand Canal Dock

If you absolutely must know about the construction and operation of Ireland's canals, you'll have to wait a bit as this interpretative centre is currently closed for renovations. Still, admiring the 'box on the docks' – as this modern building is nicknamed – is plenty good enough for the average enthusiast of artificial waterways.

If you are here in summer and are wondering why it needs to employ a security guard, it's to keep local kids from storming up to the centre's roof and using it as a diving platform into the basin. Sometimes the kids content themselves with diving off the shed on the bridge, terrorising those on board the Viking Splash Tour boats that pass beneath.

PHOENIX PARK

Dubliners are rightly proud of this humungous patch of greenery at the northwestern edge of the city centre, a short skip from Heuston Station and the Liffey quays. The hugely impressive 709 hectares that comprise the park make up one of the largest set of inner-city green lungs in the world. To put it into perspective, it dwarfs the measly 337 hectares of New York's Central Park and is larger than all of the major London parks put together. The park is a magnificent playground for all kinds of activities, from running to polo, and it's a fitting home to the president of Ireland, the American ambassador and a shy herd of fallow deer who are best observed – from a distance – during the summer months. It is also where you'll find Europe's oldest zoo, not to mention dozens of playing fields for all kinds of sport. How's that for a place to stretch your legs?

From the Anglo-Norman invasion up to 1537, the park – whose name is a corruption of *fionn uisce* (clear water), rather than anything to do with the legendary bird – was part of the lands owned by the Knights of Jerusalem, keepers of an important priory on what is now the site of the Royal Hospital Kilmainham (p98). After King Henry VIII dissolved the monasteries, the lands passed into the hands of the king's viceroys. In 1671 the Duke of Ormonde, James Butler, introduced a herd of fallow deer, 1000 pheasants and some partridge, and turned it into a royal deer park, soon enclosed by a wall. It remained the preserve of the British Crown and its Irish court until 1745, when the viceroy, Lord Chesterfield, threw it open to the public.

In an episode that set back the cause of Irish Home Rule, the British chief secretary for Ireland, Lord Cavendish, and his assistant were murdered in 1882 outside what is now the Irish president's residence, by an obscure Irish nationalist group called the Invincibles. Lord Cavendish's home is now called Deerfield, and is used as the US ambassador's residence.

Needless to say, this is very much a visit-only kind of neighbourhood – besides a teahouse in the park there are virtually no places to eat and absolutely no places to stay.

Take bus 10 from O'Connell St or bus 25 or 26 from Middle Abbey St to get here. The best way to get around the park is to hop on the new Phoenix Park Shuttle Bus (☉ hourly 7am-5pm Mon-Fri, 10am-5pm Sat & Sun; adult/child €2/1), which departs from just outside the main gate on Parkgate St.

DUBLIN ZOO Map p119

☎ 677 1425; www.dublinzoo.ie; adult/concession/family €14/9.50/40; ☉ 9.30am-6pm Mon-Sat, 10.30am-6pm Sun Mar-Sep, 9.30am-dusk Mon-Fri, 9.30am-dusk Sat, 10.30am-dusk Sun Oct-Feb; ☒ 10 from O'Connell St, or 25 or 26 from Middle Abbey St Established in 1830, the 12-hectare Dublin Zoo just north of the Hollow is one of the oldest in the world, and as thrilling or depressing as any other old zoo trying to drag itself into the 21st century. The zoo is well known for its lion-breeding program, which dates back to 1857, and includes among its offspring the lion that roars at the start of MGM films. You'll see these tough cats, from a distance, on the 'African Plains', which has doubled the size of the zoo and made it a much nicer place to stroll around in.

The zoo has several hundred different species, ranging from owls to hippos, most of which are housed in the old-fashioned part of the complex, which includes a 'World of Primates' section and 'Fringes of the Arctic', where similar animals have been grouped together as part of the zoo's modern restructuring. The one thing they haven't managed to fix, however, is the depression that seemingly afflicts the polar bears, who seem rightly incapable of coming to terms with the narrow confines of their world, a far cry from the northern tundra.

Still, the zoo has gone to great lengths to make itself visitor-friendly, and the presence of new babies or animals on breeding loans from other zoos will surely generate a couple of 'oohs' and 'aahs' from the kids. There are also plenty of children's activities, including a Meet the Keeper program, which has events approximately every half-hour from 11am to 3.30pm, where children get to feed the animals. Our favourite section is the City Farm, which brings you within touching distance of chickens, cows, goats and pigs, the luckiest animals here. There's also a zoo train and a nursery for infants.

Although there are places to eat, they're not very good and you'd be much better off bringing a picnic but, for God's sake, don't feed the animals.

ÁRAS AN UACHTARÁIN Map p119

☎ 617 1000; Phoenix Park; ☉ guided tours hourly 10.30am-4.30pm Sat; ☒ 10 from O'Connell St, or 25 or 26 from Middle Abbey St

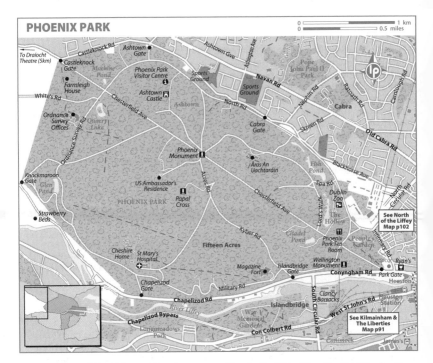

PHOENIX PARK

The residence of the Irish president is a Palladian lodge that was built in 1751 and enlarged a couple of times since, most recently in 1816. It was home to the British viceroys from 1782 to 1922, and then to the governors general until Ireland cut ties with the British Crown and created the office of president in 1937. Queen Victoria stayed here during her visit in 1849, when she appeared not to even notice the Famine. The candle burning in the window is an old Irish tradition, to guide 'the Irish diaspora' home.

Tickets for the free one-hour tours can be collected from the Phoenix Park Visitor Centre (below), where you'll see a 10-minute introductory video before being shuttled to the Áras itself to inspect five state rooms and the president's study. If you can't make it on a Saturday, just become elected president of your own country or become a Nobel laureate or something, and then wrangle a personal invite.

PHOENIX PARK VISITOR CENTRE
Map p119

☎ 677 0095; adult/concession/family €2.75/1.25/7; ☽ 10am-6pm Apr-Sep, 10am-5pm Oct, 10am-5pm Mon-Sat Nov & Dec, 10am-5pm Sat & Sun Jan-Mar; 🚌 10 from O'Connell St, or 37 or 29 from Middle Abbey St

In the north of the park, near the Ashtown Gate, this visitor centre occupies what were the stables of the papal nunciature, and explores the wildlife and history of the park through film and two floors of exhibits. Visitors are also taken on a tour of the adjacent four-storey Ashtown Castle, a 17th-century tower-house that was concealed inside the later building of the papal nunciature and was only 'discovered' when the latter was demolished in 1986. Box hedges surrounding the tower trace the ground plan of the lost building. Children keen on all things furry will love the Great Slumber Party exhibition upstairs, a walk-through tunnel that looks at the sleeping habits of animals such as foxes and badgers.

FARMLEIGH HOUSE Map p119

☎ 815 5900; www.farmleigh.ie; admission free; ☽ 10.45am-5pm Sat, Sun & bank holidays Easter-Oct; 🚌 10 from O'Connell St, or 25 or 26 from Middle Abbey St

Situated in the northwest corner of Phoenix Park, this opulent house is the state's official

PHOENIX PARK MISCELLANY

Chesterfield Ave runs northwest through the entire length of the park from the Parkgate St entrance to the Castleknock Gate. Near the Parkgate St entrance is the 63m-high Wellington Monument obelisk, which took almost 50 years to build because the duke fell from favour during its construction. It was finally completed in 1861. Nearby is the People's Garden, dating from 1864, and the bandstand in the Hollow. Across Chesterfield Ave from the Áras an Uachtaráin – and easily visible from the road – is the massive Papal Cross, which marks the site where Pope John Paul II preached to 1.25 million people in 1979 and drove around waving to the crowds in what was best described as a Tic-Tac box with wheels. In the centre of the park the Phoenix Monument, erected by Lord Chesterfield in 1747, looks so unlike a phoenix that it's often referred to as the Eagle Monument.

The southern part of the park has many football and hurling pitches; although they actually occupy about 80 hectares (200 acres), the area is known as the Fifteen Acres. To the west, the rural-looking Glen Pond corner of the park is extremely attractive.

At the northwestern end of the park near the White's Gate entrance are the offices of Ordnance Survey Ireland (OSI; ☎ 802 5300; www.osi.ie), the government mapping department. This building was originally built in 1728 by Luke Gardiner, who was responsible for the architecture in O'Connell St and Mountjoy Sq in north Dublin. In the building's map shop (☎ 802 5349; ☿ 9am-4.45pm Mon-Fri) you can buy all of the OSI maps for any of the 26 counties of Ireland.

Back towards the Parkgate St entrance is the Magazine Fort (closed to the public) on Thomas's Hill. Like the nearby Wellington Monument, the fort was no quick construction, the process taking from 1734 to 1801. It provided useful target practice during the 1916 Easter Rising, and was raided by the Irish Republican Army (IRA) in 1940 when the entire ammunition reserve of the Irish army was nabbed, but recovered a few weeks later.

B&B, where visiting dignitaries rest their very important heads – at least in theory. The truth is that after spending more than €52 million on purchasing and restoring the house, it was used to provide accommodation for just three weeks in the first two years after it opened in mid-2001. It has drawn savage criticism from some commentators who consider it money wasted on an already ugly house. It can only be visited by joining one of the 30-minute house tours.

The open days have been hugely popular with locals who, as taxpayers, reckon it's as much their pad as anyone else's. The estate takes up 79 acres and there are many beautiful features. The main house is a bit blowsy and overblown but it's a pleasant enough example of Georgian-Victorian architecture. The real highlight is the garden, where regular shows are held. There is also an extensive program of cultural events in summer, ranging from food fairs to classical concerts. Because the property is used for state business, schedules may change and you should telephone in advance.

BEYOND THE GRAND CANAL

Drinking p182; Eating p167; Shopping p146; Sleeping p220

It has long been said that a 'real' Dubliner is born within the confines of the two canals that encircle the city centre – the older Grand Canal to the south and the newer Royal Canal to the north – but the rapid expansion of the city, coupled with the shockingly high price of central real estate makes it more a case of *older* Dubliners being born within the canal boundaries.

Built to connect Dublin with the River Shannon in the centre of Ireland, the Grand Canal makes a graceful 6km loop around south Dublin and enters the Liffey at Ringsend, through locks that were built in 1796. The large Grand Canal Dock, flanked by Hanover and Charlotte Quays, is now used by windsurfers and canoeists and is the site of major new development. Here you'll find the Waterways Visitor Centre (p117), which illustrates the gleaming new development of the area that, for now, sits side by side with the workaday, historical and even quaint auld Dublin of Ringsend and Irishtown. At the northwestern corner of the dock is Misery Hill, once a very macabre place where it was the practice to bring the corpses of those already hanged at Gallows Hill, near Upper Baggot St, to be strung up for public display for anything from six to 12 months.

The canal hasn't been used commercially since 1960, but some stretches are attractive and enjoyable to stroll or cycle along. The poet Patrick Kavanagh was particularly enamoured with the 2km stretch from Mount St Bridge west to Richmond St, which has grassy, tree-lined banks and – as you might have guessed – a cluster of pubs. Among Kavanagh's compositions is the hauntingly beautiful *Raglan Road*, which was put to music and sung most memorably by Luke Kelly of the Dubliners. In another, he requested that he be commemorated by 'a canal bank seat for passers-by'. His friends obliged with a seat beside the lock on the northern side of the canal. A little further along on the northern side you can sit down by Kavanagh himself, cast in bronze, comfortably lounging on a bench and staring at his beloved canal.

Beyond the Grand Canal and into the southern outer reaches of Dublin are inner suburbs that have developed along the main roads into the city. Lively Rathmines – for generations the favoured stomping ground of students and migrants from the rest of the country – has seen its stock rise higher and higher as gentrification marches ever onwards, converting student digs into chic studio apartments, and cheap cafes into tapas bars. Barely half a mile away is Ranelagh, which makes Rathmines seem distinctly dowdy – its cosy village atmosphere barely disguises the elegance and sophistication of its bars, restaurants and wonderful Victorian and Edwardian architecture. For cashed-up Dubliners, this is definitely the place to live…unless they already reside in 'Dublin 4' further east, a postal address that is synonymous with money and affectation. Elegant and embassy-laden Ballsbridge is a great place to base yourself, especially if you don't mind being a 30-minute stroll or 10-minute bus ride from the city centre: it has some wonderful restaurants, a host of great bars and some of the most beautiful townhouse hotels in the city.

NATIONAL PRINT MUSEUM Map p122

☎ 660 3770; www.nationalprintmuseum.ie; Garrison Chapel, Haddington Rd, Beggar's Bush; adult/concession €3.50/2; ☼ 9am-5pm Mon-Fri, 2-5pm Sat & Sun; ® Grand Canal Dock; ⊟ 7, 45 or 63 from Trinity College

You don't have to be into printing to enjoy this quirky little museum, where personalised guided tours are offered in a delightfully casual and compelling way. First watch a video relating to printing and its place in Irish history, then take a wander amid the smell of ink and metal, and through the various antique presses that are still worked for small jobs by a couple of retired printers doing it for the love of the craft. The guides are excellent and can tailor the tours to suit your special interests – for example, anyone interested in history can get a detailed account of the difficulties encountered by the rebels of 1916 when they tried to get the proclamation printed. Upstairs, there are lots of old newspaper pages that record important episodes in Irish history over the last century.

ROYAL DUBLIN SOCIETY SHOWGROUND Map p122

☎ 668 9878; Merrion Rd, Ballsbridge; ⊟ 5, 7, 7A, 8, 18 or 45 from city centre

Founded in 1731, the Royal Dublin Society (RDS) was involved in the establishment of the National Museum, Library, Gallery

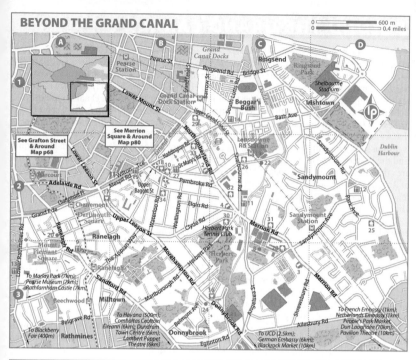

BEYOND THE GRAND CANAL

INFORMATION
Baggot St Hospital	1	B2
Italian Embassy	2	B2
UK Embassy	3	C3
US Embassy	4	C2
Well Woman Centre	5	B2

SIGHTS (p121)
National Print Museum	6	C2
Patrick Kavanagh Statue	7	B2
Royal Dublin Society		
Showground	8	C3

EATING (p167)
Café Bardeli	9	A3
Expresso Bar	10	B2
French Paradox	11	C2
Itsa4	12	D2
Jo'Burger	13	A3

Juniors	14	C1
La Peniche	15	B2

DRINKING (p182)
Ice Bar	(see 28)	
Kiely's	16	C3
O'Brien's	17	A2
Searson's	18	B2

NIGHTLIFE & THE ARTS (p185)
Royal Dublin Society		
Showground Concert		
Hall	(see 8)	

SPORTS & ACTIVITIES (p201)
Aviva Stadium	19	C2
Bellaza Clinic	20	A2
Donnybrook Rugby		
Ground	21	C3

Dublin Spa @ Four		
Seasons	(see 28)	
Irish Rugby Football		
Union	22	C2
Royal Dublin Society	(see 8)	
Shelbourne Park	23	C1
Spar	24	B3

SLEEPING (p220)
Aberdeen Lodge	25	D2
Ariel House	26	C2
Dylan	27	B2
Four Seasons	28	C3
Grand Canal Hotel	29	B1
Herbert Park Hotel	30	C2
Merrion Hall	31	C2
Pembroke Townhouse	32	C2
Schoolhouse Hotel	33	B2
Waterloo House	34	B2

and Botanic Gardens. The showground is used for various exhibitions throughout the year, but the main event is the Dublin Horse Show (p18), which reflects the society's agricultural background. The horse show takes place in the first week of August and includes a prestigious international show-jumping contest among other events. It is also home to Leinster's rugby games (see p208).

PEARSE MUSEUM Off Map p122
☎ 493 4208; www.heritageireland.ie; St Enda's, Grange Rd, Rathfarnham; admission free; ⏱ 9.30am-5.30pm Mon-Sat, Mar-Oct, 9.30am-4pm Mon-Sat Nov-Jan & 9.30am-5pm Mon-Sat Feb; 🚌 16 from O'Connell St
This handsome Palladian mansion was home to St Enda's, an experimental Gaelic school established by nationalist poet and 1916 martyr Pádraig Pearse (for more

on Pádraig Pearse, see the boxed text, p29). The fascinating exhibition focusing on Pearse's life and pedagogical theories is centred on a 20-minute audio-visual show called 'This Man Kept a School'. The beautiful grounds, gardens and grottoes surrounding the house are also worth an amble.

RATHFARNHAM CASTLE Off Map p122

☎ 493 9462; www.heritageireland.ie; Rathfarnham Rd, Rathfarnham; admission free; ☒ 9.30am-5.30pm Jun-Sep; ☒ 16, 16A or 17 from O'Connell St

Less castle and more fortified house, this was originally built by Adam Loftus, the archbishop of Dublin, around 1583 and is most interesting as a restoration in progress. Several of the rooms – including 18th-century interiors by William Chambers – have been returned to their original splendour, while others are clearly struggling under the ravages of time. The guides have an infectious enthusiasm for the project. It's 6km south of the city centre.

BEYOND THE ROYAL CANAL

Drinking p183; Sleeping p222

Constructed from 1790, when the usefulness of such waterways was already on the wane, the Royal Canal was a total commercial flop. It was founded by Long John Binns, a director of the Grand Canal who quit the board in a huff after condescending remarks were made over his profession as a shoemaker. He established the Royal Canal principally for revenge, but it never made money and he became a bit of a laughing stock. Adding insult to injury, his waterway came to be known as the 'Shoemaker's Canal'. In 1840 the canal was sold to a railway company, and rail tracks still run alongside much of the canal's route.

Beyond the Royal Canal, which provides the northern boundary of the city centre, lie the down-to-earth Dublin suburbs of Glasnevin, Marino and Drumcondra, the stomping ground of former taioseach Bertie Ahern (you could probably run into him in his local pub, Fagan's). Although traditionally working- and lower-middle-class suburbs, in recent years property prices have soared, transforming most of these 'burbs into some pretty choice postal districts.

Unless you have a particular interest in how Dubliners decorate their semidetached suburban houses, there are only a handful of sights to drag you beyond the Royal Canal's boundaries, but they're well worth the effort – and they're quite easy to get to by bus, unless of course you fancy a walk along the towpath that runs along the canal. You can join it beside Newcomen Bridge at North Strand Rd, just north of Connolly Station, and follow it to the suburb of Clonsilla and beyond, more than 10km away. The walk is particularly pleasant beyond Binns Bridge in Drumcondra. At the top of Blessington St a large pond, used when the canal also supplied drinking water to the city, attracts waterbirds.

The mighty Croke Park, HQ of Gaelic games and home to a terrific museum of the association, offers a unique and compelling insight into the history and passion of these most Irish pastimes, while the architecturally magnificent Casino at Marino, the historic Glasnevin Cemetery and the soothing National Botanic Gardens are among the best attractions the city has to offer.

You can also crash in these neighbourhoods, most notably Drumcondra – which is on the road to the airport and has dozens of B&Bs in well-maintained Victorian and Edwardian houses – and Clontarf, which stretches out along the northern edge of Dublin Bay, offering the compelling prospect of waking with the scent of brine in your nostrils.

CROKE PARK & GAA MUSEUM
Map p125

☎ 819 2323; www.crokepark.ie; New Stand, Croke Park, Clonliffe Rd; adult/child/student museum €5.50/3.50/4, museum & tour €9.50/6/7; ⏺ 9.30am-5pm Mon-Sat, noon-5pm Sun Jan-Jun & Sep-Dec, 9.30am-6pm Jul-Aug; 🚌 3, 11, 11A, 16, 16A or 123 from O'Connell St

Uniquely important in Irish culture, the magnificent stadium at 'Croker' is the fabulous fortress that protects the sanctity and spirit of Gaelic games in Ireland, as well as being the administrative HQ of the Gaelic Athletic Association (GAA), the body that governs them. Sound a little hyperbolic? Well, the GAA considers itself not just the governing body of a bunch of Irish games, but the stout defender of a cultural identity that is ingrained in Ireland's sense of self (see p205). It goes without saying that this is the country's largest stadium; after being virtually rebuilt in recent years, it's actually the fourth-largest stadium in

Europe, with a capacity of some 82,000 people, and all for sports that are only played in this tiny little country! There are stadium tours available twice a day, although these are largely for hard-core GAA and sports stadia fans and are not available on match days. It's much better to get a ticket for a match, when you can watch these brilliant games, soak up the unique atmosphere and have a squiz at the arena. Hogan Stand ticket holders can visit the museum on match days.

In the 1870s, the site was developed as the 'City & Suburban Racecourse', but was bought by the GAA in 1913 and immediately renamed Croke Park in honour of the association's first patron, Archbishop Croke of Cashel. Since its foundation it has been entwined with Irish nationalism. The famous Hill 16, which is traditionally where the hardcore Dublin fans stand during matches, was so-called because its foundations were built with rubble taken from

O'Connell St after the Easter Rising of 1916. This was also the site of the first Bloody Sunday in Irish history, the greatest single atrocity of the War of Independence.

Bloody Sunday is one of the episodes recounted in the outstanding Croke Park Experience in the GAA Museum, where the history and culture of these most Irish of games is explored in fascinating, interactive style. As well as going into exhaustive detail about Gaelic games, the exhibitions feature audiovisual displays that are sure to get the hairs on the back of any GAA fan's neck to stand up, and many relics from other sports and episodes that have captured the mood of the nation. There are terminals set up where you can watch highlights from any All-Ireland football or hurling final that has been recorded, but the highlight, for us at least, is the opportunity to test one's skills with a football or a hurley and *sliothar* (small leather ball), and imagine the glories that might have been.

GLASNEVIN CEMETERY Map p125

☎ 882 6590; www.glasnevin-cemetery.ie; Finglas Rd; admission free; ⌚ 24hr; 🚍 40, 40A or 40B from Parnell St

Glasnevin Cemetery was established in 1832 as a cemetery for Roman Catholics, who faced opposition when they conducted burials in the city's Protestant cemeteries. Many monuments and memorials have staunchly patriotic overtones, with numerous high crosses, shamrocks, harps and other Irish symbols. The single most imposing memorial is the colossal monument to Cardinal

McCabe (1837–1921), archbishop of Dublin and primate of Ireland.

A modern replica of a round tower holds the tomb of Daniel O'Connell, who died in 1847 and was re-interred here in 1869, when the tower was completed. Charles Stewart Parnell's tomb is topped with a huge granite rock. Other notable people buried here include Sir Roger Casement, who was executed for treason by the British in 1916 and whose remains weren't returned to Ireland until 1964; the republican leader Michael Collins, who was assassinated during the Civil War; the docker and trade unionist Jim Larkin, a prime force in the 1913 general strike; and the poet Gerard Manley Hopkins.

There's a poignant 'class' memorial to the men who starved themselves to death for the cause of Irish freedom over the last century, including 10 men in the 1981 H Block hunger strikes. The most interesting parts of the cemetery are at the southeastern Prospect Sq end. The towers were once used to keep watch for body snatchers. The cemetery is mentioned in *Ulysses* and there are several clues for Joyce enthusiasts to follow.

In 2010 a new museum (€6; ⌚ 10am-5pm Mon-Fri, 11am-6pm Sat & Sun) opened, which tells the social and political story of Ireland through the lives of the people known and unknown that are buried in the cemetery. The City of the Dead covers the burial practice and religious beliefs of the roughly 1.5 million people whose final resting place is here, while the Milestone Gallery

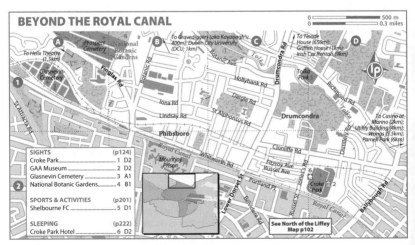

BEYOND THE ROYAL CANAL

SIGHTS	(p124)
Croke Park....................	1 D2
GAA Museum................	2 D2
Glasnevin Cemetery.........	3 A1
National Botanic Gardens....	4 B1

SPORTS & ACTIVITIES	(p201)
Shelbourne FC..............	5 D1

SLEEPING	(p222)
Croke Park Hotel............	6 D2

features a 10m-long digitally interactive timeline outlining the lives and links of the cemetery's most famous residents.

The best way to visit the cemetery is to take one of the daily tours (€5; ☽ 11.30am, 12.30 & 2.30pm) which will (ahem) bring to life the rich and important stories of those buried in what is jokingly referred to by Dubs as 'Croak Park'.

NATIONAL BOTANIC GARDENS
Map p125

☎ 837 7596; Botanic Rd, Glasnevin; admission free; ☽ 9am-6pm Mon-Sat, 11am-6pm Sun Apr-Oct, 10am-4.30pm Mon-Sat, 11am-4.30pm Sun Nov-Mar; ▣ 13, 13A or 19 from O'Connell St, or 34 or 34A from Middle Abbey St

This 19.5-hectare treasure is a delightful blend of exoticism and tousled gentility. Although only established in 1795, the area was used as a garden long before it was christened so, and the area of Yew Walk (Addison's Walk) features trees dating back to the first half of the 18th century.

The architectural highlight in the gardens is a series of curvilinear glasshouses that date from 1843 to 1869. They were created by Dubliner Richard Turner, who was also responsible for creating the Palm House at London's Kew Gardens. Within these Victorian masterpieces you will find the latest in botanical technology, including a series of computer-controlled climates that reproduce environments from around the world.

The gardens also have a palm house, which was built in 1884. Among the pioneering botanical work conducted here was the first attempt to raise orchids from seed, back in 1844. Pampas grass and the giant lily were first grown in Europe in these gardens.

CASINO AT MARINO Off Map p125

☎ 833 1618; www.heritageireland.ie; Cherry-mount Crescent, off Malahide Rd, Marino; adult/concession/family €3/2; ☽ by guided tour only 10am-5pm May-Sep, last tour 45min before closing; ▣ Clontarf Rd; ▣ 20A, 20B, 27, 27B, 42, 42C or 123 from city centre

No, not that kind of casino; perhaps it's the images of blackjack and slot machines that make so many visitors overlook this bewitching 18th-century architectural folly, which is a *casino* in the Italian sense of the word, as in a 'house of pleasure' or summer home. Off Malahide Rd, it was built for the Earl of Charlemont (1728–99), who returned from his grand European tour with a huge art collection and a burning passion for the Italian Palladian style of architecture. He appointed the architect Sir William Chambers to build the casino, a process that spanned three decades and was never really concluded because the earl frittered away his fortune.

Externally, the building's 12 Tuscan columns, forming a templelike facade, and huge entrance doorway suggest that it encloses a simple single open space. Only when you go inside do you realise what a wonderful extravagance it is. The interior is a convoluted maze, planned as a bachelor's retreat, but eventually put to quite a different use. Flights of fancy include carved draperies, ornate fireplaces, chimneys for central heating disguised as roof urns, downpipes hidden in columns, beautiful parquet floors built of rare woods, and a spacious wine cellar. All sorts of statuary adorn the outside, the amusing fakes being the most enjoyable. The towering front door is a sham, and a much smaller panel opens to reveal the interior. The windows have blacked-out panels to disguise the fact that the interior is a complex of rooms rather than a single chamber. Entry is by guided tour only, and the last tour departs 45 minutes before closing.

When the earl married, the casino became a garden retreat rather than a bachelor's quarters. The casino was designed to accompany another building where he intended to house the art and antiquities he had acquired during his European tour, so it's perhaps fitting that his townhouse on Parnell Sq, also designed by Sir William Chambers, is now the Dublin City Gallery (p104).

Despite his wealth, Charlemont was a comparatively liberal and free-thinking aristocrat. He never enclosed his demesne and allowed the public to use it as an open park. Nor was he the only eccentric in the area at that time. In 1792 a painter named Folliot took a dislike to the earl and built Marino Crescent at the bottom of Malahide Rd purely to block his view of the sea.

After Charlemont's death his estate, crippled by his debts, quickly collapsed. The art collection was dispersed and in 1870 the townhouse was sold to the government. The Marino estate followed in 1881 and the casino in 1930, though it was in a decrepit condition when the government acquired it. Not until the mid-1970s did serious restoration begin, and it still continues. Although the current casino grounds are a tiny fragment of the original Marino estate, trees around the building help to hide the fact that it's now surrounded by a housing estate.

WALKING TOURS

The walks included here take on three of the city's major themes, beginning with Dublin's well-earned reputation as a hive of literary genius, followed by a traipse through the city's faded Viking and medieval past. There's also the staggered walk that most people come to Dublin for – the pub crawl. Finally, we want you to explore the northern half of the city before straddling the southern boundary of the city centre and the suburbs.

LITERARY DUBLIN

1 Shaw Birthplace

Start your walk just north of the Grand Canal at the Shaw Birthplace (p77). Barely visited, this elegant Victorian home was where Nobel Prize–winner George Bernard Shaw (1856–1950), author of *Pygmalion* (later hammed

> ### WALK FACTS
>
> Start Shaw Birthplace, 33 Synge St
> End Dublin Writers Museum, North Parnell Sq
> Distance 3.5km
> Duration 2½ to three hours
> Fuel Stop Palace Bar
> Transport ⬜ 11, 11A, 13B or 48A from Trinity College; 🚇 Harcourt St

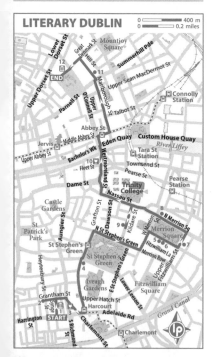

LITERARY DUBLIN

up and turned into the much-loved stage musical and film *My Fair Lady*), lived during his early years.

2 Cornelius Ryan Birthplace

Walk north along Synge St, take a left along Grantham St and at the very end, you can see Ryan's birthplace. There's not much to see, save the frontage of the house at 32 Heytesbury St where the author (1920–74) of *The Longest Day*, *The Last Battle* and *A Bridge Too Far* was born.

3 Bleeding Horse

Retrace your steps along Grantham St and keep going along until you get to the intersection with Lower Camden St. Across Camden St is this popular watering hole, where a certain Captain Bligh, of mutiny on the *Bounty* fame, lived upstairs while he was overseeing the construction of the North Wall.

4 Sir Edward Carson Birthplace

Walk along Charlotte St, take a left onto Harcourt St and head up to No 4. This is the birthplace of the founder of Northern Irish Unionism, who was a barrister in Dublin before going all political. Carson (1854–1935) made his legal bones by prosecuting Oscar Wilde in 1898, which ultimately resulted in the writer going to prison for the-then crime of homosexuality.

5 George (AE) Russell Residence

Continue walking straight along West St Stephen's Green and onto North St Stephen's Green. Take a left onto Merrion Row and continue to Merrion Sq. The former residence of self-proclaimed poet, mystic, painter and cooperator George Russell (1867–1935) is at 84 Merrion Sq South.

6 WB Yeats Residence (Part One)

The great poet, dramatist and nationalist agitator WB Yeats (1865–1939) answered the door at 82 Merrion Sq South...

7 WB Yeats Residence (Part Two)

…before moving around the square to 52 Merrion Sq East, although he later claimed not to like living on the square.

8 Oscar Wilde House

The self-professed genius (1854–1900) was born and raised at 1 Merrion Sq North; fortunately, he grew up to prove himself right.

9 Bram Stoker House

From Merrion Sq's northern corner, walk straight down Nassau St. Kildare St runs off to your left, and No 36 was once the home of Bram Stoker (1847–1912), the creator of the greatest vampire of them all (er, that's *Dracula*).

10 Palace Bar

Head back up Nassau St, past the main entrance to Trinity College and then down Westmoreland St. Off the street to your left, on Fleet St, is the Palace Bar (p179), traditionally a favourite haunt of journos and scribblers, including one Brendan Behan, who was regularly barred from here.

11 James Joyce Cultural Centre

Cross the Liffey onto O'Connell St, take a right onto Lower Abbey St, then left into Marlborough St and head north until you reach North Great George's St. On your right, at No 35, in this lovingly restored period home, is the James Joyce Cultural Centre (p108), which is the home of all things Joycean.

12 Dublin Writers Museum

Walk to the end of North Great George's St, head left into Great Denmark St and finish your literary walk at this interesting literary centre (p109) on the northern flank of Parnell Sq.

VIKING & MEDIEVAL DUBLIN

1 Essex Gate

Begin your walk at the corner of Parliament St and Essex Gate, once a main entrance gate to the city. A bronze plaque on a pillar marks the spot where the gate once stood. Further along, you can see the original foundations of Isolde's Tower through a grill in the pavement, in front of the pub of the same name.

2 Church of St Francis

Head west down Essex Gate and West Essex St until you reach Fishamble St; turn right towards the quays and left into Wood Quay. Cross Winetavern St and proceed along Merchant's Quay. To your left you'll see the Church of St Francis, otherwise known as Adam & Eve's, after a tavern through which worshippers gained access to a secret chapel during Penal Law times during the 17th and 18th centuries.

3 Father Mathew Bridge

Further down Merchant's Quay you'll spot this bridge, built in 1818 on the spot of the fordable crossing that gave Dublin its Irish name, Baile Átha Cliath (Town of the Hurdle Ford).

4 Brazen Head

Take a left onto Bridge St and stop for a drink at Dublin's oldest pub (p180), dating from 1198 (although the present building dates from 1668).

5 St Audoen's Arch

Take the next left onto Cook St, where you'll find one of the only remaining gates of 32 that were built into the medieval city walls, dating from 1240.

6 St Audoen's Church

Climb through the arch up to the ramparts to see one of the city's oldest existing churches (p99). It was built around 1190, and is not to be confused with the newer Catholic church next door.

7 Dvblinia

Leave the little park, join High St and head east until you reach the first corner. Here on your left is the former Synod Hall, now a museum (p97), where medieval Dublin has been interactively re-created.

8 Christ Church Cathedral

Turn left and walk under the Synod Hall Bridge, which links it to one of the city's most important landmarks and, in medieval times, the most important church (p96) inside the city walls.

9 Tailors' Hall

Exit the cathedral onto Christ Church Pl, cross over onto Nicholas St and turn right onto Back Lane. Proceed to Dublin's oldest surviving guild hall, built between 1703 and 1707 (though it says 1770 on the plaque) for the Tailors Guild. It's now the headquarters of An Taisce, the National Trust for Ireland.

10 St Patrick's Cathedral

Do an about-turn, head back along the lane and turn right into Nicholas St, which becomes Patrick St. To your left you'll see Dublin's most important cathedral (p93), which stood outside the city walls.

11 Marsh's Library

Along St Patrick's Close, beyond the bend on the left, is this stunningly beautiful library (p95), named after Archbishop Narcissus Marsh, dean of St Patrick's. Further along again on your left is the Dublin Metropolitan Police building, once the Episcopal Palace of St Sepulchre.

12 Dublin Castle

Finally, follow our route up Bride St, Golden Lane and Great Ship St, and finish up with a long wander around Dublin Castle (p76). Be sure not to miss the striking powder-blue Bermingham Tower and the nearby Chester Beatty Library (p72), south of the castle, which houses one of the city's most fascinating collections of rare books and manuscripts, and is well worth a visit.

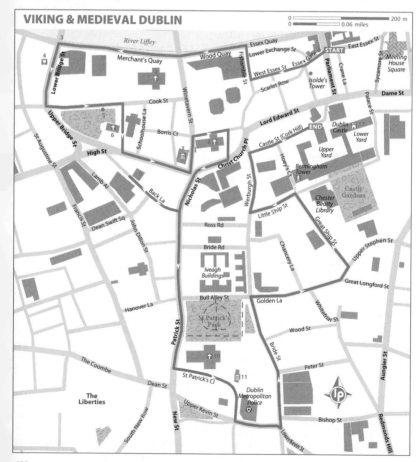

VIKING & MEDIEVAL DUBLIN

PINTLY PERAMBULATION

1 Merrion Hotel
Before your walk, start with an elegant afternoon tea, complete with scones and cucumber sandwiches, at this hotel (p216); it's the perfect lining for the road ahead.

2 Fitzwilliam Hotel
Leave the Merrion Hotel, turn left and then right along Merrion Row. Walk around St Stephen's Green until you get to the Fitzwilliam (p213), which is the perfect place to kick off the boozing with a killer cocktail in hoity-toity style.

3 Dawson Lounge
Retrace your steps back around the Green, take a left down Dawson St, then stop for a diminutive tipple in Dublin's smallest pub (p175).

4 Kehoe's
Head north up Dawson St, take a left onto South Anne St and sink a pint of plain in one of the city centre's most atmospheric bars, Kehoe's (p176).

5 South William
Turn right onto Grafton St, take a left onto Johnson's Ct and then another left into South

WALK FACTS

Start Merrion Hotel, Upper Merrion St
End Anseo, Camden St
Distance 4km
Duration There's booze involved, so how long is a piece of string?
Transport 🚌 7, 7A, 10, 11, 13 or 172 from city centre

PINTLY PERAMBULATION

131

William St. Head down to No 52 and order a drink in one of Dublin's coolest bars, South William (p175), the place to be seen.

6 Grogan's Castle Lounge
Backtrack up South William St to No 15 to enjoy this pub (p175), favoured haunt of artists, frustrated writers and various other bohemian types.

7 Long Hall
Take a left onto Castle Market, left down Drury St and right onto Fade St. Cross South Great George's St and nip into the Long Hall (p176) to discuss the vicissitudes of life in a sombre Victorian setting.

8 Sin É
Head up South Great George's St, and into South Temple Lane, cross the Millennium footbridge and turn left along the pleasant waterside boardwalk. Nearby is this narrow, deep bar (p181), which has a great reputation for top-class music and can be relied upon for a terrific night out.

9 Porterhouse
Cross the Liffey at Grattan Bridge and stop for a tipple at our favourite of the quarter's drinking establishments (p178), which serves a range of great microbrews.

10 Globe
Head south down Parliament St, turn left onto Dame St and then right onto South Great George's St. Stop off at the granddaddy of Dublin's cool bars, the Globe (p174), still going strong.

11 Swan
Stroll down South Great George's St, into Aungier St and pull up a stool at the Swan (p177). Usually quiet and always beautiful, this terrific bar is very popular with locals and students from the nearby College of Surgeons.

12 Anseo
Make the final push southwards, walking the length of the street until you get to Camden St and this seriously hip and totally unpretentious bar (p174) with fabulous DJs. If you've followed the tour correctly, you should no longer be referring to this guide. How many fingers?

TAKE A WALK ON THE NORTH SIDE

1 Mountjoy Square
Start your walk in slightly dilapidated, yet elegant Mountjoy Sq, formerly one of Dublin's most beautiful and prestigious addresses.

2 St George's Church
Take a left at the northwestern corner of the square and walk down Gardiner Pl, turning right onto North Temple St. Up ahead is this fine, but now deconsecrated Georgian church, designed by architect Francis Johnston (who lived close by in a now-demolished house at 64 Eccles St).

3 Abbey Presbyterian Church
Take a left onto Hardwicke St and left again onto North Frederick St. On your right you'll spot this distinctive building. Built in 1864, it's often referred to as Findlater's Church after the grocery magnate who financed the building's construction.

4 Garden of Remembrance
The northern slice of Parnell Sq houses this garden (p111), opened in 1966 to commemorate the 50th anniversary of the 1916 Easter Rising.

5 Dublin City Gallery – The Hugh Lane
North of the square, facing the park, is this excellent gallery (p104). Next door to the Dublin Writers Museum (p109), the Hugh Lane is home to some of the best modern art in Europe as well as Francis Bacon's recreated studio.

6 Rotunda Hospital
The southern part of Parnell Sq is occupied by this hospital (p111), a wonderful example of public architecture in the Georgian style, which was built in 1757.

7 Gate Theatre
In the southeastern corner of the square is the Gate Theatre (p198). Part of the old Rotunda complex, it's now a major theatre for top-end drama.

8 Spire
Head south down O'Connell St, passing by this 120m-high monument (p110). Erected in 2001, it has already become an iconic symbol of the city.

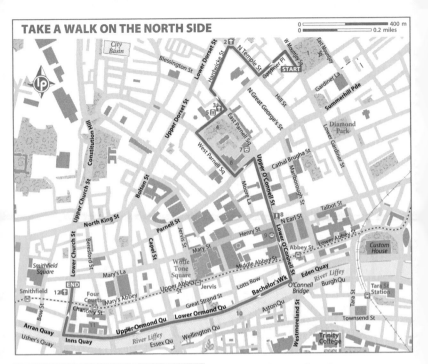

WALK FACTS

Start Mountjoy Sq
End St Michan's Church, Church St
Distance 2.5km
Duration Two hours
Transport 🚌 134 from city centre; 🚇 Four Courts

9 General Post Office
On the western side of O'Connell St, this stunning neoclassical building (p107) towers over the street. Its role as HQ for the 1916 Easter Rising (p29) makes it an important historical site.

10 Ha'penny Bridge
Head south until you hit the river, turn right and walk along the handsome boardwalk until you reach the city's most distinctive bridge (it got its name from the charge that was levied on those who used it).

11 Four Courts
Continue west along Ormond Quay to one of James Gandon's Georgian masterpieces (p108), home to the most important law courts in Ireland.

12 St Michan's Church
Finally take a right onto Church St to admire this beautiful Georgian church (p110), with grisly vaults populated by the remains of the long departed.

ALONG THE GRAND CANAL
1 Portobello
Begin at this popular watering hole (☎ 475 2715; 33 South Richmond St), which was built to service the solid (and liquid) hungers of workers building the canal.

2 Portobello College
Across the street is this technical college. Painter Jack B Yeats (1871–1957) lived here in the years leading up to his death.

3 Patrick Kavanagh Statue
Turn left at the Grand Canal and begin your stroll along the towpath. About 300m past Leeson St Bridge is the Kavanagh statue, relaxing on a bench. The Monaghan-born poet is immortalised in the spot he loved most in Dublin – where he couldn't get barred (see boxed text, p123).

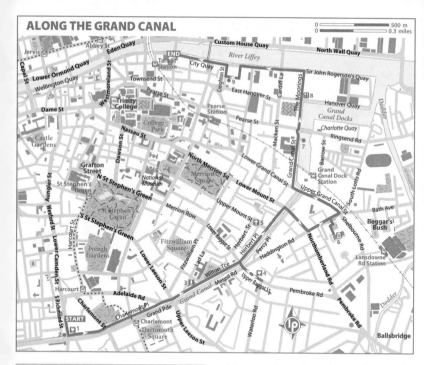

ALONG THE GRAND CANAL

4 Searson's
When you get to Baggot St Bridge take a right onto Baggot St and refuel at this popular bar (☎ 660 0330; 42 Upper Baggot St) .

5 St Stephen's Church
Return to the canal and continue eastwards, diverting left at Mount St for St Stephen's Church (p85), a Greek Revival structure known as the 'pepper canister' on account of its curious shape.

6 National Print Museum
Back on the towpath, turn right at Northumberland Rd and left onto Haddington Rd for this museum (p121). Housed in an old barracks, this is a surprisingly interesting museum, especially if you're a fan of old books.

7 Waterways Visitor Centre
Turn left onto Upper Grand Canal St, then right into Grand Canal Quay for this centre (p117), where you can find out everything you could possibly want to know on the construction of the country's canals and waterways.

8 Ely HQ
Before heading back to the city, stop for brunch or a drink at this supertrendy wine bar and restaurant (p166), which overlooks the Grand Canal Docks.

9 Windmill Lane Studios
Walk north to Sir John Rogerson's Quay, turn left and left again at Windmill Lane. Here you'll find Dublin's very own Abbey Road Studios, where U2 have their offices and recorded all of their early records up to *The Unforgettable Fire*. Back on Rogerson's Quay, walk west along the quays and back into the city.

SHOPPING

top picks

- Avoca Handweavers (p138)
- Barry Doyle Design Jewellers (p141)
- Bow Boutique (p139)
- Cathach Books (p137)
- Claddagh Records (p143)
- Costume (p139)
- Designyard (p141)
- Meeting House Square Market (p145)
- Sheridan's Cheesemongers (p140)

What's your recommendation? www.lonelyplanet.com/dublin

SHOPPING

In 2007 Europe's busiest shopping street was Dublin's very own Henry St, which saw an average of 16,000 frothing retail junkies *an hour*, each pram-pushing family and consumer couple playing catch-me-if-you-can with the credit-card companies. That was *before* the global credit crunch.

On the surface, nothing seems to have changed. Dubliners still throng the main shopping streets both north and south of the Liffey, but the numbers have dipped: both footfall (the numbers walking in and out of shops) and retail spend has dropped; according to some sources, by as much as one quarter. A low pound sterling rate and the government's ill-advised decision to bump up value-added tax (VAT) by half a percent to raise much-needed revenue has also hit retailers hard, and in early 2009 it was estimated that €70m of potential business in a six-month period was lost to Northern Ireland, as shoppers flocked north of the border where *everything* became cheaper. In 2010 the government reversed its decision and cut VAT by half a percent, but the city's shop owners are struggling to deal with the new realities of a population cut off from the cheap and easy credit that fuelled its purchasing power for the guts of a decade.

OK, that's the background. Now for the stuff on the shelves. If it's made in Ireland – or pretty much anywhere else – chances are you can find it here. Fashionistas can ogle at the Prada frocks in Brown Thomas, Dublin's most stylish department store, or head to the warren of streets west of Grafton St, where trendy little boutiques share the narrow streets with funky secondhand shops, popular pubs and cute little restaurants. At its heart is Castle Market, where you can really let loose your retail chi.

Men's bespoke tailoring is rather thin on the ground. Designers have tried to instil a sense of classical style in the Dublin male, but the species doesn't seem too interested – any pressed shirt and leather shoe seems to suffice.

Not surprisingly, streetwear is very trendy and the most obvious buyers are the city's younger consumers, who pour into every midrange fashion outlet spread throughout the city centre and pore over the trendy, mass-produced clobber within. They spend their Saturdays, off-days and lunch hours ambling about Grafton St and its side streets on the south side, or Henry St and its surrounds on the far side of the Liffey; and then there's the consumer cathedral in the southern suburb of Dundrum, easily reached by Luas and open aggressively long hours, seven days a week. Stacked with every hot name in the retail black book, it has raised the bar on shopping and turned it into a serious occupation.

At the other end of the fashion spectrum, you'll find all the knit and tweed you want at Avoca Handweavers (p138) or Blarney Woollen Mills (p141). While souvenir hunters can still buy toy sheep, Guinness magnets and shamrock tea towels, a new breed of craft shop offers one-off or limited-edition crafts and art. Traditional Irish products such as crystal and knitwear remain popular choices, and you can increasingly find innovative modern takes on the classics. But steer clear of that mass-produced junk whose joke value isn't worth the hassle of carting it home on the plane: trust us, there's no such thing as a genuine *shillelagh* (Irish fighting stick) for sale anywhere in town.

A good website for shopping tips and designer sales is www.thesavvyshopper.ie.

OPENING HOURS

The majority of the city's shops open 9.30am to 6pm Monday to Saturday. Thursday has late-night shopping, and most places stay open until 7pm or 8pm. With only a handful of exceptions, most shops also open from noon to 6pm on Sunday. Shopping centres keep the same hours with the rather pronounced exception of the Dundrum Town Centre, which opens until 9pm Monday to Friday and until 7pm on Saturday and Sunday.

DUTY FREE

Non-EU residents can claim VAT (Value Added Tax – a sales tax, 21% of the purchase price) back on their purchases so long as the store operates either the Cashback or Taxback refund program (they should display a sticker). You'll get a voucher with your purchase that must be stamped at the *last point of exit* from the EU. If you're travelling on to Britain or mainland Europe from Dublin, hold on to your voucher until you pass through your final customs stop in the EU; it can then be stamped and you can post it back for a refund of duty paid. Remember that no VAT is charged on books, children's clothing or educational items.

GRAFTON STREET & AROUND

Pedestrianised Grafton St has traditionally been *the* shopping street – but despite the sprinkling of older Dublin shops, the preponderance of British-owned chain stores means that you'll find the same kind of stuff you'll get almost anywhere else. To really get the most of the area's retail allure, it's best to get off Grafton St and head into the grid of streets surrounding it, especially to the west, where you'll find some of Dublin's most interesting outlets, from bookstores to boutiques, as well as two extraordinary shopping centres. The Victorian structure of George's St Arcade houses a wonderful collection of poky little shops and stalls while the exquisite Powerscourt Townhouse Shopping Centre is Dublin's most prestigious shopping mall. As well as being accessible by all city-centre buses, all listings around Grafton St can be accessed from the St Stephen's Luas stop.

BLUE ERIU Map p70 — Beauty
☎ 672 5776; www.nueblueeriu.com; 7 South William St; ✆ 10am-6pm Mon, Fri & Sat, 10am-8pm Tue-Thu; ☐ all city centre
Less of a cosmetics shop and more a beauty experience with a Celtic twist, this supertrendy retreat reopened in mid-2010 after its own major makeover. Its customers breathed a sigh of relief and got on with the business of getting the best facial in town (or so we're told); the products used are strictly from the top shelf, including Kiehls, Chantecaille and Shu Uemura.

CATHACH BOOKS Map p70 — Books
☎ 671 8676; www.rarebooks.ie; 10 Duke St; ✆ 9.30am-5.45pm Mon-Sat; ☐ all city centre
Our favourite bookshop in the city stocks a rich and remarkable collection of Irish-interest books, with a particular emphasis on 20th-century literature, including a large

top picks

GUARANTEED IRISH

You want to buy something Irish-made to take home? This is our quick pick.
- Avoca Handweavers (p138) Our favourite department store in the city has myriad homemade gift ideas.
- Barry Doyle Design Jewellers (p141) Exquisite handcrafted jewellery with unique contemporary designs.
- Cathach Books (left) For that priceless 1st edition or a beautiful, leather-bound copy of Joyce's *Dubliners*.
- Costume (p139) Elegance, originality and sophistication – and that's just the Irish designers represented at this fabulous shop.
- Louis Copeland (p139) Dublin's very own top tailor with his made-to-measure suits.

selection of first editions, including some rare ones by the big guns: Joyce, Yeats, Beckett and Wilde.

DUBRAY BOOKS Map p70 — Books
☎ 677 5568; 36 Grafton St; ✆ 10am-6pm Mon-Sat, to 8pm Thu, noon-6pm Sun; ☐ all city centre
Three roomy floors devoted to bestsellers, recent releases, coffee-table books and a huge travel section make this one of the better bookshops in town. It can't compete with its larger, British-owned rivals, but it holds its own with a helpful staff and a lovely atmosphere that encourages you to linger.

HODGES FIGGIS Map p70 — Books
☎ 677 4754; www.waterstones.com; 57 Dawson St; ✆ 9.30am-7pm Mon-Sat, to 8pm Thu, noon-6pm Sun; ☐ all city centre
The mother of all Dublin bookstores has books on every subject for every kind of reader spread across its three huge floors, including a substantial Irish section (fiction, history, contemporary issues) on the ground floor.

MURDER INK Map p70 — Books
☎ 677 7570; 15 Dawson St; ✆ 10am-5.30pm Mon-Sat, noon-5pm Sun; ☐ all city centre
All manner of murder-mystery and crime novels are in this small specialist book-

store, which has categorisation down to a fine art – choose from historical mystery, romantic crime, sci-fi, true crime and more.

STOKES BOOKS Map p70 Books
☎ 671 3584; 19 George's St Arcade; ⌚ 11am-6pm Mon-Sat; 🚌 all city centre
A small bookshop specialising in Irish history books, both old and new. Other titles, covering a range of subjects, include a number of beautiful, old, leather-bound editions.

WATERSTONE'S Map p70 Books
☎ 679 1415; 7 Dawson St; ⌚ 9am-7pm Mon-Sat, to 8pm Thu, noon-6pm Sun; 🚌 all city centre
Although it is large and multistoreyed, Waterstone's somehow manages to maintain that snugly, hide-in-a-corner ambience that book lovers adore. The broad selection of books is supplemented by five bookcases of Irish fiction, as well as poetry, drama, politics and history. There are book-signings every Thursday evening; check the board outside for details. There's also a cafe on the 2nd floor.

GREAT OUTDOORS
Map p70 Camping & Outdoors
☎ 679 4293; www.greatoutdoors.ie; 20 Chatham St; ⌚ 9.30am-5.30pm Mon-Sat, to 8pm Thu; 🚌 all city centre
This is Dublin's best outdoors store, with gear for hiking, camping, surfing, mountaineering, swimming and more. Fleeces, tents, inflatable dinghies, boots and gas cookers – they're all here as well as an info-laden noticeboard and superbly patient staff.

DECENT CIGAR EMPORIUM
Map p70 Cigars
☎ 671 6451; www.decent-cigar.com; 46 Grafton St; ⌚ 10am-6pm Mon-Sat, to 8pm Thu, 1.30-5.30pm Sun; 🚌 all city centre
When the clamour of Grafton St gets too much, slip up this discreet staircase, recline

in a plush leather armchair and run your nose along a sweet hand-rolled, long-filler cigar over a glass of decent red wine or a cup of Illy coffee. In a country that has a smoking ban, this is indeed a rare pleasure.

AVOCA HANDWEAVERS
Map p70 Department Store & Irish Crafts
☎ 677 4215; www.avoca.ie; 11-13 Suffolk St; ⌚ 10am-6pm Mon-Sat, to 8pm Thu, 11am-6pm Sun; 🚌 all city centre
Combining clothing, homewares, a basement food hall and an excellent top-floor cafe (p157), Avoca promotes a stylish but homey brand of modern Irish life – and is one of the best places to find an original present. Many of the garments are woven, knitted and naturally dyed at its Wicklow factory. The children's section, with unusual knits, fairy outfits, bee-covered gumboots and dinky toys, is fantastic.

BROWN THOMAS
Map p70 Department Store
☎ 605 6666; www.brownthomas.ie; 88-95 Grafton St; ⌚ 9am-8pm Mon-Fri, to 9pm Thu, to 7pm Sat, 10am-6pm Sun; 🚌 all city centre
Soak up the Jo Malone–laden rarefied atmosphere of Dublin's most exclusive store, where presentation is virtually artistic. Here you'll find fantastic cosmetics, shoes to die for, exotic homewares and a host of Irish and international fashion labels such as Balenciaga, Stella McCartney, Lainey Keogh and Philip Treacy. The 3rd-floor Bottom Drawer outlet stocks the finest Irish linen you'll find anywhere.

DUNNES STORES
Map p70 Department Store
☎ 671 4629; 62 Grafton St; ⌚ 9am-6.30pm Mon-Sat, to 9pm Thu, noon-6pm Sun; 🚌 all city centre
A favourite choice with Irish mothers for its affordable everyday family clothing. The Savida fashion range is remarkably on the pulse though, and its excellent homewares

ARMCHAIR SHOPPING
Want to avoid the leg-numbing march of the pavements in search of a bargain or much sought-after souvenir? Relax, grab a cuppa and do it online.
- Buy4Now (www.buy4now.ie) A catch-all website of Irish shops that offers nearly everything you can think of, from ski holidays to boxed sets of *Fair City*.
- Moytura (www.shopirishwithmoytura.com) Irish-themed items include *bodhráns* (Irish drums), Paddy's day souvenirs and Irish biscuits.

department is giving Habitat a run for its money. Look for branches across the city including the new Dunnes Home (Map p70; ☎ 415 5044; South Great George's St).

MARKS & SPENCER

Map p70 — Department Store

☎ 679 7855; 15-20 Grafton St; ⏰ 9am-6.30pm Mon-Sat, to 9pm Thu, noon-6pm Sun; 🚋 all city centre

Good-quality clothing and virtually everything else that the body and house might need – at affordable prices – make this British chain store one of Dublin's most popular. There's a supermarket in the basement and a popular cafe on the ground floor.

OPTICA Map p70 — Eyewear

☎ 677 4705; 1 Royal Hibernian Way; ⏰ 9.30am-5.30pm Mon-Wed, Fri & Sat, to 6.30pm Thu; 🚋 all city centre

Who says guys don't make passes at girls who wear glasses? Knock 'em dead in head-turning specs and shades by Chanel, D&G, Stella McCartney and Oliver Peoples.

ALIAS TOM Map p70 — Fashion & Designer

☎ 671 5443; Duke Lane; ⏰ 9.30am-6pm Mon-Sat, to 8pm Thu; 🚋 all city centre

Dublin's best designer menswear store, where friendly staff guide you through casuals by bling labels Burberry, Prada and whatever else makes for a classy fit. Downstairs it's classic tailored suits and designer shoes.

BOW BOUTIQUE Map p70 — Fashion & Designer

☎ 604 0044; www.bowboutique.ie; ground fl, Powerscourt Townhouse Shopping Centre; ⏰ 10am-6pm Mon-Sat, to 8pm Thu; 🚋 all city centre

The collective brainchild of four Irish designers – Eilis Boyle, Matthew Doody, Margaret O'Rourke and Wendy Crawford – this beautiful new boutique showcases original designs and made-to-measure items as well as promoting 'ecofashion' by stocking fairtrade labels from around the globe like People Tree and Camilla Nordback.

BT2 Map p68 — Fashion & Designer

☎ 605 6666; www.brownthomas.ie; 28-29 Grafton St; ⏰ 9am-6.30pm Mon-Sat, to 9pm Thu, to 7pm Sat, 10am-6.30pm Sun; 🚋 all city centre

The kiddies' table in Brown Thomas' exquisitely laid-out dining room, BT2 is the annexe shop for the city's trendy young things, targeting an audience that wants to look the contemporary part and set the tone for tomorrow. Brands include DKNY, Custom, Diesel, Ted Baker and Tommy Hilfiger.

COSTUME Map p70 — Fashion & Designer

☎ 679 4188; 10-11 Castle Market; ⏰ 10am-6pm Mon-Sat, to 7pm Thu, 2-6pm Sun; 🚋 all city centre

Costume is considered a genuine pacesetter by Dublin's fashionistas; it has exclusive contracts with some of Europe's most innovative designers, such as Isabel Marant and Anna Sui. It also has the city's best range of Tempereley and American Retro. Local designers represented here are Helen James, whose Japanese-influenced obis are enormously popular, and Leighlee.

DESIGN CENTRE

Map p70 — Fashion & Designer

☎ 679 5718; www.designcentre.ie; Powerscourt Townhouse Shopping Centre; ⏰ 10am-6pm Mon-Wed & Fri, to 8pm Thu, 9.30am-6pm Sat; 🚋 all city centre

Mostly dedicated to Irish designer womenswear, featuring well-made classic suits, evening wear and knitwear. Irish labels include N&C Kilkenny, Pauric Sweeney, Roisín Linnane and Philip Treacy. Ben De Lisi, Ophelie and La Petite Salope also get a look in.

KILKENNY SHOP

Map p70 — Fashion & Designer, Irish Crafts

☎ 677 7066; www.kilkennyshop.com; 6 Nassau St; ⏰ 8.30am-6pm Mon-Fri, to 8pm Thu, 9am-6pm Sat, 11am-6pm Sun; 🚋 all city centre

A large, long-running repository for contemporary, innovative Irish crafts, including multicoloured, modern Irish knits, designer clothing, Orla Kiely bags and some lovely silver jewellery. The glassware and pottery is beautiful and sourced from workshops around the country. A great source for presents.

LOUIS COPELAND Map p70 — Fashion & Designer

☎ 872 1600; www.louiscopeland.com; 18-19 Wicklow St; ⏰ 9am-5.30pm Mon-Sat, to 7.30pm Thu; 🚋 all city centre

Dublin's answer to the famed tailors of London's Saville Row, this shop makes fabulous suits to measure, but also stocks plenty of ready-to-wear suits by a host of international designers.

SMOCK Map p70 — Fashion & Designer

☎ 613 9000; 31 Drury St; ⏱ 10.30am-6pm Mon-Fri, 10am-6pm Sat; 🚇 all city centre

This tiny designer shop sells quirky (and very exclusive) international womenswear from investment labels Easton Pearson, Veronique Branquinho and AF Vandevorft, as well as a small range of interesting jewellery. It survives by focusing its attentions on the needs of a select (read: moneyed) clientele.

TOMMY HILFIGER

Map p70 — Fashion & Designer

☎ 633 7010; 13-14 Grafton St; ⏱ 9.30am-7pm Mon-Tue, to 8pm Wed & Fri, to 9pm Thu, 9am-7pm Sat, 11am-6pm Sun; 🚇 all city centre

'Traditional with a twist' is how Tommy Hilfiger describes his own fashions, and he's right, if the twist is designing clothes that are as appealing to a yummy mummy as to a rapper. The American designer himself landed in Dublin in 2008 to cut the ribbon on this elegant store on the city's most prestigious shopping street.

ASIA MARKET Map p70 — Food & Drink

☎ 677 9764; 18 Drury St; ⏱ 10am-7pm Mon-Sat; 🚇 all city centre

This large, friendly food emporium should be your first port of call if you want to whip up an Oriental feast. For a start it's really good value and you'll find everything here from kitchen implements to hard-to-come-by ingredients like grass jelly, habanero chillies, brown basmati rice or – should you wish – chicken's feet.

BRETZEL BAKERY Map p68 — Food & Drink

☎ 475 2724; www.bretzel.ie; 1a Lennox St; ⏱ 8.30am-3pm Mon, 8.30am-6pm Tue, Wed & Fri, 8.30am-7pm Thu, 9am-5pm Sat, 9am-1pm Sun; 🚌 14, 15, 65 or 83

The bagels might be a bit on the chewy side, but they've got their charms – as do the scrumptious selections of breads, savoury snacks, cakes and biscuits that have locals queuing out the door on weekends. Recertified as kosher since 2003, the bakery has been on this Portobello site since 1870.

FALLON & BYRNE Map p70 — Food & Drink

☎ 472 1000; www.fallonandbyrne.com; 11-17 Exchequer St; ⏱ 9am-8pm Mon-Sat, 11am-6pm Sun; 🚇 all city centre

This upmarket food hall in the style of New York's Dean & Deluca falls short of that Manhattan holy grail but still offers an abundance of delectable edibles such as white truffles from Alba, 30-year-old balsamic vinegar and Wicklow organic veg. Downstairs, a marvellous wine cellar dispenses bottles for every occasion.

MAGILLS Map p70 — Food & Drink

☎ 671 3830; 14 Clarendon St; ⏱ 9.30am-5.45pm Mon-Sat; 🚇 all city centre

With its characterful old facade and tiny dark interior, Magills' old-world charm reminds you how Clarendon St must have once looked. At this family-run place, you get the distinct feeling that every Irish and French cheese, olive oil, packet of Italian pasta and salami was hand-picked.

SHERIDAN'S CHEESEMONGERS

Map p70 — Food & Drink

☎ 679 3143; www.sheridanscheesemongers.com; 11 South Anne St; ⏱ 10am-6pm Mon-Fri, from 9.30am Sat; 🚇 all city centre

If heaven were a cheese shop, this would be it. Wooden shelves are laden with rounds of farmhouse cheeses, sourced from around the country by Kevin and Seamus Sheridan, who have almost

---

HELEN JAMES, DESIGNER

Dublin-born designer Helen James, who cut her teeth cutting cloth for the likes of Donna Karan, Katayone Adeli and Club Monaco in New York, loves her boutiques, and Dublin has enough to satisfy.

'My favourite shops are Costume (p139), Smock (p140) and Bow Boutique (p139). They're great shops because they're imbued with the personality of their owners, who in turn make sure that the items they stock suit the shop and the customers who frequent them. As a shopper, you know that the boutique owner has you in mind when they go on buying trips', she says.

Her favourite Irish designers? Helen is quick to list them off: Leighlee, Eilis Boyle, Sphere One by Lucy Downes and Tim Ryan.

Outside the city centre, Helen rates Havana (p146) in Donnybrook as one of the best boutiques in Ireland and the place where you will find some of her favourite names in fashion.

single-handedly revived cheese-making in Ireland. You can taste any one of the 60 cheeses on display and pick up some wild Irish salmon, Italian pastas and olives while you're at it.

BLARNEY WOOLLEN MILLS
Map p70   Irish Crafts

☎ 671 0068; www.blarney.com; 27 Nassau St; ☽ 9am-6pm Mon-Sat, 11am-6pm Sun; ▣ all city centre

This is the Dublin branch of the best-known Irish shop in the country – the actual mills are located in County Cork, within sight of the famous castle and its gab-bestowing rock. This branch shouldn't disappoint, with a particularly wide range of cut crystal, porcelain presents and its trademark woolly things.

DESIGNYARD Map p70   Irish Crafts, Jewellery

☎ 474 1011; www.designyardgallery.com; 48-49 Nassau St; ☽ 9.30am-6.30pm Mon-Wed & Fri, to 8pm Thu, 9am-6.30pm Sat, 10am-6pm Sun; ▣ all city centre

A high-end, craft-as-art shop where everything you see – glass, batik, sculpture, painting – is one-off and handmade in Ireland. It also showcases contemporary jewellery stock from young international designers. Perfect for that bespoke engagement ring or a very special present.

H DANKER Map p70   Irish Crafts

☎ 677 4009; www.hdanker.com; 10 South Anne St; ☽ 9.30am-5pm Mon-Sat; ▣ all city centre

Chock-full of exquisite treasures, this shop specialises in Irish and English antique silver, jewellery and objets d'art. You can find period suites of antique cutlery, candlesticks and candelabra as well as unusual items like potato rings – dish rings to insulate tables from hot bowls.

HOUSE OF NAMES Map p70   Irish Crafts

☎ 679 7287; www.houseofnames.ie; 26 Nassau St; ☽ 10am-6pm Mon-Sat, to 8pm Thu, 11am-6pm Sun; ▣ all city centre

Impress your friends by serving them drinks on coasters emblazoned with your family's coat of arms, matching the sweatshirt you're wearing and, of course, the glasses or mugs your drinks are served in. All this and more can be yours from the House of Names, so long as you have a surname with Irish roots.

KNOBS & KNOCKERS
Map p70   Irish Crafts

☎ 671 0288; www.knobsandknockers.ie; 19 Nassau St; ☽ 10am-6pm Mon-Sat, to 8pm Thu, 11am-6pm Sun; ▣ all city centre

Replica Georgian door-knockers are highly recommended as a great souvenir of your Dublin visit, but there are plenty of other souvenir door adornments to look at here.

ANGLES Map p70   Jewellery

☎ 679 1964; Westbury Mall; ☽ 10am-6pm Mon-Sat, to 7pm Thu; ▣ all city centre

You won't find Claddagh rings or charm bracelets here, just cabinets full of handmade, contemporary Irish jewellery, most of it by up-and-coming Dublin craftspeople. Commissions are taken and can be sent on to you abroad.

APPLEBY Map p70   Jewellery

☎ 679 9572; 5-6 Johnson's Ct; ☽ 9.30am-5.30pm Mon-Sat, to 7pm Thu, to 6pm Sat; ▣ all city centre

The best known of the jewellery shops that line narrow Johnson's Court, Appleby is renowned for the high quality of its gold and silver jewellery, which tends towards more conventional designs. This is the place to shop for serious stuff – diamond rings, sapphire-encrusted cufflinks and Raymond Weil watches.

BARRY DOYLE DESIGN JEWELLERS
Map p70   Jewellery

☎ 671 2838; 30 George's St Arcade; ☽ 10am-6pm Mon-Sat, to 7pm Thu; ▣ all city centre

Goldsmith Barry Doyle's upstairs shop is one of the best of its kind in Dublin. The handmade jewellery – using white gold, silver, and some truly gorgeous precious and semiprecious stones – is exceptional in its beauty and simplicity. Most of the pieces have Afro-Celtic influences.

RHINESTONES Map p70   Jewellery

☎ 679 0759; 18 St Andrew's St; ☽ 9am-6.30pm Mon-Wed, Fri & Sat, to 8pm Thu, noon-6pm Sun; ▣ all city centre

Exceptionally fine antique and quirky costume jewellery from the 1920s to 1970s, with pieces priced from €25 to €2000. Victorian jet, 1950s enamel, art deco turquoise, 1930s mother-of-pearl, cut-glass and rhinestone necklaces, bracelets, brooches and rings are displayed by colour in old-fashioned cabinets.

WEIR & SON'S Map p70 — Jewellery

☎ 677 9678; www.weirandsons.ie; 96-99 Grafton St; ⊙ 9am-5.30pm Mon-Sat, to 8pm Thu; 🚌 all city centre

The largest jeweller in Ireland, this huge store on Grafton St first opened in 1869 and still has its original wooden cabinets and a workshop on the premises. There's new and antique Irish jewellery (including Celtic designs) and a huge selection of watches, Irish crystal, porcelain, leather and travel goods.

HMV Map p70 — Music

☎ 679 5334; www.hmv.com; 65 Grafton St; ⊙ 9am-7pm Mon-Wed & Sat, to 9pm Thu, to 8pm Fri, 11am-7pm Sun; 🚌 all city centre

This giant entertainment retailer's main Dublin branch stocks CDs, vinyl, DVDs, games and even books across its three floors. It's exactly what you'd expect from a huge music store.

ROAD RECORDS Map p70 — Music

☎ 671 7340; www.roadrecs.com; 16 Fade St; ⊙ 10am-6pm Mon-Sat, to 7pm Thu; 🚌 all city centre

This small record shop, a favourite with the indie music crowd, closed in 2009, seemingly another victim of the digital music industry. But then a concerted fundraiser by those same indie fans (and presumably their mates) saw the shop reopen and retake its place as the best spot for all the latest indie sounds.

WALTON'S Map p70 — Music

☎ 475 0661; 69-70 South Great George's St; ⊙ 9am-6pm Mon-Sat, to 7pm Thu; 🚌 all city centre

This is the place to go if you're looking for your very own *bodhrán* (goat-skin drum) or indeed any other musical instrument associated with Irish traditional music. It also has an excellent selection of sheet music and recorded music.

DUBLIN CAMERA EXCHANGE

Map p70 — Photography

☎ 478 4125; www.cameraexchange.ie; 63 South Great George's St; ⊙ 9am-6pm Mon-Sat, to 7pm Thu; 🚌 all city centre

This is one of the best photographic equipment shops in town and a reputable developer of prints. Staff are friendly and knowledgable, and will usually assist in

answering any camera-related query, even if the equipment is not bought here. It has a smaller branch (Map p70; ☎ 679 3410; 9B Trinity St) that also opens on Sunday from 1 to 5pm.

GEORGE'S ST ARCADE

Map p70 — Shopping Arcade

www.georgesstreetarcade.ie; btwn South Great George's St & Drury St; ⊙ 9am-6.30pm Mon-Sat, to 8pm Thu, noon-6pm Sun; 🚌 all city centre

Dublin's best nonfood market (there's sadly not much competition) is sheltered within an elegant Victorian Gothic arcade. Apart from shops and stalls selling new and old clothes, secondhand books, hats, posters, jewellery and records, there's a fortune teller, some gourmet nibbles and a fish and chipper who does a roaring trade.

WESTBURY MALL

Map p70 — Shopping Arcade

Clarendon St; ⊙ 10am-6pm Mon-Sat, noon-5pm Sun; 🚌 all city centre

Wedged between the five-star Westbury Hotel and the expensive jewellery stores of Johnson's Court, this small mall has a handful of pricey, specialist shops selling everything from Persian rugs to buttons and lace or tasteful children's wooden toys.

POWERSCOURT TOWNHOUSE SHOPPING CENTRE

Map p70 — Shopping Centre

☎ 679 4144; www.powerscourtcentre.com; 59 South William St; ⊙ 10am-6.30pm Mon-Sat, to 9pm Thu, noon-6pm Sun; 🚌 all city centre

This absolutely gorgeous and stylish centre is in a carefully refurbished Georgian townhouse, built between 1741 and 1744 (see p77). These days it's best known for its cafes and restaurants but it also does a top-end, selective trade in high fashion, art, exquisite handicrafts and other chichi sundries.

ST STEPHEN'S GREEN SHOPPING CENTRE Map p70 — Shopping Centre

☎ 478 0888; www.stephensgreen.com; King St South & St Stephen's Green; ⊙ 9am-6pm Mon-Sat, to 9pm Thu, noon-6pm Sun; 🚌 all city centre; 🚊 St Stephen's Green

A 1980s version of a 19th-century shopping arcade, the dramatic, balconied interior and central courtyard are a bit too grand for the nondescript chain stores within. There's a Boots, Benetton and large Dunnes Store with supermarket, though, as well as last-season designer warehouse TK Maxx.

HARLEQUIN
Map p70   Vintage Clothing & Accessories
☎ 671 0202; 13 Castle Market; ⏲ 10.30am-6pm Mon-Sat, to 7pm Thu; 🚇 all city centre
A fantastically cluttered shop, jam-packed with authentic vintage clothing gems from the 1920s onwards, as well as satin gloves, top hats, snakeskin bags and jet-beaded chokers.

JENNY VANDER
Map p70   Vintage Clothing & Accessories
☎ 677 0406; 50 Drury St; ⏲ 10am-5.45pm Mon-Sat; 🚇 all city centre
More *Breakfast at Tiffany's* chic than the cast-offs from *Hair*, this secondhand store oozes elegance and sophistication. Discerning fashionistas and film stylists snap up the exquisite beaded handbags, fur-trimmed coats, richly patterned dresses and costume jewellery priced as if it were the real thing.

TEMPLE BAR

Dublin's most touristy neighbourhood has a pretty diverse mix of shops. Apart from the usual crap you might expect to find in any tourist trap, Temple Bar's stores traditionally specialise in peddling secondhand clothing and flogging the weird and the (sometimes) wonderful; it's a place where you can get everything from a Celtic-design wall-hanging to a handcrafted bong. In recent years, however, the western end of the quarter has been developed and a number of new shops have opened up, mostly of the high-end luxury design kind, with prices to boot. A couple of Dublin's best markets take place in this area on Saturday (for more information see the boxed text, p145).

GUTTER BOOKSHOP Map p87   Books
☎ 679 9206; www.gutterbookshop.com; Cow's La; ⏲ 10am-6.30pm Mon-Wed & Fri & Sat, 10am-7pm Thu, 11-6pm Sun; 🚇 all city centre
Taking its name from Oscar Wilde's famous line from *Lady Windermere's Fan*, 'we are all in the gutter, but some of us are looking at the stars', this new bookshop is flying the flag for the downtrodden independent bookstore, stocking a mix of new novels, children's books, travel literature and other assorted titles.

CLOTHING SIZES

Women's clothing

Aus/UK	8	10	12	14	16	18
Europe	36	38	40	42	44	46
Japan	5	7	9	11	13	15
USA	6	8	10	12	14	16

Women's shoes

Aus/USA	5	6	7	8	9	10
Europe	35	36	37	38	39	40
France only	35	36	38	39	40	42
Japan	22	23	24	25	26	27
UK	3½	4½	5½	6½	7½	8½

Men's clothing

Aus	92	96	100	104	108	112
Europe	46	48	50	52	54	56
Japan	S		M	M		L
UK/USA	35	36	37	38	39	40

Men's shirts (collar sizes)

Aus/Japan	38	39	40	41	42	43
Europe	38	39	40	41	42	43
UK/USA	15	15½	16	16½	17	17½

Men's shoes

Aus/UK	7	8	9	10	11	12
Europe	41	42	43	44½	46	47
Japan	26	27	27½	28	29	30
USA	7½	8½	9½	10½	11½	12½

Measurements approximate only; try before you buy

URBAN OUTFITTERS
Map p87   Fashion, Music
☎ 670 6202; www.urbanoutfitters.com; 4 Cecilia St; 🚇 all city centre
With a blaring techno soundtrack, the only Irish branch of this American chain sells ridiculously cool clothes to discerning young buyers. Besides clothing, the shop stocks all kinds of interesting gadgets, accessories and furniture. On the 2nd floor you'll find a hypertrendy record shop (hence the techno).

CLADDAGH RECORDS
Map p87   Music
☎ 677 0262; www.claddaghrecords.com; 2 Cecilia St; 🚇 all city centre
An excellent collection of good-quality traditional and folk music is the mainstay at this centrally located record shop. The profoundly knowledgable staff should be able to locate even the most elusive recording for you.

THINGS YOU DIDN'T KNOW ABOUT DUBLIN

The world's first purpose-built department store was the Palatial Mart, which opened its doors to the public on Sackville St in 1853. The street has since changed its name to O'Connell St, while the department store is still going strong as Clery's & Co.

FLIP Map p87   Vintage Clothing & Accessories

☎ 671 4299; 4 Upper Fownes St; ⏱ 10am-6pm Mon-Wed & Fri, 10am-7pm Thu & Sat, 1.30-6pm Sun; 🚌 all city centre

This hip Irish label takes the best male fashion moods of the 1950s and serves them back to us, minus the mothball smell. US college shirts, logo T-shirts, Oriental and Hawaiian shirts, Fonz-style leather jackets and well-cut jeans mix it with the genuine secondhand gear upstairs.

KILMAINHAM & THE LIBERTIES

Some of the most interesting – and wacki-est – shopping is done along Francis St in the Liberties, the home of antiquarians and art dealers of every hue. Although you mightn't fancy transporting the hand luggage, you can have that original Edwardian fireplace you've always wanted, shipped to you by the shop.

FLEURY ANTIQUES Map p91   Antiques

☎ 473 0878; 57 Francis St; ⏱ 9.30am-6pm Mon-Sat; 🚌 123, 206 or 51B from city centre

This blue-fronted antiques shop does a steady connoisseur's trade in all manner of oil paintings (there's something for virtually every taste), vases, candelabras, silverware, porcelain and decorative pieces from the 18th century right up to the 1930s.

O'SULLIVAN ANTIQUES

Map p91   Antiques

☎ 454 1143; 43-44 Francis St; ⏱ 10am-5pm Mon-Sat; 🚌 123, 206 or 51B from city centre

Fine furniture and furnishings from the Georgian, Victorian and Edwardian eras are the speciality of this respected antiques shop, where a rummage might also reveal some distinctive bits of ceramic and crystal, not to mention medals and uniforms from a bygone era that will win you first prize at the costume ball.

OXFAM HOME Map p91   Antiques

☎ 402 0555; 86 Francis St; ⏱ 10am-5.30pm Mon-Fri, 10am-1pm Sat; 🚌 123, 206 or 51B from city centre

They say charity begins at home so get rummaging among the veneer cast-offs in this furniture branch of the charity chain where you might stumble across the odd 1960s Subbuteo table or art deco dresser. Esoteric vinyl from the '80s is another speciality of the house.

NORTH OF THE LIFFEY

With only a handful of exceptions, north-side shopping is all about the high-street chain store and the easy-access shopping centre, which is mighty convenient for Dubliners looking for everyday wear at decent prices, but will hardly make for a satisfying long-distance retail pilgrimage. But if you want to do as Dubliners do…

EASON'S Map p102   Books

☎ 873 3811; 40 Lower O'Connell St; 🚌 all city centre

The biggest selection of magazines and foreign newspapers in the whole country can be found on the ground floor of this huge bookshop near the GPO, along with literally dozens of browsers leafing through mags with ne'er a thought of purchasing one.

WINDING STAIR Map p102   Books

☎ 873 3292; 40 Lower Ormond Quay; ⏱ 9.30am-6pm Mon-Sat; 🚌 all city centre

There was a public outcry when this creaky old place closed a few years ago. It's just reopened its doors and Dublin's bohemians, students and literati can once more thumb the fine selection of new and secondhand books crammed into heaving bookcases. When you've had enough of browsing, head up the winding stairs to the excellent restaurant (p164).

ARNOTT'S Map p102   Department Store

☎ 805 0400; 12 Henry St; ⏱ 9am-6.30pm Mon-Sat, to 9pm Thu, noon-6pm Sun; 🚌 all city centre; 🚇 Jervis

Occupying a huge block with entrances on Henry, Liffey and Abbey Sts, this is our favourite of Dublin's department stores. It stocks virtually everything you could possibly want to buy, from garden furniture to high fashion, and it's all relatively affordable.

CLERY'S & CO Map p102   Department Store

☎ 878 6000; O'Connell St; ⏱ 9am-6.30pm Mon-Sat, to 9pm Thu, noon-6pm Sun; 🚇 all city centre
This elegant department store is Ireland's most famous retailer, and a real Dublin classic. Recently restored to its graceful best, Clery's has sought to shed its conservative reputation by filling its shelves with funkier labels to attract younger buyers.

DEBENHAMS Map p102   Department Store

☎ 873 0044; www.debenhams.com; 54-62 Henry St; ⏱ 9am-6.30pm Mon-Sat, to 9pm Thu, noon-6pm Sun; 🚇 all city centre

This UK giant hit these shores in 2006; bold and glass-fronted on the outside with street-smart fashion labels like Zara, Warehouse and G-Star inside, as well as the obligatory homewares and electrical sections.

PENNEY'S Map p102   Department Store

☎ 888 0500; www.primark.co.uk; 47 Mary St; 🚇 all city centre
Ireland's cheapest department store is a north-side favourite, a place to find all kinds of everything without paying a fortune for it – it's the best place in town for men's socks and jocks. True, the stuff you'll find here isn't guaranteed to last, but at prices like these, why quibble over quality?

DUBLIN MARKETS

In recent years Dublin has gone gaga for markets. Which is kind of ironic, considering that the city's traditional markets, like Moore St, were ignored by those same folks who now can't get enough of the homemade hummus on sale at the new gourmet spots. It's all so…continental.

Blackberry Fair (off Map p122; Lower Rathmines Rd; ⏱ 10am-5pm Sat & Sun) You'll have to rummage through a lot of junk to find a gem in this charmingly rundown weekend market, which stocks furniture, records and a few clothes stalls. It's cheap though.

Blackrock Market (off Map p122; Main St, Blackrock; ⏱ 11am-5.30pm Sat, 10am-5.30pm Sun; 🚆 Blackrock) The long-running Blackrock Market takes place in an old merchant house and yard in the seaside village, and has all manner of stalls selling everything from New Age crystals to futons.

Book Fair (Map p87; Temple Bar Sq; ⏱ 10am-5pm Sat) Bad, secondhand potboilers, sci-fi books, picture books and other assorted titles invite you to rummage about on Saturday afternoons. If you look hard enough, you're bound to find something worthwhile.

Cow's Lane Designer Mart (Map p87; ⏱ 10am-5.30pm Sat) A real market for hipsters, on the steps of Cow's Lane, this market brings together over 60 of the best clothing, accessory and craft stalls in town. Buy cutting-edge designer duds from the likes of Drunk Monk, punky T-shirts, retro handbags, costume jewellery by Kink Bijoux and even clubby babywear. It's open from June to September; the rest of the year it moves indoors to St Michael's and St John's Banquet Hall, just around the corner.

Meeting House Square Market (Map p87; Meeting House Sq; ⏱ 10am-5pm Sat) From sushi to salsa, this is the city's best open-air food market, a compact stroll through gourmet lane where you can pick, prod and poke your way through the organic foods of the world. There are tastes of everywhere, from cured Spanish chorizos and paellas to Irish farmhouses cheeses, via handmade chocolates and freshly made crêpes, homemade jams and freshly squeezed juices.

Moore Street Market (Map p102; Moore St; ⏱ 8am-4pm Mon-Sat) An open-air, steadfastly 'Old Dublin' market, with fruit, fish and flowers. Traditional vendors hawk cheap cigarettes, tobacco and chocolate among the new wave of Chinese and Nigerians selling phonecards and hair extensions. Don't try to buy just one banana though – if it says 10 for €1, that's what it is.

Toejam Carboot Sale (Map p68; Bernard Shaw, 11-12 South Richmond St; ⏱ 1-5pm, second Sat of every month; 🚇 14, 15, 65 or 83 from city centre) Vintage goodies, accessories, clothing and other unwanted sundries from the attic make their way onto the tables at this extremely popular monthly yard sale.

WALTON'S Map p102   Music

☎ 874 7805; 2 North Frederick St; ☒ 36 or 36A from city centre

This is the main branch of the well-known Walton's music stores (p142).

CLARK'S Map p102   Shoes

☎ 872 1841; www.clarks.com; 25 Henry St; ☒ all city centre

This well-known shoe store stocks not only its own brand but others too; it also has an excellent selection of Birkenstocks. The branch (Map p102; ☎ 872 7665; 43 O'Connell St) on O'Connell St stocks women's shoes only.

SCHUH Map p102   Shoes

☎ 873 0621; www.schuh.ie; 10 O'Connell St; ☒ all city centre

Two floors of footwear, from trainers to formal shoes, and pretty much everything in between. The labels represented here are of the high-street variety, so don't expect Manolo or Gucci.

JERVIS CENTRE Map p102   Shopping Centre

☎ 878 1323; Jervis St; ⏱ 9am-6pm Mon-Sat, to 9pm Thu, noon-6pm Sun; ☒ all city centre; ☒ Jervis

This ultramodern, domed mall is a veritable shrine to the British chain store. Boots, Topshop, Debenhams, Argos, Dixons, M&S and Miss Selfridge all get a look-in.

DOCKLANDS

Isn't there enough shopping for you around Grafton St? For a long time the Docklands development crowd didn't think so and imagined a new shopping oasis by the banks of the Liffey. Things didn't *quite* go as planned and the Docklands remains largely bereft of the kind of retail distractions envisaged, with one notable exception.

TOWER CRAFT DESIGN CENTRE
Map p115   Irish Crafts

☎ 677 5655; Pearse St; ⏱ 9.30am-6pm Mon-Sat, to 8pm Thu; ☒ all city centre

Housed in a 19th-century warehouse that was Dublin's first iron-structured building, this design centre has studios for local craftspeople. They produce jewellery in both contemporary and Celtic-inspired designs, and work with Irish pewter, ceramics, silk and other fabrics. Besides jewellery they knock out pottery, rugs, wall hangings, cards, leather bags and various other handcrafted items. It's immediately opposite the Waterways Visitors Centre, off Lower Grand Canal St.

BEYOND THE GRAND CANAL

Every suburban village has its own little shopping centre, but only one can rule them all... Apart from Dundrum, there's also one of the city's best fashion boutiques.

HAVANA Off Map p122   Fashion & Designer

☎ 260 2707; 2 Anglesea House, 68 Donnybrook Rd; ⏱ 10am-5.30pm Mon-Fri, 10am-1pm Sat; ☒ 10 or 46X from city centre

This is as exclusive as Dublin fashion boutiques get, but the rewards for a trek out here are the best of Irish design – Lucy Downe's Sphere One cashmeres, Joanne

---

MUSEUM SHOPS

Most museums have a basic gift shop, but you'll find a few in Dublin that offer more than the usual baubles and trinkets, including the following.

Chester Beatty Library (p72) A wonderful little gift shop, with postcards, books, posters and other memorabilia of this extraordinary museum.

Dublin City Gallery – The Hugh Lane Shop (p104) A cultural playground for adults, where you can dig out cubist fridge magnets, huge po-mo hanging mobiles, masterpiece colour-by-number prints, cloth puppets, unusual wooden toys and beautiful art and pop culture hardbacks.

Irish Museum of Modern Art (p98) Offers a comprehensive selection of coffee-table books on Irish contemporary art.

National Gallery (p82) Sells books covering the whole history of Irish and European art.

Trinity Library Shop (Map p67; East Pavilion, Library Colonnades, Trinity College) The big sellers are the titles on the *Book of Kells*, but you can also get all kinds of other mementoes and curios.

Hynes' elegant evening wear – as well as a host of other top international names. Shoes, jewellery and accessories fill out the rest of the stock.

DUNDRUM TOWN CENTRE
Off Map p122   Shopping Centre
☎ 299 1700; www.dundrum.ie; Sandyford Rd, Dundrum; ⏱ 9am-9pm Mon-Fri, to 7pm Sat, 10am-7pm Sun; 🚌 17, 44C, 48A or 75 from city centre; 🚊 Dundrum or Ballaly

Europe's largest shopping and entertainment centre is either globalisation's hideous hydra or the greatest thing to happen to retail since the invention of money. There are over 100 retail outlets, including every imaginable high-street shop, cinemas, restaurants and bars and even a crèche so that you can keep the tiny 'uns amused while you load up on gear. A whole generation of Dubliners will grow up in its enormous shadow, the first true Dublin mall rats.

EATING

top picks

- **Chapter One** (p164)
- **Coppinger Row** (p156)
- **Dunne & Crescenzi** (p156)
- **Good World** (p156)
- **Juniors** (p167)
- **L'Gueuleton** (p155)
- **Larder** (p163)
- **Restaurant Patrick Guilbaud** (p160)
- **Silk Road Café** (p157)

EATING

Of all of the transformations brought on by prosperity, none has been so dramatic, so downright *revolutionary,* as how Dubliners deal with grub. Gone are the days when food was nothing more than a biological necessity to be endured: today, the city is brimming with self-appointed gourmands who know their tagines from their terrines. Food – how it's eaten, where it's eaten, even how it's talked about – has been the drug of choice for many Dubliners over the last decade; for them you aren't so much *what* you eat as much as *where* you eat.

And where is pretty much everywhere. The city is awash with all kinds of eateries for almost every taste and nearly every budget, each vying for a clientele no longer willing to accept shoe leather for steak or boiled-to-death vegetables – the shadows of Dublin's culinary past, where to complain would be unseemly and ungrateful. Now everyone's a food critic, and this once dormant dining town has become a culinary bear pit where restaurateurs paying exorbitant rents are in a perpetual dogfight for the patronage of a clientele that no longer feels awkwardly grateful crossing the hearth of the latest themed epicurean fantasy.

Staying in business was tough enough until late 2008, but since the crash it's been near improbable, especially for those restaurants toward the upper end of the scale. Within a year, several of the city's best-known restaurants had closed, with many others facing an uncertain future: some of the ones we've listed below may well have gone by the time you visit; we've endeavoured to include only those that stand a better-than-even shot of making it through these difficult times.

But it's not all bad news, for diners at least. Restaurateurs have rolled their sleeves up and have re-imagined their menus to suit the shrinking budgets of their punters. Prices have come down, but the real difference is in the menu itself, with lots of enticing recession-buster specials now available to ensure that you will keep coming back – which is why we've noticed the dramatic return of the wholesome, filling and generally affordable burger to menus that a couple of years ago wouldn't deign to descend to such unimaginative lows.

SPECIALITIES

Although many old Dublin staples have been consigned to the scrapheap of culinary history, some have earned their longevity while others are kept around for the sake of the tourists.

Perhaps the most feared Irish speciality is the fry – the heart attack on a plate that is the second part of so many B&B deals. It's really three meals in one – who can say no to a plate of fried bacon, sausages, black pudding, white pudding, eggs and tomatoes, washed down with lots of tea or coffee and usually accompanied by a basket of toast? But hysterical health fears have seen the fry disappear from the menus of most Dubliners and, with only a handful of exceptions, your best chance of a fry is in the hotel breakfast room.

The most Dublin of dishes is coddle, a working-class concoction of rashers, sausages, onions, potato and plenty of black pepper. Another specific to the capital is gurr cake, which 19th-century bakers made out of stale bread and cakes mixed with candied peel and dried mixed fruit. Because it was very cheap, it became popular with street urchins 'on the gurr'

from school. The term 'gurrier' entered the Dublin dialect to describe rough tearaways. Bacon and cabbage – once the epitome of bad, flavourless Irish cooking – is making a comeback, but its rich and delicious reincarnation proves that there was never anything wrong with the produce, just the person boiling it to death.

The most famous Irish bread, and one of the signature tastes of Ireland, is soda bread. Irish flour is soft and doesn't take well to yeast as a raising agent, so Irish bakers of the 19th century leavened their bread with bicarbonate of soda. Combined with buttermilk, it makes a superbly light-textured and tasty bread, and is often on the breakfast menus at B&Bs.

Scones, tarts and biscuits are specialities too. Barm brack (from the Irish for 'speckled bread') is a spicy, fruity cake long associated with Halloween. Various charms are traditionally baked in the brack, and the one you get decides your destiny for the following year. Discover the ring and you'll get married, while into the penny and you'll be wealthy (which is some consolation for the cracked tooth); the pea denotes impending poverty while a little stick cheerfully prophesises domestic violence.

Soda bread is a wonderful platform for smoked salmon, and you should take every opportunity to sample the fruits of the Irish seas, be it on a platter or wrapped in batter from a traditional chipper. Of course, you should also sample the cockles and mussels that Molly Malone made famous, oysters from the west coast, and Dublin Bay prawns – which are actually local lobsters and taste superlative at their best. If you get a chance, be sure to down a Dublin lawyer. Before you go getting yourself into trouble, this is a lobster dish cooked with whiskey and cream.

Better known as the national edible icon, Irish stew, the slow-simmered one-pot wonder of lamb, potatoes, onions, parsley and thyme (note, no carrots). In summer look out for mountain lamb from Connemara or Kerry.

Savour the dairy produce, which is some of the best you'll taste anywhere (all that rain's got to be good for something); the butter is deliciously rich and the thick and luscious cream is a joy to behold. The resurgence of cheese-making has been one of the most exciting culinary developments of recent years and Irish farmhouse cheeses win many international awards and plaudits.

WHERE TO EAT

The epicentre of decent dining is on the south side of the city centre, where the vast majority of Dublin's best and most popular eateries sit cheek by jowl. The most concentrated restaurant area is Temple Bar, but except for a handful of places the bulk of eateries offer bland, unimaginative fodder and cheap set menus for tourists. Merrion Row, St Stephen's Green and the swathe of streets west of Grafton St have plenty of options, but prohibitively high rents round these parts have forced restaurateurs to serve their specialities a little further afield, including south along the Grand Canal and east towards Grand Canal Dock.

The same pecuniary logic has forced a re-evaluation of the north side as a gourmet hotspot. Besides the plethora of greasy diners, crappy fast-food outlets and a few grand dames that have been part of the scene for decades, the north side has seen the arrival of some pretty fancy restaurants and – most excitingly – a whole new world of genuinely ethnic cuisines, from Chinese to Polish, especially

along Parnell St, which runs a perpendicular line off the northern end of O'Connell St, and Capel St, which runs parallel to O'Connell St. There are some excellent restaurants in the northern seaside suburbs of Malahide and Howth; see p227 for more.

If you're really lucky – or just smile and make nice with the right people – you'll get the chance to share a home-cooked meal, which remains the best way to cut right to the heart of this unique culture. Irish cuisine isn't just about sampling sensational seafood, fine farmhouse cheeses and mountain-bred lamb, it's defined by the warmth and conviviality around the dinner table, the chat over a cup of tea and the sizzle of the traditional Sunday roast.

PRACTICALITIES
Opening Hours

Dubliners follow a fairly rigid fuelling schedule; they like to eat their evening meal early, generally between 7pm and 9.30pm, while lunch goes down between 1pm and 2pm. Cafes are open 8.30am to 6.30pm Monday to Saturday, and 10am to 6pm Sunday. Most restaurants are open Monday to Saturday for lunch between noon and 3pm, and dinner from 5.30pm until 10.30pm, although many midrange restaurants stay open throughout the day. Top-end joints are more likely to close for Saturday lunch. Throughout these listings you can presume every place is open daily, unless otherwise specified. While we've noted where places stray from the standard, if you're going out of your way to get to a particular place it's always safest to telephone ahead.

How Much?

It's a frustrating cliché at this stage, but food is bloody expensive in Dublin and, until recently, value for money was as rare as hen's teeth. Enter the economic collapse, and restaurants all over town have started offering all kinds of lunch deals, fixed-price menus and other incentives to keep the punters coming in and the liquidator out. You can eat surprisingly well for around €15 or less – especially at lunchtime. For more memorable experiences in the city's more salubrious eateries, a main course will cost anything between €18 and €40, although at the top end of the scale you'll probably be eating in a place given a thumbs-up by Monsieur Michelin. And while most restaurants are attracting diners by lowering their food prices, the better establishments are making up the shortfall on their wine lists, which have proved resilient in the face of cuts: even a mediocre wine will cost you the guts of €20, while a known vintage will go for twice that.

In these pages, we've given you an even spread of the city's eateries, from the choicest cheap to choosiest chic – scan them well before you go out.

Booking Tables

Reserving a table has become just about compulsory for most of the city's restaurants from Thursday to Saturday, and for the hippest ones all week. Many of the latter have also gone for the multiple-sittings system, which means 'yes, we have a table for you at 7pm but could you please vacate by 9pm?'. In response, some places have snubbed the reservations system entirely in favour of the (equally annoying) get-on-the-list, get-in-line policy that usually encourages a pre-dinner drink in a nearby pub.

Tipping

It's industry standard these days to tip between 10% and 12% of the bill, unless the waiter has dumped the dinner in your lap and given you the finger, while the gratuity for exceptional service is only limited by your generosity and/or level of inebriation. If you're really unhappy don't be afraid to leave absolutely nothing, though it will very rarely come to that.

The rule of thumb is simple: the classier the restaurant, the classier the service, but even at midrange and basic places you will be treated with courtesy and attention. Dubliners are not especially obsequious and generally eschew the kind of I'm-your-slave-for-the-evening take on serving tables, but that doesn't mean that you won't get quality service with politeness and a smile. The real treat among Dublin waitstaff is a bit of personality – they might be serving your table but they're not afraid to have a laugh and share a joke.

Self-Catering

Dubliners' new taste for food extends to cooking and market shopping, and a number of artisan street markets have opened up in recent years. If you're keen to self-cater – or just to take advantage of a sunny afternoon and an empty park – the most famous and authentic market is on Moore St, where the colour of the produce is matched by the language of the dentally challenged spruikers – but in recent years some excellent organic produce markets have opened up (see boxed text, p154). The more discerning shopper should head south of the river where there are a few terrific delis, cheesemongers and bakeries.

GRAFTON STREET & AROUND

There's no doubt about it: south of the Liffey is where all the eating action is…well mostly anyway. It is impossible to walk 10 paces south of the river without coming across a menu in a window. The diversity of eating options will satisfy most palates and the wide variety in taste is matched by a range in prices, from good and groovy cheap eats to world-class cuisine.

THORNTON'S Map p70   French, Irish €€€
☎ 478 7015; www.thorntonsrestaurant.com; Fitzwilliam Hotel, West St Stephen's Green; 3-course set lunch €49, dinner menu €79; 🕑 Tue-Sat; 🚍 all city centre; 🚇 St Stephen's Green

Kevin Thornton shrugged his shoulders when Michelin saw fit to strip him of one of his two stars, and replied by ordering a refurb of his ubertrendy room on the 1st floor of the Fitzwilliam Hotel, which overlooks St Stephen's Green. The food – a mouthwatering Irish interpretation of new French cuisine – remains as good as ever, offering a mix of succulent seafood and gamey dishes like roast woodcock. A nice touch is Kevin himself making a round of the tables, to answer questions and explain dishes.

SHANAHAN'S ON THE GREEN
Map p68   American €€€
☎ 407 0939; www.shanahans.ie; 119 West St Stephen's Green; steaks €40-52; 🕑 from 6pm Mon-Thu & Sat & Sun, from noon Fri; 🚍 all city centre; 🚇 St Stephen's Green

'American-style steakhouse' hardly does justice to this elegant restaurant where JR Ewing and his cronies would happily have done business. Spread across three floors of a stunning Georgian building are four elegant dining areas, where impeccable service and a courteous bonhomie attract the great, the good and the not-so-good to its well-laid-out tables. Although the menu features seafood, this place is all about meat, notably the best cuts of impossibly juicy and tender Irish Angus beef you'll find anywhere on the island. The mountainous onion rings are the perfect accompaniment, while the sommeliers are among the best in the business.

MARCO PIERRE WHITE STEAKHOUSE & GRILL Map p70   Steakhouse €€-€€€
☎ 677 1155; www.marcopierrewhite.ie; 51 Dawson St; mains €19-32; ☺ noon-11pm; 🚌 all city centre
The long-established Fitzer's restaurant group scored quite a coup when they enlisted bad-boy chef Marco Pierre White (he who once made Gordon Ramsay cry) to lend his name to their newest venture, which opened in 2009. Steaks, grilled meats and chunks of fish are the fare, presented with minimal fuss but with plenty of taste. There are some nice surprises, like the rib-eye, garnished with snails on the side.

TOWN BAR & GRILL
Map p70   Modern European €€-€€€
☎ 662 4724; www.townbarandgrill.com; 21 Kildare St; mains €22-29; ☺ closed lunch Sun; 🚌 all city centre
One of our favourite restaurants in town, with its clientele of affluent and influential people, came within a hair's breadth of closing in 2010 due to the credit crunch, but it was rescued by one of its regulars. Thank goodness for that – otherwise we'd no longer be able to treat ourselves to the simply mouth-watering food, which ranges from basics like lamb liver to slow-roasted rabbit or sweet-pepper-stuffed lamb.

BALZAC Map p70   French €€-€€€
☎ 677 8611; www.lastampa.ie; 35 Dawson St; mains €18-30; ☺ 6-11pm; 🚌 all city centre
It's official: one of the best chefs in Ireland

is Paul Flynn, who made his name with the simply stunning Tannery in Dungarvan, County Waterford. His first Dublin venture will only serve to cement his growing reputation. The elegant old-world dining room is a fitting setting for the superb cuisine on offer; how about oysters mignonette followed by champagne and truffle risotto?

TROCADERO Map p70   International €€-€€€
☎ 677 5545; www.trocadero.ie; 3 St Andrew's St; mains €18-28; ☺ dinner Mon-Sat; 🚌 all city centre
What the Troc may have lost in dynamism it more than makes up for in character – much like the ageing actors who still frequent the place. This art deco classic has been around for so long that you would never come here for the food – nothing too exciting, just a bunch of classics solidly made – but you'd stay for the atmosphere, which rarely disappoints. Here's a good game to play: match the faces of the better-known diners to their picture on the walls.

TIGER BECS Map p70   Thai €€-€€€
☎ 677 8677; www.lastampa.ie; 35 Dawson St; mains €18-28; ☺ dinner Mon-Sat, plus lunch Mon-Sat Dec only; 🚌 all city centre
Below SamSara (p174), this long and cavernous restaurant serves high-end Thai nosh to Dublin's beautiful young things. The lamb massaman, a mild curry from southern Thailand, is a popular choice on a menu that sparkles but doesn't often shine. You'll probably feel you're paying a little too much for the sense of style, but nevertheless this loud, buzzing venue has oodles of atmosphere and is a great place to launch yourself into a night on the razzle.

FALLON & BYRNE
Map p70   Modern European €-€€€
☎ 472 1000; www.fallonandbyrne.com; 11-17 Exchequer St; deli mains €6-9, brasserie mains €18-27; ☺ deli 9am-8pm Mon-Sat, 11am-6pm Sun, brasserie noon-4.30pm & 6.30-10.30pm Mon-Wed, to 11.30pm Thu-Sat, 11am-4pm Sun; 🚌 all city centre
Dublin's very own Dean and Deluca–style upmarket food hall (see p140), wine cellar

ORGANIC & FARMERS MARKETS

Dublin Food Co-op (Map p91; ☎ 454 4258; www.dublinfoodcoop.com; 12 Newmarket; ⌚ 2-8pm Thu, 9.30am-4.30pm Sat) A buzzing community market specialising in organic veg, homemade cheeses and organic wines; there's also a baker and even baby-changing facilities.

Coppinger Row Market (Map p70; Coppinger Row; ⌚ 9am-7pm Thu) It's small – only a handful of stalls – but it packs a proper organic punch, attracting punters with the waft of freshly baked breads, delicious hummus and other goodies.

Harcourt Street Food Market (Map p68; Park Pl, Station Bldgs, Upper Hatch St; ⌚ 10am-4pm Thu) Organic vegies, cheeses, olives and meats made into dishes from all over the world.

People's Park Market (off Map p122; ☎ 087 957 3647; People's Park, Dun Laoghaire; ⌚ 11am-4pm Sun) Organic meat and veg, local seafood, Irish fruit and farm cheeses are the mainstay at this popular market in the south Dublin suburb of Dun Laoghaire. Grab a burger and sit on the lawn.

For more info on local markets, check out www.irishfarmersmarkets.ie, www.irishvillagemarkets.com or local county council sites such as www.dlrcoco.ie/markets.

and restaurant has been an absolute smash hit since it opened in 2006. The queues for the delicious deli counter are constant (which is partly due to the often inefficient staff), while the chic buzzy brasserie upstairs – with long red banquettes, a diverse menu of creamy fish pie, beef carpaccio or roast turbot and excellent service – hasn't failed to impress either.

PICHET Map p70   French, Irish €€
☎ 677 1060; www.pichet-restaurant.com; 14-15 Trinity St; mains €16-26; ⌚ lunch & dinner; 🚌 all city centre
It's not the most obvious spot to open a fancy new restaurant, but that didn't stop Nick Munier, made famous on the English TV show *Hell's Kitchen,* and Stephen Gibson, formerly of L'Ecrivain (p160), who've brought their version of modern French cuisine to this elongated dining room replete with blue leather chairs and lots of windows to stare out of. The result is pretty good indeed, the food excellent– we expected nothing less – and the service impeccable. Sit down the back – the atmosphere is better.

YAMAMORI Map p70   Japanese €€
☎ 475 5001; www.yamamorinoodles.ie; 71-72 South Great George's St; sushi €3-3.50, mains €16-25; ⌚ closed lunch Sun; 🚌 all city centre
Hip, inexpensive and generally pretty good, Yamamori rarely disappoints with its bubbly service and vivacious cooking that swoops from sushi and sashimi to whopping great plates of noodles, with plenty

in between. It's a great spot for a sociable group – including vegetarians – although you'll have to book at the weekend to be one of the happy campers. The lunch bento (€9.95) is one of the best deals in town. There's another branch north of the river (p164).

ODESSA Map p70   Mediterranean €-€€
☎ 670 7634; www.odessa.ie; 13 Dame Ct; mains €13-26; ⌚ 11.30am-4.30pm Sat & Sun, 6pm-late daily; 🚌 all city centre
Odessa and the hangover brunch go hand in hand like Laurel and Hardy. But this stylish eatery's dining credentials have long been maintained by its excellent dinner menu, which combines solid favourites like the homemade burger with more adventurous dishes like roast fillet of hake served with chorizo, clams, white bean stew and serrano ham. Although it's been around for more than a decade, the loungy atmosphere with comfy sofas and retro standard lamps have kept it a perennial fave with the cool crowd.

SEAGRASS Map p68   Mediterranean €-€€
☎ 478 9595; 30 South Richmond St; mains €15-22; ⌚ dinner; 🚌 14, 15, 65 or 83 from city centre
Utterly unassuming from the outside, this is one of Dublin's best new openings of the last couple of years: the locally sourced, roughly Mediterranean menu (baked seafood penne, pan-fried lamb livers and a bacon and cabbage risotto are typical) is uniformly excellent, the dining room is quietly elegant and the service absolutely perfect.

EATING GRAFTON STREET & AROUND

JAIPUR Map p70   Indian €€
☎ 677 0999; www.jaipur.ie; 41 South Great George's St; mains €19-23; ☒ all city centre
A stylish and contemporary room sets the scene for some of the best Indian cuisine in town. Critics rave about the subtle and varied flavours produced by Jaipur's kitchen, which is down to its refusal to skimp on even the smallest dash of spice; what you get here is as close to the real deal as you'll get anywhere outside India.

CEDAR TREE Map p70   Lebanese €€
☎ 677 2121; 11a St Andrew's St; mains €17-20; ☽ to midnight; ☒ all city centre
An old stalwart of Dublin's restaurant scene, this marvellously low-key Lebanese eatery is still a top spot to while away an evening in the company of friends, delicious meze (such as falafel, spicy sausage, dips), meatballs, kofta and several bottles of red wine. The service here is warm and personable.

L'GUEULETON Map p70   French €-€€
☎ 675 3708; 1 Fade St; mains €12-25; ☽ to 11pm; ☒ all city centre
Dubliners have a devil of a time pronouncing the name (which means 'a gluttonous feast' in French) and have had their patience tested with the no-reservations-get-in-line-and-wait policy, but they just can't get enough of this restaurant's robust take on French rustic cuisine that makes twisted tongues and sore feet a small price to pay. The steak is sensational, but the Toulouse sausages with *choucroute* and Lyonnaise potatoes is proof that when it comes to the pleasures of the palate, the French really know what they're doing.

EL BAHIA Map p70   Moroccan €€
☎ 677 0213; www.elbahia.com; 1st fl, 37 Wicklow St; mains €14-20; ☽ closed lunch Sun; ☒ all city centre
Dark and sultry, Ireland's only Moroccan restaurant looks a little like how we imagine a desert harem might be. Or maybe we just got carried away with the Moroccan sounds and smells. There are some rather fetching geometric designs on the ceilings and walls, and the gimme-gimme food includes the likes of tasty tagines (stews), couscous and *bastile* (pastry stuffed with chicken), while the sweet-and-spicy Moroccan coffee is an unusual treat.

SABA Map p70   Asian €-€€€
☎ 679 2000; www.sabadublin.com; 26-28 Clarendon St; mains €12-23; ☽ to 11.30pm; ☒ all city centre
The name means 'happy meeting place' and so far this Thai-Vietnamese fusion restaurant has proven to be just that, packed virtually every night with all sorts tucking into the extensive Southeast Asian menu amid the kind of contemporary decor that screams designer cool. We thought both the menu and the look were good without being exceptional, but it's really popular, so what the hell do we know?

IMPERIAL CHINESE RESTAURANT
Map p70   Chinese €-€€
☎ 677 2580; 12a Wicklow St; lunch from €4, mains €12-20; ☽ noon-midnight; ☒ all city centre
This long-established restaurant is a favourite with the Chinese community and is noted for its lunchtime dim sum and its we-don't-smile-but-we're-efficient service. If you're looking for some genuine Chinese dishes in an authentic atmosphere, there's no better time to go than Sunday, when the Imperial serves brunch Chinese-style in what is known as yum cha, or 'drink tea', the traditional accompaniment to dim sum.

SIXTY6 Map p70   International €-€€
☎ 400 5878; www.brasseriesixty6.com; 66 South Great George's St; mains €12-20; ☽ 8am-11.30pm Mon-Sat, from 11am Sun; ☒ all city centre
This swanky New York–style brasserie is one of the most popular party-dinner spots in town – the kind of place at which you'd want to celebrate your birthday with friends. It does a mean rotisserie chicken, four different ways at any given time. Besides its signature dish, the meat-heavy menu features things like lamb shank and a particularly good bit of liver. For that special occasion, there's a whole roast pig, but you need to order seven days in advance and be in a group of eight.

CHEZ MAX Map p68   French €-€€
☎ 633 7215; 1 Palace St; mains €13-19; ☽ from 7.30am; ☒ 50, 54, 56A, 77 or 77A
Guarding the main gate to Dublin Castle is a French cafe that is Gallic through and through, from the fixtures imported from gay Paree to the beautiful, sultry staff who ignore you until they're ready and then turn the sexy pout into a killer smile. The

lunchtime *tartines* – basically open sand-wiches – are good enough to get us misty-eyed for Montmartre. They've recently opened a sister restaurant on Baggot St (see p161).

CAFÉ MAO Map p68 Vietnamese, Thai €-€€
☎ 670 4899; www.cafemao.com; 2-3 Chatham Row; mains €12-19; ⏱ to 10.30pm; 🚌 all city centre

Mao's often spicy mix of Vietnamese and Thai specialities, cooked to order and served with a musical soundtrack that declares its super-cool credentials, is one of the city's most successful restaurants. You can feast on the likes of nasi goreng and *bulkoko* here or at its other spots in the Dundrum Town Centre (☎ 296 2802; The Mill Pond) and Dun Laoghaire (☎ 214 8090; The Pavilion Seafront).

LA MAISON Map p70 French €€
☎ 672 7258; www.lamaisonrestaurant.ie; 15 Castle Market; mains €15-18; ⏱ Mon-Sat; 🚌 all city centre

Fans of Olivier Quenet's cafe and ground-floor *boulangerie* were a little put out when he gutted the lot in 2009 and turned it into this chic little restaurant spread over two floors. The menu is all about French classics done just right: sea bass with fennel ratatouille, shin of Irish beef pot-au-feu and *andouillette* sausage with wholegrain mustard and Lyonnaise potatoes are timely reminders that *la cuisine française* is still as great as ever.

DUNNE & CRESCENZI
Map p70 Italian €-€€
☎ 677 3815; www.dunneandcrescenzi.com; 14-16 South Frederick St; mains €9-20; ⏱ Mon-Sat; 🚌 all city centre

This exceptional Italian eatery delights its regulars with a basic menu of rustic pleasures, such as *panini*, a single pasta dish and a superb plate of mixed antipasto drizzled in olive oil. It's always full, and the tables are just that little bit too close to one another, but the coffee is perfect and the desserts are sinfully good.

COPPINGER ROW Map p70 Mediterranean €€
☎ 672 9884; www.coppingerrow.com; Coppinger Row; mains €12-17; ⏱ all city centre; 🚌 all city centre

The South William boys (see p175) have applied their criteria of cool to this new eatery just around the corner from their bar and come up trumps – chefs Troy Maguire (ex-L'Gueuleton and Locks) and Billy Scurry (ex-Gruel) have combined to create a tasty, unfussy menu of Mediterranean treats, to be enjoyed as main courses or as bar bites. We like the roast guinea fowl with borlotti beans but will settle for the meatball linguini.

LENNOX CAFE BISTRO
Map p68 Modern Irish €-€€
☎ 478 9966; 31 Lennox St; mains €9-15; ⏱ to 5pm; 🚌 14, 15, 65 or 83

Tucked away in the warren of handsome streets that make up Portobello, Huibrecht and Sally Ann Luykx's relatively new restaurant has garnered loyal customers for its fine Irish cuisine (try the smoked haddock with creamed potatoes) and its leisurely atmosphere – perfect for a long, wine-fuelled lunch. There were plans to open up the 2nd floor, which would be most welcome as it can get a little cramped.

CHILLI CLUB Map p70 Thai €-€€
☎ 677 3721; 1 Anne's Lane; mains €13-19; ⏱ lunch & dinner; 🚌 all city centre

Cosy, comfy and a million miles from the hubbub of modern Dublin – well, a block – this is one of the longest-serving Thai restaurants in town. It has built its reputation on unfailingly good – and unremittingly hot – curries, satays and soupy broths served in a slightly cramped but stylish room. A great choice for a quiet first date!

GOOD WORLD Map p70 Chinese €-€€
☎ 677 5373; 18 South Great George's St; mains €11-18; ⏱ to 3am; 🚌 all city centre

A hands-down winner of our best-Chinese-restaurant competition, the Good World has two menus, but to really get the most of this terrific spot, steer well clear of the Western menu and its unimaginative dishes. With listings in two languages, the Chinese menu is literally packed with dishes and delicacies that keep us coming back for more.

WAGAMAMA Map p70
Japanese €-€€

☎ 478 2152; www.wagamama.ie; South King St; mains €11-18; ☽ lunch & dinner; 🚌 all city centre
There's ne'er a trace of raw fish to be seen, but this popular chain dishes up some terrific Japanese food nonetheless. Production-line rice and noodle dishes served pronto at canteen-style tables mightn't seem like the most inviting way to dine, but boy this food is good, and the basement it's served up in is surprisingly light and airy – for a place with absolutely no natural light.

JUICE Map p70
Vegetarian €-€€

☎ 475 7856; www.juicerestaurant.ie; Castle House, 73 South Great George's St; smoothies €3.75-6.50, mains €11-16; ☽ 11am-11pm; 🚌 all city centre
Lighten up, folks, it's just food! If the staff at this trendy, self-conscious vegetarian restaurant lost some of their attitude and smiled occasionally, we might actually forget the cool-out and focus on the terrific Pacific Rim–style cuisine, as well as tasty stir-fries, soups, wraps, soya desserts, organic wines and delicious fresh juices and smoothies. Isn't yoga supposed to be *relaxing*?

GREEN HEN Map p70
French €-€€

☎ 670 7238; 33 Exchequer St; lunch mains €11-15, dinner mains €16-25; ☽ lunch & dinner Mon-Fri, brunch & dinner Sat & Sun; 🚌 all city centre
Borrowing a page out of New York's book of how to successfully re-imagine the French brasserie, the Green Hen is Dublin's version of a buzzing, stylish Soho eatery. Elegance and economy live side-by-side here, so if you don't fancy gorging on oysters or tucking into a divine Irish Hereford rib-eye, you can opt for the *plat du jour* or avail of the early-bird menus; watch out for their killer cocktails.

AVOCA Map p70
Cafe €

☎ 677 4215; www.avoca.ie; 11-13 Suffolk St; mains €11-14; ☽ breakfast & lunch; 🚌 all city centre

The waiters are easy on the eye for a reason: the upstairs cafe of the city's best designer crafts store has long been the favourite spot of the Ladies Who Lunch. Designer bags can get very heavy, so there's nothing better to restore flagging energy than the simple, rustic delights on offer: organic shepherd's pie, roast lamb with couscous, or sumptuous salads from the Avoca kitchen. There's also a takeaway salad bar and hot-food counter in the basement. For more information on the handicrafts, see p138.

CAFÉ BARDELI Map p70
Italian €

☎ 672 7720; www.cafebardeli.ie; Bewley's Bldg, Grafton St; mains €10-14; ☽ breakfast, lunch & dinner; 🚌 all city centre
With two branches in the south city centre, the folks behind Café Bardeli have created a winning formula: great crispy pizzas with imaginative toppings such as spicy lamb and tzatziki, fresh homemade pastas or salads like broccoli, feta and chickpea, all served within the stylish environs of what were once branches of Dublin's most beloved cafe, Bewley's. No reservations allowed, so prepare to wait on a busy night. There's a second city branch (Map p70; ☎ 677 1646; 12-13 South Great George's St; ☽ lunch & dinner; 🚌 all city centre) and another in Ranelagh (see p167).

THE PIG'S EAR Map p70
Modern Irish €€€

☎ 670 3865; www.thepigsear.ie; 4-5 Nassau St; mains €11.95; ☽ Mon-Sat; 🚌 all city centre
Looking over the playing fields of Trinity College – which counts as a view in Dublin – this fashionably formal restaurant is spread over two floors and is renowned for its exquisite and innovative Irish cuisine, but not especially of the porky kind. Grilled sea trout with bubble 'n' squeak (cabbage, bacon, ham, onion and leftover potatoes), roast winter pumpkin with warm sheep's ricotta…who knew that Irish home-cooking could be so good?

SILK ROAD CAFÉ
Map p68
Middle Eastern €

☎ 407 0770; www.cbl.ie; Chester Beatty Library, Dublin Castle; mains around €11; ☽ 11am-4pm Mon-Fri; 🚌 50, 54, 56A, 77 or 77A
Museum cafes don't often make you salivate, but this vaguely Middle Eastern–North African–Mediterranean gem is the exception. On the ground floor of the Chester

Beatty Library, it is the culinary extension of the superb collection upstairs, gathering together exotic flavours into one outstanding menu that is about two-thirds vegie. Complementing the house specialities like Greek moussaka and spinach lasagne are daily specials like *djaj mehshi* (chicken stuffed with spices, rice, dried fruit, almonds and pine nuts and served with okra and Greek yoghurt). For dessert, there's Lebanese baklava and coconut kataif, or you could opt for the juiciest dates this side of Tyre. All dishes are halal and kosher.

GREEN NINETEEN Map p68   Organic €

☎ 478 9626; 19 Lower Camden St; mains €10-12; ☽ 10am-11pm Mon-Sat, noon-6pm Sun; ☐ 16, 16A, 19, 19A, 65X or 83 from city centre

The newest addition to Camden St's growing corridor of cool is this sleek restaurant that specialises in locally sourced, organic grub – without the fancy price tag. Braised lamb chump, corned beef, pot roast chicken and the ubiquitous burger are but the meaty part of the menu, which also includes salads and vegie options. We love it.

GOURMET BURGER KITCHEN
Map p70   Burgers €

☎ 679 0537/672 8559; 14 South William St & 5 South Anne St; ☽ to 10pm Sun-Wed, to 11pm Thu-Sat; burgers €9-13; ☐ all city centre

Burgers are back, and they don't get any better than the ones served at the three city centre branches of this new restaurant (including one in Temple Bar; see p163). The menu has a large range, from your straight-up beef burger with cheese, to something a little more adventurous: how about a Kiwiburger – a beef burger topped with beetroot, egg, pineapple, cheese, salad and relish? They also have decent vegie options.

LISTONS Map p68   Deli €

☎ 405 4779; 25 Camden St; lunch €5-12; ☽ Mon-Sat; ☐ 16, 16A, 19, 19A, 65X or 83 from city centre

The lunchtime queues streaming out the door of this place are testament to its reputation as Dublin's best deli. Its sandwiches (with fresh and delicious fillings), roasted-vegetable quiches, rosemary potato cakes and sublime salads will have you coming back again and again – the only problem is there's too much choice! On fine days, take your gourmet picnic to the nearby Iveagh Gardens (p78).

BOTTEGA TOFFOLI Map p68   Italian €

☎ 633 4022; 34 Castle St; sandwiches & salads €9-14, pizzas €9-13; ☽ 8am-4pm Tue-Wed, to 9pm Thu-Fri, 11am-8pm Sat, 1-8pm Sun ☐ 50, 54, 56A, 77 or 77A

Tucked away on a side street that runs alongside Dublin Castle is this superb Italian cafe (which you'd miss unless you were specifically looking for it), the loving creation of its Irish-Italian owners. Not only is it home to our favourite sandwich in town – beautifully cut prosciutto, baby tomatoes and rocket salad drizzled with imported olive oil on homemade *piadina* bread that is just too good to be true – but its pizzas are as good as any you'd get out of a Neapolitan oven.

BOBO'S Map p68   Burgers €

☎ 400 5750; 22 Wexford St; burgers €8-11; ☽ 9.30am-11pm Mon-Sat, from 1pm Sun; ☐ 16, 16A, 19, 19A, 65X or 83 from city centre

Cow-hide leather banquettes suggest a burger joint with a difference, and Bobo's is just that: a dozen different kinds of organic burgers with Irish names flesh out the menu at this cute spot that promotes the notion that fast food can be healthy. The burgers are exceptional but the home-cut chips, which promise so much in their old-fashioned metal bucket, are disappointing.

MARKET BAR Map p70   Tapas €

☎ 613 9094; www.marketbar.ie; 14a Fade St; mains €6-12; ☐ all city centre

This one-time sausage factory, now fashionable watering hole (see p173), also has a super kitchen that knocks out Spanish tapas and other Iberian-influenced bites in a light-filled, cavernous room, which is just perfect for a slow lunch. The dishes also come in convenient half-size portions, so you can mix and match without feeling like you've gorged.

CAKE SHOP Map p68   Pastries €

☎ 633 4477; Pleasants Pl; mains €2-8; ☽ 10am-6pm; ☐ 16, 16A, 19, 19A, 65X or 83 from city centre

Dublin's best-kept pastry secret is this great little cafe on a tiny lane parallel to Camden St. The easiest way in is through Daintree (61 Camden St) stationery shop; through the back is the self-contained yard, which in good weather is the best spot to enjoy a coffee and a homemade cake.

CAFE CULTURE & BEST COFFEES

Dublin's coffee junkies are everywhere, looking for that perfect barista fix that will kill the hunger until the next one. You can top-up at any of the chains – including that one from Seattle – but we reckon your caffeine craving will get the best fix at these individual locales:

Brown's Bar (Map p70; ☎ 679 5666; Brown Thomas, Grafton St) Not as cool as it used to be, thank God; this is in Dublin's finest department store and is the best place to stop for a mid-shop reviver.

Butler's Chocolate Café (Map p70; ☎ 671 0591; 24 Wicklow St) Heavenly hedonistic; the coffee might not be the *very* best in town, but the combination of a delicious handmade chocolate and damn good coffee is hard to beat. Actually, sod the coffee and double up with its famous hot chocolate for an unforgettable treat. There are branches around the south side.

Coffee Society (Map p102; ☎ 878 7984; 2 Lower Liffey St) It looks most uninviting from the outside and only has paper cups, so it's a good job that this place has some of the best coffee-to-go in the city. There are various branches around town.

Milk Bar (Map p68; ☎ 487 8450; 18 Montague St; ⏱ Mon-Fri) Don't go to Iveagh Gardens (p78) without visiting this groovy little sandwich bar, which serves some of the best coffee in Dublin. The blend is a little mild, but if its standard offerings don't hit the mark, these are the most benevolent baristas in Dublin and are happy to tweak their coffee – a little cooler, warmer, stronger, milkier, sweeter – until you get your fix exactly how you like it.

Milk & Honey (Map p68; ☎ 475 9144; www.milkandhoney.ie; 68 Aungier St) Arguably the best coffee in town is the work of 2009 Irish Latte Art champion Fan Zhang, who mans his station like a smiling magician, carefully creating while engaging in friendly banter with his customers. The decor is a little suspect – too much 1970s going on – but the coffee is perfect.

HONEST TO GOODNESS
Map p70   Cafe €
☎ 633 7727; www.honesttogoodness.ie; 25 George's St Arcade; mains €6.95; ⏱ 9am-6pm Mon-Sat, noon-4pm Sun; 🚇 all city centre
Wholesome sandwiches (made with freshly baked bread), tasty soups and a near-legendary Sloppy Joe, all made on the premises using ingredients sourced from local producers, have earned this lovely spot in the George's St Arcade a bevy of loyal fans who want to keep it all to themselves. No place this good can stay secret for long.

NUDE Map p70   Sandwich Bar €
☎ 675 5577; 21 Suffolk St; wraps €5-6; ⏱ Mon-Sat; 🚇 all city centre
This environmentally friendly take on Dublin fast food looks like the juice bar at the end of the universe. The massive kitchen is fronted by a space-age counter and the communal benches are very human and sociable. Just checking out the huge pre-packaged display, with all its juices, salads and cold dishes, makes your vitamin count surge, while the hot menu mainly features hunky and healthy Asian-style filled wraps.

LEMON Map p70   Crêperie €
☎ 672 9044; 66 South William St; crêpes from €5; ⏱ to 7pm, 8pm Thu; 🚇 all city centre

Dublin's best pancake joint has branches on both sides of Grafton St, one on South William and the other on Dawson St (Map p70; ☎ 672 8898; 60 Dawson St). Each serves up a wide range of sweet and savoury crêpes – those paper-thin ones stuffed with a variety of goodies and smothered in toppings – along with super coffee in a buzzy atmosphere that is popular with literally everyone.

SIMON'S PLACE Map p70   Cafe €
☎ 679 7821; George's St Arcade; ⏱ to 6pm Mon-Sat; 🚇 all city centre
Simon hasn't had to change the menu of doorstep sandwiches and wholesome vegetarian soups since he first opened shop two decades ago – and why should he? His grub is as heartening and legendary as he is. It's a great place to sip a coffee and watch life go by in the old-fashioned arcade. Downstairs is dingy and appropriately popular with Goths and other types with an aversion to sunlight.

MERRION SQUARE & AROUND

Most of the city's Michelin stars are collected by the restaurants surrounding Merrion Sq, but it's not all about top-end cuisine either, as

top picks

IRISH CUISINE

- Chapter One (p164)
- Winding Stair (p164)
- Bentley's Oyster Bar & Grill (p153)
- The Pig's Ear (p157)
- Avoca (p157)

a host of cheaper eateries and sandwich bars cater to the busy lunchtime trade. Needless to say, reservations are essential if you're going for a splurge; the good news is that even the best of the best have felt the squeeze and have reacted to tough times by creating more affordable lunch and dinner specials to entice reticent customers.

RESTAURANT PATRICK GUILBAUD Map p80   French €€€

☎ 676 4192; www.restaurantpatrickguilbaud.ie; Merrion Hotel, 21 Upper Merrion St; 2-/3-course set lunch €38/50, mains €38-60; ⏰ Tue-Sat; 🚇 all city centre

Handing out the title of 'Best in the Country' involves some amount of personal choice, but few disagree that this exceptional restaurant is a leading candidate, not least those good people at Michelin, who have put two stars in its crown. As a result, this is the most prestigious restaurant in the country, where the service is formal but surprisingly friendly, the setting elegant but not stuffy, the wine list simply awesome and head chef Guillaume Lebrun's haute cuisine proudly French. The food is innovative without being fiddly, beautifully cooked and superbly presented. The lunch menu is an absolute steal, at least in this stratosphere.

L'ECRIVAIN Map p80   French €€€

☎ 661 1919; www.lecrivain.com; 109a Lower Baggot St; 3-course lunch menu €25-45, dinner menu €50-60, mains €40-42; ⏰ closed Sun, lunch Sat; 🚇 all city centre

A firm favourite with the bulk of the city's foodies, L'Ecrivain trundles along with just one Michelin star to its name, but the plaudits just keep coming. Head chef Derry Clarke is considered a gourmet god for the exquisite simplicity of his creations, which put the emphasis on flavour and the use of the best local ingredients – all

given the French once over and turned into something that approaches divine dining. The €50 dinner menu, available between 6pm and 7pm Monday to Wednesday, is a virtual steal.

DOBBINS Map p80   French €€€

☎ 676 4679; www.dobbins.ie; 15 Stephen's Lane; mains €26-35; ⏰ closed Sun, lunch Sat; 🚇 all city centre

This old stalwart, opposite a row of council houses, was where the privileged came for lunch before the Celtic Tiger brought privilege to half the city. Its traditional French fare, homely setting and old-fashioned hospitality have served it well over the last quarter of a century, and it's still a favourite with politicians, journalists and spin doctors (often at the same table).

DAX Map p80   French €€€

☎ 676 1494; www.dax.ie; 23 Upper Pembroke St; mains €21-34; ⏰ lunch & dinner Tue-Fri, dinner Sat; 🚇 all city centre

Olivier Meisonnave, convivial ex-maître d' of Thornton's, stepped out on his own with Irish chef Pól ÓhÉannraich to open this posh-rustic restaurant named after his home town, north of Biarritz. In this bright basement venue, serious foodies will be able to sate their palate on sea bass with celeriac purée, pork wrapped in serrano ham or truffle risotto.

UNICORN Map p80   Italian €€€

☎ 676 2182; www.unicornrestaurant.com; 12b Merrion Ct, Merrion Row; mains €19-32; ⏰ Mon-Sat; 🚇 all city centre

Saturday lunch at this Italian restaurant in a laneway off Merrion Row is a tradition for Dublin's media types, socialites, politicos and their cronies who guffaw and clink glasses in conspiratorial rapture. At lunch many opt for the extensive antipasto bar, but we still prefer the meaty á la carte menu – a particular favourite are the kidneys on a bed of risotto, but there are pastas and fish dishes to cater to all palates.

DIEP LE SHAKER Map p80   Asian €€-€€€

☎ 661 1829; www.diep.net; 55 Pembroke Lane; mains €19-29; ⏰ closed Sun & lunch Sat; 🚇 all city centre

Diep le Shaker is a modern, light-filled space tucked down an alley off prestigious Pembroke St. It is popular with the local business crowd, establishment movers and shakers, and people generally consumed by their own self-importance. The predominantly Thai grub is inventive and excellent, but you get the impression you're paying for the company and it ain't worth it.

BANG CAFÉ
Map p80   Modern European €€-€€€
☎ 400 4229; www.bangrestaurant.com; 11 Merrion Row; mains €19-28; ☾ Mon-Sat; 🚌 all city centre

The highest-profile victim of the big bust was this stylish spot owned by the handsome Stokes twins, which closed suddenly in 2009 despite being one of the few enterprises of their empire to actually be in the black. But you can't keep a good restaurant down, it seems, and within months it had reopened under new management, which has sworn to keep up Bang's reputation for excellent fare. Only time will tell.

ELY
Map p80   Wine Bar €€-€€€
☎ 676 8986; www.elywinebar.ie; 22 Ely Pl; mains €15-29; ☾ lunch & dinner Mon-Sat; 🚌 all city centre

Scrummy homemade burgers, bangers and mash, or wild smoked salmon salad are some of the dishes you'll find in this basement restaurant. Meals are prepared with organic and free-range produce from the owner's family farm in County Clare, so you can rest assured of the quality. There's a large wine list to choose from, with more than 70 sold by the glass. There are two more branches on either side of the Liffey – see p166.

CHEZ MAX
Map p80   French €-€€
☎ 661 8899; 133 Baggot St; mains €13-19; ☾ from 10am, Mon-Sat; 🚌 all city centre

Following the success of its sister restaurant by the gates of Dublin Castle (see p155), this version of Chez Max has taken pretty much the same formula (brasserie-style dining room, authentic French cuisine) and thrown in a tree-filled yard for extra measure. And it works a treat. If you're looking for a top notch midrange bite, this could be the one.

TEMPLE BAR
Scattered among the panoply of overpriced and underwhelming eateries in Temple Bar are some excellent spots to get a bite that will suit a variety of tastes and depth of pocket.

MERMAID CAFÉ
Map p87   Seafood €€-€€€
☎ 670 8236; www.mermaid.ie; 69-70 Dame St; mains €19-28; 🚌 all city centre

The largely seafood-serving Mermaid is one of the city's favourite restaurants, as much for the superb cuisine as for the friendly and informal atmosphere. The menu is loaded with inventive ingredient-led organic food, such as roast monkfish tail with sweet potato and chorizo mash and roast poussin with cassava chips, lentils and shallots. But what makes this place that little bit extra special is the atmosphere, fostered as much by the excellent staff as by little touches like free coffee refills at brunch. Call now and make a booking.

EDEN
Map p87   Modern European €€-€€€
☎ 670 5372; www.edenrestaurant.ie; Meeting House Sq; mains €18-28; ☾ lunch & dinner; 🚌 all city centre

The epitome of Temple Bar chic, Eden's minimalist look – designed to look something like the interior of an (empty) swimming pool – and contemporary European menu has earned plenty of kudos over the last decade. The menu, which offers dishes as diverse as braised lamb shank with Moroccan spices and organic beef and Guinness stew, is generally excellent, but we enjoy it best at brunch on the much-sought-after ground-floor terrace. Try to avoid the upstairs dining room, which can get very hot.

TEA ROOMS
Map p87   Modern Irish €€
☎ 670 7766; www.theclarence.ie; Clarence, 6-8 Wellington Quay; two-/three-course menu €21.50/26; ☾ dinner Thu-Sat, Sun brunch noon-4pm; 🚌 all city centre

Mathieu Melin is performing small miracles in this elegant restaurant, its soaring ceiling and double-height windows designed to resemble a church. There are few places in all of Dublin where you'll get such superb

TASTE OF DUBLIN
Since 2005 the city's best restaurateurs have shared their secrets and their dishes with each other and the public at the wonderful Taste of Dublin (☎ 210 9290; www.tasteofdublin.ie; Iveagh Gardens; tickets €15-65), which takes place over a long weekend in June and features talks, demonstrations and lessons as well as the chance to eat some extraordinary grub.

LOCAL VOICE: AINGEALA FLANNERY, FOOD CRITIC

Times are tough for Dublin's restaurants, but is there any silver lining? Yes, most definitely. The boom years saw an explosion of mediocre and just plain bad restaurants in Dublin. The recession has weeded out the worst of them and, in fact, several really excellent restaurants have opened.

The best thing about eating out in Dublin? The south side city centre is so small, you can walk from place to place in a matter of minutes and check out menus and atmosphere and decide where you want to eat. Now that Dublin isn't awash with money and people who are dying to flaunt it, you don't always have to have a reservation, even on the weekends.

Your favourite restaurant for…a special occasion: The upstairs restaurant at Fallon & Byrne (p153) is sophisticated, but not as formal and stuffy as the city's older fine-dining restaurants. The dining room is gorgeous and the wine list is excellent. And of course it's always nice to breeze by the shoppers in the downstairs food hall when you know you're going to upper echelons of the establishment.

A quick bite: During the day, Honest to Goodness (p159) serves the best roast-beef sandwich in town. At night, the Market Bar (p158) does decent food, big portions and snappy service, plus you can drink before or after at the bar.

For a cheap meal: Green Nineteen (p158). Proper food and Irish Mammy dinners for a tenner. Brunch is also stunning. This place set the benchmark for budget dining in the recession and its success made others follow suit. Close to some of the best live music venues too.

A romantic night out: Chez Max (p161) on Baggot St (Dublin Castle is good, too); the lighting is very kind, the music is seductive, the staff are good looking and charming, there's a smoking area, and the wine flows freely.

Any other tips? Look for early-bird and set-price dinner menus. Do not buy bottled water, ask for tap water; the public water supply in Dublin is excellent. Check to make sure that service hasn't already been added to your bill before you leave a tip. Ten per cent is enough if you think the service was good.

Aingeala is a food critic with the Irish Independent (www.independent.ie).

fare – an ambitious marriage of classic French cuisine and typically Irish produce – at such reasonable prices.

TANTE ZOÉ'S Map p87   Cajun, Creole €€-€€€
☎ 679 4407; www.tantezoes.com; 1 Crow St; mains €16-26; ☾ Mon-Sat; ⊜ all city centre
This well-established favourite serves up a Mardi Gras for the senses almost every night, with its menu of gumbos, jambalayas, bayou steaks, Cajun-blackened this and Creole-infused that. It ain't subtle and it won't win a lot of gourmet foodie awards, but the crowd couldn't care less: they come to *laisser rouler les bons temps* and that's exactly what they get.

CHAMELEON Map p87   Indonesian €€
☎ 671 0362; www.chameleonrestaurant.com; 1 Lower Fownes St; mains €16.50-19.50; ☾ dinner Tue-Sun; ⊜ all city centre
Friendly, cute and full of character, Chameleon is draped in exotic fabrics and serves up perky renditions of Indonesian classics, such as satay, gado gado and nasi goreng. If you can't decide what dish to have, you can always plump for the rijsttaffel, a selection of several dishes with rice. The top floor has low seating on cushions, which is perfect for intimate group get-togethers.

IL BACCARO Map p87   Italian €€
☎ 671 4597; www.ilbaccarodublin.com; Meeting House Sq; mains €13-23; ☾ dinner daily, lunch Sat; ⊜ all city centre
Want a free Italian lesson? Drop into this fabulous trattoria and eavesdrop in this rustic piece of the Old Boot, where the food is exuberantly authentic, and includes bruschetta, homemade pasta, Italian sausage and the like. The Italian wines are *buonissimi*.

AR VICOLETTO Map p87   Italian €-€€
☎ 670 8633; 5 Crow St; mains €13-25; ☾ lunch & dinner Mon-Sat, from 3pm Sun; ⊜ all city centre
When it's good, this cosy little *osteria* is very, very good, with excellent Italian dishes washed down with splendid Italian reds and enjoyed in a convivial atmosphere. But it's a little inconsistent and sometimes the standard menu of pasta, meaty mains and seafood misses the mark. At these times it doesn't seem like good value at all, although the warm gorgonzola salad never disappoints. Absolutely worth the risk.

MONTY'S OF KATHMANDU
Map p87   Nepalese €-€€
☎ 670 4911; www.montys.ie; 28 Eustace St; mains €14-18; ☾ lunch Mon-Sat, dinner daily; ⊜ all city centre

It has won a ton of ethnic dining awards, but Monty's still leaves us a little flat. The food is good if not exceptional, focusing primarily on Nepalese dishes like *gorkhali* (chicken cooked in chilli, yoghurt and ginger) or *kachela* (raw marinated meat). The atmosphere is muted, but on weeknights it can tend towards the moribund.

LARDER Map p87 International €-€€

☎ 633 3581; 8 Parliament St; mains €10-18; ⊗ lunch & dinner; 🚌 all city centre

This welcoming cafe-restaurant has a positively organic vibe to it, what with its wholesome porridge breakfasts, gourmet sandwiches with fillings such as serrano ham, gruyere and rocket, and speciality Suki teas (try the China gunpowder). It's confident about its food – we like the fact that it lists suppliers – and so are we.

GOURMET BURGER KITCHEN

Map p87 Burgers €

☎ 670 8343; Temple Bar Sq; ⊗ noon-11pm Mon-Sat, noon-10pm Sun; burgers €9-13; 🚌 all city centre

The Temple Bar branch of this popular and tasty burger restaurant is perfectly placed to feed the throngs of revellers looking for the party in Temple Bar – for many of them it's an important prep to a big night out, as you really shouldn't drink on an empty stomach! By closing relatively early it is avoiding those same people with the post-club munchies.

ZAYTOON Map p87 Middle Eastern €

☎ 677 3595; 14-15 Parliament St; chicken shish-kebab meal €11; ⊗ to 4am; 🚌 all city centre

It's the end of the night and you've got a desperate case of the munchies. Head straight for this terrific kebab joint and gobble the house speciality, the chicken shish-kebab meal, complete with chips and a soft drink. There's another branch on Camden St (Map p68; ☎ 400 5006; 44-55 Lwr Camden St).

QUEEN OF TARTS Map p87 Cafe €

☎ 670 7499; Cork Hill, Lord Edward St; cakes & pastries from €4; ⊗ 7.30am-6pm; 🚌 all city centre

Diet dodgers rejoice, for this doughty little cafe is to cakes what Willie Wonka was to chocolate, and you'll think you're in a dream when you see the displays of tarts, meringues, crumbles, cookies and brownies, never mind taste them. There are also great brekkies – such as potato-and-chive cake with mushroom and egg, plus the coffee is splendid and the service sweet. This is a treasure so popular that they opened a bigger version around the corner on Cow's Lane (Map p87; ☎ 633 4681; 3-4 Cow's La; ⊗ 7.30am-6pm).

KILMAINHAM & THE LIBERTIES

Gourmet experiences are a little thin on the ground west of the south city centre, but if you are traipsing towards the Guinness Storehouse, IMMA or Kilmainham Gaol and are looking for something to sustain you, there's one spot worth considering.

LEO BURDOCK'S Map p91 Fish & Chips €

☎ 454 0306; 2 Werburgh St; fish & chips €7-9; ⊗ to 11pm; 🚌 50, 54, 56A, 77 or 77A

You will often hear that you haven't eaten in Dublin until you've queued in the cold for a cod 'n' chips wrapped in paper from the city's most famous chipper. Total codswallop, of course, but there's something about sitting on the street, balancing the bag on your lap and trying to eat the chips quickly before they go cold that smacks of Dublin in a bygone age. It's nice to revisit the past, especially if you don't have to get stuck there.

NORTH OF THE LIFFEY

Like just about every facet of Dublin life, cafes and restaurants north of the Liffey tend to be more down-to-earth than their southern counterparts. O'Connell St itself is lined with fast-food factories, although there are a couple of cracking restaurants close by. The area around Parnell St has exploded in the last couple of years and is now chock-a-block with ethnic eateries, mostly Chinese, but also Korean and Polish.

CHAPTER ONE Map p102   Modern Irish €€€

☎ 873 2266; www.chapteronerestaurant.com; Dublin Writers Museum, 18 Parnell Sq; mains €32-72; ☾ closed Sun, lunch Sat; 🚌 3, 10, 11, 13, 16, 19 or 22 from city centre

One of the best restaurants in Dublin, this venerable old trooper sets its ambitions no further than modern Irish cuisine, which it has realised so brilliantly that those Michelin lads saw fit to throw one of their sought-after stars its way. Menus change regularly but the dishes are always top-notch, the service first class and the atmosphere reassuringly reserved – although its success means that you have to book well in advance. Get there between 6pm and 7.40pm for the three-course pre-theatre special (€37.50), a favourite with those heading to the Gate (p198) around the corner.

WINDING STAIR

Map p102   Modern Irish €€-€€€

☎ 873 3292; www.winding-stair.com; 40 Lower Ormond Quay; mains €21-27; ☾ noon-4pm & 6-10pm Tue-Sat, from 1pm Sun; 🚌 all city centre

Housed within a beautiful Georgian building that was once home to the city's most beloved bookshop (the ground floor still is one, see p144), the Winding Stair's conversion to elegant restaurant has been faultless. The wonderful Irish menu – creamy fish pie, bacon and organic cabbage, steamed mussels, and Irish farmyard cheeses – coupled with an excellent wine list makes for a memorable meal.

HALO Map p102   Modern Irish €€€

☎ 878 2999; www.morrisonhotel.ie; Morrison Hotel, Lower Ormond Quay; two/three-course dinner €30/34; ☾ dinner; 🚌 all city centre

Housed in this superslick hotel, the visually stunning Halo has soaring ceilings, a wall of mirrors and striking artwork, but don't let this distract you from the Ireland-meets-continental Europe fusion fare that includes the likes of fillet of sea bream and Carlow lamb rump. Its critics complain that the menu competes with the staff to see who can be more stuffy, but in truth it's the moneyed clientele that win hands down.

YAMAMORI SUSHI

Map p102   Japanese €€-€€€

☎ 475 5001; www.yamamorinoodles.ie; 38-39 Lower Ormond Quay; sushi €3-3.50, mains €16-35; ☾ lunch Sun-Wed, dinner daily; 🚌 all city centre

Sushi arrives on the north side and immediately proves successful, but that's hardly surprising considering that its south side sister has been doing the Japanese thang

---

VEGIE BITES

Vegetarians are having it increasingly easier in Dublin as the capital has veered away from the belief that food isn't food until your incisors have had to rip flesh from bone, and towards an understanding that healthy eating leads to, well, longer lives. There's a selection of general restaurants that cater to vegetarians beyond the token dish of mixed greens and pulses – places like Nude (p159), Yamamori (p154) and Chameleon (p162). Solidly vegetarian places include the following:

Blazing Salads (Map p70; ☎ 671 9552; 42 Drury St; mains €3-7) Organic breads (including many special diet varieties), Californian-style salads, smoothies and pizza slices can all be taken away from this delicious deli.

Cornucopia (Map p70; ☎ 677 7583; 19 Wicklow St; mains from €7) For those escaping the Irish cholesterol habit, Cornucopia is a popular wholefood cafe turning out healthy goodies. There's even a hot vegetarian breakfast as an alternative to muesli.

Fresh (Map p70; ☎ 671 9552; top fl, Powerscourt Townhouse Shopping Centre; lunch €6-12) This long-standing restaurant serves a variety of salads and filling, hot daily specials. Many dishes are dairy- and gluten-free, without compromising on taste. The baked potato, topped with organic cheese (€5.50), comes with two salads, is very reasonable and is a hearty meal in itself.

Govinda's (www.govindas.ie; mains €6-10) Aungier St (Map p70; ☎ 475 0309; 4 Aungier St); Merrion Row (Map p80; ☎ 661 5095; 18 Merrion Row); Middle Abbey St (Map p102; ☎ 872 7463; 83 Middle Abbey St) An authentic beans-and-pulses place run by the Hare Krishna, with three branches in the city centre. Its cheap, wholesome mix of salads and Indian-influenced hot daily specials are filling and tasty.

with great aplomb for a very long time. The menus in both are largely the same, but we prefer this newer location – right on the river – because it's just that little bit more airy and spacious. The bento boxes are a popular choice – especially at lunchtime – but we really just can't get enough of the *nami moriawase*.

BON GA Map p102 Korean €-€€
☎ 872 7934; 52 Capel St; buffet €10-18, karaoke rooms €25-60; ✆ 5.30pm-midnight; ☒ all city centre

Korean barbecue (usually grilled marinated meats) is all well and – in this instance – very good, but there's something extra about this large, friendly place that is always buzzing with locals, visitors and immigrants alike: oh yeah, it's the karaoke rooms, where you can dine and sing 'til your heart's content. To get the vocal chords going try the *dongdong ju* rice wine or *soju*, basically a Korean vodka. Top night out.

MELODY Map p102 Chinese €-€€
☎ 878 8988; 122 Capel St; buffet €10-18, karaoke rooms €25-60; ✆ 5.30pm-midnight; ☒ all city centre

Lots of red lacquer, black marble, a couple of fish tanks and the biggest TV we've ever seen is clear evidence that this place was designed to suit the sensibilities of the city's substantial Chinese community, but it works for the Irish too: they come, preferably in big groups, and tuck into the fairly standard Chinese fare. Downstairs, a warren of tunnels leads to the karaoke dining rooms – probably the real reason this place is so popular.

BAR ITALIA Map p102 Italian €
☎ 874 1000; 28 Lower Ormond Quay, Quartier Bloom; mains €9-15; ☒ all city centre

One of a new generation of eateries that's showing the more established Italian restaurants how the Old Country *really* eats, Bar Italia's specialities are its ever-changing pasta dishes, homemade risottos and excellent Palombini coffee.

TASTE OF EMILIA Map p102 Italian €
☎ 878 8188; 28 Lower Liffey St; mains €4-10; ✆ 7.30am-7pm Mon-Wed & Fri & Sat, to 9.30pm Thu; ☒ all city centre

Half bar, half Italian deli, this warm, buzzing locale does a wonderful trade in cured meats and cheeses from all over Italy, paying particular attention to the produce of

the true heartland of Italian cuisine, Emilia-Romagna. The sandwiches are made with homemade *piadina* bread or *tigelle,* and you can wash it down with a light sparkling wine from the north of Italy. Italians love the joint, and it's no wonder.

KIMCHI/THE HOP HOUSE
Map p102 Korean, Irish €
☎ 872 8318; www.hophouse.ie; 160 Parnell St; mains €8-13; ✆ closed lunch Sun; ☒ all city centre

Two distinct halves – one strictly Korean, the other very Irish – make up this buzzy eatery on one of Dublin's most ethnically diverse streets. The food – a mixture of Korean with the odd Japanese bento thrown in for good measure – is served in Kimchi (which refers to a pickled vegetable ever-present in Korean cuisine), while just across the room is the Hop House, Korea's version of an Irish bar, where you can wash it all down with a beer, local or imported.

DUBLIN CITY GALLERY – THE HUGH LANE Map p102 International €
☎ 874 1903; www.hughlane.ie; 22 North Parnell Sq; mains €8-12; ✆ to 6pm Mon-Thu, to 5pm Fri-Sun; ☒ 3, 10, 11, 13, 16, 19 or 22 from city centre

There's hardly a better way to ruminate over the art in the gallery than over lunch in the new gallery cafe, an airy room in the basement next to a small garden. The menu tends largely towards the healthy-eating side of things, offering a range of scrumptious tarts and exotic seasonal salads.

PANEM Map p102 Cafe €
☎ 872 8510; 21 Lower Ormond Quay; mains €7-10; ✆ to 5pm, closed Sun; ☒ all city centre

Pasta, focaccia and salads are the standard fare at this diminutive quay-side cafe, but the specialities are wickedly sweet and savoury pastries, which are all made on-site. The croissants and brioche – filled with Belgian chocolate, almond cream or hazelnut *amaretti* – are the perfect snack for a holiday stroll along the Liffey Boardwalk. Lunchtimes are chaotic.

COBALT CAFÉ & GALLERY
Map p102 Cafe €
☎ 873 0313; 16 North Great George's St; mains €6-10; ✆ 10am-4.30pm Mon-Fri; ☒ 3, 10, 11, 13, 16, 16A, 19, 19A or 22 from city centre

A splendid little cafe just opposite the James Joyce Cultural Centre (p108), the Cobalt occupies the ground floor of an elegant Georgian building and serves honest-to-goodness sandwiches stuffed with lots of lovely fillings. The big fireplace is the spot to warm those winter toes.

LA TAVERNA DI BACCO
Map p102   Italian €
☎ 873 0040; Quartier Bloom; salads & sandwiches €5-8, mains €8-9; ☷ closed lunch Sun; ▣ all city centre

Football-mad developer Mick Wallace has managed to single-handedly create a thriving new Italian quarter with cafes and eateries popping up all over Quartier Bloom, the lane from Ormond Quay to Great Strand St. La Taverna and Enoteca Delle Langhe (Map p102; ☎ 888 0834), just a few doors up, serve simple pastas, antipasti and Italian cheeses along with the delicious produce of Wallace's own vineyard and others in Piemonte.

SOUP DRAGON Map p102   Soup Bar €
☎ 872 3277; 168 Capel St; soups €5-10; ☷ closed Sun; ▣ all city centre

Eat in or takeaway one of 12 tasty varieties of homemade soups, including shepherd's pie or spicy vegetable gumbo. Bowls come in three different sizes and prices include fresh bread and a piece of fruit. Kick-start your day (or afternoon) with a healthy all-day breakfast selection: fresh smoothies (€4.50), generous bowls of yoghurt, fruit and muesli (€5) or poached egg in a bagel (€4).

EPICUREAN FOOD HALL
Map p102   International €
Lower Liffey St; ☷ Mon-Sat; ▣ all city centre

This place is essentially just a food court, but some of Dublin's best eateries have outlets here, and it's a worthy daytime stop-off for a snack, a coffee, lunch or specialist supplies. The food court is perfect if you're not sure what you feel like or if there's discord among your number, because once you get here you can choose between bagels, Italian, French, Mexican, Japanese, Indian and Lebanese, to name just a few.

DOCKLANDS
Although the crash has put paid to some of the grander plans for restaurant openings in the Docklands, there are a couple of good options that reflect the best of new dining in the city.

QUAY 16
Map p115   Modern European €€-€€€
☎ 817 8760; www.mvcillairne.com; MV Cill Airne, North Wall Quay; mains €19.50-32, bar food €12-16; ☷ noon-3pm Mon-Fri, 6-10pm Mon-Sat; ▣ 33D, 53A or 151 from city centre

The MV Cill Airne, commissioned in 1961 as a passenger liner tender, is now permanently docked along the north quays, where it serves the public as a bar, bistro and fine restaurant. The food in this restaurant is surprisingly good – dishes such as seared beef fillet, and monkfish on saffron risotto are expertly prepared and are served alongside an excellent variety of wines.

ELY CHQ BAR & BRASSERIE
Map p115   Modern European €€
☎ 672 0010; www.elywinebar.ie; Custom House Quay; mains €15-24; ☷ lunch & dinner Mon-Fri, from 4pm Sat; ▣ 33D, 53A or 151 from city centre

Scrummy homemade burgers, bangers and mash, and wild smoked salmon salad are some of the meals you'll find in this restaurant, which is contained within a converted tobacco warehouse in the heart of the International Financial Services Centre (IFSC). Dishes are prepared with organic and free-range produce from the owner's family farm in County Clare, so you can be assured of the quality. There's a large wine list to choose from, with over 70 sold by the glass. There's another branch, Ely HQ (Map p115; ☎ 633 9986; Hanover Quay; ☷ lunch & dinner Mon-Sun) located on the other side of the river just alongside the Grand Canal Square, which has been branded a gastropub.

HERBSTREET Map p115   International €-€€
☎ 675 3875; www.herbstreet.ie; Hanover Quay; mains €13-19; ☷ noon-3pm Mon-Fri, 6-10pm Mon-Sat; ▤ Grand Canal Dock

The hand-driers use low power, the LED lighting uses just one watt per bulb, the chairs date from circa 1956 and the wines are European only: this eatery is taking its green responsibilities seriously by making sure its carbon footprint is as shallow as possible. The fish used here is farmed locally, and all of the other dishes – they're nothing too radical, just fine, delicious portions of sandwiches, burgers and salads – are sourced as close to the restaurant as they possibly can be.

PHOENIX PARK

Europe's largest enclosed expanse of green has nothing in the way of restaurants, but there is one spot that is just marvellous on a warm, sunny day.

PHOENIX PARK TEA ROOM

Map p119   Cafe €

☎ 677 0090; www.phoenixpark.ie; Chesterfield Ave, Phoenix Park; mains €3-6; ⏲ 10am-5pm Apr-Sep, to 4pm Oct-Mar; 🚌 10 from O'Connell St, or 25 or 26 from Middle Abbey St

This Victorian tea room just next to Dublin Zoo is the real deal. Built in the late 19th century to serve refreshments to the ladies and gentlemen who perambulated in Phoenix Park, the building has been carefully maintained and today serves pretty much the same function for the modern walker, zoo-visitor or couple on a first date (it's a great spot to make a good first impression with). Homemade soups and desserts, sandwiches and wraps are the extent of the menu, along with coffees, teas and soft drinks.

BEYOND THE GRAND CANAL

It's not surprising that the fancier neighbourhoods of the inner southern suburbs that ring the Grand Canal have a selection of local eateries worth making the effort for. This is especially true of Ranelagh and Sandymount, where you can find some excellent nosh.

EXPRESSO BAR Map p122   French €€-€€€

☎ 660 0585; www.expressobar.ie; 1 St Mary's Rd; mains €17-29; ⏲ lunch & dinner Mon-Sat, brunch Sun; 🚌 10 from city centre

Hidden away on a leafy suburban road off Baggot St, this hip, minimalist place with leather seating and subdued lighting attracts local rock stars and other types normally seen only in the social columns. Top nosh such as lamb shank or baked sea bass with lime-and-mint potatoes should keep most folk happy when they're not people-watching over *Hello!* magazine.

JUNIORS Map p122   Irish €€

☎ 664 3648; www.juniors.ie; 2 Bath Ave, Sandymount; mains €15-24; ⏲ lunch & dinner; 🚌 5, 7, 7A, 8, 45 or 46 from city centre; 🚆 Sandymount

---

Cramped and easily mistaken for any old cafe, Juniors is anything but ordinary: the food (mostly Irish dishes, all locally sourced produce) is delicious, the atmosphere always buzzing (it's often hard to get a table) and the ethos top-notch, due to the two brothers who run the place.

FRENCH PARADOX Map p122   French €€

☎ 660 4068; 53 Shelbourne Rd; mains €16-18; ⏲ closed Sun dinner; 🚌 5, 7, 7A, 8, 45 or 46 from city centre

This bright and airy wine bar over an excellent wine shop of the same name serves fine authentic French dishes such as cassoulet, a variety of foie gras, cheese and charcuterie plates, and large green salads. All there to complement the main attraction: a dazzling array of fine wines, mostly French (unsurprisingly), sold by the bottle, glass or even 6.25cL taste! A little slice of Paris in Dublin.

ITSA4 Map p122   Modern Irish €€

☎ 219 4676; www.itsabagel.com; 6a Sandymount Green; mains €12-18; ⏲ lunch & dinner; 🚆 Sandymount

Although Itsa4's funky flamboyant interior has been used for many fashion shoots, its organic chef and writer Domini Kemp is far from frivolous. Her latest venture continues her ambition to deliver well-sourced, quality food in delicious, down-to-earth ways. The lamb shank with Lyonnaise potatoes, or the chicory, blue cheese and glazed-pear salad are incredible. Serious food for fun people.

CAFÉ BARDELI Map p122   Italian €

☎ 496 1886; www.cafebardeli.ie; 62 Ranelagh Rd; mains €11-15; ⏲ 12.30-11pm Mon-Sat, to 10pm Sun; 🚌 11, 11A, 11B, 18, 44, 44N or 48A from city centre; 🚆 Ranelagh

If it ain't broke, do it again: CBD hit Ranelagh a few years back with the same no-fuss menu that made its city-centre sisters such roaring successes on Grafton and South Great George's Sts (see p157) and it just hasn't looked back.

JO'BURGER Map p122   Burgers €

☎ 491 3731; www.joburger.ie; 137 Rathmines Rd, Rathmines; burgers €8.95-12; ☒ noon-midnight; ☒ 14, 14A, 15, 15A, 15B, 15E, 15F, 15N, 18, 49N, 65, 65B, 74, 74A, 83, 128 or 142 from city centre

A playful, kids-in-the-'70s theme, DJs playing great music loud enough to hear but not too loud to be annoying, and a sensational burger menu make this the coolest burger joint in the city. The organic burgers – beef, lamb, fish, vegie – come in a variety of options, all with funky names. The mapetla has beetroot salad, rocket and relish; the zondi comes with green Thai curry mayo, coriander and chilli.

DRINKING

top picks

- Anseo (p174)
- Gravediggers (aka Kavanagh's) (p183)
- Grogan's Castle Lounge (p175)
- James Toner's (p177)
- Kehoe's (p176)
- Long Hall (p176)
- Long Stone (p176)
- Bar With No Name (p173)
- Hartigan's (p177)
- Sin É (p181)

What's your recommendation? www.lonelyplanet.com/dublin

DRINKING

If there's one constant about life in Dublin, it's that Dubliners will always take a drink. Come hell or high water, the city's pubs will never be short of customers, and we suspect that exploring a variety of Dublin's legendary pubs and bars ranks pretty high on your list of why you're here.

You'd be absolutely right, too: like getting bumped on the streets of New York or being the victim of haughty rudeness in Paris, you cannot fully experience Dublin without spending at least some of your time here in a pub. The city may have gone through some pretty dramatic changes over the last few years, but the pub remains the heart of its social existence, the broadest window through which you can examine and experience the very essence of the city's culture, in all its myriad forms. It's the great leveller where status and rank hold no sway, where generation gaps are bridged, inhibitions lowered, tongues loosened, schemes hatched, songs sung, stories told and gossip embroidered. It's a unique institution: a theatre and a cosy room, a centre stage and a hideaway, a debating chamber and a place for silent contemplation. It's whatever you want it to be, and that's the secret of the great Irish pub.

Talk – whether it is frivolous, earnest or incoherent – is the essential ingredient. Once tongues are loosened and the cogs of thought oiled, your conversation can go anywhere and you should follow it to its natural conclusion. An old Irish adage suggests you should never talk about sport, religion or politics in unfamiliar company. But just be mindful and you needn't restrict yourself too much. While it's a myth to say you can walk into any Dublin pub and be befriended, you probably won't be drinking on your own for long – unless that's what you want of course. There are few more spiritual experiences than a solitary pint in a Dublin pub in the midafternoon.

There are pubs for every taste and sensibility, although the *truly* traditional haunts populated by flat-capped pensioners bursting with insightful anecdotes are about as rare as hen's teeth; the city has been overwhelmed by designer bars and themed locales that could be found pretty much anywhere else in the world. But despair not, for it is not the spit or sawdust that makes a great Dublin pub (although it can help with the setting) but the patrons themselves, who provide a reassuring guarantee that Dublin's reputation as the pub capital of the world remains in perfectly safe (if occasionally unsteady!) hands.

PUB ETIQUETTE

The rounds system – the simple custom where someone buys you a drink and you buy one back – is the bedrock of Irish pub culture. It's summed up in the Irish saying: 'It's impossible for two men to go to a pub for one drink.' Nothing will hasten your fall from social grace here like the failure to uphold this pub law. The Irish are extremely generous and one thing they can't abide is tightfistedness.

Another golden rule about the system is that the next round starts when the first person has finished (preferably just about to finish) their drink. It doesn't matter if you're only halfway through your pint, if it's your round get them in.

Your greatest challenge will probably be trying to keep up with your fellow drinkers, who may keep buying you drinks in every round even when you've still got a clatter of unfinished pints in front of you and you're sliding face first down the bar.

Banter is the fibre of sociability. 'Slagging', or teasing, is the city's favourite pastime and a far more reliable indicator of the strength of friendship than virtually any kind of compliment: a fast, self-deprecating wit and an ability to take a joke in good spirits will win you plenty of friends.

IRISH DRINKS

You can get every conceivable international brew and distillation of booze that is made for export – and the vast majority of Dubliners are happy to declare a foreign tipple as their favourite, with one exception. You would be criminally negligent if you didn't wet your teeth with at least one local liquid, the black stuff that virtually symbolises the city.

A Pint of Plain

They've been brewing beer in Ireland possibly since the Bronze Age and definitely since the arrival of Christianity. The most famous beer of all though, stout, was in fact brewed in Britain, and became known as porter because of its popularity among London market porters. A mere accident of geography, say Dubliners, all the while pointing to the very large Guinness brewery (p90) that has occupied the same premises at St James's Gate since 1759 and whose product is as much a part of the furniture of the Dublin pub as the counter-top itself.

If you're looking for another taste and want to avoid the same beers you can get in any other city, seek out the blossoming microbrews. In the following listings we have included pubs serving speciality beers on draught – proof that the pub is serious about their beers.

Whiskey, not Whisky

Irish whiskey shares equal billing as the national drink, but in the home it is paramount and if your host produces their best bottle it means you're either very welcome, very wealthy or very lucky. Besides the spelling and the fact that it is distilled three times, Irish whiskey differs from its Scotch cousins in that Scottish malt barley is dried over peat fires, which gives the drink its smoky flavour, whereas Irish malt is dried in smokeless kilns. Finally, while most punters (including most Dubs) would be hard pressed to name more than a handful of Irish whiskeys, at last call there were almost 100 different types, albeit brewed by only three distilleries – Jameson's, Bushmills and Cooley's. If the history, creation (and the drinking) of whiskey is your bag, check out the Old Jameson Distillery (p105).

WHERE TO DRINK

There are about 1000 pubs across the city, so there's bound to be one to suit every mood. Many visitors begin – and sadly end – their exploration of the city's pub scene within the cobbled confines of Temple Bar, the city's most frequented nightlife quarter. It's busy, sure, but the pubs here cater to out-of-towners rather than locals, frantically selling a plastic paddy version of the Dublin experience that most locals avoid like the plague. Still, if the 'Ibiza in the Rain' cheesefest is what you're looking for, you won't be disappointed.

The pubs around Grafton St and St Stephen's Green are a mix of authentic Dublin boozers and stylish contemporary bars that cater to a broad range of punters, from penniless students cadging pints of cider off one another to moneyed execs buying rounds of Mojitos for the table. If the former is more your bag, stay west and southwest of Grafton St, especially along the newish corridor of cool that extends from Aungier St south to Wexford and Camden Sts. If a more designer drink is to your liking, Dawson St, east of Grafton St, and Ballsbridge and Donnybrook, beyond the Grand Canal, have plenty of bars to suit those tastes.

The area around Merrion Sq has pubs and bars that are popular with office workers winding down – but that's not nearly as unattractive a proposition as it might sound elsewhere. Most Dubliners like to leave work behind once they cross the pub's hearth and many a wild Friday night is regretted on a Saturday morning!

The quays north and south of the river, for so long in a state of perilous abandonment, have come to life in recent years and now play host to a number of excellent pubs well worth checking out. There are many unreconstructed boozers north of the Liffey, although O'Connell St and its environs are not particularly pleasant or safe places to hang around at night, and you should keep your wits about you when out and about.

But we won't leave this section on that note. From centuries-old taverns to slick DJ bars, there's plenty to please in Dublin these days whether you're supping Guinness, quaffing wine or sipping cocktails. While some still bemoan the loss of the traditional and the proliferation of slick designer bars, we've accepted the development now and like to think that it leaves more room for us in our favourite snugs.

Finally, if you're looking for traditional music pubs, you'll find them listed under Traditional and Folk (p195).

PRACTICALITIES
Opening Hours & Licensing Laws

Last orders are at 11.30pm Monday to Thursday, 12.30am Friday and Saturday and 11pm Sunday, with 30 minutes drinking-up time each night. However, many central pubs have secured late licences to serve until 1.30am, 2.30am and – in the case of those with a super-special 'theatre licence' – until 3am. As part of the 2003 licensing laws, happy hours have been banned and pubs instructed to get tougher on underage drinkers (so if you look young, bring ID).

top picks

DJ BARS

- Anseo (p174) Old and new alternative favourites.
- Dice Bar (p180) Dive bar with an eclectic range, from rock to lounge and dance.
- Bia Bar (p174) Dance, R&B and hip hop every night.
- Hogan's (p188) Contemporary dance music.
- Sin É (p181) Down-to-earth ambience and great music – classic rock, hip hop and party tunes.

Tipping

The American-style gratuity has never been a part of Irish drinking culture, mostly because hard-pressed drinkers in less prosperous times would have needed every penny to continue keeping reality at bay. At best, a regular may opt to leave coppers on the bar for the bartender to pick up, but this practice would only happen in quieter bars among locals.

Which of course doesn't mean that you *can't* tip. If you want to reward your hard-working barkeep for good service (watch them sweat on a busy night and you'll know how hard it is) feel absolutely free to do so. They'll probably look at you with bemused gratitude.

Nonsmoking

Ireland went smoke-free in March 2004 (with smoking banned in all workplaces, including pubs). Which is why you'll see a fairly busy social scene outside the front doors of most pubs, as smokers gather to puff away; the most intrepid publicans have converted hitherto unused yard space behind their bars into 'beer gardens' where smokers can indulge the habit without having to leave the bar (see the boxed text, p175, for the best of them).

GRAFTON STREET & AROUND

Amid the designer shops and trendy eateries of the Grafton St area, a few top-notch Victorian pubs combine elegance and traditional style to pull in punters from far and near. Dawson St is popular with straight professional types, the area immediately west of

Grafton St has something for everyone, and trendy Wexford and Camden Sts tick the arty, alternative box.

BAILEY Map p70   Contemporary Bar
☎ 670 4939; www.baileybar.ie; 2 Duke St; 🚍 all city centre
Perpetually popular with self-appointed shakers and movers – and a few frustrated office workers looking to shake and move – the Bailey has wall-mounted light boxes and comfortable seating, perfect for an evening schmooze. Outside gas braziers allow you to sit on the pavement and observe the street life by day. It also does a mean trade in continental lunches.

BANK Map p70   Contemporary Bar
☎ 677 0677; www.bankoncollegegreen.com; 20-22 College Green; 🚍 all city centre
This architecturally dazzling bar occupies the site of a former Victorian bank and has opulent decoration, including a stained-glass ceiling, hand-carved plasterwork and mosaic-tiled floors to occupy your eyes while you wait for your pint of Guinness to settle. The atmosphere is conversational, and the bar staff are excellent.

CAFÉ EN SEINE Map p70   Contemporary Bar
☎ 677 4369; 40 Dawson St; 🚍 all city centre
The wildly extravagant art-nouveau style of this huge bar has been a massive hit since it first opened in 1995, and while it may not be the 'in' place it once was, it is still very popular with suburbanites, the after-work crowd and out-of-towners. Maybe it's the glass panelling, or the real 12m-high trees; but most likely it's the beautiful people propping up the wood-and-marble bar.

DAKOTA Map p70   Contemporary Bar
☎ 672 7696; 8 South William St; 🚍 all city centre
Surprisingly chilled out for a superpub, Dakota is distinguished by dimmed lights, funky tunes, crafty cocktails and a slick modern layout. Unfortunately, we found the weekend bouncers to be goons, the beer patchy and the bar staff so frosty that if you stuck your tongue out at them it might stick.

DAVY BYRNE'S Map p70   Contemporary Bar
☎ 677 5217; www.davybyrnes.com; 21 Duke St; 🚍 all city centre
James Joyce would barely recognise the bar that Leopold Bloom popped into for

a gorgonzola sandwich and a glass of burgundy in *Ulysses*. It doesn't stop Davy Byrne's from making the most of its Joycean connections, even though today's version is strictly for out-of-towners and the rugby crowd.

DICEY REILLY'S Map p68   Contemporary Bar
☎ 478 4066; Russell Court Hotel, 21-25 Harcourt St; 🚌 all city centre; 🚉 St Stephen's Green/Harcourt

One of Dublin's most popular bars is this absolutely massive place spread across a couple of levels and with about three different styles, including old-style pub, modern superbar and European beer garden. It is the favourite destination for the after-work crowd, which mixes it up with all kinds of revellers from all over the country who come for the cheap booze, the charty music and the lack of pretention. Which makes us wonder why exactly the bouncers are so notoriously difficult?

HORSESHOE BAR
Map p70   Contemporary Bar
☎ 676 6471; www.theshelbourne.ie; Shelbourne Hotel, 27 St Stephen's Green; 🚌 all city centre; 🚉 St Stephen's Green

The refurb of the Shelbourne has brought us a brand new Horseshoe Bar, a thoroughly modern version of the old one beloved of politicians, hacks and journalists, where many an important decision was made, celebrated and even regretted around the once-horsehoe-shaped-but-now-rectangular bar.

MARKET BAR Map p70   Contemporary Bar
☎ 613 9094; www.marketbar.ie; 14a Fade St; 🚌 all city centre

An architectural beauty, this giant redbrick and iron girder room that was once a Victorian sausage factory is now a large, breezy bar that stands as a far more preferable

alternative to many of the city's superbars. Unlike virtually every other new pub in town, there's no music. It also does a roaring trade in Spanish-influenced pub grub (see p158).

MERCANTILE Map p70   Contemporary Bar
☎ 670 1700; 28 Dame St; 🚌 all city centre

A big, sprawling bar spread across three floors, the Mercantile's stock-in-trade has been tourists, mostly of the stag-and-hen type, who fill the place at weekends and lend it a party atmosphere which then attracts local lads and lasses looking for a bit of 'fun'. The music is as loud as the atmosphere is boisterous – you know what to expect!

BAR WITH NO NAME
Map p70   Contemporary Bar
☎ 675 3708; 3 Fade St; 🚌 all city centre

A low-key entrance just next to the trendy French restaurant L'Gueuleton (see p155) leads upstairs to one of the nicest bar spaces in town, consisting of three huge rooms in a restored Victorian townhouse plus a sizeable heated patio area for smokers. There's no sign or a name – folks just refer to it as the No Name Bar or, if you're a real insider, Number 3.

ODEON Map p68   Contemporary Bar
☎ 478 2088; www.odeon.ie; Old Harcourt St Station, 57 Harcourt St; 🚌 all city centre; 🚉 Harcourt

This former train station is light, airy, and jam-packed with art-deco elegance and Red Bull–loaded punters getting ready for a gig next door at Tripod. The comfy sofas are too scarce but this is the kind of place to be parading or standing along its impossibly long bar rather than sitting down anyway. Sunday afternoons are all about indulgence and taking it nice and easy with Bloody Marys, the newspapers and comfort foods.

IRISH DRINK IS MADE TO MEASURE

When drinking stout, beer or ale, the usual measure is a 'pint' (568mL). Half a pint is called a 'glass' and these are generally drunk by women – or visitors from Italy and Spain, unless of course they buy one pint to share among the whole group. Sound sexist and chauvinistic? Truth is that even if they only want a half, and are in a rush, most Dublin males will buy a half-measure and pour into a pint glass rather than be seen drinking from the half-pint glass. That's not to say that the pint glass is the sole preserve of the Dublin male; many a member of the Fair City's fairer sex are equally comfortable with the bigger measure, without any eyebrows being raised.

If you come to Ireland via Britain and drink spirits (or 'shorts' as they're called here), watch out: the English measure is a measly 25mL, while in Dublin you get a whopping 35mL, nearly 50% more.

PYGMALION Map p70 · Contemporary Bar

☎ 674 6712; www.bodytonicmusic.com; Powerscourt Townhouse Shopping Centre, 59 South William St; 🚌 all city centre

Currently one of the busiest bars in town, the 'Pyg' caters to a largely student crowd with its €10 pitchers, pounding music and labyrinthine nooks and crannies (perfect for a naughty hideaway). The owner thought it best to line the wall with carpet – perhaps they're worried that the action on the dance floor might get a little too crazy?

RON BLACK'S Map p70 · Contemporary Bar

☎ 672 8231; www.ronblacks.ie; 37 Dawson St; 🚌 all city centre

Big, brash and dripping with affluent young players seemingly insulated against the worst ravages of the economic collapse, Ron Black's is a suitably elegant kind of place, where budding business impresarios and sexy young barristers come to play and mate over expensive cocktails and tall tales.

SAMSARA Map p70 · Contemporary Bar

☎ 671 7723; www.lastampa.ie; 35 Dawson St; 🚌 all city centre

This huge Middle Eastern–themed drinking emporium is packed at weekends with gorgeous young things and thingies, air-kissing and comparing their designer ware. The seats are too uncomfortable and there's an overwhelming vibe of 'me, me, me!' but you can get through it by meditating on samsara – the endless cycle of suffering and reincarnation. Or just enjoy the eye candy.

ANSEO Map p68 · DJ Bar

☎ 475 1321; 28 Camden St; 🚌 all city centre

Unpretentious, unaffected and incredibly popular, this cosy alternative bar – which is pronounced 'an-shuh', the Irish for 'here' – is a favourite with those who live by the credo that to try too hard is far worse than not trying at all. Wearing cool like a loose garment, the punters thrive on the mix of chat and terrific DJs, who dig into virtually every crate to provide the soundtrack, whether it be Peggy Lee or Lee Perry.

BERNARD SHAW Map p68 · DJ Bar

☎ 085 712 8342; www.bodytonicmusic.com; 11-12 South Richmond St; 🚌 16, 19 or 122 from Trinity College; 🚆 Harcourt

This deliberately ramshackle boozer is probably the coolest bar in town for its

marvellous mix of music (courtesy of its owners, the Bodytonic production crew that also runs Twisted Pepper, see p189) and diverse menu of events such as afternoon car-boot sales, storytelling nights and fun competitions like having a 'tag-off' between a bunch of graffiti artists. This place looks like a dump, but it works because it is the effortless embodiment of the DIY, low-cost fun that is very much the city's contemporary Zeitgeist.

BIA BAR Map p70 · DJ Bar

☎ 405 3563; www.biabar.ie; 30 Lower Stephen St; 🚌 all city centre

This trendy watering hole is as popular with the after-work crowd as it is with young hipsters who come for the excellent music policy, which has brought some of the city's best DJs to ply their craft on the decks. It goes 'til late Thursday through Saturday, when the dance floor gets pretty packed – and there's no admission charge!

GLOBE Map p70 · DJ Bar

☎ 671 1220; www.globe.ie; 11 South Great George's St; ☽ from 5pm Mon-Fri; 🚌 all city centre

The granddaddy of the city's hipster bars, the Globe has held on to its groover status by virtue of tradition and the fact that the formula is brilliantly simple: wooden floors, plain brick walls and a no-attitude atmosphere that you just can't fake. The bar doubles as a chill-out room for the popular Rí Rá (p188).

HOGAN'S Map p70 · DJ Bar

☎ 677 5904; 35 South Great George's St; 🚌 all city centre

Once an old-style traditional bar, Hogan's is now a gigantic boozer spread across two floors. Midweek it's a relaxing hang-out for young professionals and restaurant and bar workers on a night off. But come the weekend the sweat bin downstairs pulls them in for some serious music courtesy of the usually excellent DJs.

NO 4 DAME LANE Map p70 · DJ Bar

☎ 679 0291; 4 Dame Lane; 🚌 all city centre

This two-storey designer bar took forever to get going – one of the pitfalls of trying to manufacture cool – but once it did it really took off, especially at weekends, when clubby kids and young professionals dressed as clubby kids try to hold a conversation above the loud DJ-led music. Upstairs is even louder, but that's OK, because – judging by some of the conversations we eavesdropped on – the music is often better than the chat. It has a late licence, so you don't have to bother with a nightclub.

SOLAS Map p68
DJ Bar

☎ 478 0583; www.solasbars.com; 31 Wexford St; 🚌 all city centre

Good DJs every night of the week are the primary attraction at this trendy little bar along trendy Wexford St; at weekends the music is loud and you'll most likely struggle to hear what's being said. Midweek the place is quieter but you might find yourself stopping the conversation with a 'hold on a minute, I love this song!'

SOUTH WILLIAM Map p70
DJ Bar

☎ 679 3701; www.southwilliam.ie; South William St; 🚌 all city centre

Its star doesn't shine quite as brightly as it did a couple of years ago when it opened, but this remains one of the hippest bars in town – which means that it caters primarily to the under-30s crowd. Behind the glass frontage you'll get top-class music, great DJs and a downstairs club.

VILLAGE Map p68
DJ Bar

☎ 475 8555; www.thevillagevenue.com; 26 Wexford St; 🚌 all city centre

Packed to overflowing every weekend, this large modern bar is where the lovely lads and gorgeous gals show off their plumage in a fun-time courting ritual that has the rest of them queuing up at the door to join in. There are live bands (see p195) and excellent DJs nightly, and Sunday night's Songs of Praise is the city's best karaoke night. The nightclub bit of the venue (see p189) opens Thursday to Saturday.

DRAGON Map p70
Gay Bar

☎ 478 1590; 64 South Great George's St; 🚌 all city centre

High-concept, high-octane and simply loaded with attitude, the Dragon is the slightly trendier alternative to the long-established George down the street (George and the Dragon; get it?). It's more popular with guys than girls, and even then with a certain type of guy – young, brash and unafraid to express themselves…on the dance floor or in the arms of another.

BEST BEER GARDENS

The most enterprising publicans in town have gone to great lengths to make sure their customers don't have the leave the pub to wreck their health. Top marks to:

- Dicey Reilly's (p173)
- Fitzsimons (p178)
- Long Stone (p176)
- Bar With No Name (p173)
- Sycamore Club (p179)

GEORGE Map p70
Gay Bar

☎ 478 2983; 89 South Great George's St; 🚌 all city centre

The purple mother of Dublin's gay bars is a long-standing institution, having lived through the years when it was the only place in town where the gay crowd could, well, be gay. There are other places to go, but the George remains the best, if only for tradition's sake. Shirley's legendary Sunday night bingo is as popular as ever.

BRUXELLES Map p70
Traditional Pub

☎ 677 5362; 7-8 Harry St; 🚌 all city centre

Although it has largely shed its heavy metal and alternative skin, Bruxelles is still a raucous, fun place to hang out and there are different music areas. It's comparatively trendy on the ground floor, while downstairs is a great, loud and dingy rock bar with live music each weekend. Just outside, a bronze Phil Lynott is there to remind us of Bruxelles' impeccable rock credentials (see the boxed text, p195).

DAWSON LOUNGE
Map p70
Traditional Pub

☎ 677 5909; 25 Dawson St; 🚌 all city centre

To see *the* smallest bar in Dublin, go through a small doorway, down a narrow flight of steps and into two tiny rooms that always seem to be filled with a couple of bedraggled drunks who look they're hiding. Psst, here's a secret: a certain sun-glassed lead singer of a certain ginormous Irish band is said to love unwinding in here from time to time.

GROGAN'S CASTLE LOUNGE
Map p70
Traditional Pub

☎ 677 9320; 15 South William St; 🚌 all city centre

This place is known simply as Grogan's (after the original owner), and it is a city-centre institution. It has long been a favourite haunt of Dublin's writers and painters, as well as others from the alternative bohemian set, most of whom seem to be waiting for the 'inevitable' moment when they are finally recognised as geniuses. A peculiar quirk of the pub is that drinks are marginally cheaper in the area with a stone floor than in the carpeted lounge, even though they are served by exactly the same bar!

INTERNATIONAL BAR

Map p70   Traditional Pub

☎ 677 9250; www.international-bar.com; 23 Wicklow St; 🚌 all city centre

This tiny pub with a huge personality is a top spot for an afternoon pint. It has a long bar, stained-glass windows, red velour seating and a convivial atmosphere. Some of Ireland's most celebrated comedians stuttered through their first set in the Comedy Cellar (p190), which is, of course, upstairs.

KEHOE'S Map p70   Traditional Pub

☎ 677 8312; 9 South Anne St; 🚌 all city centre

This is one of the most atmospheric pubs in the city centre and a favourite with all kinds of Dubliners. It has a beautiful Victorian bar, a wonderful snug, and plenty of other little nooks and crannies. Upstairs, drinks are served in what was once the publican's living room – and looks it!

LONG HALL Map p70   Traditional Pub

☎ 475 1590; 51 South Great George's St; 🚌 all city centre

Luxuriating in full Victorian splendour, this is one of the city's most beautiful and best-loved pubs. Check out the ornate carvings in the woodwork behind the bar and the elegant chandeliers. The bartenders are experts at their craft, an increasingly rare attribute in Dublin these days.

LONG STONE Map p115   Traditional Pub

☎ 671 8102; 10-11 Townsend St; 🚇 Tara St; 🚌 all city centre

Don't be fooled by the 'Old Man Pub' feel of this place – the flagstone floors, earthenware jugs and lace curtains are merely the dressing for what is the traditional pub equivalent of an uberbar. The difference here is that unlike so many obviously trendy places, this place is just about a good night out – so grab a table, get some drinks and settle in for the night.

MCDAID'S Map p70   Traditional Pub

☎ 679 4395; 3 Harry St; 🚌 all city centre

One of Dublin's best-known literary pubs, this classic boozer was Brendan Behan's 'local' (until he was barred) and it still oozes character. The pints are perfect, and best appreciated during the day when it's not full of our type. Thankfully, there's no music – just conversation and raucous laughter.

MULLIGAN'S Map p115   Traditional Pub

☎ 677 5582; 8 Poolbeg St; 🚇 Tara St; 🚌 all city centre

This brilliant old boozer was established in 1782 and has barely changed over the years. In fact, the last time it was renovated was when Christy Brown and his rowdy clan ran amok here in the film My Left Foot. It has one of the finest pints of Guinness in Dublin and a colourful crew of regulars. It's just off Fleet St, outside the eastern boundary of Temple Bar.

NEARY'S Map p70   Traditional Pub

☎ 677 8596; 1 Chatham St; 🚌 all city centre

One of a string of off–Grafton St, classic Victorian boozers once patronised by Dublin's legless literati, Neary's is a perfect stop-off day or night. It combines great service, a bohemian atmosphere and attractively

UNA MALLALLY: LGBT DUBLIN

How would you describe the gay scene in Dublin? Within the gay scene itself, everything is quite vibrant, with lots going on all the time. But the lines between the gay and straight scenes have become very blurred and things like club nights have become very mixed, which is a good thing. There are lots of 'polysexual' club nights, where the crowd is gay, straight, young and old.

Your favourite places to go? The Front Lounge (p179) is a beautiful, chilled-out bar with lovely staff and it's the perfect spot to start your night or have a relaxing Sunday afternoon drink. Pantibar (p181) is the city's only independently owned gay bar and club. It's wild and fun, but it's also like Cheers in that there's a good community of people there, people who aren't necessarily into dancing on the podium with their shirts off!

Una Mullally is features writer for the Sunday Tribune (www.tribune.ie).

worn furnishings, and is popular with actors from the nearby Gaiety Theatre (p198).

OLD STAND Map p70 — Traditional Pub
☎ 677 7220; 37 Exchequer St; 🚌 all city centre
Refreshingly unreconstructed, this is one of the oldest pubs in Dublin and seems to be just sauntering along at the same pace it was 10 years ago, as if the whole Celtic Tiger thing never happened. It's named after the old stand at Lansdowne Rd Stadium, and is a favourite with sports fans and reporters.

PETER'S PUB Map p70 — Traditional Pub
☎ 677 8588; 1 Johnston Pl; 🚌 all city centre
A pub for a chat and a convivial catch up, this humble and friendly place is more like Peter's Living Room, and is one of the few remaining drinking dens in this area that hasn't changed personality in recent years, and is all the better (and popular) for it.

STAG'S HEAD Map p70 — Traditional Pub
☎ 679 3701; 1 Dame Ct; 🚌 all city centre
The Stag's Head was built in 1770, remodelled in 1895 and thankfully not changed a bit since then. It's a superb pub: so picturesque that it often appears in films and also featured in a postage-stamp series on Irish bars. While you're waiting for your steak and chips you may find yourself philosophising in the ecclesiastical atmosphere, as James Joyce did. It's probable that some of the fitters that worked on this pub would have also worked on churches in the area, so the stained-wood-and- polished-brass similarities are no accident. A bloody great bar, no doubt.

SWAN Map p68 — Traditional Pub
☎ 647 5272; 70 Aungier St; 🚌 all city centre
John Lynch's pub (known to all as the Swan) is home to two kinds of punter: the in-for-a-pint-and-a-chat tippler that doesn't venture far from the Victorian front bar; and the more animated younger person, who finds solace and music in the side bar. A beautiful marriage that works because neither troubles the other.

WHELAN'S Map p68 — Traditional Pub
☎ 475 8555; www.whelanslive.com; 28 Wexford St; 🚌 all city centre
The traditional pub attached to the popular live music venue (see p195) was one of the best places to wind down a week over a pint and a chat, until it closed its doors for a major refurb. What it'll become is anyone's guess – we just hope that it keeps its old-fashioned ambience.

MERRION SQUARE & AROUND

Away from the city centre there are a number of fine pubs that are worthy of the trek. Many fill up with office workers straight after (or just before) clocking-off time and then get quieter as the night progresses.

DOHENY & NESBITT'S
Map p80 — Traditional Pub
☎ 676 2945; 5 Lower Baggot St; 🚌 all city centre
A standout, even in a city of wonderful pubs, Nesbitt's is equipped with antique snugs and is a favourite place for high-powered gossip among politicians and journalists; Leinster House (p83) is only a short stroll away.

HARTIGAN'S Map p80 — Traditional Pub
☎ 676 2280; 100 Lower Leeson St; 🚌 all city centre; 🚇 St Stephen's Green
This is about as spartan a bar as you'll find in the city, and is the daytime home to some serious drinkers, who appreciate the quiet, no-frills surroundings. In the evening it's popular with students from the medical faculty of University College Dublin (UCD).

JAMES TONER'S Map p80 — Traditional Pub
☎ 676 3090; 139 Lower Baggot St; 🚌 all city centre
Toner's, with its stone floors and antique snugs, has changed little over the years and is the closest thing you'll get to a country pub in the heart of the city. The shelves and drawers are reminders that it once doubled as a grocery shop. The writer Oliver St John Gogarty once brought WB Yeats here, after the upper-class poet – who only lived around the corner – decided he wanted to visit a pub. After a silent sherry in the noisy bar, Yeats turned to his friend and said, 'I have seen the pub, now please take me home'. We always suspected he was a little too precious for normal people, and he would probably be horrified by the good-natured business crowd making the racket these days too. His loss.

O'DONOGHUE'S Map p80   Traditional Pub

☎ 661 4303; 15 Merrion Row; 🚌 all city centre

Once the most renowned traditional music bar in all Dublin, this is where the world-famous folk group the Dubliners refined their raspish brand of trad in the 1960s. On summer evenings a young, international crowd spills out into the courtyard beside the pub. It's also a famous rugby pub and the Dublin HQ for many Irish and visiting fans.

TEMPLE BAR

Temple Bar's loud and busy pubs are a far cry from authentic, but they're undoubtedly fun – that is if your idea of fun is mixing it with a bunch of lads and lasses from the north of England, egging each other on to show off their family jewels and daring one another to drain 10 Fat Frogs in a row, all in front of a bemused audience of Spanish and Italian tourists, all sharing three glasses of Guinness. You've been warned!

FITZSIMONS Map p87   Contemporary Bar

☎ 677 9315; www.fitzsimonshotel.com; 21-22 Wellington Quay; 🚌 all city centre

The epitome of Temple Bar's commitment to a kind of loud and wonderfully unsophisticated nightlife is this sprawling hotel bar, which serves booze, sports and cheesy music to a throbbing crowd of pumped revellers. At weekends, it gets so busy that the bouncers don't even try to keep the crowd from spilling out onto the cobbled

streets. If you want a no-nonsense night out, this is the place for you.

MESSRS MAGUIRE

Map p87   Contemporary Bar

☎ 670 5777; 1-2 Burgh Quay; 🚌 all city centre

This uber-bar and microbrewery is spread across three levels, connected by a truly imperious staircase, and is a disconcerting mix of young and old, intimate and brash. Its own beers are worth contemplating, but not on the weekend when the place is absolutely jammers.

OCTAGON BAR

Map p87   Contemporary Bar

☎ 670 9000; www.theclarence.ie; Clarence Hotel, 6-8 Wellington Quay; 🚌 all city centre

Temple Bar's trendiest watering hole is where you'll find many of Dublin's celebrities (including mates of the owners, U2) and their hangers-on, swaggering and sipping expertly made cocktails in front of stylish wood panelling and amid perpetual daylight. Drinks are expensive, but if such things concern you, don't even try getting past the bouncers.

PORTERHOUSE BREWING COMPANY

Map p87   Contemporary Bar

☎ 679 8847; www.porterhousebrewco.com; 16-18 Parliament St; 🚌 all city centre

The second-biggest brewery in Dublin, the Porterhouse looks like a cross between a Wild West bar and a Hieronymus Bosch painting – all wood and full of staircases –

MARC BEREEM, PUBLICAN

'The days of the traditional Dublin pub, where all they do is serve a good pint of Guinness, are gone. The contemporary bar has to offer more, but it can't lose sight of the past either.' A bold statement, but Marc Bereem knows a thing or two about the city's bars. As one of the two brothers who own one of Dublin's trendiest bars, the South William (p175), Bereem (in his mid-30s) believes that the essence of a great Dublin pub is not the old-fashioned look but the personality behind the bar.

'If the staff feel a sense of ownership of the place and are to serve and entertain the clientele, then you have the makings of a great bar.' Marc is pretty adamant as to why so many other modern bars are so infinitely forgettable: 'Most of them are owned by companies who don't care about anything other than the bottom line.'

This is hardly the case with the South William, lovingly designed by Marc and his younger brother Conor in a style influenced as much by their extensive travels as their love of the simple lines of a traditional boozer. 'We wanted to create a simple space where young creative people would feel inspired…by the food, the music and the decor, which has lots of little things we collected over the years.'

The South William opened its doors in December 2006 and so far, so very good. Its mix of New York bar, trendy Parisian cafe and Dublin boozer hits the spot just right and manages to avoid the label of trying too hard. But where does Marc go when he wants a night off? 'My favourite pub is Peter's, which is conveniently just up the street!' Why aren't we surprised that he's chosen such a quiet and classy pub as his favourite?

on the fringe of Temple Bar. We love it, and although it inevitably gets crowded, this pub is for the discerning drinker and has lots of its own delicious brews, including its Plain Porter (some say it's the best stout in town) as well as unfamiliar imported beers.

PURTY KITCHEN
Map p87   Contemporary Bar

☎ 677 0945; 35 East Essex St; 🚍 all city centre
Three floors of mayhem, the Purty Kitchen is a typical Temple Bar superpub, packed to the rafters with students, tourists and other hedonists all intent on drinking as much as they can, dancing until their legs hurt and meeting that special someone with whom to share a brief but passionate burst of romance. It's especially crazy on Bank Holiday Sundays. The roof is where you'll find the fancy Sycamore Club (☎ 474 3942; www.sycamore club.com; 9 Sycamore St; ⏲ 6pm-2.30am Thu-Sat & bank holiday Sun), nominally a private members' club for over-25s, but easy enough to get into these days; here you'll rub shoulders with a trendier crowd and the occasional visiting band. The entrance is around the corner on Sycamore St.

THOMAS READ'S
Map p87   Contemporary Bar

☎ 670 7220; 1 Parliament St; 🚍 all city centre
The clientele at this spacious and airy bar, spread across two levels, seems to favour a selection of wine and coffee over beer. During the day, it's a great place to relax and read a newspaper. For a more traditional setting its annexe, the Oak, is still a great place for a pint.

TURK'S HEAD Map p87   Contemporary Bar

☎ 679 9701; 27-30 Parliament St;
🚍 all city centre
This superpub is decorated in two completely different styles – one really gaudy, the other a re-creation of LA c 1930 – and is

one of the oddest and most interesting in Temple Bar. It pulsates nightly with a young pumped-up crowd of mainly tourists, out to boogie to chart hits. Be mindful of hidden steps all over the place.

FRONT LOUNGE Map p87   Gay Bar

☎ 670 4112; 33-34 Parliament St;
🚍 all city centre
The unofficially gay 'Flounge' is a sophisticated and friendly bar that stands out from other gay joints in that it is quieter, more demure and popular with a mixed crowd. Sexual orientation here is strictly secondary to having a drink and a laugh with friends, even though the 'Back Lounge' toward the back of the bar is traditionally predominantly gay.

AULD DUBLINER
Map p87   Traditional Pub

☎ 677 0527; 17 Anglesea St; 🚍 all city centre
Predominantly patronised by tourists, 'the Auld Foreigner', as locals have dubbed it, has a carefully manicured 'old-world' charm that has been preserved – or refined – after a couple of renovations. It's a reliable place for a singsong and a laugh, as long as you don't mind taking 15 minutes to get to and from the jax (toilets).

BROGAN'S Map p87   Traditional Pub

☎ 679 9570; 75 Dame St; 🚍 all city centre
Only a couple of doors down from the Olympia Theatre (p194), this is a wonderful old-style bar where conversation – not loud music – is king. The beer is also pretty good.

OLIVER ST JOHN GOGARTY
Map p87   Traditional Pub

☎ 671 1822; www.gogartys.ie; 58-59 Fleet St;
🚍 all city centre
You won't see too many Dubs ordering drinks in this bar, which is almost entirely given over to tourists, who come for the carefully manufactured slice of authentic traditionalism…and the knee-slappin', toe-tappin' sessions that run throughout the day (see p196). The kitchen serves up dishes that most Irish cooks have consigned to the culinary dustbin.

PALACE BAR Map p87   Traditional Pub

☎ 677 9290; 21 Fleet St; 🚍 all city centre
With its mirrors and wooden niches, this is one of Dublin's great Victorian pubs and

used to be the unofficial head office of the *Irish Times*. Throughout the 1990s it steadfastly refused to accommodate the cubs of the Celtic Tiger and has always had a reputation as a place where yuppie bullshit is barred. While the Temple Bar vibe is encroaching on it a little, the staff's razor-sharp sarcasm can still bring uppity patrons down the required peg or two. Upstairs is where you'll hear some of the city's best traditional music (see p197).

TEMPLE BAR Map p87   Traditional Pub
☎ 677 3807; 48 Temple Bar; 🚌 all city centre
The most photographed pub facade in Dublin, perhaps the world, the Temple Bar (aka Flannery's) is smack bang in the middle of the tourist precinct and is usually chock-a-block with visitors. It's good craic though, and presses all the right buttons, with traditional musicians, a buzzy atmosphere and even a beer garden. It's also one of the most expensive pubs in Dublin.

KILMAINHAM & THE LIBERTIES
Like what's happening in the rejuvenated Smithfield across the river, some of the pubs in Dublin's oldest area are now being rediscovered by new crowds jaded with the super-pub phenomenon.

BRAZEN HEAD Map p91   Traditional Pub
☎ 679 5186; 20 Lower Bridge St; 🚌 51B, 78A or 123 from city centre
Reputedly Dublin's oldest pub, the Brazen Head has been serving thirsty patrons since 1198 when it was set up as a Norman tavern. Though its history is uncertain, the sunken level of the entrance courtyard clearly indicates how much street levels have altered since its construction. It's a bit away from the city centre, and the clientele is made up of foreign-language students, tourists and some grizzly auld locals. Robert Emmet was believed to have been a regular visitor, while in *Ulysses,* James Joyce reckoned 'you get a decent enough do in the Brazen Head'.

FALLON'S Map p91   Traditional Pub
☎ 454 2801; 129 The Coombe; 🚌 123, 206 or 51B from city centre
Just west of the city centre, in the heart of medieval Dublin, this is a fabulously

old-fashioned bar that has been serving a great pint of Guinness to a most discerning clientele since the end of the 17th century. Prize fighter Dan Donnelly, the only boxer ever to be knighted, was head bartender here in 1818. It's a genuine Irish bar filled with Dubs.

NORTH OF THE LIFFEY
The north side's pubs just don't get the same numbers of visitors as their south side brethren, which just means that if you're looking for a truly authentic pub experience, you're more likely to get it here. Around O'Connell St you'll also get the rough with the smooth, and we suggest you keep your wits about you late at night so as to avoid the potential for trouble that can sadly beset the city's main thoroughfare after dark.

MORRISON BAR
Map p102   Contemporary Bar
☎ 878 2999; Upper Ormond Quay; 🚌 all city centre; 🚇 Jervis
This is the north side's version of the Octagon Bar (p178), only far more difficult to get into if you don't look the part. If you haven't spent a fortune on your outfit (or managed to fake it), forget it. You wouldn't have enjoyed the luxurious John Rocha–designed dark-oak and cream interior, the views over the Liffey, and the suave and sophisticated clientele. Nah, you didn't miss much.

PRAVDA Map p102   Contemporary Bar
☎ 874 0076; www.pravda.ie; 35 Lower Liffey St; 🚌 all city centre; 🚇 Jervis
As un-Irish as you could probably get, this huge, multilevel Russian-themed bar was all the rage when it opened a few years ago. It has got a party atmosphere and is a great pick-up joint for young tourists, but you can forget about conversation at night (because the music is so loud) and the bouncers seem especially dim-witted.

DICE BAR Map p102   DJ Bar
☎ 674 6710; 79 Queen St; 🚌 25, 25A, 38, 39 or 39A from Burgh Quay; 🚇 Smithfield
Co-owned by Huey from the Fun Lovin' Criminals, the Dice Bar looks like something you might find on New York's Lower East Side. Its dodgy locale, black-and-red painted interior, dripping candles and stressed seating, combined with rocking

DJs most nights, make it a magnet for Dublin's beautiful beatnik crowds. It has Guinness and local microbrews.

SIN É Map p102 — DJ Bar
☎ 878 7078; 14-15 Ormond Quay; 🚌 all city centre

This is unquestionably one of the best bars on the north side, if not all of Dublin. The name (pronounced shin-ay) means 'that's it' in Irish and pays tribute to the legendary 1990s Irish cafe-bar in New York's East Village where Jeff Buckley first performed. Like its American namesake, style is forsaken over substance: the theme is (vaguely) Irish pub meets western saloon, with lots of wood and long banquettes, but it's really all about ambience. The crowd is a terrific mix of students, professionals, the hip and the indifferent. The DJs are uniformly excellent as are the bar staff, who keep the place ticking over just nicely. Recommended.

PANTIBAR Map p102 — Gay Bar
☎ 874 0710; www.pantibar.com; 7-8 Capel St; 🕔 from 5pm; 🚌 all city centre; 🚊 Jervis

It's not as big as the George (p175) or as in-your-face as the Dragon (p175), but Pantibar is just as bold and brash as both, mostly because it's owner, the eponymous Panti, is an outrageous entertainer and goes to great lengths to make sure that a night in her bar is going to be one to remember. The floor shows – both on and off the stage – are fabulous. It's open late Friday and Saturday.

FLOWING TIDE Map p102 — Traditional Pub
☎ 874 0842; 9 Lower Abbey St; 🚌 all city centre; 🚊 Abbey

This beautiful, atmospheric old pub is directly opposite the Abbey (p197) and is popular with theatre-goers – it can get swamped around 11pm, after the curtain comes down. They blend in with some no-bullshit locals who give the place a vital edge, and make it a great place for a drink and a natter.

GILL'S Map p102 — Traditional Pub
☎ 855 4128; 555 North Circular Rd; 🚌 10, 38 or 122 from city centre

Just a stone's throw from Croke Park, this unashamedly old-fashioned boozer was one of Brendan Behan's favourites and the place where his friends chose to wake his passing when he died. If you're on your way to

A NON-ALCOHOLIC NIGHT OUT
Need a drink but don't fancy the pub? Make your way down the (slightly questionable entrance) of Tea Garden (Map p102; ☎ 086 219 1010; www.tea-garden.eu; 7 Lwr Ormond Quay; pot of tea €5-13; 🕔 3-11pm Mon-Thu, from 1pm Fri-Sun), one of the coolest places to hang out in all of Dublin. Laid out like an Asian teahouse, with low tables and lighting, soft cushions and a shoes-off policy, the Slovak owners will happily explain their own teahouse culture before expertly advising you on a selection of teas from around the globe. The menu also has coffees, smoothies and hookah pipes. Each pot is enough for two to three people.

Croker for a match, or just want to try out a good old-style pub, there are few better.

NEALON'S Map p102 — Traditional Pub
☎ 872 3247; Capel St; 🚌 all city centre; 🚊 Jervis

The warm and cosy decor of this traditional pub is matched by the exceptionally friendly staff. It's a bit of old Dublin on a street getting ready to take off, so catch it while you can. There's live jazz on Sunday.

OVAL Map p102 — Traditional Pub
☎ 872 1259; 78 Middle Abbey St; 🚌 all city centre; 🚊 Abbey

This is a great little pub, where young and old come together in conversation and rich, creamy pints go down a treat. The Tardis effect is evident once you walk through the door: it is much bigger than it looks from the outside, spreading over three floors.

PATRICK CONWAY'S
Map p102 — Traditional Pub
☎ 873 2687; 70 Parnell St; 🚌 all city centre

This gem of a pub has been lining up drinks since 1745 and joyous fathers – including Colm Meaney's character in The Snapper (see p43) – have been skulling celebratory pints at its bar since the day the Rotunda Maternity Hospital opened across the road in 1757. Upstairs is the fantastic Boom Boom Room, one of the best places in the city for good live music.

SACKVILLE LOUNGE
Map p102 — Traditional Pub
☎ 874 5222; Sackville Pl; 🚌 all city centre; 🚊 Abbey

This tiny 19th-century, one-room, wood-panelled bar lies just off O'Connell St and is popular with actors from the nearby Abbey and Peacock theatres (see p197), as well as a disproportionate number of elderly drinkers. It's a good pub for a solitary pint.

SEAN O'CASEY'S Map p102   Traditional Pub
☎ 874 8675; 105 Marlborough St; 🚌 all city centre; 🚇 Abbey
The antithesis of the Dublin superpub, this is the kind of place where the male drinkers (and there seems to be *only* male drinkers) look up and grunt when you walk through the door. It's a Kerry pub, decked out in the county's Gaelic Athletic Association (GAA) colours, and is particularly lively when Kerry are playing in Croke Park.

WELCOME INN Map p102   Traditional Pub
☎ 874 3227; 93 Parnell St; 🚌 1 or 2 from city centre
This musty, scruffy, wonderful bar has been a favourite with the city's college slackers for a couple of generations. They love the oversized lounge and its assorted cast of characters, which these days include groups of Spanish and Italian tourists looking to check out Dublin alcoholics up close.

DOCKLANDS
The Docklands area isn't great for pubs, with one exception. There is another spot where you can sample some pretty fine wines.

KENNEDY'S Map p115   Traditional Pub
☎ 677 0626; 10 George's Quay; 🚇 Tara St; 🚌 all city centre
This is a proper traditional pub where literally nothing has changed in 50 years, including some of the clientele. Tread softly and speak even quieter so as not to disturb the contemplative atmosphere of a bar that seems oblivious to what's happened to Dublin in the last 20 years.

LA CUVEE @ ENO WINE BAR
Map p115   Wine Bar
☎ 636 0616; Irish Financial Services Centre, Mayor Sq; 🚌 151 from city centre
A wine bar in a financial services centre sounds like a formula for insufferable pretentiousness, but this remarkable venture is unique to the city so we thought we'd give it a try – and we weren't disappointed. Basically, this is a wine-tasting centre where you buy a card for whatever amount you

like and are then free to try any of the 60-plus wines that are available, deducting the cost of it from your card as you go along. The Shiraz is to die for, darling.

PHOENIX PARK
There are no pubs in the park itself, but at the city side of the main park gates is one of Dublin's classic Victorian haunts, which has a mixed clientele of guidebook-toting visitors and bemused regulars.

RYAN'S Map p119   Traditional Pub
☎ 677 6097; 28 Parkgate St; 🚇 Heuston
Near the main entrance to the Phoenix Park, this is one of only a handful of city pubs that has retained its Victorian decor virtually intact, complete with ornate bar and snugs. An institution among Dublin's public houses, this is truly worth the trip.

BEYOND THE GRAND CANAL
Southern suburban bars are among the most popular in town, especially those in the chichi Dublin 4 area, where the bold and the beautiful swap tales of new cars bought with old money over vodka gimlets and gin and tonics.

ICE BAR Map p122   Contemporary Bar
☎ 665 4000; Four Seasons Hotel, Simmonscourt Rd; 🚌 5, 7, 7A, 8, 18 or 45 from city centre
Not to be confused with the Dice Bar (p180) in a taxi – practise your elocution because the bars are worlds apart in every sense. Young, single 20-somethings with infinite disposable incomes come here to see and be seen, making this either the most sought-after destination in town or somewhere to

OUR THREE FAVOURITE PUB JOKES

- A man walks into a pub with a roll of tarmac under his arm and says, 'Pint please, and one for the road'.
- A duck walks into a bar. The barman says, 'Hey, your pants are down'. (Think about it.)
- A white horse walks into a bar and orders a drink. The barman says 'Hey! We've a whiskey named after you!' The horse looks confused and replies, 'You've a whiskey called Dobbin?'

avoid like a bad dose of plague. Flash your convertible-beemer car keys at the door for speedy access. The all-white chichi interior with central chrome and marble bar is softened by some lovely, specially commissioned wall hangings by Irish artists. Vodka-based cocktails are the house speciality.

KIELY'S Map p122   Contemporary Bar
☎ 283 0209; 22 Donnybrook Rd; 🚌 10 or 46X from city centre
Fans of satirist Paul Howard's lovable D4 monster Ross O'Carroll-Kelly will instantly recognise the favourite hang-out of the rugby-loving southsider, where the fortunes of Drico, Shaggy and the Darce are discussed in earnest by hard bodies wrapped in Leinster jerseys…and that's just the girls. If you're going to the next-door Donnybrook Rugby Ground, this is the perfect pre- and post-match place to be.

O'BRIEN'S Map p122   Traditional Pub
☎ 668 2851; 8-9 Sussex Tce, Upper Leeson St; 🚌 18 from city centre
The unofficial HQ of media types and advertising execs, old-fashioned O'Brien's is the embodiment of all the aspirations of the Celtic Tiger, a place where prosperity and forward-thinking can flourish amid the powerfully nostalgic reminders of a time gone by. Which pretty much means that O'Brien's hasn't changed its decor all that much, but the bathrooms are absolutely spotless.

SEARSON'S Map p122   Traditional Pub
☎ 660 0330; www.searsons.ie; 42-44 Upper Baggot St; 🚌 10, 10A or 66D from city centre

What could easily be dismissed as yet another characterless superpub, with the warmth and ambience of a train station, is actually a pretty decent bar with the option of Old Man pub at the front and trendy, modern bar at the back. Something for everyone then: lunchtimes it's packed with office workers, weekend nights it's packed with the same crowd in jeans and designer shirts and, when the rugby's on, the Irish green. Two Havana Clubs and Coke, please.

BEYOND THE ROYAL CANAL

It is just beyond the north side's canal that you can find some of the best traditional pubs in Dublin, and this place is highly recommended.

GRAVEDIGGERS (AKA KAVANAGH'S)
Off Map p125   Traditional Pub
☎ 830 7978; 1 Prospect Sq, Glasnevin; 🚌 13 from city centre
The gravediggers from the adjacent Glasnevin Cemetery (p125) had a secret serving hatch so that they could drink on the job – hence the pub's nickname. Founded in 1833 by one John Kavanagh and still in the family, this pub is one of the best in Ireland, virtually unchanged in 150 years. In summer time the green of the square is full of drinkers basking in the sun, while inside the hardened locals ensure that ne'er a hint of sunshine disturbs some of the best Guinness in town. An absolute classic.

NIGHTLIFE & THE ARTS

top picks

- Abbey Theatre (p197)
- Button Factory (p188)
- Devitt's (p196)
- Dublin Fringe Festival (p198)
- JJ Smyth's (p193)
- Lighthouse Cinema (p191)
- O2 (p195)
- Tripod (p195)
- Sugar Club (p195)
- Whelan's (p195)

Wait a minute…we've already included a chapter devoted to drinking, what else is there that falls under 'nightlife' in this town? Doesn't *everybody* come here to drink the beer and discover their inner poet? Even the most hard-nosed business deal is discussed and delivered at some point with a pint (or two) in one of the city's 1000-or-so boozers.

Believe it or not, there is life beyond the pub or, more accurately, *around* it. Dublin's status as an entertainment giant has been hyped out of all proportion by the tourist authorities and other vested interests, but it is – for its size at least – a pretty good town to amuse yourself in, with a range of options to satisfy most tastes. There are comedy clubs and opera nights, recitals and readings, cinemas and concert halls. There is the theatre, where you can enjoy a light-hearted musical alongside the more serious stuff by Beckett, Yeats and O'Casey – not to mention a host of new talents. There is music, and lots of it – you can trawl through the listings virtually every day and find a live gig, from classical to contemporary, featuring musicians both home-grown and internationally renowned. There are festivals, dozens of them running throughout the year, devoted to film, theatre, literature, dance and music. And when everything else has closed its doors for the night, you can go back to the pub, or negotiate your way past club bouncers, and strut your funky stuff on a packed dance floor. Whatever it is that floats your boat, you can be sure you will find a version of it in Dublin.

A word to the wise: if you really want to get a full slice of what's available, look beyond Temple Bar. We're not saying you should avoid it – a night of sloppy hedonism should always feature on the schedule – but we do believe that the district is a victim of its own success. The south side remains the part of Dublin with most to offer, but ignore the north side at your peril; not only does it have the city's most important theatres, but the nightlife is constantly evolving, thanks in large part to the influx of nationals from all over the world who have added new flavour to the business of having fun.

BOOKINGS

Theatre, comedy and classical concerts are usually booked directly through the venue. Tickets for touring international bands and big-name local talent are either sold at the venue or through a number of booking agencies, including Road Records (☎ 671 7340; www.road recs.com; 16 Fade St), which sells tickets to smaller alternative gigs and DJ sets, HMV (Map p70; ☎ 24hr credit-card booking line 679 5334; 65 Grafton St), which sells tickets to pop and rock gigs (see also p142), and Ticketmaster (Map p70; ☎ 0818 719 300, 456 9569; www.ticketmaster.ie; St Stephen's Green Shopping Centre), which sells tickets to every genre of big- and medium-sized show – but be aware that it charges between 9% and 12.5% service charge *per ticket*.

CLUBBING

It's been an interesting ride since the halcyon days of the early 1990s, when exploring the underground scene fuelled by ecstasy (lovingly referred to as 'disco biscuits') and dancing to the pounding beats of white-label floor-killers virtually defined a whole generation's experience of what a good night out really was. A brief few years of unregulated excess were followed by the general move to the middle of the road, as venue owners cottoned on to the fact that there was a lot of money to be made from kids in DayGlo tops and crazy smiles.

To be fair, club owners were forced to worry about the bottom line as a result of the late-night bar licence (see the boxed text, p189), which created real competition for pay-in clubs in the shape of free entry and late-night bars that closed only an hour earlier than the clubs, thereby prompting thousands of punters to keep their euro in their pockets and stay put; the music was just as loud and the booze (marginally) cheaper.

For a few years the other victim of the bottom line was musical variety, as clubs were forced to appeal to as broad an audience as possible, putting an end to the likes of Afrobeat nights and other sounds of the musical margins in favour of a tried-and-tested menu of unchallenging dance music, rock and charty stuff.

These days, pop is the Zeitgeist of the dance floor, but lest you think that it's all gone bubblegum, there's been a wonderful reaction to the sameness of the last few years with the rise of so-called 'creative clubbing', an explosion of imaginatively themed nights that try to give the clubbers something more than just loud music and a dance floor. These run the gamut from dressing up as your favourite Edwardian literary figure to a tropical hula-hoop night.

Dublin may not be able to match other European capitals in the clubbing stakes, but it more than makes up for its shortcomings with the anything-goes atmosphere generated by the clubbers themselves. Dubliners love to dance and will not let the total absence of rhythm or style get in the way of getting down – a lack of inhibition brought on by a long night's drinking. The other bonus is the city's fixed position on the gigging schedules of some of the world's best DJs, who complement the cream of local talent and help generate some truly memorable nights.

The busiest club nights are Thursday to Saturday, but there's something going on virtually every other night of the week except Sunday. The listings publications and websites (see boxed text, below) have comprehensive, night-by-night coverage of who and what's playing where and when. Admission to most places is between €5 and €8 Monday to Thursday, rising to up to €15 or €20 on Friday and Saturday. For discounts, look out for the thousands of fliers that are distributed around most of the city centre's pubs.

ACADEMY Map p102

☎ 877 9999; www.theacademydublin.com; 57 Middle Abbey St; ⏰ Fri & Sat; 🚌 all city centre; 🚆 Abbey

A terrific midsized venue, the Academy's music policy runs the gamut from disco and R & B to alternative rock and hard dance…whatever keeps them dancing, so long as it's not sell-out commercial.

ANDREW'S LANE THEATRE Map p70

☎ 478 0766; Andrew's La; ⏰ Thu–Sun; 🚌 all city centre

Recently converted from a much-loved theatre, club purists will enjoy ALT's stripped-down look: a huge dance floor, a kick-ass sound system and a bar are the essentials to a good night. Add a couple of regular nights (Sunday's Italian Factory is a banging

WHAT'S ON

To make sense of Dublin's entertainment options, a number of resources will come in handy. Listings of virtually every event appear in the following websites and publications – available at all newsagents except for the *Dublin Event Guide*, which is found in hostels, cafes and bars.

Newspapers

Dublin Event Guide (www.eventguide.ie; free) A comprehensive fortnightly listings newspaper.

Evening Herald (www.unison.ie; €1) The Thursday edition features listings of pop and rock concerts, movies and other popular activities.

Hot Press (www.hotpress.com; €3.95) Dublin's premier weekly entertainment magazine lists all gigs and events.

Irish Times (www.irishtimes.com; €1.80) The Friday edition has an excellent pull-out section called the *Ticket,* with reviews and listings of upcoming events.

Irish Independent (www.independent.ie; €1.80) The Friday edition's pull-out section is called Night/Day and covers entertainment as well as reviews.

Websites

Dublinks (www.dublinks.com) Good for all kinds of entertainment in the capital.

Dublinpubscene.com (www.dublinpubscene.com) An exhaustive list of where to go for night-time fun, including club nights.

Entertainment.ie (www.entertainment.ie) An excellent, catch-all listings page detailing what's on.

MCD (www.mcd.ie) Ireland's biggest promoter provides a comprehensive list of upcoming gigs.

Nialler9 (www.nialler9.com) Fabulous listings website for gigs compiled by one of the most trustworthy reviewers of the Dublin musical scene.

top picks

CLUB NIGHTS

- **War** (Spy, opposite; Friday) Glitter, gold and glamour is the order of the day with great sounds delivered by DJs Mixen Vixen, Bitches with Wolves and Cooler than You. If you like Lady Gaga…
- **Antics** (PoD, right; Wednesday) Two rooms: one with classic indie and rock, the other with electro and new wave. Great night out.
- **Soundcheck** (Spy, opposite; Thursday) One of the most interesting nights in town; no week is ever the same but the music is always fresh and interesting.
- **Sunday Night @ Ukiyo** (Ukiyo, p192; Sunday) Not technically a club night, but Sunday nights in this Korean restaurant are the place to be if you want to hear some fabulous DJs play some killer tunes to a mellow, appreciative audience. Dancing is very much permitted!
- **Pogo** (Twisted Pepper, opposite; Friday) The best techno night in town features excellent local DJs and a rotating menu of top-class international names like Carl Craig and Derrick May.

night of European hard house), a regular menu of visiting DJs and live gigs and you've got the makings of a *great* night.

BUTTON FACTORY Map p87

☎ 670 9202; www.buttonfactory.ie; Curved St; admission €8-12; ⏲ Thu-Sun; 🚌 all city centre
Temple Bar's best venue is a top-class joint for both gigs and clubs that deserves a merit badge on two counts: firstly for offering something to the left of the usual Temple Bar cheese; and secondly for being swanky and carpeted. Great sound, big room, terrific spot.

COPPER FACE JACKS Map p68

☎ 475 8777; www.jackson-court.ie; Jackson Court Hotel, 29-30 Harcourt St; admission €6-12; 🚌 all city centre; 🚇 Harcourt/St Stephen's Green
Dublin's ultimate meat market packs them in and has a reputation for being the destination of choice for off-duty police officers, nurses and anyone looking to avoid music that didn't chart. Don't let the presence of the law put you off though. From what we've heard, they're the biggest miscreants of the lot, especially if there are nurses about!

HOGAN'S Map p70

☎ 677 5904; 35 South Great George's St; admission free; ⏲ Thu-Sun; 🚌 all city centre
The basement of this popular bar (p174) is where you'll hear some of Dublin's best DJs spin to a sweaty, appreciative floor – the music policy is not overly precious, but you won't hear anything charty. On Fridays, Mr Moto and Nelly Romano play Latin-fused house.

KRYSTLE Map p68

☎ 478 4066; www.krystlenightclub.com; Russell Court Hotel, 21-25 Harcourt St; ⏲ Thu-Sat; 🚌 all city centre; 🚇 Harcourt/St Stephen's Green
The favourite venue of many a Celtic cub, Krystle (annoyingly pronounced 'cris-*tal*' by its snootiest devotees) is where you'll most likely find the current crop of celebrities and their hangers-on, although you'll have to wade your way through the huge main floor and gain access to the upstairs VIP lounge for maximum exposure. Chart hits and club classics are the mainstay here.

LILLIE'S BORDELLO Map p70

☎ 679 9204; www.lilliesbordello.ie; Adam Ct; admission €5-15; ⏲ Mon-Sat; 🚌 all city centre
Dublin's most prestigious nightclub is not nearly as exclusive as it was a couple of years ago – it just can't afford to be. Still, the door policy is stricter here than anywhere else: either look good or be famous or 'not tonight, buddy'. And if you do get in, you still won't rub shoulders with whatever Cristal-swilling visiting megarapper is in town: they're safely ensconced in the ultra-VIP Jersey Lil's private members' bar. Bad music, bad attitude.

POD Map p68

☎ 478 0025; www.pod.ie; 35 Harcourt St; admission €5-20; ⏲ Wed-Sat; 🚌 all city centre; 🚇 Harcourt
Dublin's once-legendary dance club has been resized to fit owner John Reynold's vision of three entertainment venues in one complex, with the now smaller PoD still hosting some excellent club nights, including Friday night's Trainwreck – all techno, house and electro.

RÍ RÁ Map p68

☎ 677 4835; www.rira.ie; Dame Ct; admission free; 🚌 all city centre

A true veteran of the city's club scene, Rí Rá – one half of the Irish expression *rí rá agus ruaile buaile* (pronounced 'ree raw aw-gus roola boola'), which translates roughly as 'devilment and good fun' – has been keeping the dance floor full with funky beats for more than 15 years. Unfortunately, it has gone through some tough financial times recently and may not be around when you read this.

SPY/WAX Map p70

☎ 677 0014; Powerscourt Town Centre, South William St; admission €6-12; 🚇 all city centre

Part of the magnificent 18th-century Powerscourt complex (p77), at Spy/Wax you get two clubs for the price of one: upstairs, spread across three levels and a host of rooms, is handsome Spy, where the music is eclectic and the crowd beautifully self-aware. In the basement is Wax, a hardcore dance sweatbox where you can really let loose.

THE GOOD BITS Map p102

☎ 819 7635; Store St; admission €5-17; 🕙 Thu-Sat; 🚉 Connolly

Dublin's newest club venue is part-run by legendary local DJ Johnny Moy, who uses his extensive contacts in the music world to bring in some of the best DJs, as well as members from various trendy bands, to try their hand behind the decks. It is very popular with a younger crowd, who appreciate the cutting-edge sounds.

THINK TANK Map p87

☎ 670 7655; www.thethinktank.ie; 24 Eustace St; admission €6-15; 🚇 all city centre

Dance DJs, Battle of the Bands nights, visiting live acts and assorted other festivities make up the menu at this basement club in Temple Bar. There's a mix of underground R & B, hip hop, trance, house and other electronic beats to keep the largely youthful crowd dancing.

TRIPOD Map p68

☎ 478 0025; www.tripod.ie; 35 Harcourt St; admission €5-20; 🕙 Wed-Sat; 🚇 all city centre; 🚉 Harcourt

Part of the PoD entertainment complex, Tripod hosts mostly live music, but it's where you'll also get to hear visiting DJs play. It's mostly four-to-the-floor stuff: house, techno and electro, but the occasional hip-hop turntablist turns up with a bag of tricks.

TWISTED PEPPER Map p102

☎ 873 4800; www.bodytonicmusic.com; 54 Middle Abbey St; 🕙 8am-midnight Mon-Wed, 10am-2.30am Thu-Sat; 🚇 all city centre; 🚉 Abbey

Dublin's coolest new venue comes in four parts: the basement is where you can hear some of the best DJs in town, the stage is for live acts, the mezzanine is a secluded bar area above the stage and the cafe is where you can get an Irish breakfast all day. All run by the Bodytonic crew, one of the most exciting music and production crowds in town. What more could you want?

VILLAGE Map p68

☎ 475 8555; 26 Wexford St; www.thevillage venue.com; admission €8-10; 🕙 Thu-Sat; 🚇 all city centre

When the live music ends (see p195), the club kicks off and takes 600-odd groovers through a consistent mix of new and old tunes, dance-floor classics and whatever else will shake that booty. A great venue, an eager crowd and a top night out overall.

WRIGHT VENUE Map p225

☎ 890 0099; South Quarter, Airside Retail Park, Swords; www.thewrightvenue.ie; admission €8-10; 🕙 Fri & Sat; 🚌 WV Bus

OK, so you'll have to traipse out to the 'burbs beyond the airport to get here, but what will greet you at the end of your journey is Dublin's most OTT club, the kind

---

OPENING HOURS

It's difficult to be one of Europe's coolest clubbing cities if everything has to shut down just as the night is getting going everywhere else. So difficult, in fact, that Dublin clubs are not too cool at all. No matter where you are, the needles come off the decks at 2.30am sharp and everyone has to clear out within half an hour. The authorities listen to the complaints about a nanny state and then do nothing about it; there are much more powerful forces exerting influence than a bunch of clubbers looking to stretch the good times by a couple of hours, namely the publicans themselves, who hate the idea of late openings and will fight tooth and nail to resist them.

of place that makes more sense in Miami. Fittingly, the VIP room is a replica of Tony Montana's office in *Scarface*! It's where sub-urbanite kids come to dream – and dance to fairly conventional club hits. The club's own WV Bus (Mansion House, Dawson St; one way/return €6/10; ☺ 11pm & midnight) is the easiest way to get there and back from the city centre.

COMEDY

The Irish can be hilarious. Off-the-cuff, in the pub, their real speciality is deflationary, iconoclastic humour as used within that other great art form, storytelling. It's all about pacing and not taking yourself too seriously. On a stage, though, they tend to take themselves far too seriously.

Still, a few names have risen out of the mire of mother-in-law jokes and earned that elusive tag of great comic. Besides stars like Dermot Morgan and Ardal O'Hanlon – who gave us the utterly brilliant *Father Ted* – these include the observational genius of Dara O'Briain, the laconic wit of Dylan Moran, the superb Deirdre O'Kane and the most popular funnyman of recent years, Tommy Tiernan.

The highlight of the comedy year is the annual Bulmers International Comedy Festival (www.bulmerscomedy.ie), which takes place at 20-odd venues over three weeks, usually in September, and features a barrel-load of local and international talent. Big laughs.

BANKER'S Map p70

☎ 679 3697; 16 Trinity St; admission €8; ☺ 9-11pm; ▣ all city centre

A Friday-night improv club takes place in the basement of this bar near Trinity College. It has yet to establish itself as a success, but it's a good spot to watch wet-behind-the-ears wannabe comics go through their (often terrified) paces. And who said *Schadenfreude* wasn't fun?

COMEDY DUBLIN

☎ 872 9199; www.comedydublin.com; admission €8; ☺ from 8pm

Some of Dublin's best comic talents have grouped together to create a comedy troupe that takes to the stage on Sunday nights in the Belvedere (Map p102; ☎ 872 9199; Great Denmark St) and Tuesday nights in Sheehan's (Map p70; ☎ 677 1914; 17 Chatham St). Some of their stuff is hilarious.

HA'PENNY BRIDGE INN Map p87

☎ 677 0616; 42 Wellington Quay; adult/concession €6/5; ☺ 9-11pm; ▣ all city centre

From Tuesday to Thursday you can hear some fairly funny comedians (as well as some truly awful ones) do their stuff in the upstairs room of this Temple Bar pub. Tuesday night's Battle of the Axe (☎ 086 815 6987; www.battleoftheaxe.com), an improvisation night that features a lot of 'crowd participation' (read 'trading insults'), is the best of them.

INTERNATIONAL BAR Map p68

☎ 677 9250; www.international-bar.com; 23 Wicklow St; admission €7.50; ☺ 9-11pm; ▣ all city centre

The room above this pub (see p176) hosts comedy every night of the week. From Monday's Comedy Improv to new-material night on Sunday's International Comedy Club, this is where you can hear the best of the country's new crop of comedians, and watch established talents try out new material.

LAUGHTER LOUNGE Map p102

☎ 1800 266 339; www.laughterlounge.com; 4-8 Eden Quay; admission from €25; ☺ doors open 7.30pm

Dublin's only specially designated comedy theatre is where you'll find those comics too famous for the smaller pub stages but

---

PARTY ON: ARVEENE JUTHAN

The Dublin scene? Dublin doesn't do full-on raves, but it has a great culture of parties hosted by smaller clubs and venues. **Essence of a good night out?** Everyone should be on the level; even if people don't know you they treat you like they do. **Best night out?** Sunday in Ukiyo (p192), where you can hear the likes of Jason O'Callaghan throw down some serious disco. Another great venue with the same kind of ethos is Twisted Pepper (p189). **Favourite club nights?** As for club nights, my choices would be Transmission on a Saturday night in the Button Factory (p188) or Antics on a Wednesday night in the PoD (p188), both of which are popular with a new generation of clubber, whose musical tastes are pretty sophisticated thanks to the influence of travel and the internet. *Arveene Juthan is one of Ireland's best-known DJs and a regular guest of the Prodigy and Soulwax.*

SODOM & BEGORRAH

Ah, those Dubs and their word plays. One of our favourites was coined by the country's first film censor, James Montgomery, appointed in 1932. He took his job very seriously and dedicated himself to protecting Irish audiences from the 'californication' of American films (Red Hot Chili Peppers, eat your hearts out). He also cast a suspicious eye on the activities of the Gate and Abbey theatres, which he dubbed Sodom and Begorrah. Brilliant.

not famous enough to sell out the city's bigger venues. Think comedians on the way up (or on the way down).

FILM

Little-known fact: in December 1909, James Joyce opened the Volta Cinematograph on Mary St in Dublin – the city's first cinema. A century later, Dublin's love affair with movies is reflected in the fact that the city has the highest number of young cinema-goers in all of Europe. The cluster of independent cinemas that were dotted around the city centre have long since gone, however, to be replaced with the ubiquitous suburban multiplex showing the usual selection of first-run films and the odd independent movie. Of the five cinemas in the city centre, three offer a more offbeat list of foreign releases and art-house films.

Save yourself the hassle of queuing and book your tickets online, especially for Sunday-evening screenings of popular first-run films. Out on the piss Friday and Saturday nights, most Dubliners have neither the energy nor the cash for more of the same, so it's a trip to the cinema at the end of the weekend. Admission prices are generally €5 to €6 for afternoon shows, rising to €9.50 after 5pm. If you have a student card, you pay only €6 for all shows.

CINEWORLD MULTIPLEX Map p102

☎ 0818 304 204; www.cineworld.ie; Parnell Centre, Parnell St; 🚌 all city centre

This 17-screen cinema replaced many smaller cinemas and shows only commercial releases. The seats are comfy, the concession stand is huge and the selection of pick 'n' mix could induce a sugar seizure. It lacks the style of the older-style cinema, but we like it anyway.

IRISH FILM INSTITUTE Map p87

☎ 679 3477; www.irishfilm.ie; 6 Eustace St; 🚌 all city centre

The Irish Film Institute (IFI) has a couple of screens and shows classics and new art-

house films, although we question some of their selections: weird and controversial can be a little tedious if the film is crap. The complex also has a bar, a cafe and a bookshop. Weekly (€1.70) or annual (€20) membership is required for some uncertified films that can only be screened as part of a 'club' – the only way to get around the censor's red pen. It's a great cinema, but sometimes it can be a little pretentious.

LIGHTHOUSE CINEMA Map p102

☎ 879 7601; www.lighthousecinema.ie; Smithfield Plaza; 🚌 all city centre; 🚇 Smithfield

The most impressive cinema in town is this snazzy four-screener in a stylish new building just off Smithfield Plaza. The menu is strictly art house, and the trendy cafe-bar on the ground floor is perfect for discussing the merits of German Expressionism.

SAVOY Map p102

☎ 0818 776 776; www.savoy.ie; Upper O'Connell St; 🚌 all city centre

The Savoy is a five-screen, first-run cinema, and has late-night shows at weekends. Savoy Cinema 1 is the largest in the country and its enormous screen is the perfect way to view really spectacular blockbuster movies.

SCREEN Map p115

☎ 671 4988; www.screencinema.ie; 2 Townsend St; 🚇 Tara St; 🚌 all city centre

If you like art-house movies or foreign films that wouldn't get a run in a multiplex, this is your best bet. Devoid of the self-awareness

MOVIES IN THE SQUARE

Every Saturday night throughout the summer (from June to August), Temple Bar's Meeting House Sq hosts free screenings of films beginning at 8pm. The movies on offer are usually classics and are often preceded by an Irish short. For tickets, contact the Temple Bar Information Centre (Map p87; ☎ 677 2255; www. visit-templebar.ie; 12 East Essex St).

DUBLIN INTERNATIONAL FILM FESTIVAL

If you're around in early spring (late February to early March), most of Dublin's cinemas participate in the Jameson Dublin International Film Festival (☎ 679 1616; www.dubliniff.com), a two-week showcase for new films by Irish and international directors, and a good opportunity to see classic movies that hardly get a run in cinemas. A major criticism of the festival, however, is that many of the films included in the schedule would have earned a cinema release regardless, making it more difficult for small-budget films to find a slot.

that afflicts the IFI, this place puts the emphasis on well-made films rather than experimental ones.

KARAOKE

Out-of-tune balladeering has become one of Dublin's best-loved activities, as scores of well-lubed vocal chords are put through their paces in a variety of venues around the city. The opening of so many authentic Asian restaurants has seen an explosion of the eat-and-sing combo; we recommend Bon Ga (p165) and Melody (see p165) on the city's north side. Also worth checking out are:

UKIYO Map p68
☎ 633 4071; www.ukiyobar.com; 7-9 Exchequer St; per hr €25; 🚍 all city centre
The basement rooms of this trendy sake bar can fit up to 10 people each for a night of singalong fun from the 30,000-odd songs on the menu (in a variety of languages).

VILLAGE Map p68
☎ 475 8555; 26 Wexford St; www.thevillage venue.com; admission free; 🕐 Sun;
Sunday nights are the ever-popular Songs of Praise, hosted by Rory, Murt and Sister Barbara: just put down your name and choice and wait for your turn to get up and belt out songs like Whitesnake's 'Here I Go Again'.

LIVE MUSIC
CLASSICAL

Classical music is constantly fighting an uphill battle in Dublin, with inadequate funding, poor management and questionable repertoires all contributing to its limited appeal. Resources are appalling, and there's neither the talent nor the funding to match their European counterparts. But before lambasting Ireland's commitment to classical

forms, it's well worth bearing in mind that this country has never had a tradition of classical music or lyric opera – the musical talents round these parts naturally focused their attentions on Ireland's home-grown repertoire of traditional music. And still they managed to produce one of the great lyric tenors of the 20th century in Count John McCormack (1884–1945).

But it's not all doom and gloom. Classical music may be small fry, but it's getting better all the time, thanks to the efforts of promoters who attract performers and orchestras from abroad; one local success has been the Anna Livia International Opera Festival (☎ 661 7544; www.opera.ie). Bookings for all classical gigs can be made either at the venues or through Ticketmaster and HMV (see Bookings on p186).

BANK OF IRELAND ARTS CENTRE
Map p70
☎ 671 1488; Foster Pl; admission free; 🚍 all city centre
The arts centre hosts a regular Wednesday lunchtime recital at 1.15pm, usually featuring a soloist with accompaniment. The performers are excellent. It also hosts an irregular evening program of concerts; call for details.

DUBLIN CITY GALLERY – THE HUGH LANE Map p102
☎ 874 1903; www.hughlane.ie; 22 North Parnell Sq; 🚍 3, 10, 11, 13, 16, 19 or 22 from city centre
Between September and June, this top-class art gallery (see p104) hosts up to 30 concerts of contemporary classical music. The concerts generally start at noon on Sundays.

GAIETY THEATRE Map p70
☎ 677 1717; www.gaietytheatre.com; South King St; 🚍 all city centre; 🚇 St Stephen's Green
Amid its repertoire of popular plays (see p198) the Gaiety occasionally plays host to the more salubrious sounds of classical

music, including some outstanding performances by Opera Ireland (www.opera ireland.com).

GRAND CANAL THEATRE Map p115

☎ 677 7999; www.grandcanaltheatre.ie; Grand Canal Sq; 🚇 Grand Canal Dock
Designed by Daniel Liebeskind, this magnificent 2000-seat auditorium opened in 2010 and has already established itself as the city's premier venue for opera, ballet and classical music, as well as West End and Broadway productions.

HELIX Off Map p125

☎ 700 7000; www.thehelix.ie; Collins Ave, Glasnevin; 🚌 11, 13A or 19A from city centre
Based in Dublin City University (DCU), the impressive Helix theatre hosts, among other things, a fantastic array of international operatic and classical recitals and performances.

NATIONAL CONCERT HALL Map p68

☎ 475 1572; www.nch.ie; Earlsfort Tce; 🚌 all city centre; 🚇 Harcourt
Leaden acoustics and a none-too-aesthetic conversion of University College Dublin's old lecture hall are the main criticisms levelled at Ireland's premier orchestral venue, but the cream of the classical crop perform here throughout the year as part of a rich and varied program of concerts and recitals. There is also a series of excellent lunchtime concerts (€9) from 1.05pm to 2pm on Tuesdays between June and September.

ROYAL DUBLIN SOCIETY SHOWGROUND CONCERT HALL
Map p122

☎ 668 0866; Merrion Rd, Ballsbridge; 🚌 7 from Trinity College
The RDS (see p121) hosts a rich line-up of classical music and opera throughout the year.

JAZZ

Jazz is a marginal art form in Dublin and mostly the preserve of a small clique of loyal listeners; for most others it's nothing more than background music. The small scene is nonetheless pretty active, promoting gigs and sponsoring the visits of international artists, although for the most part the gigs are held in pubs. Keeping the jazz flame burning is the Improvised Music Company (☎ 877 9001; www.improvisedmusic.ie), whose website will keep you abreast of the jazzy goings on in the city, including a yearly series of summer lunchtime gigs at a number of changing venues.

GLOBE Map p70

☎ 671 1220; www.globe.ie; 11 South Great George's St; admission free; 🕙 5.30-7.30pm Sun; 🚌 all city centre
This trendy cafe-bar (see p174) has a popular Sunday afternoon session. The atmosphere is usually terrific, and the players are generally pretty good, even though you're unlikely to hear John Coltrane's successor.

JJ SMYTH'S Map p70

☎ 475 2565; 12 Aungier St; admission €8-12; 🕙 8-11.30pm Thu & Sun; 🚌 all city centre
The best place in Dublin to hear good jazz is at this pub, located in an upstairs lounge where the stage is almost on top of the punters. Sunday's Pendulum Club, run by the Improvised Music Company, is a consistently good night. The intimacy of the place, coupled with the generally high standard of musicians performing here, make this a definite must for any fans of the genre.

POPULAR

Dublin rocks. The city is now a definite stop on the international touring schedule of virtually every rock and pop act in the world. In part it's because Dublin is no longer a pissant capital, but mostly it's because promoters

HANDEL WITH CARE

In 1742 the nearly broke GF Handel conducted the very first performance of his epic work *Messiah* in the since-demolished Neal's Music Hall, on the city's oldest street, Fishamble St. Ironically, Jonathon Swift – author of *Gulliver's Travels* and dean of St Patrick's Cathedral – suggested the choirs of St Patrick's and Christchurch participate, but then he revoked his invitation, vowing to 'punish such vicars for their rebellion, disobedience and perfidy'. The concert went ahead nonetheless, and the celebrated work is now performed in Dublin annually at the original spot – now a hotel that bears the composer's name (Map p87).

TOP U2 MOMENT

Need proof that Bono can still belt them out? Just listen to the live version of *Miss Sarajevo*, recorded in Milan in 2005 and available on the *All Because of You* single. Luciano Pavarotti wasn't around to sing his bit as he did on the studio version (on U2 and Brian Eno's *Passengers* soundtrack album from 1995), so Bono does the honours – in Italian, and with a power and intensity that has reduced us to tears. Grazie, maestro.

promise big fees (the cost of which is duly handed down to you, the out-of-pocket fan) and big crowds (it seems the high fees offer little deterrent!) to anyone willing to stand in front of thousands of screaming, cheering fans who do a damn fine job of making you feel like you're the biggest star in the world. From MGMT to Neil Diamond, they've all come, sung and gone away very, very happy.

Yet Dublin's newish international reputation is merely a welcome adjunct to a musical scene that has thrived since the 1970s. Thousands of bands have come and gone, and while most of them didn't achieve the broader success they presumably dreamed of when they first starting practising in the drummer's parents' garage, every one of them has contributed to a rich landscape that makes Dublin such a great place to hear live music. As for the bands that did manage to make names for themselves beyond the city's boundaries, they all pale in the shadow of U2, who have come to define not just Dublin rock but Irish culture with their extraordinary success. For more on Dublin's contemporary music scene, see p39.

Big and small, Dublin has venues to suit every taste and crowd requirement. The city is also awash with music festivals, especially in summer – check p16 for the list of the ones you don't want to miss. Check the newspapers for upcoming events, or even better, go online: www.entertainment.ie and www.nialler9.com are two of the best gig guides around.

You can sometimes buy tickets at the venue itself, but you're probably better off going through an agent. Prices for gigs range dramatically, from as low as €5 for a tiny local act to anywhere up to €140 for the really big international stars.

ACADEMY Map p102
☎ 877 9999; www.theacademydublin.com; 57 Middle Abbey St; 🚌 all city centre; 🚈 Abbey
A terrific midsized venue, the Academy's stage has been graced by an impressive list

of performers, from Nick Cave's Bad Seeds to '80s superstar Nik Kershaw. It's also the place to hear those unknown names who stand a better than evens chance of making it somewhere.

AMBASSADOR THEATRE Map p102
☎ 1890 925 100; Parnell Sq West; 🚌 all city centre
The Ambassador started life as a theatre and then became a cinema. Not much has changed inside, making it a cool retro place to see visiting and local rock acts perform.

BUTTON FACTORY Map p87
☎ 670 0533; Curved St; 🚌 all city centre
This venue offers a wide selection of musical acts, from traditional Irish music to drum and bass (and all things in between), to a non-image-conscious crowd. One night you might be shaking your glow light to a thumping live set by a top DJ and the next you'll be shifting from foot to foot as an esoteric Finnish band drag their violin bows over their electric guitar strings.

CRAWDADDY Map p68
☎ 478 0225; www.pod.ie; 35a Harcourt St; 🚌 all city centre; 🚈 Harcourt
Named after the London club where the Stones launched their professional careers in 1963, Crawdaddy is an intimate barvenue that specialises in putting on rootsy performers – from African drum bands to avant-garde jazz artists and flamenco guitarists. It's part of the PoD/Tripod entertainment complex.

MARLAY PARK Off Map p122
☎ 1890 925 100; Rathfarnham, Dublin 14; 🚌 15C, 16, 16A, 16C or 17 from city centre
In recent years, this park in the south Dublin suburb of Rathfarnham has been transformed into a major outdoor venue for some fairly heavy-hitting international acts, with Metallica headlining here in 2009 followed by Green Day in 2010. But it also hosts slightly more muted affairs throughout the summer.

OLYMPIA THEATRE Map p87
☎ 679 3323; 72 Dame St; 🚌 all city centre
This beautiful Victorian theatre generally puts on light plays, musicals and pantomime (see p198), but also caters to a range

of midlevel performers and fringe talents that are often far more interesting than the superstar acts – this is one of the best places for a more intimate gig.

O2 Map p115

☎ 819 8888; www.theo2.ie; East Link Bridge, North Wall Quay; 🚌 142 or 151 from city centre

A complete overhaul of what was once a rail terminal (built in 1878) has resulted in this superb new venue, formerly known as the Point Depot, with a capacity of around 10,000. The acoustics are sublime and the performing acts picked out of the very top drawer: Black Eyed Peas, Rod Stewart and Rihanna are just some of the names that played here during 2010.

SUGAR CLUB Map p80

☎ 678 7188; www.thesugarclub.com; 8 Lower Leeson St; admission €8-10; ⏲ Tue-Sun; 🚌 all city centre; 🚇 St Stephen's Green

Table service and a cocktail bar draw in a slightly more sophisticated (read older) crowd who come for the cabaret-style acts performing here regularly.

TRIPOD Map p68

☎ 478 0025; www.tripod.ie; 35 Harcourt St; admission €15-40; ⏲ Wed-Sat; 🚌 all city centre; 🚇 Harcourt

R & B stars, reggae masters, indie guitar heroes, dance music monsters… You can see a full range of live shows at this excellent venue, which has quickly developed a reputation as one of the best in the city, as much for the quality of its acts as the acoustics and surroundings.

VICAR STREET Map p91

☎ 454 5533; 58-59 Thomas St; 🚌 51B, 51C, 78A or 123 from city centre

Smaller performances take place at this intimate venue near Christ Church Cathedral. It has a capacity of 1000, between its table-serviced group seating downstairs and theatre-style balcony. Vicar Street offers a varied program of performers, with a strong emphasis on soul, folk, jazz and foreign music.

VILLAGE Map p68

☎ 475 8555; www.thevillagevenue.com; 26 Wexford St; 🚌 all city centre

An attractive midsize venue that is a popular stop for acts on the way up and down, the Village has gigs virtually every night of the week, featuring a diverse range of rock bands and solo performers. It's also a good showcase for local singer-songwriters.

WHELAN'S Map p68

☎ 478 0766; www.whelanslive.com; 25 Wexford St; 🚌 all city centre

Whelan's near-legendary status as the home of the soul-searching sensitive singer – and where gigs are treated like semimystical experiences by their devoted fans – is inevitably the cause of much derision in some Dublin quarters, but there's no denying the venue's special place in the Dublin musical scene. It's a pretty intimate space, perfect if you're looking to 'connect' with your favourite artists, who will most likely be cadging drinks off fans in the bar afterwards.

TRADITIONAL & FOLK

Dublin's ambivalent relationship with traditional music stems from its peculiar separation from the heart of traditional Irish culture; the capital has always seemed more concerned with the cultural goings on across the water in Britain and, latterly, continental Europe.

THE PEOPLE'S ROCKER

Just in case you didn't recognise the bronze figure outside Bruxelles (p175), it is none other than arguably the greatest of all Dublin rockers, Thin Lizzy frontman Phil Lynott (1949–86). Lynott's immense popularity with Dubliners is not especially hard to fathom – not only did Thin Lizzy lead the Irish charge onto the international rock stage but they turned out to be one of the best bands of their time – though it is reflective of more than just Lynott's talent or success. Dubliners loved Lynott because he was always one of their own, a true Dub who remembered where he came from long after his star had risen. And, just to prove that Dubliners aren't so easily understood, they loved him because he was an outsider – a black kid raised in a working-class Dublin suburb during the 1950s and '60s – and a tortured genius who died young from drugs and alcohol, but who left a musical legacy that we should all be proud of and cherish. So, find a copy of Live and Dangerous and listen to 'Still in Love with You'; U2 fans may disagree, but it never did get better than this.

By the way, take a close look at Philo's face: isn't it uncannily like the face on the James Joyce statue (Map p102) on North Earl St? Joyce with an afro or wha'?

THE NUTS & BOLTS OF TRADITIONAL MUSIC

Despite popular perception, the harp isn't widely used in traditional music (it *is* the national emblem, but that probably has more to do with the country traditionally being run by people pulling strings). The *bodhrán* (bow-rawn) goat-skin drum is much more prevalent, although it makes for a lousy symbol. The uilleann pipes, played by squeezing bellows under the elbow, provide another distinctive sound although you're not likely to see them in a pub. The fiddle isn't unique to Ireland but it is one of the main instruments in the country's indigenous music, along with the flute, tin whistle, accordion and bouzouki (a version of the mandolin). Music fits into five main categories (jigs, reels, hornpipes, polkas and slow airs) while the old style of singing unaccompanied versions of traditional ballads and airs is called *sean-nós*.

Many middle-class Dubliners, eager to bask in a more 'cosmopolitan' light, have dismissed the genre as the preserve of rural types with nicotine-coloured fingers and beer-stained beards, all the while packing their own CD collections with the folk and traditional music of *other* cultures – inevitably found in the 'world music' section of their local CD store.

The irony has become all too apparent and in recent years there has been a slow (and often grudging) acknowledgement that one of the richest and most evocative veins of traditional expression is on their very doorstep – and it's *not* Riverdance, or any of the other versions of sex-and-reels that have led to Irish music becoming popular all over the world.

The best place to hear traditional music is in the pub, where the 'session' – improvised or scheduled – is still best attended by foreign visitors who appreciate the form far more than most Dubs and will relish any opportunity to drink and toe-tap to some extraordinary virtuoso performances.

Also worth checking out is the Temple Bar Trad Festival (☎ 677 2397; http://templebartrad.com), which takes place in the pubs of Temple Bar over the last weekend in January.

COBBLESTONE Map p102
☎ 872 1799; 77 North King St; admission free; ⊕ Smithfield

This pub in the heart of Smithfield has a great atmosphere in its cosy upstairs bar, where there are superb nightly music sessions performed by traditional musicians (especially Thursday) and up-and-coming folk acts.

COMHALTAS CEOLTÓIRÍ ÉIREANN
Off Map p122
☎ 280 0295; www.comhaltas.com; 32 Belgrave Sq, Monkstown; admission €5-10; ⊙ Mon, Wed & Fri; ⊕ Monkstown

The Friday evening traditional *céilidh* (communal dance) is the big draw at this infor-

mal venue, which is really a community club for the preservation of the traditional form, be it played or danced. Other nights feature regular sessions, but you'll find something just as good in the city centre.

DEVITT'S Map p68
☎ 475 3414; 78 Lower Camden St; admission free; ⊙ from 9.30pm Thu-Sat; ⊕ all city centre

Devitt's – aka the Cussak Stand – is one of the favourite places for the city's talented musicians to display their wares, with sessions as good as any you'll hear in the city centre. Highly recommended.

HA'PENNY BRIDGE INN Map p87
☎ 677 0616; 42 Wellington Quay; adult/concession €6/5; ⊙ 9-11pm Fri; ⊕ all city centre

An excellent session takes place upstairs on Friday at this lovely pub, best known for its comedy nights (see p190).

HUGHES' BAR Map p102
☎ 872 6540; 19 Chancery St; admission free; ⊙ from 9pm; ⊕ 25, 25A, 66, 67, 90 or 134 from city centre; ⊕ Four Courts

Traditional purists love the nightly sessions at this pub, which by day caters to barristers, solicitors and their clients from the nearby Four Courts (p108) – all of whom probably need a pint, but for different reasons! Although the playing is very good, the atmosphere is a little lacking and the sessions can be a bit dead.

OLIVER ST JOHN GOGARTY Map p87
☎ 671 1822; 58-59 Fleet St; admission free; ⊙ from 2pm; ⊕ all city centre

The best thing about this popular Temple Bar watering hole (see p179) is not that it's ram-packed with tourists or that the 'craic' is slightly manufactured, but that the sessions run virtually all day from 2pm, making this the only place you'll hear trad before nightfall. And it's pretty good stuff too.

PALACE BAR Map p87

☎ 677 9290; 21 Fleet St; admission free; ⏰ from 8.30pm Tue, Wed & Sun; 🚌 all city centre
Some of the best traditional music in Dublin can be heard at the excellent sessions laid on in the gorgeous upstairs lounge of this venerable boozer. If you want to hear the real deal in the city centre, this is the place.

THEATRE

Dublin has a reputation for being a theatrical heavyweight, and while it's true that Irish theatre is going through something of a revival after several decades in the doldrums, theatre remains under threat by the overwhelmingly oppressive force of commerce. The prohibitively high price of real estate has drastically impeded theatre's ability to stretch its legs by reducing the amount of available space for theatrical ventures to operate in.

Despite the recent revival, no new theatres have opened up and companies have been forced to improvise – usually by going outdoors or co-opting non-theatrical spaces like pubs or offices. It makes for some interesting experimentation, but the jury is out on whether it makes for lasting theatre.

Theatre bookings can usually be made by quoting a credit-card number over the phone, then you can collect your tickets just before the performance. Expect to pay anything between €12 and €25 for most shows, with some costing as much as €30. Most plays begin between 8pm and 8.30pm. Check www.irishtheatreonline.com and other online listings (see p186) to see what's playing.

ABBEY THEATRE Map p102

☎ 878 7222; www.abbeytheatre.ie; 26 Lower Abbey St; admission €13-38; 🚌 all city centre; 🚇 Abbey
Ireland's national theatre has been plagued by uncertainty over its future for so long that few can quite remember a time when all was well in the box on Abbey St. Nobody likes the building it's in – built to replace the original building that burnt down in the 1950s – but plans to move it a purpose-built facility in the Docklands have been derailed by the economic crisis, leading to a proposal to move it to the GPO (see p107). However, even that has been the subject of controversy. What was staged here in the past also provoked grumblings of disapproval, but current director Fiach MacConghail has transformed the hitherto stale program by rendering old classics by

SMALLER THEATRES & WORKSHOPS

Ark (Map p87; ☎ 670 7788; www.ark.ie; 11a Eustace St; admission free; ⏰ 9.30am-4pm Tue-Fri,10am-4pm Sat; 🚌 all city centre) This children's centre has a 150-seat venue that stages shows for kids aged between three and 14. See also p88.

Bewley's Café Theatre (Map p70; ☎ 086 878 4001; www.bewleyscafetheatre.com; Bewley's Bldg, 78/79 Grafton St; adult/concession €15/13; ⏰ 1.10pm; 🚌 all city centre) Fancy a bowl of soup and a sandwich with your theatre ticket? This marvellous space puts on interesting, experimental work by Irish playwrights in a suitably bohemian atmosphere. Mind your slurping.

Crypt Arts Centre (Map p68; ☎ 671 3387; Dublin Castle; 🚌 50, 54, 56A, 77 or 77A) The beautiful church crypt located within Dublin Castle (p76) has this space used by adventurous young Irish companies for experimental work.

International Bar (Map p70; ☎ 677 9250; 23 Wicklow St; ⏰ 6-8.30pm; 🚌 all city centre) Early evening plays in the upstairs space of this bar (p176) by nonestablished actors can offer up some worthwhile stuff; they're on early because they have to clear the room for the established comedy shows (see p190).

Lambert Puppet Theatre (Off Map p122; ☎ 280 0974; www.lambertpuppettheatre.com; 5 Clifton Lane, Monkstown; adult/child €12.50/9; 🚇 Monkstown/Salthill; 🚌 7, 7A or 8 from Trinity College) You think Gameboy and Xbox have spoilt the magic of puppetry for your kids? Let the Lambert prove you wrong with its excellent performances, staged every Saturday (and daily at Christmas and Easter).

Samuel Beckett Theatre (Map p67; ☎ 608 2266; www.tcd.ie; Trinity College; admission €5-20; 🚇 Pearse; 🚌 all city centre) Used mainly by drama students, the theatre also features the occasional show by established troupes. It's all pretty cerebral stuff.

the great stalwarts of the Irish theatrical firmament (JM Synge, Sean O'Casey et al), and supporting the work of new play-wrights such as Mark O'Rowe, Marina Carr and contemporary international stars such as Sam Shepard. Monday performances are cheaper. Work by up-and-coming writers and more experimental theatre is staged in the adjoining Peacock Theatre (☎ 878 7222; admission €13-17).

CIVIC THEATRE Off Map p91
☎ 462 7477; www.civictheatre.ie; The Square, Tallaght; adult/child €19/16; 🚈 Tallaght
This purpose-built 350-seat theatre is inconveniently located in the southern suburb of Tallaght, but its state-of-the-art facilities are top notch and include an art gallery. The plays it puts on, an interesting mix of Irish and European works, are uniformly good. The easiest way to get here is by Luas: the theatre is at the terminus of the red line.

DRAÍOCHT THEATRE Off Map p119
☎ 885 2622; www.draiocht.ie; Blanchardstown Shopping Centre; adult/child from €16/12; 🚌 38, 38A, 39, 39X, 236 or 239
This multipurpose arts centre (named after the Irish word for 'magic') is one of the most interesting venues in the city. Two separate theatres feature all kinds of work, from reinterpretations of classic plays to brand-new material by cutting-edge writers and performers.

GAIETY THEATRE Map p70
☎ 677 1717; www.gaietytheatre.net; South King St; adult/child & student €35/20 plus booking fee; 🚌 all city centre; 🚈 St Stephen's Green
The Gaiety's program of plays is strictly of the fun-for-all-the-family type: West End hits, musicals, Christmas pantos and classic Irish plays keep the more serious-minded away, but it leaves more room for those simply looking to be entertained.

GATE THEATRE Map p102
☎ 874 4045; www.gate-theatre.ie; 1 Cavendish Row, East Parnell Sq; admission from €25; 🚌 all city centre
The city's most elegant theatre, housed in a late-18th-century building, features a generally unflappable repertory of classic American and European plays. Orson Welles' first professional performance was here, and James Mason played here early in his career. Even today it is the only theatre in town where you might see established international movie stars work on their credibility with a theatre run.

NEW THEATRE Map p87
☎ 670 3361; www.thenewtheatre.com; 43 East Essex St; adult/child €15/8; 🚌 all city centre
This small theatre's location above a left-wing bookshop should be a guide to the kind of thinking that informs most of the performances taking place on its small stage. It's all about having a social conscience, whether by promoting new work by emerging playwrights or putting on established works that highlight society's injustices.

OLYMPIA THEATRE Map p87
☎ 677 7744; www.olympia.ie; 72 Dame St; admission from €21; 🚌 all city centre
You won't find serious critics near the place, but the much-loved Olympia, a Victorian beauty that began life as a music hall, attracts the crowds for its program of variety shows and musicals. At Christmas time, it's the place to come for the traditional panto.

PAVILION THEATRE Off Map p122
☎ 231 2929; www.paviliontheatre.ie; Pavilion Complex, Dun Laoghaire; adult/child €22/14; 🚈 Dun Laoghaire
This modern space in the seaside suburb of Dun Laoghaire offers a dynamic program of

WHO WANTS BECKETT'S COAT?

The last great shadow cast by an Irish dramatist was that of Samuel Beckett (1906–89), who moved from Dublin to Paris before he wrote a single word. Thereafter, only Brian Friel has really come close to inheriting the mantle of the 'greatest Irish playwright'. Today, Irish theatre is at an exciting but uneasy crossroads. A new generation of talented dramatists has certainly emerged since 1990 – Conor McPherson, Mark O'Rowe, Marie Jones and Marina Carr among them – but their path to theatrical greatness is littered with the high expectations of critics and a media that is uncomfortable with the fact that Irish theatre currently has no outstanding behemoth, and that is chomping at the bit to proclaim the next Beckett, Wilde or Shaw. There are plenty of dramatists about (see p42), but if we had to pick one who has the mark of greatness rather than merely the rubber stamp of commercial success, it would be Eugene O'Brien, whose first play, *Eden*, was one of the best to hit a Dublin stage since Vladimir and Estragon sat around waiting for a guy who never showed up.

theatre and performance art, much like the Draíocht Theatre (opposite) and Civic Theatre (opposite).

PROJECT ARTS CENTRE Map p87
☎ 1850 260 027; www.projectartscentre.ie; 39 East Essex St; adult/child €18/15; 🚌 all city centre
This is the city's most interesting venue for challenging new work – be it drama, dance, live art or film. Three separate spaces, none with a restricting proscenium arch, allow for maximum versatility. You never know what to expect, which makes it all that more fun: we've seen some awful rubbish here, but we've also seen some of the best shows in town.

TIVOLI THEATRE Map p91
☎ 454 4472; 135-136 Francis St; adult/child & student €15/10; 🚌 51B, 51C, 78A or 123 from city centre
This commercial theatre offers a little bit of everything, from a good play with terrific actors to absolute nonsense with questionable comedic value.

SPORTS & ACTIVITIES

top picks

- A match at **Croke Park** (p207)
- A round of golf at **Carton House** (p203)
- Heineken Cup rugby at the **Aviva Stadium** (p207)
- A night at the dogs at **Shelbourne Park** (p207)
- A massage at **Melt** (p202)

To many Dubliners, sport is a religion. For an ever-increasing number, it's all about faith through good works such as jogging, amateur football, cycling and yoga; for everyone else, observance is enough, especially from the living-room chair or the pub stool.

Sporting facilities are pretty good, but for the most part they're in private hands – there are only a handful of public tennis courts in the whole city, for instance (and they're not that good) – which means that you'll have to pay some kind of fee or membership to participate in most sports. We assume you're only visiting, so there's little point in telling you how to join one of the city's myriad soccer, rugby or GAA teams; instead, you'll have to settle on watching them play.

HEALTH & FITNESS

Dubliners have only really noticed the shapes of their own bodies in the last decade or so. All of a sudden, it was de rigueur to tackle those droopy bits by joining a gym, although whatever good work managed midweek was generally undone by the end of the weekend thanks to a couple of nights out and the kebab on the way home – that didn't stop memberships soaring. The recent crash has seen prices drop dramatically, but most city-centre gyms are private affairs that demand three- to six-month membership commitments. Most hotels above a certain standard have a fitness room where guests can stretch a muscle or two, and anywhere that wants to rock star fans to provide the ultimate in self-care: the spa. We're suckers for the kinds of mysterious treatments administered to a body that just murmurs in delight, but we leave a dangling, cynical question mark over some of these mystical Indian- and Irish-named treatments that are little more than an oily massage to whale music. The gyms and spas listed here are all open to the public.

BELLAZA CLINIC Map p122

☎ 496 3484; www.bellazabeauty.com; 27 Ranelagh Rd, Ranelagh; treatments €50-600; ☉ 9.30am-6pm Mon-Wed & Fri & Sat, to 8pm Thu; 🚆 Ranelagh

Cult facialist Sue Machesney uses all her considerable skills to treat, repair, nurture and love all kinds of skins – using facials, vein zapping, laser hair removals and other non-surgical methods that leave you feeling beautiful without the post-op doldrums.

DUBLIN SPA @ FOUR SEASONS Map p122

☎ 665 4000; www.fourseasons.com; Four Seasons Hotel; Simmonscourt Rd, Ballsbridge; day packages €150-420; ☉ 9am-9pm; 🚌 5, 7, 7A, 8, 18 or 45 from city centre

Every conceivable treatment, from a basic 55-minute facial to the three-hour Swiss Bliss, working the body from head to toe with a range of La Prairie products, is available at this top spa in arguably the city's finest hotel. Day packages also allow you full use of the gym, swimming pool and fitness facilities.

MANDALA DAY SPA Map p70

☎ 671 7099; www.mandala.ie; La Stampa Hotel, 35 Dawson St; 70min massage €110; ☉ 10am-6pm Tue-Wed & Sun, to 8pm Thu & Fri, to 7pm Sat; 🚌 all cross-city; 🚆 St Stephen's Green

It sells itself as the 'essence of Eastern solace', but even the cringeworthy feng shui nonsense doesn't detract from the fact that this is a terrific little spa where you genuinely can iron out those stress creases and get back in touch with your inner softness (there is such a thing as too much spa treatment).

MARKIEVICZ LEISURE CENTRE Map p115

☎ 672 9121; www.dublincity.ie; Townsend St; adult/child €6/3; ☉ 7am-10pm Mon-Thu, 7am-9pm Fri, 9am-6pm Sat, 10am-4pm Sun; 🚆 Tara St; 🚌 all cross-city

This excellent fitness centre has a swimming pool, a workout room (with plenty of gym machines) and a sauna. You can swim for as long as you please, but children are only allowed at off-peak times (10am to 5.30pm Monday to Saturday).

MELT Map p87

☎ 679 8786; www.meltonline.com; 2 Temple Lane; full body massage 30min/1hr €60/90; ☉ 9am-7pm Mon-Sat; 🚌 all city centre

A full range of massage techniques – from Swedish to shiatsu and many more in between – are doled out by expert practitioners at Melt, aka the Temple Bar Healing Centre. Also available are a host of other left-of-centre healing techniques, including acupuncture, Reiki and polarity therapy. It's all very alternative, but the touchy-feely vibe never obscures the fact that these folks really know what they're doing. They have also set up shop in the Westin (Map p70; ☎ 679 9352; Westin Dublin; Westmoreland St; 🚌 all city centre).

WELLS SPA
☎ 040 236 444; www.brooklodge.com; Brook Lodge, Macreddin, Co Wicklow; whole-day packages €150-220; 🚌 Bus Eireann 133 from city centre to Rathdrum

OK, so it's not technically in Dublin, but this extraordinary spa in a luxurious country house is the favourite chill-out spot for Dublin's high-flyers. Mud and flotation chambers, Finnish and aroma baths, Hammam massages and a full range of Decleor and Carita treatments make this one of the top spas in the country. Whole-day treatments include a light lunch and full use of all the pool and gym facilities. Your credit card will never have nestled in softer hands. It is 3km west of Rathrum in the village of Macreddin.

ACTIVITIES
It's tough to join in a sport if you're breezing through the city; there are virtually no opportunities to join in besides a round of golf, which is always popular.

GOLF
Pádraig Harrington's triple-Major success (two British Opens and a USPGA Championship in 2007–08) has inspired a new generation of kids to take up the world's most frustrating game. However, golf has always been popular in Ireland, where playing doesn't quite have the same cliquish exclusivity as it does in other countries.

Although the best golf is generally played on a seaside links, the Celtic Tiger saw a slew of inland American-style resort courses open their doors, most of which are facing increasingly tough times in the face of a big drop in members able to afford the expensive joining fees. The good news for you is that

top picks

DUBLIN SPORTING MOMENTS

- Dubliner Pádraig Harrington winning the Open Championship in 2007 – the first Irish golfer to win a major since Fred Daly in 1947.
- Dublin beating Kerry in the 1976 All-Ireland Final, the only victory in four finals meetings that decade against the Kingdom.
- Ireland beating England 1-0 in 1988 during the European Championship finals in Stuttgart, the first – and only – time the Irish soccer team has ever beaten England competitively.
- The Irish rugby team beating England by a record-margin 43-13 on 24 February 2007 at Croke Park: history and victory wrapped up in one delicious moment.
- England losing at anything, preferably sports that they think they're good at (hey, Dubliners love a little schadenfreude).

they'll do almost anything to encourage you to play, including offering some fantastically reduced green fees, especially if you book online beforehand.

You'll generally need your own transport if you wish to head to any of the courses listed below.

CARTON HOUSE
☎ 505 2000; www.cartonhousegolf.ie; Maynooth, Co Kildare; green fees Mon-Wed €55, Thu-Sun €76.50

Two outstanding courses designed by Colm Montgomerie and Mark O'Meara respectively.

DRUID'S GLEN Map p225
☎ 287 3600; www.druidsglen.ie; Newtown-mountkennedy, Co Wicklow; green fee €120

One of the country's older breed of championship courses, Druid's Glen is a spectacular place to play, with some stunningly beautiful holes.

K CLUB Map p225
☎ 601 7297; www.kclub.com; Kildare Hotel & Golf Club, Straffan, Co Kildare; green fee €100

Two golf courses: one, with Arnold Palmer's design imprimatur, is one of the best in Ireland and hosted the PGA European Open until 2008; the second course opened in 2003.

KILLEEN CASTLE Map p225

☎ 689 3000; www.killeencastle.com; Dunsany, Co Meath; green fee €90

A Jack Nicklaus–designed resort course just outside Dunshaughlin, Co Meath. Killeen will host the Solheim Cup in 2011 – the women's equivalent of the Ryder Cup. In the meantime, you can try to break par on its well-manicured holes.

SPECTATOR SPORT

Sport has a special place in the Irish psyche, probably because it's one of the few occasions when an overwhelming expression of emotion won't cause those around you to wince or shuffle in discomfort. Sit in a pub while a match is on and watch the punters foam at the mouth as they yell pleasantries at the players on the screen, such as 'they should pay me for watching you!'.

What is absolutely true, however, is that sport – for the few who play and the majority who are happy to watch it on TV or from the sidelines – is a major bonding activity in Dublin, and it's by no means an exclusively male domain. Ask any adult in Dublin for their top five sporting moments and they could probably reel them off as quickly as they could remember their five closest friends.

FOOTBALL

Dublin is football mad, although local fans – and the national broadcaster – are much more enthusiastic about the likes of Manchester United, Liverpool and Glasgow Celtic than the struggling pros and part-timers that make up the League of Ireland (www.leagueofireland.com). It's just too difficult for domestic teams to compete with the multimillionaire glitz and glamour of the English Premiership, which has always drawn the cream of Irish talent. The best-known Dubliners playing across the water are Damien Duff (Fulham) and Robbie Keane (Glasgow Celtic).

Nevertheless, if you want to feel the excitement of actually attending a game rather than just watching it on TV, Dublin is currently home to five teams in the League of Ireland Premier division (see the boxed text, p206). The season runs from April to November; tickets are easily available at all grounds.

The national side, made up of Irish players playing nowhere near the League of Ireland, has had some notable successes, especially in the late 1980s and 1990s, but things haven't gone so well since their last appearance in a major tournament, the World Cup of 2002. They are – in the words of Irish soccer's governing body, the Football Association of Ireland (FAI; ☎ 676 6864; www.fai.ie) – in a 'period of rebuilding', which saw them misfire for a few years before finally seeming to turn the corner in 2008 with the appointment of legendary Italian coach Giovanni Trapattoni as manager. 'Trap' has taken a fairly mediocre crop of talent and turned them into an efficient (if unattractive) team and while their wait for qualification to a major finals goes on, they

---

IT'S NOT ONLY A GAME

Paris, 18 November 2009: the Irish football team are playing the second leg of their World Cup–qualifying play-off against France. The Irish lost the first leg 1-0 at home the previous week, but now, against Les Bleus on their own turf, they've responded doggedly and have taken the lead, squaring the tie at 1-1. Then, disaster: the French captain, Thierry Henry, handles the ball twice in passing it to William Gallas, who scores what proves to be the winner. France go through, Ireland are out.

Following the match, Ireland erupts in a frenzy of rage and recrimination, with newspapers, call-in radio shows and even politicians demanding that the game be replayed, that France be thrown out of the World Cup or that Thierry Henry be tried by the International Court of Justice in The Hague.

Irish anger was not really about the handball or the fact that France were going to the World Cup instead of Ireland. It was about a country that was reeling in the wake of the global economic collapse, a population shocked by the depths to which their own politicians and bankers had mismanaged the economy and incensed by the apparent lack of any real accountability.

In short, in late 2009 Ireland was punch-drunk and low in confidence: qualification for the World Cup in South Africa would have given the country a boost, much as qualification for the World Cup in Italy had done in 1990, when the country was still in the doldrums. But it wasn't just about good vibes, either: qualification would have been a boon to the economy, some argued, as the national spend would have gone up as many thousands of fans would have gone to the pub to watch the games. The Irish aren't great for taking to the street in protest, but on 19 November, 300 fans marched on the FAI headquarters to demand that justice be done. And they say it's only a game...

THE FAST & THE FURIOUS

Gaelic games are fast, furious and not for the faint-hearted. Challenges are fierce, and contact between players is extremely aggressive. Both games are played by two teams of 15 players whose aim is to get the ball through what resembles a rugby goal: two long vertical posts joined by a horizontal bar, below which is a soccer-style goal, protected by a goalkeeper. Goals (below the crossbar) are worth three points, whereas a ball placed over the bar between the posts is worth one point. Scores are shown thus: 1-12, meaning one goal and 12 points, giving a total of 15 points.

Gaelic football is played with a round, soccer-size ball, and players are allowed to kick it or hand-pass it, like Australian Rules football. Hurling, which is considered by far the more beautiful game, is played with a flat ashen stick or bat known as a hurley or *camán*. The small leather ball, called a *sliothar*, is hit or carried on the hurley; hand-passing is also allowed. Both games are played over 70 action-filled minutes.

Both sports are county-based games. The dream of every club player is to represent his county, with the hope of perhaps playing in an All-Ireland final, the climax of a knockout championship that is played first at a provincial and then interprovincial level.

And if you thought that only men would be so bold as to get involved, you'll be surprised to know that there's also an equally tough women's version of hurling called *camogie*, which is now being promoted as 'chicks with sticks' in an attempt to rejuvenate the sport. Women's football is growing all the time, with the Dublin senior team one of the country's best, along with Waterford, Mayo and Monaghan.

came pretty close to making it to South Africa for the World Cup in 2010, losing in a play-off to a France side that benefitted from Thierry Henry's infamous hand ball (see boxed text, opposite).

As Ireland prepared for a new round of qualifying matches – for the 2012 European Championships, hosted jointly by Poland and Ukraine – the fans have a renewed sense of hope, and a brand new stadium to yell about it in, with the opening of the genuinely world-class Aviva Stadium (Map p122; ☎ 647 3800; www.aviva stadium.ie; 11-12 Lansdowne Rd), which holds 50,000 in ultramodern seated comfort. Tickets range from €25 to €50, but fan interest and corporate buyouts make getting a ticket for a really competitive match pretty tough without having to deal with a tout.

GAELIC FOOTBALL & HURLING

Gaelic games are at the core of Irishness; they are enmeshed in the fabric of Irish life and hold a unique place in the heart of its culture. Their resurgence towards the end of the 19th century was entwined with the whole Gaelic revival and the march towards Irish independence. The beating heart of Gaelic sports is the Gaelic Athletic Association (GAA), set up in 1884 'for the preservation and cultivation of National pastimes'. The GAA is still responsible for fostering these amateur games and it warms our hearts to see that after all this time – and amid the onslaught of globalisation and the general commercialisation of sport – they are still far and away the most popular sports in Ireland.

They are simultaneously the most divisive and unifying activity in Irish culture. Although the GAA club is at the heart and soul of virtually every parish in the country, in Dublin the organisation holds its greatest sway in the northern half of the city and the traditionally working- and lower-middle-class enclaves on the south side.

Here football – commonly referred to as 'gaah' (but only by Dubs) – is king, and hurling is a game for country folk and crazy people with a death wish – although in recent years the hurling team has improved to such a degree that they're now second-tier contenders (although still a few leagues behind the likes of Cork, Tipperary and the current kings of them all, Kilkenny). We've outlined the basic rules in a boxed text above.

Support for the Dubs verges on the fanatical, but it's a support that grows from the ground up, beginning with the local parish club that virtually everyone – man, woman and child – in the community can be a member of. And, because the GAA is a volunteer-based amateur organisation, local communities come together to raise money for the club, through cake sales, raffles, bingo nights and other fund-raising efforts that further strengthen the ties that bind.

Community bonding aside, club matches are intensely competitive and provoke fierce local rivalries, especially among the major teams in north Dublin: Na Fianna from the Finglas/Glasnevin area, St Brigid's from Castleknock and St Vincent's from Raheny. Throw in a little south side rivalry with Kilmacud Crokes and the support can get pretty vocal. But when the best players from the club teams are selected to put on the blessed blue jersey, local rivalries are cast aside and replaced by intercounty ones as supporters unite behind their beloved Dubs. As fervent as this rivalry is, and as polarised as the support may be, there's rarely a cross word between opposing fans who are ultimately united in their love of the game and shared heritage; there's nothing like it anywhere else in the world, and we love it.

They might be good at football, but the Blues haven't held Sam in their mitts since 1995 – 'Sam' being the Sam Maguire Cup, awarded to the winner of the All-Ireland Football Championship, contested at a county level from April onwards to the final in Croke Park on the third Sunday of September. They have won the Leinster Senior Football championship every year since 2005, but they just can't cross that final hurdle and add to their tally of 22 All-Ireland wins, an impressive haul that is second only to their great nemesis Kerry, who added yet another win in 2009 to make it a face-rubbing 36.

The All-Ireland's poorer cousin is the National Football League (and National Hurling League), which runs from February until mid-April. All of the county teams fight it out for the title of their respective divisions in a tournament that is generally seen as the warm-up for the All-Ireland Championship, which begins a couple of weeks after the league has wrapped up its affairs.

Dublin plays all of its championship matches at Croke Park (p124), Ireland's largest stadium and the venue for both semifinals and the final, irrespective of whether the Dubs are involved. League matches, however, are played at the far less impressive Parnell Park (off Map p125; Clantarkey Rd, Donnycarney; adult/child €10/7; 20A, 20B, 27, 27A, 42, 42B, 43 or 103 from Lower Abbey St or Beresford Pl), but it's still a great venue to see this fast game up close.

Although tickets for the NFL and NHL are easy to come by (you can just buy one at the grounds), they're tougher to get for the championship games, particularly past the quarterfinal stages. Dublin's hurling team invariably gets beaten before then, but the football team is expected to make the quarterfinals at least. You can buy tickets for the All-Ireland championship games at the GAA Ticket Office (Map p102; ☎ 865 8657; 53A Dorset St).

Ticket prices range from €25 in the stand and €15 in the terrace for the early rounds, €36 and €16 respectively for the quarterfinals,

---

LOCAL FOOTBALL TEAMS

Local die-hards will insist that 'real' football is played on bumpy pitches by 'honest' semipros who aren't wandering about the pitch thinking about their image rights. You can find out for yourself between April and November by going to see one of the Dublin clubs in action.

Bohemians FC (Map p64; ☎ 868 0923; www.bohemians.ie; Dalymount Park, Phibsboro; adult/child €15/10; 10, 19 or 19A from city centre) Known as the Gypsies, this club is the north side's pride and joy, and one of only two totally professional teams playing in the league.

Shamrock Rovers FC (off Map p91; ☎ 709 3620; www.shamrockrovers.ie; Tallaght Stadium, Whitestown Way, Tallaght; adult/child €15/10; 49, 54A, 65 or 65B from city centre; Tallaght) After wandering in the wilderness for nearly 20 years, the Hoops have finally found a home in a purpose-built stadium in Tallaght, from where they can once again go about becoming the most dominant team in Irish football history.

Shelbourne FC (Map p125; ☎ 837 5536; www.shelbournefc.ie; Tolka Park, Richmond Rd, Drumcondra; adult/child €15/5; 3, 11, 11A, 13, 16 or 16A from city centre) Premier League champions in 2006, Shels was ignominiously booted out of the top division straight afterwards for financial irregularities, lost all its good players and spent the last four years struggling in Division 1 – which is really the second division.

St Patrick's Athletic (Map p91; ☎ 454 6332; www.stpatsfc.com; Richmond Park, Inchicore, Dublin 8; adult/child from €15/10; 19, 51, 51B, 68 or 69 from city centre; Drimnagh or Goldenbridge) Four league titles in the 1990s, and one since the turn of the century...the Saints are an accomplished club whose ground is slangily known as the Stadium of Lights, in tribute to the infinitely more impressive ground once played on by Benfica.

UCD (off Map p122; ☎ 716 2142; www.ucdsoccer.com; Belfield, Clonskeagh; adult/child from €10/5; 10, 10A or 46A from city centre) The Students have been yo-yoing up and down the league but in 2010 found themselves respectively mid-table in the Premier Division. They play in the lovely Belfield stadium, part of the University College Dublin (UCD) campus.

€40 and €26 for the semis, and €60 and €30 for the final – although good luck hunting down a ticket for the big game. Kids are entitled to a €7 juvenile ticket, but then must be seated in the stand; if you want to take your kid into the terrace, you'll have to pay full price. The stand is more comfortable and usually has better views, but if the Dubs are playing and you want to get right into the partisan thick of things, go for the Hill 16 terrace.

The website for all Dublin-related info is www.hill16.ie.

HORSE & GREYHOUND RACING

Dubliners love the gee-gees, but most of all, they love betting on them. There are several picturesque racecourses within easy driving distance of the city centre and there are good quality meetings throughout the year.

The flat racing season runs from March to November, while the National Hunt season – when horses jump over things – is October to April. There are also some events in summer.

Traditionally the poor-man's punt, greyhound racing (the dogs) has been smartened up in recent years and partly turned into a corporate outing. It offers a cheaper, more accessible and more local alternative to horse racing. The action all happens at the following venues:

CURRAGH Map p225
☎ 045-441 205; www.curragh.ie; County Kildare; admission €12-55; 🚌 special from Busáras
The home of Irish racing, 35km west of Dublin, hosts five classic flat races between May and September: the 1000 Guineas, 2000 Guineas, Oaks, St Leger and Irish Derby.

FAIRYHOUSE Map p225
☎ 825 6167; www.fairyhouseracecourse.ie; Ratoath, County Meath; admission €10-22; 🚌 special from Busáras
The National Hunt season has its yearly climax with the Grand National, held here on Easter Monday. The course is 25km north of Dublin.

HAROLD'S CROSS PARK Map p61
☎ 497 1081; www.igb.ie; 151 Harold's Cross Rd; admission €10; ⏰ from 8pm Mon, Tue & Fri; 🚌 16 from city centre
This greyhound track is close to the city centre and offers a great night out for a fraction of what it would cost to go to the horses.

LEOPARDSTOWN Map p225
☎ 289 3607; www.leopardstown.com; Foxrock; admission €10-55; 🚌 special from Eden Quay
Specialising in both flat and steeplechase races, Leopardstown's big event is the prestigious Hennessey Gold Cup in February.

PUNCHESTOWN Map p225
☎ 045-897 704; www.punchestown.com; Naas, Co Kildare; admission from €15; train to Naas; 🚌 Bus Éireann 8, 12, 13, 14, 15 & 126 from Busáras
Although it specialises mostly in flat racing, Punchestown is home to the extremely popular Steeplechase Festival in April. The course is 40km southwest of the city.

SHELBOURNE PARK Map p122
☎ 668 3502; www.shelbournepark.com; South Lotts Rd; admission €10; ⏰ 7-10.30pm Wed, Thu & Sat; 🚌 3, 7, 7A, 8, 45 or 84 from city centre
All the comforts, including a restaurant in the covered stand overlooking the track, make going to the dogs one of the best nights out in town. Table service – including betting – means that you don't even have to get out of your seat. Shelbourne Football Club (see the boxed text, p206) doesn't play here; its home is Tolka Park. Don't worry, even some Dubs get confused.

RUGBY

Read any of Ross O'Carroll-Kelly's hilarious tales of life in Dublin and you'll understand how important rugby is in certain social circles, especially the affluent ones of SoCoDu (that's South County Dublin to you and me). Attendance at one of the dozen or so rugby-playing schools in Dublin is advantage enough, but being a rugby star, especially at Blackrock College, the *primus inter pares* of rugger schools, is a virtual guarantee of status, recognition and of course a bloody good career.

Rugby is but a sporting extension of a privileged caste, but it helps to be passionate about the game, especially the fortunes of Leinster, the provincial side. It's currently captained by the Mr Dreamy of most young rugger-bugger huggers (as the girls who like rugby and rugby players are so affectionately known), Brian O'Driscoll (who was born and raised on the north side). Drico also happens to be the main man on the Irish national team, which pretty much ensures that a bit of Dublin 4 will one day bear his name.

The association with privilege has pretty much always been there with rugby, until the game decided to go global, kick its branding into a whole new gear and Dublin began witnessing some pretty successful local teams at both inter-provincial and international level. Irish rugby's governing body, the Irish Rugby Football Union (IRFU; Map p122; ☎ 660 0779; www. irishrugby.ie; 62 Lansdowne Rd), has done a brilliant job of selling rugby outside its traditional domain, so much so that the game has finally generated a genuinely national interest.

The Six Nations championship sees Ireland pitted against Scotland, Wales, France, Italy and the old enemy, England, in an annual league that, in 2009, saw Ireland win the Grand Slam (a clean sweep of all their games) for the first time since 1948. They lost to France in 2010 but Irish rugby has never been in better health. Ireland's three home matches, played between February and April, are played at the brand-spanking new Aviva Stadium (Map p122; ☎ 647 3800; www.avivastadium.ie; 11-12 Lansdowne Rd), formerly Lansdowne Road. Tickets for internationals are like gold dust – they're generally divided between corporate buyers and the network of small clubs throughout the country, of which you need to be a member if you want a ticket. You can try

getting them through the IRFU (which also has a limited online purchasing service), but chances are you'll draw a blank.

Leinster's fortunes have mirrored those of the national side – in 2009 it won the Heineken European Cup for the first time, the premier provincial tournament that sees sides from the Six Nations countries play each other between December and May. In 2010 they lost in the semifinals to the eventual champions Toulouse before losing their inspirational head coach Michael Cheika to French side Stade Français. Leinster have also performed well in the secondary provincial tournament, the Magners League (played between teams from Ireland, Scotland, Wales and, from 2010–11, two Italian teams), which runs from September to May and is used to determine qualification for the European Cup; Leinster won it in 2008 but lost to Welsh team the Ospreys in the 2010 final.

Leinster plays its home games at the Royal Dublin Society (RDS; Map p122; ☎ 269 3224; www.leinster rugby.ie; 158 Shelbourne Rd; adult/child from €20/10; 🚍 7 from Trinity College) showgrounds. Tickets for both competitions are available at Elvery's (Map p70; ☎ 679 4142; Suffolk St) on Suffolk St or at its other branch (Map p70; ☎ 679 1141; Dawson St) on Dawson St; at the Spar (Map p122; ☎ 269 3261; 54-56 Donnybrook Rd) opposite Aviva Stadium; or online from the IRFU or Leinster rugby.

SLEEPING

top picks

- **Aberdeen Lodge** (p221)
- **Four Seasons** (p220)
- **Grafton Guesthouse** (p214)
- **Herbert Park Hotel** (p221)
- **Irish Landmark Trust** (p216)
- **Isaacs Hostel** (p220)
- **Number 31** (p216)
- **Pembroke Townhouse** (p221)
- **Shelbourne** (p212)
- **Trinity College** (p215)

SLEEPING

If you're looking for concrete evidence of what happens when a buoyant economy gets the beating of a lifetime, book a hotel room in Dublin. For more than a decade Dublin's room rates have hovered near the top end of the scale, making this one of Europe's most expensive capitals to sleep in and rarely (if ever) offering value for money.

No more. The city's hoteliers have been forced to scramble in the face of the economic crisis and the resultant dip in tourist numbers, and their primary response (in 2010 at least) was cheaper beds – as much as 40% cheaper in the middle and upper brackets – as they desperately sought to guarantee their hotels' futures, so many that were built or renovated during the boom at huge costs. Although it is difficult to predict what will happen, it is clear that not every hotel will survive the lean years.

Which isn't bad news for you, as everyone competes for your dime and is willing to try virtually anything to make sure that you dribble on their pillows: there are so many deals on offer that room rates can vary wildly from day to day, never mind season to season. Always check online (see Booking Services, p212) and query the rack rate: discounts are more available now than ever before.

The pillows in question are pretty snazzy, too: Dublin has hotels that can stand up to any of the European greats, while a host of others has cottoned on to the fact that the contemporary traveller doesn't think worn sheets are part of the charm and that grapefruit isn't some kind of exotic fruit that has no place at the breakfast buffet. Those that haven't just don't get a mention, least of all in these pages. As ever, we've only selected for your enjoyment what we consider the best options in each category.

So where to stay? If you're only in Dublin for the weekend, you'll want to be in the city centre or a short stroll away. The prices are higher, but pay the money. Believe us, it's worth it. Besides the obvious advantage of being central, you will avoid the potential nightmare of transport to and from the suburbs. The construction of the Luas tram line has made some suburbs far more accessible, but public transport more or less disappears shortly after midnight, with the exception of hourly night buses packed full of drunken youngsters (an experience that can often be a cutting-edge anthropological experiment). Get a taxi, you'll think, and we say good luck: there's you and thousands of others all queuing up in the wee hours for the same thing. Still, some of our favourite properties – the ones with all the charm and character – are just outside the city centre in the outlying suburbs south of the Grand Canal, so you may have to rely on some kind of motorised transport if you can't handle the 20- to 30-minute walk.

So, what exactly is available in this fair city?

ACCOMMODATION STYLES

Top-end and deluxe hotels fall into two categories – period Georgian elegance and cool, minimalist chic. No matter what the decor, you can expect luxurious surrounds, king-size beds, satellite TV, in-room DVDs, full room service, broadband or wi-fi and discreet, professional pampering. While the luxury of the best places is undeniable, their inevitable affiliation to the world's most celebrated hotel chains has introduced the whiff of corporate homogeneity into the carefully ventilated air.

Dublin's midrange accommodation is more of a mixed bag, ranging from no-nonsense but soulless chains to small B&Bs in old Georgian townhouses. These days, hotel connoisseurs the world over have discovered the more intimate, but equally luxurious, boutique hotel, where the personal touch is maintained through fewer rooms, each of which is given lavish attention. Dublin's townhouses and guesthouses – usually beautiful Georgian homes converted into lodgings – are this city's version of the boutique hotel, and there are some truly outstanding ones to choose from.

These are beautifully decked out and extremely comfortable, while at the lower end, rooms are simple, a little worn and often rather overbearingly decorated. Here you can look forward to kitsch knick-knacks, chintzy curtains, lace doilies and clashing floral fabrics so loud they'll burn your retinas. Breakfast can range from home-baked breads, fruit and farmhouse cheeses to a traditional, fat-laden fry-up.

Budget options are few and far between in a city that has undergone a dramatic tourist revolution and if you want to stay anywhere close to the city centre you'll have to settle for a hostel. Thankfully, most of these maintain a pretty high standard of hygiene and comfort. Many offer various sleeping arrangements, from a bed in a large dorm to a four-bed room or a double. There are plenty to choose from, but they tend to fill up very quickly and stay full.

Groups, families or those on extended stays may prefer to do their own thing so you'll also find a list of central self-catering apartments (see boxed text, p215).

CHECK-IN & CHECK-OUT TIMES

Check-out at most establishments is noon, but some of the smaller guesthouses and B&Bs require that you check out a little earlier, usually around 11am. Check-in times are usually between noon and 2pm.

ROOM RATES

Hardly surprising, but the closer to the centre you stay, the more you'll pay – and the rack rates are comparable to Europe's most expensive cities. With prices, it's not just quality that counts, but position. For instance, a large-roomed comfortable B&B in the north-side suburbs may cost you as little as €50 per person, while the owners of a small, mediocre guesthouse within walking distance of Stephen's Green won't blink when asking €100 for a room the size of a shoebox. A quality guesthouse or midrange hotel can cost anything from €80 to €150, while rates at the city's top digs usually start at around €150 – even (and it bears repeating here) if in this climate you'd be mad not to check around for deals or call the hotel directly and make polite enquiries along the lines of 'is that the best price you can offer me?' At the other end of the scale there's the ubiquitous hostel, the bedrock of cheap accommodation: their standards have uniformly gone up, but so have their prices and a bed will cost anything from €18 to as much as €34 (note that hostel rates don't include breakfast; exceptions are noted).

BOOKINGS

Despite the slowdown, Dublin is still a busy, popular city, which makes getting a last-

ROOM RATES

The categories used in this chapter indicate the cost per night of a standard double room in high season.

€€€	over €150
€€	€80-150
€	under €80

minute room in the high season (May to September) still a challenging proposition, especially if you're looking for a bed in the city centre. If you can make a reservation, it will make life easier. If you arrive without accommodation, staff at Dublin Tourism's walk-in booking offices (see p256) will find you a room for €4 plus a 10% deposit. Sometimes this may require a great deal of phoning around so it can be money well spent.

If you want to book a hotel from elsewhere in Ireland or abroad, the easiest way is to go through Gulliver Infores, Dublin Tourism's computerised reservations service, via their website, www.visitdublin.com, or book directly yourself from the accommodation's own website. See p256 for a list of Dublin Tourism offices and Gulliver contact numbers.

There are also great savings if you book online (see the boxed text, p212). These rates are generally available year-round, but are tougher to find during high season. Be sure to book ahead and ask for a pre-booking rate.

Longer-Term Rentals

Finding long-term accommodation in Dublin is difficult for Dubliners, never mind visitors from abroad. Gulliver Ireland's Reservation Service (☎ 1800 668 668; www.gulliver.ie) specialises in reserving accommodation. However, while it can find places for up to six months, or even a year, it charges a nonrefundable deposit of 10% of the total price.

There are several letting agencies in Dublin. Abbott & Matthews Letting & Management (Map p70; ☎ 679 2434; www.abbottmatthews.com; 40 Dame St) specialises in long- and short-term leases of apartments and houses, furnished or unfurnished. One-bedroom apartments rent for between €700 and €1400 per month. Home Locators (Map p68; ☎ 679 5233; www.homelocators.ie; 35 Dawson St) has a wide selection of properties on its books; the agency charges a €15 registration fee and then helps you locate suitable accommodation.

BOOKING SERVICES

Advance internet bookings are your best bet for deals on accommodation. These are just a handful of services that will get you a room at a competitive rate.

All Dublin Hotels (www.all-dublin-hotels.com)

Dublin City Centre Hotels (http://dublin.city-centre-hotels.com)

Dublin Hotels (www.dublinhotels.com)

Dublin Tourism (www.visitdublin.com)

Go Ireland (www.goireland.com)

Hostel Dublin (www.hosteldublin.com)

A few British newspapers, notably the *Daily Telegraph*, carry advertisements for long-term rentals in Dublin. Websites such as www.daft.ie are well worth checking too.

GRAFTON STREET & AROUND

Grafton St itself has only one hotel – one of the city's best – but you'll find a host of choices in the area surrounding it. Not surprisingly, being so close to the choicest street in town comes at a premium, but the competition for business is fierce, which ensures that quality is top rate.

WESTBURY HOTEL Map p70   Hotel €€€
☎ 679 1122; www.doylecollection.com; Grafton St; s/d/ste from €170/260/500; 🚌 all city centre; Ⓟ 🖥 🛜
Visiting celebs looking for some quiet time have long favoured the Westbury's elegant suites, where they can watch TV from the jacuzzi before retiring to a four-poster bed. Mere mortals tend to make do with the standard rooms, which are comfortable enough but lack the sophisticated grandeur promised by the luxurious public

spaces – which are a great spot for an afternoon drink.

SHELBOURNE Map p68   Hotel €€€
☎ 676 6471; www.theshelbourne.ie; 27 St Stephen's Green; r from €200; 🚌 all city centre; Ⓡ St Stephen's Green; Ⓟ 🖥 🛜
Dublin's most iconic hotel has been the best address in town since it was founded in 1824, which inevitably leads to any changes being scrutinised more than most. A major refurbishment has been greeted with general approval – many of the rooms and most of the public spaces were given the once over – but the management style of its new owners, the Marriott group, has led to grumblings that this is no longer at the top of its five-star game. Whatever your experiences, you're staying in a slice of history: it was here that the Irish Constitution was drafted in 1921, and this is the hotel in Elizabeth Bowen's eponymous novel. Afternoon tea in the refurbished Lord Mayor's Lounge remains one of the best experiences in town.

WESTIN DUBLIN Map p70   Hotel €€€
☎ 645 1000; www.westin.com; Westmoreland St; s/d from €210/260; 🚌 all city centre; Ⓟ 🖥 🛜
Formerly a grand branch of the Allied Irish Bank, this fine old building was gutted and reborn as a stylish upmarket hotel. The rooms, many of which overlook a beautiful atrium, are decorated in elegant mahogany and soft colours that are reminiscent of the USA's finest. You will sleep on 10 layers of the Westin's own trademark Heavenly Bed, which is damn comfortable indeed. The hotel's most elegant room is the former banking hall, complete with gold-leaf plasterwork on the ceiling, now used for banquets. Breakfast will set you back €27.

HILTON Map p68   Hotel €€€
☎ 402 9988; www.dublin.hilton.com; Charlemont Pl; r from €155; Ⓡ Charlemont; Ⓟ 🖥 🛜

What is it about hotels that assume that just because you're here on business you couldn't care less about style, decor or the basics of good taste? The Hilton group's Dublin offering is comfortable and convenient – right on the Grand Canal by a Luas stop – but about as pretty as a photocopier. You'll sleep just fine here, but that's about it. We expected more.

BROOKS HOTEL Map p70　　Hotel €€€

☎ 670 4000; www.sinnotthotels.com; 59-62 Drury St; s/d from €135/145; 🚌 all city centre; 🅿 ✖
About 120m west of Grafton St, this small, plush place has an emphasis on familial, friendly service. The decor is nouveau classic with high-veneer-panelled walls, decorative bookcases and old-fashioned sofas, while bedrooms are extremely comfortable and come fitted out in subtly coloured furnishings. The clincher for us though is the king- and superking-size beds in all rooms, complete with…a pillow menu. Go figure. The intimate Jasmine bar and on-site cinema are popular with media industry schmoozers.

FITZWILLIAM HOTEL Map p70　　Hotel €€€

☎ 478 7000; www.fitzwilliam-hotel.com; St Stephen's Green; r from €164; 🚌 all city centre; 🚇 St Stephen's Green; 🅿 ✖ 🖥 🛜
You couldn't pick a more prestigious spot on the Dublin Monopoly board than this minimalist Terence Conrad–designed number overlooking the Green. Ask for a corner room on the 5th floor (502 or 508) with balmy balcony and a view. The hotel is also home to one of the city's best restaurants, Thornton's (p152).

RADISSON BLU ROYAL HOTEL

Map p68　　Hotel €€-€€€
☎ 898 2900; www.radissonblu.ie; Golden Lane; r/ste from €130/210; 🚌 all city centre; 🅿 ✖ 🖥 🛜
This stunning modern hotel is an excellent example of how sleek lines and muted colours can combine beautifully with luxury to ensure a memorable night's stay. From the hugely impressive public areas (the bar alone is worth the visit) to the sophisticated bedrooms – each with flat-screen digital TVs embedded in the wall to go along with all the other little touches – this is bound to be one of the most popular options for the business traveller and our favourite hotel in town at this price range.

STEPHEN'S GREEN HOTEL

Map p68　　Hotel €€
☎ 607 3600; www.ocallaghanhotels.com; St Stephen's Green; r from €99; 🚌 all city centre; 🚇 Stephen's Green; 🅿 🖥 🛜
Past the glass-fronted lobby are 75 thoroughly modern rooms that make full use of the visual impact of primary colours, most notably red and blue. This is a business hotel par excellence; everything here is what you'd expect from a top international hotel (including a gym and a business centre), but what you won't find elsewhere is the marvellous view of St Stephen's Green below. There are extraordinary online deals available.

LA STAMPA HOTEL

Map p70　　Boutique Hotel €€
☎ 677 4444; www.lastampa.ie; 35 Dawson St; s/d from €120/160; 🚌 all city centre; 🚇 St Stephen's Green; 🅿 🖥 🛜
La Stampa is an atmospheric boutique hotel on trendy Dawson St with 29 Asian-influenced white rooms with oriental rattan furniture and exotic velvet throws. The Mandala Day Spa (p202) is a luxurious, all-frills ayurvedic spa, but to fully benefit from your restorative treatments, ask for a top-floor bedroom away from the revelling at SamSara bar (p174) below.

TRINITY LODGE Map p70　　Guesthouse €€

☎ 617 0900; www.trinitylodge.com; 12 South Frederick St; s/d €120/150; 🚌 all city centre; 🚇 St Stephen's Green; 🛜
Martin Sheen's grin greets you upon entering this cosy, award-winning guesthouse, which he declared his favourite spot for an Irish stay. Marty's not the only one: this

SLEEPING GRAFTON STREET & AROUND

HERE TODAY, GONE TOMORROW

For the first time in its history, the Irish hospitality industry is confronted by the spectre of the 'zombie hotel' – properties so in debt that they will never manage to cover their costs. Nationally, up to 30% of all hotels – a total of around 15,000 bedrooms – were categorised as such, and while proportionally fewer of these are in the capital, the years 2010–11 will be extremely challenging for the whole sector. Even the widespread price slash so evident in nearly all accommodation won't be enough to save a bunch of them, including ones listed in this chapter – we just don't know who they are yet.

place is so popular that they've added a second townhouse across the road, which has also been kitted out to the highest standards. Room 2 of the original house has a lovely bay window.

MERCER HOTEL Map p70 Hotel €€
☎ 478 2179; www.mercerhotel.ie; Lower Mercer St; s/d from €99/140; 🚌 all city centre; 🚆 St Stephen's Green; 🅿 🛜

Not a stone's throw from Grafton St, a fairly plain frontage hides a pretty decent hotel, with largish rooms dressed in antiques, giving the whole place an elegant, classical look. There are a dizzying array of room deals available; the off-peak rates are sensational.

BUSWELL'S HOTEL Map p70 Hotel €€
☎ 614 6500; www.quinnhotels.com; 23-27 Molesworth St; r from €130; 🚌 all city centre; 🚆 St Stephen's Green; 🅿 🎮 🖥

In business since 1882, this elegant hotel made up of five Georgian townhouses is a Dublin institution. Like the Shelbourne (p212), it has a long association with politicians, who wander across the road from Dáil Éireann to wet their beaks at the hotel bar. The 69 bedrooms have all been given the once-over, but have left its Georgian charm intact. In 2010 the hotel's parent company went into administration so the hotel's future remains somewhat uncertain, but we have no doubt that this gem of a place will survive – if only because the politicos from Dáil Éireann across the street will need somewhere to meet!

CAMDEN COURT HOTEL
Map p68 Hotel €€
☎ 475 9666; www.camdencourthotel.com; Camden St; s/d from €99/130; 🚌 all city centre; 🚆 Harcourt; 🅿 🎮 🖥 🛗

Big and bland ain't such a bad thing this close to St Stephen's Green, especially if the mainstay of your clientele is the business crowd. They like the standardised rooms but love the amenities, which include a 16m pool, health club (with jacuzzi, sauna and steam room) and a fully equipped gym.

HARRINGTON HALL
Map p68 Guesthouse €€
☎ 475 3497; www.harringtonhall.com; 69-70 Harcourt St; s/d from €99/129; 🚆 Harcourt; 🅿 🖥 🛜

Want to fluff up the pillows in the home of a former Lord Mayor of Dublin? The traditional Georgian style of Timothy Charles Harrington's home – he wore the gold chain from 1901 to 1903 – has thankfully been retained and this smart guesthouse stands out for its understated elegance. The 1st- and 2nd-floor rooms have their original fireplaces and ornamental ceilings. Guests can avail of the late bar and nightclub in the Harcourt Hotel next door.

STAUNTON'S ON THE GREEN
Map p68 Guesthouse €€
☎ 478 2300; www.stauntonsonthegreen.ie; 83 St Stephen's Green; s/d from €88/119; 🚌 all city centre; 🚆 St Stephen's Green

Bargains and a St Stephen's Green address are mutually exclusive, so surely there must be a catch to this handsome Georgian house two doors down from the Department of Foreign Affairs smack in the middle of the most expensive spot in town? There isn't really, not unless the worn decor reminiscent of another decade really bothers you. The place is clean, the staff are friendly and professional, and the front-facing rooms have floor-to-ceiling windows overlooking the Green. Any closer and you're sleeping with the Lord Mayor.

CENTRAL HOTEL Map p70 Hotel €€
☎ 679 7302; www.centralhotel.ie; 1-5 Exchequer St; s/d from €60/100; 🚌 all city centre; 🅿 🛜

The rooms are a modern – if miniaturised – version of Edwardian luxury. Heavy velvet curtains and custom-made Irish furnishings (including beds with draped backboards) fit a little too snugly into the space afforded them, but they lend a touch of class. Note that street-facing rooms can get a little noisy. The wonderful Library Bar, all leather armchairs and roaring fireplaces, is also one of the finest spots for an afternoon drink in the whole city. Location-wise, the name says it all.

GRAFTON GUESTHOUSE
Map p70 Guesthouse €€
☎ 679 2041; www.graftonguesthouse.com; 26-27 South Great George's St; s/d from €60/90; 🚌 all city centre; 🖥 🛜

This slightly off-beat guesthouse in a Gothic-style building gets the nod in all three key categories: location, price and style. Just next to George's St Arcade, the Grafton offers the traditional friendly features of a B&B (including a terrific breakfast), coupled with a funky design – check out the psychedelic wallpaper. Hard to beat at this price.

TRINITY COLLEGE
Map p67   Campus Residence €
☎ 608 1177; www.tcd.ie; Accommodations Office, Trinity College; s/d from €60/81; ☷ mid-Jun–Sep; ☐ all city centre; 🅿 ☐ ☎
The closest thing to living like a student at this stunningly beautiful university is crashing in their rooms when they're on holidays. The location is second to none, and the rooms are large and extremely comfortable. Rooms and two-bed apartments in the newer block have their own bathrooms; the others in the older (and more beautiful) blocks share facilities, though there are private sinks. Breakfast is included.

GRAFTON CAPITAL HOTEL
Map p70   Hotel €
☎ 648 1221; www.capital-hotels.com; Lower Stephen's St; r from €69; ☐ all city centre; 🅿 🕸
It's hardly recognisable as such today, but this centrally located hotel just off Grafton St is actually a couple of converted Georgian townhouses. Its 75 modern rooms are designed along the lines of function before form, which makes them perfect for the weekend visitor who wants to bed down somewhere central and still keep some credit-card space for a good night out. Breakfast is included.

AVALON HOUSE Map p68   Hostel €
☎ 475 0001; www.avalon-house.ie; 55 Aungier St; dm/s/d €18/30/60; ☐ all city centre; ☐ ☎

Before there was tourism, this large, listed Victorian building catered to the thin trickle of adventurers who landed in Dublin. They flood in now, and Avalon House is one of the city's most popular hostels, a welcoming house with pine floors, high ceilings and large, open fireplaces that create the ambience for a good spot of meet-the-backpacker lounging. Some of the cleverly designed rooms have mezzanine levels, which are great for families. Book well in advance.

MERCER COURT CAMPUS ACCOMMODATION
Map p70   Campus Residence €
☎ 478 0328; www.mercercourt.ie; Lower Mercer St; r from €35; ☷ late Jun–late Sep; ☐ all city centre; 🚇 St Stephen's Green; ☐ ☎
Owned and run by the Royal College of Surgeons, this is the most luxurious student-accommodation option in the city. Cheaper than Trinity, but just as central, it's close to Grafton St and St Stephen's Green. The rooms are modern and up to hotel standard.

MERRION SQUARE & AROUND

It's the most sought-after real estate in town, so it's hardly surprising that it's home to the lion's share of the city's top hotels. But although you'll pay for the privilege of bedding down in luxury, there are some excellent deals available at many of these well-located properties, which are within a gentle stroll of the best restaurants, bars and attractions the city has to offer.

HOME AWAY FROM HOME

Self-catering apartments are a good option for visitors staying a few days, for groups of friends, or families with kids. Apartments range from one-room studios to two-bed flats with lounge areas, and include bathrooms and kitchenettes. A decent two-bedroom apartment will cost about €100 to €150 per night. Good, central places include the following:

Clarion Stephen's Hall (Map p80; ☎ 638 1111; www.premgroup.com; 14-17 Lower Leeson St; ☐ all city centre; 🅿 🕸 ☐) Deluxe studios and suites, with in-room safe, fax, modem facilities and CD players.

Home From Home Apartments (Map p115; ☎ 678 1100; www.yourhomefromhome.com; The Moorings, Fitzwilliam Quay) Deluxe one- to three-bedroom apartments in the south-side city centre.

Latchfords (Map p80; ☎ 676 0784; www.latchfords.ie; 99-100 Lower Baggot St; ☐ all city centre) Studios and two-bedroom flats in a Georgian townhouse.

Oliver St John Gogarty's Penthouse Apartments (Map p87; ☎ 671 1822; www.gogartys.ie; 18-21 Anglesea St; ☐ all city centre) Perched high atop the pub of the same name, these one- to three-bedroom places have views of Temple Bar.

MERRION Map p80   Hotel €€€

☎ 603 0600; www.merrionhotel.com; Upper Merrion St; r from €199; 🚌 all city centre; 🅿 🖵 🛜 🛒

This resplendent five-star hotel, in a terrace of beautifully restored Georgian townhouses, opened in 1988 but looks like it's been around a lot longer. Try to get a room in the old house (with the largest private art collection in the city), rather than the newer wing, to sample its truly elegant comforts. Located opposite government buildings, its marble corridors are patronised by politicos, visiting dignitaries and the odd celeb. Even if you don't stay, come for the superb afternoon tea (€34), with endless cups of tea served out of silver pots by a raging fire.

CONRAD DUBLIN INTERNATIONAL
Map p80   Hotel €€€

☎ 602 8900; www.conradhotels.com; Earlsfort Tce; r from €169; 🚌 all city centre; 🅿 🖵 🛜

Kudos to the Conrad: Dublin's first truly international business hotel has worked hard to keep up with the ever-growing needs of its primary clientele, folks in suits. The king-size rooms have every gizmo and gadget your computer, PDA or mobile phone might ever need, while the state-of-the-art fitness centre should take good care of the rest of you. The hotel offers a dizzying array of special discount rates – at the last minute, room prices are often slashed by half – for both business and leisure travellers.

NUMBER 31 Map p80   Boutique Hotel €€€

☎ 676 5011; www.number31.ie; 31 Leeson Cl; s/d/tr €115/150/225; 🚌 11, 11A, 13B, 46, 58 or 58B; 🅿 🛜

Probably the city's most distinctive property, this is the former home of modernist architect Sam Stephenson (see p50), who created here a stunning homage to the

TRAVELLING WITH CHILDREN

Finding reasonable accommodation for a young family can be difficult in Dublin. Your best bet is a larger chain hotel (where a flat room rate usually applies), a serviced apartment, or a hostel where you can house the whole family in one room, usually with en suite. Almost all deluxe and top-end hotels offer 24-hour babysitting services and extra beds or cots.

style and cool of the 1960s: cue the theme music to *Austin Powers*. As you enter this magnificent home, only five minutes' walk from St Stephen's Green, with its sunken sitting room, leather sofas, mirrored bar, Perspex lamps and ceiling-to-floor windows, you are enveloped in an oasis of stylish calm. Its 21 bedrooms are split between the retro coach house, with its fancy rooms, and the more gracious Georgian house, through the garden, where rooms are individually furnished with tasteful French antiques and big comfortable beds. Gourmet breakfasts with kippers, homemade breads and granola are served in the conservatory. Yeah, baby!

DAVENPORT HOTEL Map p80   Hotel €€

☎ 607 3500; www.ocallaghanhotels.com; Merrion Sq; r from €130; 🚌 all city centre; 🅿 🍴 🖵 🛜

A great location just a stone's throw from Merrion Sq and Trinity College, this fine hotel is located in Merrion Hall, which was built in 1863 for the religious Plymouth Brethren. It is still a popular spot for meetings, only of a more commercial kind, and its 114 rooms are tailored to suit the needs of the business visitor (voicemail, ISDN line, wi-fi and European and American sockets are all standard). Leisure travellers also like the large rooms, which come with orthopaedic beds. There's a well-equipped workout room downstairs.

TEMPLE BAR

If you're here for a weekend of wild abandon and can't fathom anything more than a quick stumble into bed, then Temple Bar's choice of hotels and hostels will suit you perfectly. Generally speaking the rooms are small, the prices large and you should be able to handle the late-night symphonies of die-hard revellers.

IRISH LANDMARK TRUST
Map p87   Self-Catering €€€

☎ 670 4733; www.irishlandmark.com; 25 Eustace St; 1 night €300, weekly €1800; 🚌 all city centre

If you're travelling in a group, instead of renting a bunch of doubles in a hotel that you'll barely remember a week after you've gone home, why not go for this fabulous 18th-century heritage house, gloriously restored to the highest standard by the Irish Landmark Trust charity? You'll have this unique house all to yourselves. It sleeps up to seven in its double, twin and triple bedrooms. Furnished with tasteful antiques, and authentic furniture and fittings (including a grand piano in the drawing room), this kind of period rental accommodation is something really unique.

CLARENCE HOTEL Map p87   Hotel €€€
☎ 407 0800; www.theclarence.ie; 6-8 Wellington Quay; r/ste from €135/439; 🚌 all city centre; Ⓟ 💻 � 🛜

If you were hoping to find TV sets cascading from windows, groupie-clad tour buses or any other evidence of the Clarence's rock-star associations, you'll be sorely disappointed, as Bono and Edge's discreet little bolthole is anything but that – although we suspect that the penthouse's rooftop hot tub has seen its fair share of frolics. The genteel atmosphere in the 50-odd smallish rooms is more 1930s gentlemen's club, but that was all going by the way of a megabucks makeover: the economic downturn (and some planning snafus) has put it on ice for the foreseeable future.

PARAMOUNT HOTEL Map p87   Hotel €€€
☎ 417 9900; www.paramounthotel.ie; cnr Parliament & Essex Sts; s/d €105/200; 🚌 all city centre; Ⓟ 💻 🛜

Behind the Victorian facade, the lobby is a faithful re-creation of a 1930s hotel, complete with dark-wood floors, deep-red leather Chesterfield couches and heavy velvet drapes. The 70-odd rooms don't quite bring *The Maltese Falcon* to mind, but they're handsomely furnished and very comfortable. Downstairs is the Turk's Head (p179), one of the area's most popular bars.

MORGAN HOTEL
Map p87   Boutique Hotel €€
☎ 643 7000; www.themorgan.com; 10 Fleet St; r from €110; 🚌 all city centre; 💻 🛜

Designer cool can often be designer cold and the hypertrendy Morgan falls on the right side of the line, but only just. It's the kind of place Victoria Beckham would have liked – before she made the real cash. The facilities are top rate, and all rooms come equipped with satellite TV, video, stereo and minibar. Aromatherapy treatments and massages are extra, as is breakfast (€21).

DUBLIN CITI HOTEL Map p87   Hotel €€
☎ 679 4455; www.dublincitihotel.com; 46-49 Dame St; s/d Sun-Thu from €60/80, Fri & Sat €100/140; 🚌 all city centre; 💻

top picks

COMFIEST PILLOWS

Our favourite pillows to rest our weary heads on are in…
- Brooks Hotel (p213)
- Merrion (p216)
- Aberdeen Lodge (p221)
- Morrison Hotel (p218)
- Westin Dublin (p212)

An unusual turreted 19th-century building right next to the Central Bank is home to this cheap and cheerful hotel. Rooms aren't huge but are simply furnished and have fresh white duvets. Prices are reasonable considering it's only a stagger (literally) from the heart of Temple Bar, hic.

ASHFIELD HOUSE Map p87   Hostel €
☎ 679 7734; www.ashfieldhouse.ie; 19-20 D'Olier St; dm/s/d from €10/22/78; 💻 🛜 all city centre; 💻 🛜

A stone's throw from Temple Bar and O'Connell Bridge, this modern hostel in a converted church has a selection of tidy four- and six-bed rooms, one large dorm and 25 rooms with private bathroom. It's more like a small hotel, but without the price tag. A continental-style breakfast is included – a rare beast indeed for hostels. Maximum stay is six nights.

GOGARTY'S TEMPLE BAR HOSTEL
Map p87   Hostel €
☎ 671 1822; www.gogartys.com; 18-21 Anglesea St; dm from €12, d with/without bathroom €50/40; 🚌 all city centre; Ⓟ 🛜

Sleeping isn't really the activity of choice for anyone staying in this compact, decent hostel in the middle of Temple Bar, next to the pub of the same name. It tends to get booked up with stag and hen parties so, depending on your mood, bring either your earplugs or bunny ears. Six self-catering apartments are also available (see p215).

ELIZA LODGE Map p87   Guesthouse €
☎ 671 8044; www.dublinlodge.com; 23-24 Wellington Quay; s/d/ste from €45/49/79; 🚌 all city centre; ▣

It's priced like a hotel, looks like a hotel, but it's still a guesthouse. The 18 rooms are

top picks

HOTEL BARS

These are our favourite hotels to hole up in with a drink:
- **Central Hotel** (p214) The Library Bar is discreet and elegant.
- **Radisson Blu Royal Hotel** (p213) Bangkok-style bar.
- **Merrion** (p216) Best afternoon tea.
- **Four Seasons** (p220) Ice, baby, Ice.
- **Westbury Hotel** (p212) I recognise him/her/them!

comfortable, spacious and – due to its position right over the Millennium Bridge – come with great views of the Liffey. The penthouses even have jacuzzis.

KINLAY HOUSE Map p87   Hostel €
☎ 679 6644; www.kinlayhouse.ie; 2-12 Lord Edward St; dm/d from €14/32; ☐ all city centre; ☐
An institution among the city's hostels, this former boarding house for boys has massive, mixed 24-bed dorms, as well as smaller rooms. Its bustling location next to Christ Church Cathedral and Dublin Castle is a bonus, but some rooms suffer from traffic noise. There are cooking facilities and a cafe, and breakfast is included. Not for the faint-hearted.

BARNACLES TEMPLE BAR HOUSE
Map p87   Hostel €
☎ 671 6277; www.barnacles.ie; 1 Cecilia St; dm/d from €10/30; ☐ all city centre; ☐ ☐
Bright and spacious, in the heart of Temple Bar, this hostel is immaculately clean, has nicely laid-out dorms and doubles with private bathrooms and, that rare commodity, in-room storage. Because of its location, rooms are quieter at the back. Top facilities include a comfy lounge with an open fire. Linen and towels are provided. A contender for the south side's best hostel, it also has a discount deal with a nearby covered car park.

NORTH OF THE LIFFEY
As a general rule you'll get more for your buck on the north side, which mightn't match its southern half for the number of fancy hotels, but has a couple of choice hotels and plenty of midrange accommodation on offer. It's also where you'll find, east of O'Connell St, the B&B heartland of Gardiner St, where virtually

every second building provides this type of accommodation. Once proudly unfussy and basic, they've had to up the game and introduce a better standard of comfort – although the further north you go the dodgier they get. Watch yourself around Upper Gardiner St and the area immediately around Connolly Station and Busáras, the central bus station.

MORRISON HOTEL Map p102   Hotel €€€
☎ 887 2400; www.morrisonhotel.ie; Lower Ormond Quay; r €120-200, ste €260-1010; ☐ all city centre; ☐ Jervis; ☐ ☐ ☐
Muted and minimalist, this ubertrendy hotel has been a favourite of visiting celebs for quite a few years, who seemingly find comfort in the Zen-like furnishings and earth-tone colour palette created by top Irish designer John Rocha. Distractions come by way of flat-screen LED TVs, iPod docking stations and Aveda goodies in every room, as well as the trendy lobby bar and Halo restaurant (see p164). For a few quid extra, nab a far superior studio den in the new wing with balcony and enough space to throw a party.

MALDRON HOTEL SMITHFIELD
Map p102   Hotel €€
☎ 485 0900; www.maldronhotels.com; Smithfield Village; r €130-150; ☐ Smithfield; ☐
This functionally modern hotel with big bedrooms and plenty of earth tones to soften the contemporary edges is your best bet in this part of town. We love the floor-to-ceiling windows: great for checking out what's going on below in the square.

TOWNHOUSE Map p102   Boutique Hotel €€
☎ 878 8808; www.townhouseofdublin.com; 47-48 Lower Gardiner St; s/d/tr €70/115/132; ☐ Connolly Station
The ghostly writing of Irish-Japanese author Lafcadio Hearn may have influenced the Gothic-style interior of his former home. A dark-walled, gilt-framed foyer with jingling chandelier leads into 82 individually designed, comfy rooms. Some rooms in the new wing at the back are larger with balconies overlooking the small Japanese garden. It shares a dining room with the Globetrotters Tourist Hostel (p220) next door.

WALTON'S HOTEL Map p102   Hotel €€
☎ 878 3131; www.waltons-hotel.ie; 2-5 North Frederick St; s/d from €75/115; ☐ 36 or 36A; ☐ ☐

Better known for their legendary musical instrument shop next door, the Walton family opened this friendly hotel in an effort to preserve the traditional Georgian heritage of the building. With the help of the Castle Hotel (below) they have done just that. This is an excellent choice with a superb location overlooking Findlater's Church and the Rotunda Hospital, and 43 clean, spacious rooms. Children under 12 stay for free.

GRESHAM HOTEL   Map p102   Hotel €€
☎ 874 6881; www.gresham-hotels.com; Upper O'Connell St; r from €99; 🚌 all city centre; 🅿 ✕ 🖳 ♿
This landmark hotel shed its traditional granny's parlour look with a major overhaul some years ago. Despite its brighter, smarter, modern appearance and a fabulous open-plan foyer, its loyal clientele – elderly groups on shopping breaks to the capital and well-heeled Americans – has stuck firmly. Rooms are spacious and well serviced, though the decor is a little brash.

CASTLE HOTEL   Map p102   Hotel €€
☎ 874 6949; www.castle-hotel.ie; 3-4 Great Denmark St; r from €99; 🚌 36 or 36A; 🅿 ⌐
In business since 1809, the Castle Hotel may be slightly rough around the edges but it's one of the most pleasant hotels this side of the Liffey. The fabulous *palazzo*-style grand staircase leads to the 50-odd bedrooms, whose furnishings are traditional and a tad antiquated, but perfectly good throughout – check out the original Georgian cornicing around the high ceilings.

ACADEMY HOTEL   Map p102   Hotel €€
☎ 878 0666; www.academyhotel.ie; Findlater Pl; r from €89; 🚌 all city centre; 🅿 🖳 ⌐
Only a few steps from O'Connell St, this solidly three-star hotel is part of the Best Western group and as such offers the kind of comfortable if unmemorable night's sleep associated with the brand. The deluxe suites come with free wi-fi and flat-screen digital TVs. There's discounted parking at the covered car park next door.

BROWN'S HOTEL   Map p102   Hotel €
☎ 855 0034; www.dublin-hotel.net; 80-90 Lower Gardiner St; s/d from €35/70; 🚇 Connolly Station
A popular hotel along the strip, Brown's 22 rooms are a fairly comfortable bunch even if they're a little shabby looking. They fill up quickly and there's usually a pretty lively atmosphere, although we could do without the noise from the hostel next door.

JURY'S INN PARNELL ST
Map p102   Hotel €
☎ 878 4900; www.jurysinns.com; Moore St Plaza, Parnell St; r from €69; 🚌 36 or 36A; ✕ 🖳 ⌐
Jury's hotels are nothing if not reliable, and this edition of Ireland's most popular hotel chain is no exception. What do you care that the furnishings were once mass-produced and flat-packed and that the decor was created to be as utterly inoffensive to everything save good taste? The location – just off Upper O'Connell St – is terrific.

CLIFDEN GUESTHOUSE
Map p102   Guesthouse €
☎ 874 6364; www.clifdenhouse.com; 32 Gardiner Pl; s/d/tr from €25/60/90; 🚌 36 or 36A; 🅿
A great place to stay in the area, the Clifden is a very nicely refurbished Georgian house with 14 tastefully decorated rooms. They all come with bathroom, are immaculately clean and extremely comfortable. A nice touch is the free parking, even after you've checked out!

ANCHOR GUESTHOUSE
Map p102   Guesthouse €
☎ 878 6913; www.anchorguesthouse.com; 49 Lower Gardiner St; s/d from €35/45; 🚇 Connolly Station; 🅿
Most B&Bs round these parts offer pretty much the same stuff: TV, half-decent shower, clean linen and tea- and coffee-making facilities. The Anchor does all of that, but it just has an elegance you won't find in many of the other B&Bs along this stretch. This lovely Georgian guesthouse, with its delicious wholesome breakfasts, comes highly recommended by readers. They're dead right.

ABBEY COURT HOSTEL
Map p102   Hostel €
☎ 878 0700; www.abbey-court.com; 29 Bachelor's Walk; dm/d from €23/89; 🚌 all city centre
Spread over two buildings, this large, well-run hostel has 33 clean dorm beds with good storage. Its excellent facilities include a dining hall, conservatory and barbecue area. Doubles with bathroom are in the

newer building where a light breakfast is provided in the adjacent cafe. Not surprisingly, this is a popular option for travellers. Reservations are advised.

GLOBETROTTERS TOURIST HOSTEL
Map p102   Hostel €

☎ 878 8088; www.globetrottersdublin.com; 46-48 Lower Gardiner St; dm/d €20/60; 🚇 Connolly
This is a really friendly place with 94 beds in a variety of dorms, all with bathrooms and under-bed storage. The funky decor is due to the fact that it shares the same artistic ethos (and dining room) as the Townhouse (p218) next door. There's a little patio garden to the rear for that elusive sunny day.

JACOB'S INN Map p102   Hostel €
☎ 855 5660; www.isaacs.ie; 21-28 Talbot Pl; dm/d from €12.50/74; 🚇 Connolly; 🛜
Sister hostel to Isaacs (below) around the corner, this clean and modern hostel offers spacious accommodation with private bathrooms and outstanding facilities, including some disabled-access rooms, a bureau de change, bike storage and a self-catering kitchen.

ISAACS HOSTEL Map p102   Hostel €
☎ 855 6215; www.isaacs.ie; 2-5 Frenchman's Lane; dm/d from €12/50; 🚇 Connolly; 🖥 🛜
The north-side's best hostel – hell, for atmosphere alone it's the best in town – is in a 200-year-old wine vault just around the corner from the main bus station. With summer barbecues, live music in the lounge, internet access and colourful dorms, this terrific place generates consistently good reviews from backpackers and other travellers. There's also a disabled-access room.

DOCKLANDS
As a hive of activity, the Docklands isn't quite what the planners had hoped it would be, which means that you'll still be making your way west along the quays to get to the action. Still, the hotels here are all good in their respective categories.

GIBSON HOTEL Map p115   Hotel €€€
☎ 618 5000; www.gibsonhotel.ie; Point Village; r €99-209; 🚇 Grand Canal Dock; 🚌 151 from city centre; 🅿 🖥 🛜
A sleek, brand-new hotel, with 250-odd rooms all decked out in snazzy Respa beds,

flat-screen TVs and internet work stations, is the ideal stopping point for the business traveller looking to press the flesh in the Docklands. The hotel is owned by the same folks who own the O2 Arena (p195) – and the rest of the Point Village – so there are some good deals if you're looking for tickets to a show and a bed for the night.

CLARION HOTEL Map p115   Hotel €€€
☎ 433 8800; www.clarionhotelifsc.com; Custom House Quay; r from €154, ste from €179; 🚇 Connolly; 🅿 🖥 🛜 🚇
This swanky business hotel in the heart of the Irish Financial Services Centre has beautiful rooms decorated in contemporary light oak furnishings and a blue-and-taupe colour scheme that is supposed to relax the mind after a long day of meetings. Relax in the Sanovitae health club downstairs.

MALDRON HOTEL CARDIFF LANE
Map p115   Hotel €€
☎ 643 9500; www.maldronhotels.com; Cardiff Lane; r €110-360; 🚇 Grand Canal Dock; 🖥 🛜 🚇
Located on the south side of the Liffey a short walk away from the Grand Canal Dock, this is one of the best midrange options in the city. The rooms are large and extremely comfortable, but the real catch is the amenities: two restaurants, a fitness centre complete with sauna and a 22m swimming pool, the largest hotel pool in town.

BEYOND THE GRAND CANAL
Just beyond the prohibitive reaches of city-centre real estate are some of Dublin's most beautiful guesthouses and hotels. They're spread out through the residential suburbs that stretch south of the Grand Canal, notably Ballsbridge and Donnybrook. Here you'll find the best examples of Dublin's take on the boutique hotel.

FOUR SEASONS Map p122   Hotel €€€
☎ 665 4000; www.fourseasons.com; Simmonscourt Rd, Ballsbridge; r from €225; 🚌 5, 7, 7A, 8, 18 or 45 from city centre; 🅿 🖥 🛜 🚇
Like Alexis Carrington gliding down the stairs in Dynasty, you know you're in the presence of a diva when you step inside the grand lobby of this enormous hotel, in the grounds of the Royal Dublin Show-

grounds. To some, the effect is a little garish, a bit like Joan Collins herself – but to others, the combination of marble, chandeliers and marvellous bedrooms scream luxury. Whatever your take, there's no denying the quality of the service, as good as anywhere in Ireland.

DYLAN Map p122   Hotel €€€
☎ 660 3001; www.dylan.ie; Eastmoreland Pl; r from €200; 🚌 5, 7, 7A, 8, 18, 27X or 45 from city centre; 🏋 🖳 🛜

A genuine contender for favourite celebrity stopover, the Dylan's designer OTT look – baroque meets Scandinavian sleek by way of neo-art nouveau and glammed-up 1940s art deco – has nevertheless been a big hit. It is perhaps a reflection of a time when too much was barely enough for the glitterati who signed contracts over cocktails before retiring to the snazzily appointed rooms.

HERBERT PARK HOTEL
Map p122   Hotel €€€
☎ 667 2200; www.herbertparkhotel.ie; Merrion Rd, Ballsbridge; s/d from €120/195; 🚌 5, 7, 7A, 8, 18 or 45 from city centre; 🅿 🖳 🛜

We'll forgive them the stripey wallpaper in the bedrooms (and it's not the worst) because this place has so much else going for it. A bright, modernist foyer opens onto two buzzing bars; gorgeous Herbert Park is right on your doorstep; there are spacious comfortable rooms; and, in our opinion, the best (and most reasonably priced) suites in town, designed with chichi New York in mind and with huge balconies overlooking Dublin's most exclusive bit of greenery.

SCHOOLHOUSE HOTEL
Map p122   Boutique Hotel €€€
☎ 667 5014; www.schoolhousehotel.com; 2-8 Northumberland Rd; s/d €115/190; 🚌 5, 7, 7A, 8, 18 or 45 from city centre; 🅿 🖳 🛜

A Victorian schoolhouse dating from 1861, this beautiful building has been successfully converted into an exquisite boutique hotel that is (ahem) ahead of its class. Its 31 cosy bedrooms, named after famous Irish people, all have king-sized beds, big white duvets and loudly patterned headboards.

PEMBROKE TOWNHOUSE
Map p122   Boutique Hotel €€€
☎ 660 0277; www.pembroketownhouse.ie; 90 Pembroke Rd; s/d €90/180; 🚌 5, 7, 7A, 8, 18 or 45 from city centre; 🅿 🖳 ♿

This super-luxurious townhouse is a wonderful example of what happens when traditional and modern combine to great effect. A classical Georgian house has been transformed into a modern boutique hotel, with each room carefully appointed to reflect the best of contemporary design and style, right down to the modern art on the walls and the lift to the upper floors. May we borrow your designer?

WATERLOO HOUSE
Map p122   Guesthouse €€
☎ 660 1888; www.waterloohouse.ie; 8-10 Waterloo Rd; s/d €89/139; 🚌 5, 7, 7A, 8, 18 or 45 from city centre; 🅿 🛜

A short walk from St Stephen's Green, off Baggot St, this plush guesthouse spread over two ivy-clad Georgian houses has 17 rooms classically furnished in authentic Georgian style and is immaculately kept right through to the manicured gardens and breakfast conservatory. There's a serene atmosphere here and the prices represent exceptional value for the swanky D4 address.

ABERDEEN LODGE
Map p122   Guesthouse €€
☎ 283 8155; www.halpinsprivatehotels.com; 53-55 Park Ave; s/d from €69/90; 🚉 Sydney Parade; 🅿 🛜

Not only is this one of Dublin's absolutely best guesthouses, but it's a carefully guarded secret, known only to those lucky enough to dare stay a short train ride from the city centre. Their reward is a luxurious house with stunning rooms, most of which come with either a four-poster, a half-tester or a brass bed to complement the authentic Edwardian furniture and tasteful art on the walls. The suites even have fully working Adams fireplaces. To top it off, there's a level of personalised service as good as any you'll find in any of the city's top hotels.

MERRION HALL Map p122   Boutique Hotel €€
☎ 668 1426; www.halpinsprivatehotels.com; 54 Merrion Rd, Ballsbridge; s/d from €79/119; 🚌 5, 7, 7A, 8, 18 or 45 from city centre; 🅿 🛜

This ivy-clad Edwardian house, directly across the street from the Royal Dublin Showground, has 12 superbly appointed rooms, each decorated with restored period furniture. The suites have four-poster beds and whirlpool baths. A nice touch in all the rooms are the aromatherapeutic toiletries, a far cry from the usual savonettes.

GRAND CANAL HOTEL

Map p122   Hotel €€

☎ 646 1000; www.grandcanalhotel.com; Upper Grand Canal St; r from €109; 🚇 Grand Canal Dock; Ⓟ 🖳 🛜

If you're looking for your hotel to be functional and largely formless – unless, of course, you have a particular thing for business hotels – then this perfectly decent hotel a stone's throw from the Grand Canal Dock is the one for you. The could-be-anywhere furnishings (lots of light wood, mood lighting and plastic flowers) are suitably bland.

ARIEL HOUSE Map p122   B&B €

☎ 668 5512; www.ariel-house.net; 52 Lansdowne Rd; r from €69; 🚇 5, 7, 7A, 8, 18 or 45 from city centre; Ⓟ

With 28 rooms, all with their own bathroom, this is hardly your average B&B, but not many B&Bs are listed Victorian homes that have been given top rating by Fáilte Ireland either. Every room is individually decorated with period furniture, which lends the place an air of genuine luxury. Ariel House beats almost any hotel.

BEYOND THE ROYAL CANAL

About 30 minutes' walk (3km, five minutes by bus) east of Upper O'Connell St, along Dorset St on the way to the airport, is the leafy suburb of Drumcondra (Map p125), a popular area for B&Bs. Most of the houses here are late-Victorian or Edwardian, and are generally extremely well kept and comfortable. As they're on the airport road, they tend to be full virtually throughout the year, so advance booking is definitely recommended.

CROKE PARK HOTEL Map p125   Hotel €€

☎ 607 0000; www.doylecollection.com; Croke Park, Jones's Rd; r from €89; 🚇 3, 11, 11A, 16, 16A or 123 from O'Connell St

Jury's, Ireland's most Irish hotel chain, hit on a sure-fire winner when it opened a hotel at the most sacred cathedral of Gaelic sports (see p124). It makes perfect sense: as tens of thousands arrive in Dublin to support their county's efforts at Croker, the clever few hundred who booked in advance won't have far to go to sleep off their celebrations – or commiserations. If you're looking for full immersion into the joys of Gaelic sports, find out when a big game is on and book early.

GRIFFITH HOUSE

Off Map p125   B&B €

☎ 837 5030; www.griffithhouse.com; 125 Griffith Ave; s/d €50/80; 🚇 41, 41B or 16A from city centre; Ⓟ

Suburban elegance should never be underestimated, especially not if it comes in the shape of this handsome Victorian home with four elegant rooms, three of which are en suite. It's a simple, traditional place that puts the emphasis on a warm welcome, a good night's sleep and a filling breakfast.

TINODE HOUSE Off Map p125   B&B €

☎ 837 2277; www.tinodehouse.com; 170 Upper Drumcondra Rd; s/d €55/70; 🚇 11A, 11B, 36 or 36A from city centre; Ⓟ

This comfortable Edwardian townhouse has four elegant bedrooms, all with bathrooms. A friendly welcome and excellent breakfast are part of the package.

DUBLIN CITY UNIVERSITY (DCU)

Off Map p125   Campus Residence €

☎ 700 5736; www.summeraccommodation.dcu.ie; Larkfield Apartments, Campus Residences, Dublin City University, Glasnevin; s/d from €50/84; 🕐 mid-Jun–mid-Sep; 🚇 11, 11A, 11B, 13, 13A, 19 or 19A from city centre; Ⓟ 🚹

This accommodation is proof that students slum it in relative luxury. The modern rooms have plenty of amenities at hand, including a kitchen, common room and a fully equipped health centre. DCU's Glasnevin campus is only 15 minutes by bus or car from the city centre.

EXCURSIONS

EXCURSIONS

Without even the smallest hint of irony Dubliners will happily tell you that one of the city's best features is how easy it is to get out of it. Whenever they get the chance – come sun, a bank holiday or a sneaky 'sick' day off work – Dubliners will stuff their families, picnic hampers, golf clubs or whatever else they need into their cars and head for the hills, the beach, the countryside or anywhere else not hemmed in by grey concrete. Ireland is pretty small, so you can get pretty much anywhere within four or five hours' drive, but you don't have to go to Kerry or Donegal to really get into the heart of the country. A short, non-rush-hour drive will literally transport you into the countryside.

Beachcombers can jump the bus or DART and within half an hour grey concrete gives way to seaside villages with cosy harbours and sandy beaches. If you want to dig a little into the country's remote and recent past, Dublin's neighbouring counties – Wicklow to the south, Kildare to the west and Meath to the north – have ruins, prehistoric sites and stately country piles that rank among the country's most important historical attractions. Or, if you just fancy a rugged walk or gentle gambol in the Irish countryside, then there are plenty of spots to indulge, from the taxing hikes around the mountains surrounding Glendalough in County Wicklow to the gorse-bracketed paths of Howth Head immediately north of Dublin Bay.

If you're on a short visit to Dublin, then obviously timing is all-important. Sure, there's plenty to keep you amused, entertained and interested within the confines of the city centre, but Dublin's environs are as much a part of the Dublin experience as a weekend in Temple Bar; to most Dubliners, in fact, even more so. All of the sights listed in this chapter are worthwhile destinations in their own right and deserving of any effort you make to get to them. But what makes them doubly attractive for the short-term visitor is that they're all a short distance from the city, and travel to and from them is generally hassle-free.

COASTAL BREAKS

You'd never think it while walking around the city centre, but Dublin is a mere stone's throw from a number of lovely seaside towns, most of which have been incorporated into the greater city but have managed to retain that quiet village feel. The traditional fishing village of Howth (p227) – that bulbous headland on the northern edge of Dublin Bay – is now one of Dublin's most prestigious addresses, primarily because the residents are fiercely protective of their unspoilt headland, dotted with fancy houses and rising above the beautiful harbour where many of them keep their pleasure boats. Further north along the coast is the ever-elegant village of Malahide (p228), fronted by a long, sandy coastal basin and an impressive marina full of shops, restaurants and – naturally – expensive boats.

To the south of Dublin Bay lies Dalkey (p229), a compact village that is virtually attached to the southern suburbs. You can rent boats at the small harbour and explore the southern reaches of the bay and, after you're back on dry land, there are a couple of great restaurants that alone make the journey worthwhile.

Visiting all three is pretty easy. All are connected to the city centre via the DART, which cuts travel time to under 45 minutes in any direction. The obvious itinerary is to visit Howth and Malahide in one day, but each is worth devoting a little more time to if you can. If golf is your thing, Howth's wonderful courses will take up the better part of half a day, leaving you the other half to explore the port and have a seafood dinner in one of the harbour's restaurants. If you feel like a good walk, then an amble across the top of Howth Head to the lighthouse is a thoroughly enjoyable experience, especially in good weather.

As Dalkey lies on the opposite end of Dublin Bay, it is really a trip in itself, but there's plenty to keep you amused for at least half a day. Besides renting a boat and exploring the nearby waters and offshore island, there are some lovely walks in the hills above the town and further south in Killiney (p230), which is also home to a fabulous beach.

THE DISTANT PAST

Dublin is old, but it ain't that old. If you really want to get stuck into Ireland's past, you need to get out of the city, but you don't have to

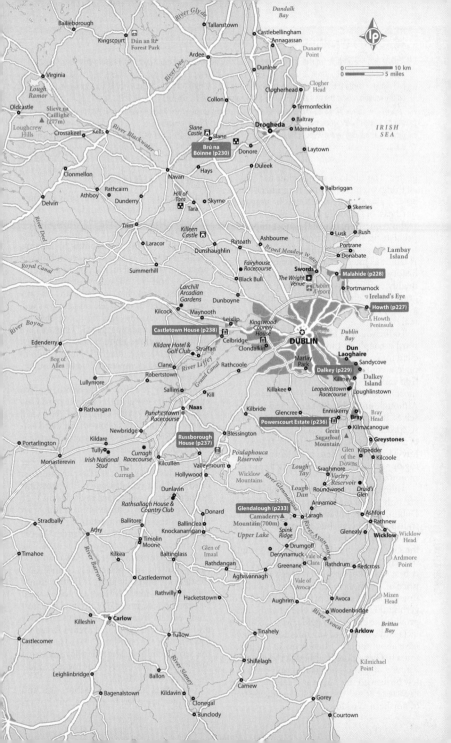

go far. The obvious destination for fans of all things prehistoric is the magnificent Brú na Bóinne (p230), an extensive Neolithic graveyard northeast of Dublin in County Meath. This is, without question, one of the most important prehistoric sites in Europe, a testament to the genius and imagination of the pre-Celts. A fabulous interpretative centre explains the history and use of the passage tombs in a thoroughly satisfying way, but a tour of the two graves themselves (Newgrange and Knowth; a third, Dowth, is under excavation) is the real treat.

To the south of Dublin, and skipping forward a couple of thousand years, is the ancient monastic settlement of Glendalough (p233), once a contemplative paradise for Ireland's first monks and now one of the country's most important sets of early-Christian ruins. Although undoubtedly fascinating in themselves, it is their setting that makes this place so special, around two glacial lakes at the foot of a secluded valley in the middle of the Wicklow Mountains. There are plenty of walking opportunities here, including a couple of mountain hikes.

Although Brú na Bóinne and Glendalough are only 40km and 25km respectively from Dublin, they are not easily accessible by public transport. A private bus company runs buses to and from Glendalough twice a day from the city centre, but Brú na Bóinne is a little harder to get to if you don't have a car and is best visited by organised coach tour – the price of which includes transport and all admission fees. Aside from leaving the hassle of getting there in someone else's hands, tours provide the bonus of a guide, who has all the facts and will answer any questions you may have about the site. There are also organised tours to Glendalough, although the main advantage of joining one is that you can kill a few birds with one stone and get in a visit to Russborough House (p237) as well as a quickie tour of northern Wicklow.

STATELY HOMES

Dublin came of age in the 18th century, when the Protestant Ascendancy committed themselves to making the city one of the most beautiful in Europe. Up went stunning Palladian townhouses around handsome, manicured squares and Georgian Dublin was born. But the actual breadth of the Palladian vision – and the full extent of the kind of cash these people had to play with – is only really revealed in the weekend getaways and country retreats they built for themselves far from the city's madding crowds. Here we have included the three finest houses of all. Each is a breathtakingly magnificent example of what vainglorious power and oodles of money can produce.

In County Wicklow, to the south, are two examples of Georgian top-dog Richard Cassels' finest work: the wonderful Powerscourt Estate (p236), built for the Power family and embellished by one of the most beautiful gardens in Europe; and Russborough House (p237), home to an extraordinary art collection built up over the years by Sir Alfred Beit. (Despite a number of robberies, it remains one of the most important private collections in the world.)

West of Dublin, County Kildare is not just home to the most important private stud farms in Ireland, but to the grandest Georgian pile of the lot, Castletown House (p238). The first complete example of the Palladian style that was all the rage between 1720 and 1820, Castletown is simply huge, without a doubt reflecting owner William Conolly's vast wealth (he was, in his day, Ireland's richest man). Not far from the house lies a relatively undiscovered delight, the Larchill Arcadian Gardens (see the boxed text, p238). Here, amid the wonderfully wild garden layout, are a number of follies, proof of the owners' oddities and eccentricities.

The actual houses at Russborough and Castletown are open to visitors, but Powerscourt House is not. Since a massive fire gutted the inside in 1974 a process of restoration has been going on that will eventually restore each room to its original splendour. However, a visit is still more than worthwhile, as the estate itself is a marvellous place to while away an afternoon, with its gardens the main draw. The nearby waterfall is the tallest in Britain and Ireland, and the surrounding countryside is perfect for a good walk.

All three houses are within about an hour and a half of Dublin's city centre, and are served by public bus. Organised tours to Glendalough also take in a visit to Powerscourt.

HOWTH

Howth is a popular excursion from Dublin and has developed as a residential suburb. It is a pretty little town built on steep streets running down to the waterfront. Although the harbour's role as a shipping port has long gone, Howth is now a major fishing centre and yachting harbour.

Most of the town backs onto the extensive grounds of Howth Castle, originally built in 1564 but much changed over the years, most recently in 1910 when Sir Edwin Lutyens gave

it a modernist makeover. Today the castle is divided into four separate – very posh and private – residences. The original estate was acquired in 1177 by the Norman noble Sir Almeric Tristram, who changed his surname to St Lawrence after winning a battle at the behest (or so he believed) of his favourite saint. The family has owned the land ever since, though the unbroken chain of male succession came to an end in 1909.

Also on the grounds are the ruins of the 16th-century Corr Castle and an ancient dolmen (a Neolithic grave memorial built of vertical stones and topped by a table stone) known as Aideen's Grave. Legend has it that Aideen died of a broken heart after her husband was killed at the Battle of Gavra near Tara in AD 184, but the legend is rubbish because the dolmen is at least 300 years older than that.

The Castle Gardens (Map p227; admission free; ☻ 24hr) are worth visiting, however, as they're noted for their rhododendrons (which bloom in May and June), for their azaleas and for the long, 10m-high beech St Mary's Abbey (Map p227; Abbey St, Howth Castle; admission free), originally founded in 1042 by the Viking King Sitric, who also founded the original church on the site of Christ Church Cathedral. In 1235 the

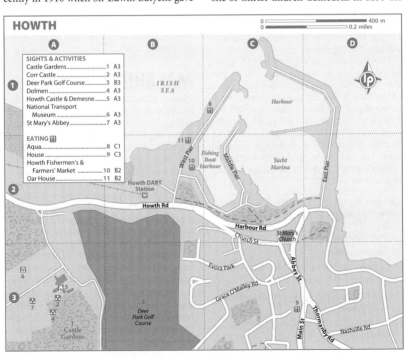

HOWTH

SIGHTS & ACTIVITIES	
Castle Gardens	1 A3
Corr Castle	2 A3
Deer Park Golf Course	3 B3
Dolmen	4 A3
Howth Castle & Demesne	5 A3
National Transport Museum	6 A3
St Mary's Abbey	7 A3

EATING 🍴	
Aqua	8 C1
House	9 C3
Howth Fishermen's & Farmers' Market	10 B2
Oar House	11 B2

abbey was amalgamated with the monastery on Ireland's Eye (a rocky island outcrop, just offshore from Howth, which is now home to a cacophony of sea birds). Some parts of the ruins date from that time, but most are from the 15th and 16th centuries. The tomb of Christopher St Lawrence (Lord Howth), in the southeastern corner, dates from around 1470. See the caretaker or read the instructions on the gate for entry.

A more recent addition is the rather ramshackle National Transport Museum (Map p227; ☎ 832 0427; www.nationaltransportmuseum.org; Howth Castle; adult €3, child & student €1.25; ☯ 10am-5pm Mon-Sat Jun-Aug, 2-5pm Sat, Sun & bank holidays Sep-May), which has a range of exhibits including double-decker buses, a bakery van, fire engines and trams – most notably a Hill of Howth electric that operated from 1901 to 1959. To reach the museum, go through the castle gates and turn right just before the castle.

The allure of history and public transport aside, most visitors set foot in the demesne armed with golf clubs, as here you'll find Deer Park Golf Course (Map p227; ☎ 832 2624; Howth Castle; 18-holes Mon-Fri €17.50, Sat & Sun €25, club rental €16; ☯ 8am-dusk Mon-Fri, 6.30am-dusk Sat & Sun), a public facility attached to a hotel. An 18-hole course, two nine-hole courses and a par-three course, all with splendid views of Dublin Bay and the surrounding countryside, are the big draw.

Howth is essentially a very large hill surrounded by cliffs, and the peak (171m) has excellent views across Dublin Bay right down to Wicklow. From the summit you can walk to the top of the Ben of Howth, which has a cairn said to mark a 2000-year-old Celtic royal grave. The 1814 Baily Lighthouse, at the southeastern corner, is on the site of an old stone fort and can be reached by a dramatic cliff-top walk. There was an earlier hill-top beacon here in 1670.

TRANSPORT: HOWTH

Distance from Dublin 9km

Direction Northeast

Bus Dublin bus 31, 31A or 31B (€2.20, 45 minutes, every 30 minutes) from Lower Abbey St.

Car Northeast along Clontarf Rd; follow the northern bay shoreline.

Train DART (€2.20, 20 minutes, every 20 minutes) to Howth.

EATING

House (Map p227; ☎ 839 6388; www.thehouse-howth.ie; 4 Main St; mains €16-22; ☯ 9am-3pm Mon-Fri, 11.30am-3pm & 6-11pm Sat & Sun) A wonderful spot on the main street leading away from the harbour, where you can feast on dishes like crunchy Bellingham blue-cheese polenta or wild Wicklow venison stew, as well as a fine selection of fish.

Oar House (Map p227; ☎ 839 4562; www.oarhouse.ie; 8 West Pier; tapas €5-12, mains €10-24; ☯ 12.30-10pm) A feast-o-fish is what the menu is all about at this newish restaurant, particularly of the locally caught variety. You can get everything on the menu in smaller, tapas portions as well as mains.

Aqua (Map p227; ☎ 832 0690; www.aqua.ie; 1 West Pier; mains €29-32; ☯ 12.30-3.30pm & 5.30-10.30pm Tue-Sat, 4-8.30pm Sun) Another contender for best seafood in Howth, Aqua serves top-quality fish dishes in its elegant dining room overlooking the harbour. The building was once home to the Howth Yacht Club.

Howth Fishermen's & Farmers' Market (Map p227; ☎ 611 5016; www.irishfarmersmarkets.ie; West Pier, Howth Harbour; ☯ 10am-5pm Sun & bank holidays) One of the best markets in Dublin. This is the place to come for fresh fish (obviously) but for organic meat, veg and homemade everything else, including jams, cakes and breads. A great option for Sunday lunch.

MALAHIDE

Malahide (Mullach Ide; Map p225) was once a small village with its own harbour, a long way from the urban jungle of Dublin, but the only thing protecting it from the northward expansion of Dublin's suburbs now is Malahide Demesne – 101 well-tended hectares of parkland dominated by a castle once owned by the powerful Talbot family. The handsome village remains relatively intact, but the erstwhile quiet marina has been massively developed and is now a bustling centre with a pleasant promenade and plenty of restaurants and shops.

Despite the vicissitudes of Irish history, the Talbot family managed to keep Malahide Castle (☎ 846 2184; www.malahidecastle.com; adult/child/student/family €7.50/4.50/6.30/18, incl Fry Model Railway €11.50/7.50/9.50/29; ☯ 10am-5pm Apr-Sep, 10am-5pm Mon-Sat, 11am-5pm Sun Oct-Mar) under its control from 1185 to 1976, apart from the time when Cromwell was in power (1649–60). The castle is now owned by the Dublin County Council.

It displays the usual hotchpotch of additions and renovations. The oldest part is a three-storey, 12th-century tower house, and the facade is flanked by circular towers, which were tacked on in 1765.

The castle is packed with furniture and paintings. Highlights include a 16th-century oak room with decorative carvings and the medieval Great Hall with family portraits, a minstrel's gallery and a painting of the Battle of the Boyne. Puck, the Talbot family ghost, is said to have last appeared in 1975.

The country's biggest collection of toy trains is the Fry Model Railway (☎ 846 3779; Malahide Castle; adult/child/student/family €6/4/5/15; ⏱ 10am-1pm & 2-5pm Tue-Sat, 1-5pm Sun Apr-Sep, closed rest of yr), a 240-sq-metre model that authentically displays much of Ireland's rail and public transport system, including the DART line and Irish Sea ferry services, in O-gauge (32mm track width). There is also a separate room featuring model trains and other memorabilia. Unfortunately, the operators suffer from the overseriousness of some grown men with complicated toys. Rather than let you simply look and admire, they herd you into the control room in groups for demonstrations.

The parkland (admission free; ⏱ 10am-9pm Apr-Oct, 10am-5pm Nov-Mar) around the castle is a good place for a picnic.

EATING

Chez Sara (☎ 845 1882; 3 Old St; mains €18-26; ⏱ 5.30pm-midnight Mon-Fri, from 1pm Sat & Sun) Irish lamb, red snapper and a beautifully cooked steak are just three of the highlights of this cosy French restaurant in the middle of the village.

Sale e Pepe (☎ 845 4600; www.saleepepe.ie; The Diamond, Main St; mains €17-29; ⏱ dinner) Despite the name, there's only a handful of Italian dishes on the menu, which emphasises well-prepared steaks, fish and chips, and homemade organic burgers.

Gibney's (☎ 845 0863; New St; dishes €4-8; ⏱ 10.30am-11.30pm Mon-Thu, 10.30am-12.30am Fri & Sat, noon-11pm Sun) Malahide's best and most popular pub does a roaring trade in sandwiches, burgers and salads.

Siam Thai Restaurant (☎ 845 4698; Gas Lane, the Marina; dishes €16-24; ⏱ 6pm-midnight) Thai classics for local palates means that you can vary the spiciness and be assured that no MSG is used.

DALKEY

Dublin's most important medieval port, Dalkey (Map p225), has long since settled into its role as an elegant dormitory village, but there are some revealing vestiges of its illustrious past, most notably the remains of three of the eight castles that once lorded over the area. Facing each other on Castle St are the 15th-century Archibold's Castle and Goat Castle. The latter (aka the Towerhouse), along with the adjoining St Begnet's Church, has been converted into the Dalkey Castle & Heritage Centre (☎ 285 8366; www.dalkeycastle.com; Castle St; adult/child/student/family €6/4/5/16; ⏱ 10am-6pm Wed-Mon May-Aug, 9.30am-5pm Mon & Wed-Fri, 11am-5pm Sat & Sun Sep-Apr), where models, displays and exhibitions are the backdrop to the 'Medieval Experience,' a live show every 30 minutes by actors from the Deilg Inis Living History Theatre.

Overlooking Bullock Harbour are the remains of Bulloch Castle, built by the monks of St Mary's Abbey in Dublin around 1150.

A few hundred metres offshore is Dalkey Island, home to St Begnet's Holy Well (admission free; boat from Coliemore Harbour per hr €25), the most important of Dalkey's so-called holy wells. This one is reputed to cure rheumatism, making the island a popular destination for tourists and the faithful alike. The island is easily accessible by boat from Coliemore Harbour; you can't book a boat, so just show up. The waters around the island are popular with

DETOUR: SANDYCOVE & JAMES JOYCE MUSEUM

About 1km north of Dalkey is Sandycove, with a pretty little beach and the Martello tower – built by British forces to keep an eye out for a Napoleonic invasion – now housing the James Joyce Museum (☎ 280 9265; Sandycove; adult/child/student €6.70/4.20/5.70; ⏰ 10am-1pm & 2-5pm Mon-Sat, 2-6pm Sun Apr-Oct, by arrangement only Nov-Mar). This is where the action begins in James Joyce's epic novel *Ulysses*. The museum was opened in 1962 by Sylvia Beach, the Paris-based publisher who first dared to put *Ulysses* into print, and has photographs, letters, documents, various editions of Joyce's work and two death masks of Joyce on display.

Below the Martello tower is the Forty Foot Pool, an open-air sea-water bathing pool that took its name from the army regiment, the Fortieth Foot, that was stationed at the tower until the regiment was disbanded in 1904. At the close of the first chapter of *Ulysses*, Buck Mulligan heads off to the Forty Foot Pool for a morning swim. A morning wake-up here is still a local tradition, whether it's winter or summer. In fact, a winter dip isn't much braver than a summer one since the water temperature varies by only about 5°C between the two seasons. Basically, it's always bloody cold.

Pressure from female bathers eventually opened this public stretch of water, originally nudist and for men only, to both sexes despite strong opposition from the 'forty-foot gentlemen'. The men eventually compromised with the ruling that a 'Togs Must Be Worn' sign would now apply after 9am. Prior to that time nudity prevails and swimmers are still predominantly male.

scuba divers; qualified divers can rent gear in Dun Laoghaire, further north, from Ocean Divers (☎ 280 1083; www.oceandivers.ie; West Pier; half-day dive with full equipment & boat €59).

To the south there are good views from the small park at Sorrento Point and from Killiney Hill. Dalkey Quarry is a popular site for rock climbers, and originally provided most of the granite for the gigantic piers at Dun Laoghaire Harbour. A number of rocky swimming pools are also found along the Dalkey coast.

About 1km south of Dalkey is the super-affluent seaside suburb of Killiney, home to some of Ireland's wealthiest people and a handful of celebrities, including Bono, Enya and filmmaker Neil Jordan. The attraction is self-evident, from the long, curving sandy beach of Killiney Bay (which 19th-century residents felt resembled Naples' Sorrento Bay, hence the Italian names of all the local roads) to the gorse-covered hills behind it, which make for a great walk. Alas, for most of us, Killiney will always remain a place to visit; on the rare occasion that a house comes on the market, it would take a cool €5 million to get the seller to bite.

EATING

Guinea Pig (☎ 285 9055; 17 Railway Rd; mains €22-42; ⏰ dinner) Despite the name, is this the best seafood restaurant in Dublin? Many a food critic seems to think so.

Caviston's Seafood Restaurant (☎ 280 9245; Glasthule Rd, Sandycove; mains €18-27; ⏰ noon-5pm Tue-Thu, noon-midnight Fri & Sat) All self-respecting crustacean-lovers should make the 1km trip to Caviston's for a seafood meal to remember.

BRÚ NA BÓINNE

One of Ireland's genuine five-star attractions, the vast Neolithic necropolis known as Brú na Bóinne (the Boyne Palace; Map p225) is one of the most extraordinary sites in Europe and shouldn't be missed. A thousand years older than Stonehenge, this is a powerful and evocative testament to the mind-boggling achievements of prehistoric humans.

The complex was built to house the remains of those who were at the top of the social heap and its tombs were the largest artificial structures in Ireland until the construction of the Anglo-Norman castles 4000 years later. The area consists of many different sites, with the three principal ones being Newgrange, Knowth and Dowth.

Over the centuries the tombs decayed, were covered by grass and trees and were plundered by everybody from Vikings to Victorian treasure hunters, whose carved initials can be seen on the great stones of Newgrange. The countryside around the tombs is littered with countless other ancient tumuli (mounds) and standing stones.

To keep visitors from mucking up the ruins at random, all visits to Brú na Bóinne have to start at the Brú na Bóinne Visitor Centre (☎ 041-988 0300; www.heritageireland.ie; Donore; adult/child visitor centre €3/2, visitor centre incl Newgrange & Knowth €11/6; ⏰ 9am-6.30pm May, 9am-7pm Jun-Sep, 9.30am-5pm Oct-Apr). Happily, this is a superb interpretive centre with an extraordinary series of interactive exhibits on the passage tombs and prehistoric Ireland in general. The building is a stunner, picking up the spiral design of Newgrange. It has regional tourism info, a good cafe and a bookstore. It's located south of the River Boyne and 2km west of Donore.

You should allow plenty of time to visit Brú na Bóinne. Plan on an hour's visit for the interpretive centre alone, two hours if you wish to include a trip to Newgrange or Knowth, and a half-day to see all three in one go (Dowth is not open to tourists).

In summer, particularly at the weekend, and during school holidays, the place gets very crowded, and you will not be guaranteed a visit to either of the passage tombs. There are only 750 tour slots and on peak days 2000 people show up. Tickets are sold on a first come first served basis (no advance booking) so the best advice is to arrive early in the morning or visit midweek and be prepared for a wait.

Brú na Bóinne is one of the most popular tourist attractions in Ireland, and there are oodles of organised tours transporting busloads of eager tourists to the visitor centre (everybody must access the sites through there) – especially from Dublin. Highly recommended are the Mary Gibbons Tours (☎ 086 355 1355; www.newgrangetours.com; tours €35), which depart from numerous Dublin hotels beginning at 9.30am Monday to Saturday, and take in the whole of the Boyne Valley. The expert guides offer a fascinating insight into Celtic and pre-Celtic life in Ireland and you'll get access to Newgrange even on days when all visiting slots are filled. Bus Éireann (☎ 836 6111; www.buseireann.ie; adult/child €29/18; Mon-Thu, Sat & Sun mid-Mar–Sep) runs Newgrange and the Boyne Valley tours, departing from Busáras (Map p102) in Dublin at 10am and returning at approximately 5.45pm.

TRANSPORT: BRÚ NA BÓINNE

Distance from Dublin 40km

Direction Northwest

Bus Bus Éireann (return €12.90, 1½ hours, one daily) and Newgrange Shuttlebus (☎ 1800 424 252; www.overthetoptours.com; return ticket €18, 1-2 daily) run to the Brú na Bóinne visitor centre from central Dublin.

Car Take M1 north to Drogheda and then N51 west to Brú na Bóinne.

NEWGRANGE

Even from afar, you know that Newgrange (adult/child visitor centre & Newgrange €6/3) is something special. Its white, round stone walls topped by a grass dome look otherworldly, and just the size is impressive: 80m in diameter and 13m high. But underneath it gets even better. Here lies the finest Stone Age passage tomb in Ireland, and one of the most remarkable prehistoric sites in Europe. It dates from around 3200 BC, predating the Pyramids by some six centuries. Besides serving as a tomb, its secondary purpose remains somewhat unclear, although it seems likely that it was a centre for ritual. The tomb's precise alignment with the sun at the time of the winter solstice also suggests it was designed to act as a calendar.

The name Newgrange derives from 'new granary' (the tomb did in fact serve as a repository for wheat and grain at one stage), although a belief more popular in the area is that it comes from the Irish for 'Cave of Gráinne', a reference to a Celtic myth taught to every Irish schoolchild. The story of 'The Pursuit of Diarmuid and Gráinne' tells of the illicit love between Gráinne, the wife of Fionn McCumhaill (or Finn McCool), leader of the Fianna, and one of his most trusted lieutenants. When Diarmuid was fatally wounded, his body was brought to Newgrange by the god Aengus in a vain attempt to save him, and the despairing Gráinne followed him into the cave, where she remained long after he died. This suspiciously Arthurian legend (for Diarmuid and Gráinne read Lancelot and Guinevere) is undoubtedly untrue, but it's still a pretty good story. Newgrange also plays another role in Celtic mythology, serving as the site where the hero Cúchulainn was conceived.

Over the centuries, Newgrange, like Dowth and Knowth, deteriorated and was even quarried at one stage. There was a standing stone on the summit until the 17th century. The site was extensively restored in 1962 and again in 1975.

A superbly carved kerbstone, with double and triple spirals, guards the tomb's main entrance and the front facade has been reconstructed so that tourists don't have to clamber in over it. Above the entrance is a slit, or roof box, which lets light in. Another beautifully decorated kerbstone stands at the exact opposite side of the mound. Some experts say that a ring of standing stones once encircled the mound, forming a Great Circle about 100m in diameter, but only 12 of these stones remain – with traces of some others below ground level.

Holding the whole structure together are the 97 boulders of the kerb ring, designed to stop the mound from collapsing outwards. Eleven of these are decorated with motifs similar to those on the main entrance stone, although only three have extensive carvings.

The white quartzite stone was originally obtained from Wicklow, 70km to the south – in an age before horse and wheel, it was transported by sea and then up the River Boyne – and there is also some granite from the Mourne Mountains in Northern Ireland. More than 200,000 tonnes of earth and stone also went into the mound.

You can walk down the narrow 19m passage, lined with 43 stone uprights – some of them engraved – which leads into the tomb chamber, about one-third of the way into the colossal mound. The chamber has three recesses, and in these are large basin stones that held cremated human bones. Along with the remains would have been funeral offerings of beads and pendants, but these must have been stolen long before the archaeologists arrived.

Above your head the massive stones support a 6m-high corbel-vaulted roof. A complex drainage system means that not a drop of water has penetrated the interior in 40 centuries.

At 8.20am on the winter solstice (sometime between the 19 and 23 of December), the rising sun's rays shine through the roof box above the entrance, creep slowly down the long passage and illuminate the tomb chamber for 17 minutes. There is little doubt that this is one of the country's most memorable, even mystical, experiences. There is a simulated winter sunrise for every group taken into the mound but to be in with a chance of witnessing the real thing add your name to the list that is drawn by lottery every 1 October.

KNOWTH

Northwest of Newgrange, the burial mound of Knowth (Cnóbha; visitor centre & Knowth adult/child €5/3; ☼ Easter-Oct) was built around the same time and seems set to surpass its better-known neighbour in both its size and the importance of the discoveries made here. It has the greatest collection of passage-grave art ever uncovered in Western Europe, and has been under excavation since 1962.

The excavations first cleared a passage leading to the central chamber, which, at 34m, is much longer than the one at Newgrange. In 1968 a 40m passage was unearthed on the opposite side of the mound. Although the chambers are separate, they're close enough for archaeologists to hear each other at work. Also in the mound are the remains of six early-Christian souterrains (underground chambers) built into the side. Some 300 carved slabs and 17 satellite graves surround the main mound.

Human activity at Knowth continued for thousands of years after its construction, which accounts for the site's complexity. The Beaker folk, so called because they buried their dead with drinking vessels, occupied the site in the Bronze Age (c 1800 BC), as did the Celts in the Iron Age (c 500 BC). Remnants of bronze and iron workings from these periods have been discovered. Around AD 800 to 900, it was turned into a rath (earthen ringfort), a stronghold of the very powerful O'Neill clan. In 965, it was the seat of Cormac MacMaelmithic, later Ireland's high king for nine years, and in the 12th century the Normans built a motte and bailey here. The site was finally abandoned in about 1400.

Excavations are likely to continue for at least the next decade so you may see archaeologists at work when you visit.

DOWTH

The circular mound at Dowth (from the Irish 'Dubhadh', meaning 'dark') is a little

---

DETOUR: NEWGRANGE FARM

One for the kids. Situated a few hundred metres down the hill to the west of Newgrange tomb (or follow the signs on the N51) is a 135-hectare working farm (☎ 041-982 4119; www.newgrangefarm.com; Newgrange; adult €8, family €12-30; ☼ 10am-5pm Easter-Aug). The truly hands-on, family-run farm allows visitors to feed the ducks and lambs, and tour the exotic bird aviaries. Amiable Farmer Bill keeps things interesting and demonstrations of threshing, sheepdog work and shoeing a horse are absorbing. Sunday at 3pm is a very special time when the 'sheep derby' is run. Finding jockeys small enough wasn't easy, so teddy bears are tied to the animals' backs. Visiting children are made owners of individual sheep for the race.

FIONN & THE SALMON OF KNOWLEDGE

One of the best-known stories in the Fenian Cycle is set around Newgrange and tells of the old druid Finnegan, who struggled for seven years to catch a very slippery salmon that, once consumed, would bestow enormous wisdom on the eater, including the gift of foresight. The young Fionn McCumhaill arrived at his riverside camp one day, looking for instruction, and no sooner did the young hero arrive than Finnegan managed to land the salmon. As befits the inevitable tragedy of all these stories, Finnegan set the fish to cook and went off for a bit, ordering Fionn to keep an eye on it without eating so much as the smallest part. You'd think that after all these years of labour Finnegan could have put off what he went off to do until after dinner, but it wasn't to be. As Fionn turned the fish on the spit a drop of hot oil landed on his thumb, which he quickly put in his mouth to soothe. Finnegan returned, saw what had happened and knew that it was too late: he bade Fionn eat the rest of the fish and so it was that Fionn acquired wisdom and foresight.

smaller than Newgrange – about 63m in diameter – but is slightly taller at 14m high. It has suffered badly at the hands of everyone from road builders and treasure hunters to amateur archaeologists, who scooped out the centre of the tumulus in the 19th century. For a time, Dowth even had a teahouse ignobly perched on its summit. Relatively untouched by modern archaeologists, Dowth shows what Newgrange and Knowth looked like for most of their history. Because it's unsafe, Dowth is closed to visitors, though the mound can be viewed from the road. Excavations began in 1998 and will continue for years to come.

There are two entrance passages, which lead to separate chambers (both sealed), and a 24m early-Christian souterrain at either end, which connects up with the western passage. This 8m-long passage leads into a small cruciform chamber, in which a recess acts as an entrance to an additional series of small compartments, a feature unique to Dowth. To the southwest of the mound is the entrance to a shorter passage and another smaller chamber.

North of the tumulus are the ruins of Dowth Castle and Dowth House.

SLEEPING & EATING

Newgrange Lodge (☎ 041-988 2478; www.newgrangelodge. com; Newgrange; dm/s/d €18/45/70; P ▣) A beautiful place just east of the Brú na Bóinne Visitor Centre, the lodge has dorm beds and hotel-standard en-suite rooms with TVs. Reception is open 24 hours and there is a cafe, outdoor patios, bicycle hire and much more.

Glebe House (☎ 041-983 6101; www.theglebehouse. ie; Dowth; s/d €60/120; P) This charming 17th-century, wisteria-clad country house has views of Newgrange and Dowth. It has four gorgeous rooms with open log fires and vibrant purple carpet. It is 7km west of Drogheda; children under 10 are not allowed.

Rossnaree (☎ 041-982 0975; www.rossnaree.ie; Newgrange; s/d €100/160; ☺ Apr-Dec; P) A magnificent Palladian-style country house between Donore and Slane, just south of the visitor centre, with exquisite bedrooms and fabulous cuisine (dinner €45). The river at the bottom of the garden is the same one where poor old Finnegan landed the Salmon of Knowledge (see the boxed text, above).

Boyle's Licensed Tea Rooms (☎ 041-982 4195; Main St, Slane) About 2km west of Knowth; this is a wonderful tea shop and cafe, with a 1940s ambience. The menu, written in 12 languages, is strictly of the tea-and-scones type (around €3).

GLENDALOUGH

If you're looking for the epitome of rugged and romantic Ireland, you won't do much better than Glendalough (Gleann dá Loch, 'Valley of the Two Lakes'; Map p225), truly one of Ireland's most beautiful corners and a highlight of any trip along the eastern seaboard.

The substantial remains of this important monastic settlement are certainly impressive, but the real draw is the splendid setting, two dark and mysterious lakes tucked into a deep valley covered in forest. It is, despite its immense popularity, a deeply tranquil and spiritual place, and you will have little difficulty in understanding why those solitude-seeking monks came here in the first place. Visit early or late in the day – or out of season – to avoid the big crowds. Remember that a visit here is all about walking, so wear comfortable shoes.

If you don't fancy doing Glendalough on your own steam, there are a couple of tours that will make it fairly effortless. The award-winning Wild Wicklow Tour (☎ 280 1899; www.discover dublin.ie; adult/student & child €28/25; ☺ departs 9am) of Glendalough, Avoca and the Sally Gap never fails to generate rave reviews for atmosphere and all-round fun, but so much craic has

Distance from Dublin 25km

Direction South

Bus St Kevin's Bus (☎ 281 8119; one way/return €9/15) takes 1½ hours and departs 11.30am and 6pm Monday to Saturday, and 11.30am and 7pm Sunday from outside the Royal College of Surgeons, St Stephen's Green West, Dublin, returning at 7.15am and 4.15pm Monday to Friday, and 9.45am and 4.15pm Saturday and Sunday.

Car N11 south to Kilmacanogue, then R755 west through Roundwood, Annamoe and Laragh.

made a casualty of informative depth. The first pick-up is at the Dublin Tourism office, but there are a variety of pick-up points throughout Dublin; check the point nearest you when booking. Alternatively, Bus Éireann (☎ 836 6111; www.buseireann.ie; Busáras; adult/child/student €28.80/22.50/25.20; ⊗ departs 10am mid-Mar–Oct) runs good but slightly impersonal whole-day tours of Glendalough and the Powerscourt Estate, which return to Dublin at about 5.45pm.

At the valley entrance, before the Glendalough Hotel, is the Glendalough Visitor Centre (☎ 0404-45325; www.heritageireland.ie; adult/child & student €3/1; ⊗ 9.30am-6pm mid-Mar–Oct, 9.30am-5pm Nov–mid-Mar). The centre screens a high-quality 17-minute audiovisual presentation, *Ireland of the Monasteries*, which does exactly what it says on the tin.

The original site of St Kevin's settlement, Teampall na Skellig, is at the base of the cliffs towering over the southern side of the Upper Lake, and is accessible only by boat; unfortunately, there's no boat service to the site and you'll have to settle for looking at it across the lake. The terraced shelf has the reconstructed ruins of a church and early graveyard. Rough wattle huts once stood on the raised ground nearby. Scattered around are some early grave slabs and simple stone crosses.

Just east of the lake and 10m above its waters is the 2m-deep artificial cave called St Kevin's Bed, said to be where Kevin lived (for more on St Kevin, see the boxed text, below). The earliest human habitation of the cave was long before St Kevin's era – there's evidence that people lived in the valley for thousands of years before the monks arrived. In the green area just south of the car park is a large circular wall thought to be the remains of an early-Christian *caher* (stone fort).

Follow the lakeshore path southwest of the car park until you find the considerable remains of Reefert Church above the tiny Poulanass River. This is a small, rather plain, 11th-century Romanesque nave-and-chancel church, with some reassembled arches and walls. Traditionally, Reefert (meaning King's Burial Place) was the burial site of the chiefs of the local O'Toole family. The surrounding graveyard contains a number of rough stone crosses and slabs, most made of shiny mica schist.

Climb the steps at the back of the churchyard and follow the path to the west and you'll find, at the top of a rise overlooking the lake, the scant remains of St Kevin's Cell, a small beehive hut.

While the Upper Lake has the best scenery, the most fascinating buildings lie in the lower part of the valley, east of the Lower Lake.

Around the bend from the Glendalough Hotel is the stone arch of the monastery gatehouse, the only surviving example of a monastic entranceway in the country. Just inside the entrance is a large slab with an incised cross.

ST KEVIN & GLENDALOUGH

In AD 498 a young monk named Kevin arrived in the valley looking for somewhere to kick back, meditate and be at one with nature. He pitched up in what had been a Bronze Age tomb on the southern side of the Upper Lake and for the next seven years slept on stones, wore animal skins, maintained a near-starvation diet and – according to the legend – became bosom buddies with the birds and animals. Kevin's ecofriendly lifestyle soon attracted a bunch of disciples, all seemingly unaware of the irony that they were flocking to hang out with a hermit who wanted to live as far away from other people as possible. Over the next couple of centuries his one-man operation mushroomed into a proper settlement and by the 9th century Glendalough rivalled Clonmacnoise as the island's premier monastic city. Thousands of students studied and lived in a thriving community that was spread over a considerable area.

Inevitably, Glendalough's success made it a key target of Viking raiders, who sacked the monastery at least four times between 775 and 1071. The final blow came in 1398, when English forces from Dublin almost completely destroyed it. Efforts were made to rebuild and some life lingered on here as late as the 17th century, when, under renewed repression, the monastery finally died.

WALKS AROUND GLENDALOUGH

The easiest and most popular walk at Glendalough is the gentle hour-long walk along the northern shore of the Upper Lake to the lead and zinc mine workings, which date from 1800. However, the better route is along the lakeshore rather than on the road, which runs 30m from the shore. You can continue on up to the head of the valley if you want to go a little further.

Alternatively, you can walk the railway sleepers that form the path along the Spink (550m), the steep ridge with vertical cliffs running along the southern flanks of the Upper Lake. You can go part of the way and turn back, or complete a 5km circuit of the Upper Lake by following the top of the cliff, eventually coming down by the mine workings and going back along the northern shore.

The third option is the 7.5km hike up and down Camaderry Mountain (700m), hidden behind the hills that flank the northern side of the valley. The walk starts on the road 50m back towards Glendalough from the entrance to the Upper Lake car park. Head straight up the steep hill to the north and you come out on open mountains with sweeping views in all directions. You can then continue up Camaderry to the northwest, or just follow the ridge west looking over the Upper Lake.

Beyond that lies a graveyard, which is still in use. The 10th-century round tower is 33m tall and 16m in circumference at the base. The upper storeys and conical roof were reconstructed in 1876. Near the tower, to the southeast, lies the Cathedral of St Peter and St Paul, with a 10th-century nave. The chancel and sacristy both date from the 12th century.

At the centre of the graveyard, to the south of the round tower, is the Priest's House. This odd building dates from 1170 but has been heavily reconstructed. It may have been the location of shrines of St Kevin. Later, during the 18th century, it became a burial site for local priests – hence the name. The 10th-century St Mary's Church, 140m southwest of the round tower, probably originally stood outside the walls of the monastery and belonged to local nuns; it has a lovely western doorway. A little to the east are the scant remains of St Kieran's Church, the smallest at Glendalough.

Glendalough's trademark is St Kevin's Church – or Kitchen – at the southern edge of the enclosure. With its miniature round-tower-like belfry, protruding sacristy and steep stone roof, it's a masterpiece. How it came to be known as a kitchen is a mystery as there's no indication that it was ever anything other than a church. The oldest parts of the building date from the 11th century – the structure has been remodelled since but it's still a classic early Irish church.

At the junction with Green Rd, as you cross the river just south of these two churches, is the Deer Stone, in the middle of a group of rocks. Legend claims that when St Kevin needed milk for two orphaned babies, a doe stood here waiting to be milked. The stone is actually a *bullaun*, used as a grinding stone for medicines or food. Many are thought to be prehistoric and they were widely regarded as having supernatural properties; women who bathed their faces with water from the hollow were supposed to keep their looks forever. The early churchmen brought them into their monasteries, perhaps hoping to inherit some of the stones' powers.

The road east leads to St Saviour's Church, with its detailed Romanesque carvings. To the west a nice woodland trail leads up the valley past the Lower Lake to the Upper Lake.

SLEEPING & EATING

Glendale (☎ 0404-45410; www.glendale-glendalough.com; Laragh East; s/d €70/80, cottage per week €355-480; P) A tidy B&B with large, comfortable rooms. Also available are five modern, fully equipped self-catering cottages that sleep six. The owners will also drop you off in Glendalough if you don't fancy the walk.

Glendalough Hotel (☎ 0404-45135; www.glendalough hotel.com; s/d €118/164; bar mains around €10, 3-course lunch €21; ☷ noon-6pm; P ▯) Forty-four luxurious bedrooms right next to the ruins. The hotel's enormous restaurant serves a very good lunch of unsurprising dishes, usually involving some chicken, beef and fish. The bar menu – burgers, sandwiches, sausages and the like – is also quite filling.

Wicklow Heather Restaurant (☎ 0404-45157; www.thewicklowheather.com; Main St, Laragh; mains €16-26; ☷ noon-8.30pm) This is the best place for anything substantial. The menu offers Wicklow lamb, wild venison, Irish beef and fresh fish (the trout is excellent) – most of it sourced locally and all of it traceable from farm to fork.

SPIRITUAL SLEEPS

Glendalough Cillíns (☎ 0404-45140, bookings 45777; www.hermitage.dublindiocese.ie; St Kevin's Parish Church, Glendalough; s/d €45/70) In an effort to re-create something of the contemplative spirit of Kevin's early years in the valley, St Kevin's Parish Church rents out six hermitages (or *cillíns*) to people looking to take time out from the bustle of daily life and reflect on more spiritual matters. In keeping with more modern needs, however, there are a few more facilities than were present in Kevin's cave. Each hermitage is a bungalow consisting of a bedroom, a bathroom, a small kitchen area and an open fire (supplemented by a storage heating facility). The whole venture is managed by the local parish, and while there is a strong spiritual emphasis here, it is not necessarily a Catholic one. Visitors of all denominations and creeds are welcome, so long as their intentions are reflective and meditative – backpackers looking for a cheap place to bed down are not. The hermitages are in a field next to St Kevin's Parish Church, about 1km east of Glendalough on the R756 to Laragh.

POWERSCOURT ESTATE

About 500m south of the charming village of Enniskerry is the entrance to the 64-sq-km Powerscourt Estate (Map p225; ☎ 204 6000; www.powerscourt.ie; adult/child/student €8/5/7; ☼ 9.30am-5.30pm Feb-Oct, 9.30am-4.30pm Nov-Jan), Wicklow's grandest country pile. This is one of the most popular day trips from Dublin, and the village – built in 1760 by Richard Wingfield, Earl of Powerscourt, so that his labourers would have somewhere to live – is a terrific spot to while away an afternoon.

If getting there under your own steam is an issue, you can visit it and Glendalough together as part of a Bus Éireann Tour (☎ 836 6111; www.buseireann.ie; Busáras; adult/child/student €28.80/22.50/25.20; ☼ 10am mid-Mar–Oct), which departs from the Dublin Tourism office. Dublin Bus Tours (☎ 872 0000; www.dublinbus.ie; 59 Upper O'Connell St; adult/child €25/12; ☼ 11am) includes a visit in its four-hour South Coast & Gardens tour, which takes in the stretch of coastline between Dun Laoghaire and Killiney before turning inland to Wicklow and on to Enniskerry. Admission to the gardens is included. Grayline Tours (☎ 872 9010; www.irishcitytours.com; Gresham Hotel, O'Connell St; adult/student/child €35/32/25; ☼ 10am Fri-Sun) takes in Wicklow's big hitters – Powerscourt, Glendalough and the lakes, a stop at Avoca, then heads to Dun Laoghaire and Dalkey.

Powerscourt Estate has existed more or less since 1300 when the LePoer (later anglicised to Power) family built themselves a castle here. The property then changed Anglo-Norman hands a few times before coming into the possession of Richard Wingfield, newly appointed Marshall of Ireland, in 1603; his descendants were to live here for the next 350 years. In 1731 the Georgian wunderkind, Richard Cassels, turned his genius to building the stunning Palladian-style mansion,

which he finished in 1743. An extra storey was added to the building in 1787 and other alterations were made in the 19th century. The house was restored after the Wingfields sold up in the 1950s, but the whole building was gutted by fire on the very eve of its re-opening in 1974.

The estate has since come into the hands of the sporting-goods giants the Slazengers, who have overseen a second restoration, as well as the addition of two golf courses, a cafe, a huge garden centre and a bunch of cutsey little retail outlets. Basically, it's all intended to draw in the punters and wring as many euros out of their pockets as possible, so as to finish the huge restoration job and make the estate a kind of profitable wonderland. If you can deal with the crowds (summer weekends are the worst) or, better still, avoid them and visit midweek, you're in for a real treat.

Easily the biggest draw is the simply magnificent 20-hectare formal gardens and the breathtaking views that accompany them. Originally laid out in the 1740s, they were redesigned in the 19th century by Daniel Robinson, who had as much a fondness for the

TRANSPORT: POWERSCOURT ESTATE

Distance from Dublin 18km

Direction South

Bus Dublin bus 44 (€2.20, 1¼ hours, every 20 minutes) from city centre (see Map p115).

Car Drive south on Ranelagh Rd (R117), right onto Milltown Rd, left onto Dundrum Rd and on through Kilternan and Enniskerry; alternatively, head south to Bray along N11 and west for 3km on R117.

Train DART to Bray (€2.70), bus 185 to Enniskerry (€1.60, 20 minutes, hourly) from station.

booze as he did for horticultural pursuits (see the boxed text, left). Perhaps this influenced his largely informal style, which resulted in a magnificent blend of landscaped gardens, sweeping terraces, statuary, ornamental lakes, secret hollows, rambling walks and walled enclosures replete with over 200 types of trees and shrubs – all beneath the stunning natural backdrop of the Great Sugarloaf Mountain to the southeast. Tickets come with a map laying out 40-minute and hour-long tours of the gardens. Don't miss the exquisite Japanese Gardens or the Pepperpot Tower, modelled on a 3-inch actual pepperpot owned by Lady Wingfield. Our own favourite, however, is the animal cemetery, final resting place of the Wingfield pets and even some of their favourite milking cows. Some of the epitaphs are astonishingly personal.

A 7km walk to a separate part of the estate takes you to the 130m **Powerscourt Waterfall** (☎ 204 6000; adult/child/student €5/3.50/4.50; ☷ 9.30am-7pm May-Aug, 10.30am-5.30pm Mar-Apr & Sep-Oct, to 4.30pm Nov-Jan). This is the highest waterfall in Britain and Ireland, and is most impressive after heavy rain. You can also get to the falls by road, following the signs from the estate. A nature trail has been laid out around the base of the waterfall, which takes you past giant redwoods, ancient oaks, beech, birch and rowan trees. There are plenty of birds in the vicinity, including the chaffinch, cuckoo, chiffchaff, raven and willow warbler.

SLEEPING & EATING

Coolakay House (☎ 286 2423; www.coolakayhouse.com; Waterfall Rd, Coolakay; s/d €40/80; ☷) Four comfortable bedrooms and a terrific restaurant (mains around €11).

Summerhill House Hotel (☎ 286 7928; www.summerhillhousehotel.com; Enniskerry; r from €100; ☷) Enniskerry's best hotel is a fabulous country mansion set amid its own woodland and landscaped park. It's off the N11.

Organic Life/Marc Michel (☎ 201 1882; Tinna Parc, Kilpedder; mains around €17; ☷ 10am-5pm, restaurant 10am-5pm) Situated just off the N11, past the turn-off for Glendalough, is the east coast's best-kept organic secret: a superb restaurant located in the middle of a lush forest.

Poppies Country Cooking (☎ 282 8869; The Square, Enniskerry; mains €9; ☷ 8.30am-6pm) A pokey little cafe serving wholesome salads, filling sandwiches and award-winning ice cream…even if the service can be slow.

THE BOOZY GARDENER

Daniel Robertson was not your typical gardener. He supervised the construction of the gardens from a wheelbarrow, in which he would lay prostrate, armed only with a bottle of sherry. To his underlings he would bark orders that, as the day passed, grew more and more incoherent as his bottle became lighter. Work usually went on until 5pm, when the tanked-up Robertson would call an end to the day's work on account of bad light. A perfectly reasonable suggestion, you may think, but considering that the summer day doesn't end until at least 10pm…

Emilia's Ristorante (☎ 276 1834; www.emilias.ie; Clock Tower, The Square; mains €12-16; ☷ 5-10.45pm Mon-Sat, noon-9.30pm Sun) A lovely 1st-floor restaurant that will satisfy even the most ardent craving for thin-crust pizzas.

RUSSBOROUGH HOUSE

Magnificent **Russborough House** (Map p225; ☎ 045-865 239; www.russborough.ie; Blessington; adult/child/student €10/5/8; ☷ 10am-6pm daily May-Sep, Sun & bank holidays only Apr & Oct) is one of Ireland's finest stately homes, a Palladian pleasure palace built for Joseph Leeson (1705–83), later the first earl of Milltown and, later still, Lord Russborough. It was built from 1741 to 1751 to the design of Richard Cassels, who was at the height of his fame as an architect. Poor old Richard didn't live to see it finished, but the job was well executed by Francis Bindon. Now, let's get down to the juicy bits.

The house has always attracted unwelcome attention, beginning in 1798 when Irish forces took hold of the place during the Rising (see p27); they were soon thrown out by the British army who got so used to the comforts that they didn't leave until 1801, and then only after a raging Lord Russborough challenged their commander, Lord Tyrawley, to a duel 'with blunderbusses and slugs in a sawpit'. Miaow.

The house remained in the Leeson family until 1931. In 1952 it was sold to Sir Alfred Beit, the eponymous nephew of the co-founder of the de Beers diamond-mining company. Uncle Alfred was an obsessive art collector, and when he died his impressive haul – which includes works by Velázquez, Vermeer, Goya and Rubens – was passed on to his nephew, who brought it to Russborough House. The collection was to attract the interest of more than just art-lovers.

TRANSPORT: RUSSBOROUGH HOUSE

Distance from Dublin 35km

Direction Southwest

Bus Dublin bus 65 (€4.50, 1½ hours, 10 daily) from Eden Quay.

Car N81 southwest via Blessington.

In 1974 the IRA decided to get into the art business by stealing 16 of the paintings. They were eventually all recovered, but 10 years later the notorious Dublin criminal Martin Cahill (aka the General) masterminded another robbery, this time for Loyalist paramilitaries. On this occasion, however, only some of the works were recovered and of those several were damaged beyond repair – a good thief does not a gentle curator make. In 1988 Beit got the picture and decided to hand over the most valuable of the paintings to the National Gallery; in return for the gift, the gallery agreed to lend other paintings to the collection as temporary exhibits. The sorry story didn't conclude there. In 2001 two thieves took the direct approach and drove a jeep through the front doors, making off with two paintings worth nearly €4 million, including a Gainsborough that had been stolen, and recovered, twice before. And then, to add abuse to the insult already added to injury, the house was broken into again in 2002, with the thieves taking five more paintings, including two by Rubens. Incredibly, however, both hauls were quickly recovered.

The admission price includes a 45-minute tour of the house and all the important paintings, which, given the history, is a monumental exercise in staying positive. Whatever you do, make no sudden moves.

Russborough hosts a monthly farmers market (☎ 087-611 5016; ⏱ 10am-4pm, 1st Sun of the month) that goes indoors during the winter months.

SLEEPING & EATING

Haylands House (☎ 045-865 183; haylands@eircom.net; Dublin Rd, Blessington; s/d €40/70; P) Highly recommended B&B with a warm welcome and lovely rooms.

Rathsallagh House & Country Club (Map p225; ☎ 045-403 112; www.rathsallagh.com; Dunlavin; s/d from €135/260; P ⏱) This fabulous country manor off the N81, converted from Queen Anne stables in 1798, has splendidly appointed rooms and a superb golf course. The restaurant offers a five-course meal (€65).

Grangecon Cafe (☎ 045-857 892; Tullow Rd, Blessington; mains €11-18; ⏱ 10am-5pm Tue-Sat) Salads, home-baked dishes and a full menu of Irish cheeses are the staples at this tiny, terrific cafe located in a converted schoolhouse.

CASTLETOWN HOUSE

In a country full of elegant Palladian mansions, it is no mean feat to be considered the grandest of the lot, but Castletown House (Map p225; ☎ 628 8252; www.castletownhouse.ie; adult/child €4.50/3.50; ⏱ 10am-6pm Mon-Fri, 1-6pm Sat & Sun Easter-Sep, 10am-5pm Mon-Fri, 1-5pm Sun Oct) simply has no peer. It is Ireland's largest and most imposing Georgian estate, and a testament to the vast wealth enjoyed by the Anglo-Irish gentry during the 18th century.

The house was built between the years 1722 and 1732 for William Conolly (1662–1729), speaker of the Irish House of Commons, and, at the time, Ireland's richest man. Born into relatively humble circumstances in Ballyshannon, County Donegal, Conolly made his fortune through land transactions in the uncertain aftermath of the Battle of the Boyne (1690).

The original design of the house was by the Italian architect Alessandro Galilei (1691–1737), who in 1718 designed the facade of the main block so as to resemble a 16th-century Italian *palazzo* (palace). Construction began in 1722 but Galilei didn't bother hanging around to supervise, having left Ireland in 1719. Instead, the project was entrusted to Sir Edward Lovett Pearce (1699–1733), who returned from his grand tour of Italy in 1724 (where he had become friends with Galilei).

Inspired by the work of Andrea Palladio, which he had studied during his visit to Italy, Pearce enlarged the original design of the

TRANSPORT: CASTLETOWN HOUSE

Distance from Dublin 21km

Direction West

Bus Dublin buses 67 and 67A (one way €3.50, about one hour, hourly) depart from D'Olier St for Celbridge and stop at the gates of Castletown House.

Car Take N4 to Celbridge.

house and added the colonnades and the terminating pavilions. The interior is as opulent as the exterior suggests, especially the Long Gallery, replete with family portraits and exquisite stucco work by the Francini brothers. Pearce's connection with Conolly was a fortuitous one, as he was commissioned in 1728 to design the House of Commons in Dublin. That building, now the Bank of Ireland (p75) on College Green, is one of the most elegant examples of the Georgian style in Dublin.

As always seems the way with these grand projects, Conolly didn't live to see the completion of his wonder-palace. His widow continued to live at the unfinished house after his death in 1729, instigating many of the improvements made to the house after the main structure was completed in 1732. Her main architectural contribution was the curious 42.6m Obelisk, known locally as the Conolly Folly. Designed to her specifications by Richard Cassels, and visible from both ends of the Long Gallery, it is 3.2km north of the house.

The house remained in the family's hands until 1965, when it was purchased by Desmond Guinness. He spent vast amounts of money on restoring the house to its original splendour, an investment that was continued from 1979 by the Castletown Foundation. In 1994 Castletown House was transferred to state care and today it is managed by the Heritage Service.

Immediately to the east of the grounds of Castletown House, and on private property that never belonged to the house, you will find the even more curious, conical Wonderful Barn (☎ 624 5448; Leixlip; closed to the public). Standing at 21m high, this extraordinary five-storey structure, which is wrapped by a 94-step winding staircase, was commissioned by Lady Conolly in 1743 to give employment to local tenants whose crops were ruined by the severe frosts in the winters of 1741 and 1742. The building was ostensibly a granary, but it was also used as a shooting tower – doves were considered a delicacy in Georgian times. Flanking the main building are two smaller towers, which were also used to store grain.

DETOUR: LARCHILL ARCADIAN GARDENS

Green thumbs and shrubbery fanatics will not want to miss a detour to the Larchill Arcadian Gardens (Map p225; ☎ 628 7354; www.larchill.ie; Kilcock; adult/child €7.50/5.50; noon-6pm Tue-Sun Jun-Aug, noon-6pm Sat & Sun Sep), Europe's only example of a mid-18th-century *ferme ornée* (ornamental farm). A 40-minute walk takes you through beautiful landscaped parklands, passing eccentric follies (including a model of the Gibraltar fortress and a shell-decorated tower), gazebos and a lake. Children will be chuffed with the adventure playground, maze and rare-breed farm animals. The gardens are 12km northwest of Castletown House.

Be warned however: the land surrounding the barn has been zoned for redevelopment and there is a scandalous plan to build 500-odd houses around it, so prepare to trundle through a building site.

SLEEPING & EATING

Kildare Hotel & Golf Club (Map p225; ☎ 601 7200; www.kclub.ie; Straffan; r from €200; P □) Better known as the K Club, the host of the 2006 Ryder Cup, the estate is home to a palatial Palladian villa that is one of the best hotels in Ireland. It is 6km southwest of Celbridge just off the R403.

Carton House (☎ 505 2000; www.cartonhouse.com; Maynooth; r from €150; P □) It really doesn't get any grander than this vast, early-19th-century estate, which is set on lavish grounds and includes two outstanding golf courses.

Kehoe's (☎ 628 6533; Main St, Maynooth; meals €6-10; 8am-4pm Mon-Sat) The place for a classic Irish breakfast, Kehoe's offers a warm, trad welcome to its small and cosy quarters. There are numerous daily lunch specials.

Mohana (☎ 505 4868; Main St, Maynooth; mains €13; noon-2.30pm & 5-11pm) Several cuts above the usual curry joint, Mohana has a wide range of excellent South Asian dishes.

TRANSPORT

Ireland's capital and biggest city is the most important point of entry and departure for the country – the overwhelming majority of airlines fly in and out of Dublin Airport. The city has two ports that serve as the main points of sea transport with Britain; ferries from France arrive in the southern port of Rosslare. Dublin is also the nation's primary rail hub. Flights, tours and rail tickets can be booked online at www.lonelyplanet.com/travel_services.

AIR

There are direct flights to Dublin from all major European centres (including a dizzying array of options from the UK) and from Boston, Baltimore, Chicago, New York and Los Angeles in the USA. Flights from further afield (Australasia or Africa) are usually routed through London.

Airlines

No airline has a walk-in office in Dublin, but most have walk-up counters at Dublin airport. Those that don't, have their ticketing handled by other airlines. The website of the Fáilte Ireland (Irish Tourist Board; www.ireland.ie) has information on getting to Dublin from a number of countries.

Airlines that serve Dublin:

Aer Árann (☎ 1890 462 726; www.aerarann.com)

Aer Lingus (☎ 01-886 8888; www.aerlingus.com)

Air Baltic (☎ +370 5 2356000; www.airbaltic.com)

Air Canada (☎ 1800 709 900; www.aircanada.ca)

Air France (☎ 01-605 0383; www.airfrance.com)

ONLINE BOOKING AGENCIES

- www.bestfares.com
- www.cheapflights.com
- www.ebookers.com
- www.expedia.com
- www.flycheap.com
- www.opodo.com
- www.priceline.com
- www.statravel.com
- www.travelocity.com

Air Malta (☎ 1800 397 400; www.airmalta.com)

Air Wales (☎ 1800 465 193; www.airwales.com)

Air Southwest (☎ +44 870 241 8202; www.airsouthwest.com)

Air Transat (☎ +44 8705 561 522; www.airtransat.com)

American Airlines (☎ 01-602 0550; www.aa.com)

BMI (☎ 01-407 3036; www.flybmi.com)

British Airways (☎ 1800 626 747; www.britishairways.com)

City Jet (☎ 01-870 0300; www.cityjet.com)

Continental (☎ 1890 925 252; www.continental.com)

Delta Airlines (☎ 1800 768 080; www.delta.com)

Etihad Airways (☎ 01-477 3479; www.etihadairways.com)

Flybe (☎ 1890 925 532; www.flybe.com)

Flyglobespan (☎ 01-874 7666; www.flyglobespan.ie)

German Wings (☎ 01-865 0125; www.germanwings.com)

Iberia (☎ 01-407 3017; www.iberia.com)

Lufthansa (☎ 01-844 5544; www.lufthansa.com)

Luxair (☎ +44 8003 899443; www.luxair.co.uk)

Malev Hungarian Airlines (☎ 01-844 4303; www.malev.com)

Ryanair (☎ 0818 30 30 30; www.ryanair.com)

S7 Airlines (☎ 01-663 3933; www.s7.ru)

Scandinavian Airlines (☎ 01-844 5440; www.flysas.com)

Swiss Airlines (☎ 1890 200 515; www.swiss.com)

Turkish Airlines (☎ 01-844 7920; www.turkishairlines.com)

US Airways (☎ 1890 925 065; www.usairways.com)

Airport

Dublin's international airport (DUB; Map p225; ☎ 814 1111; www.dublinairport.com) is located 13km north of the city centre. Along with the usual selection of pubs, restaurants, shops, ATMs and car-hire desks, there is a variety of airport facilities in the one passenger terminal:

Aer Rianta Information Desk (Irish Airport Authority; ☾ 24hr Jun-Sep, 6am-1am Oct-May)

Bank of Ireland (⊙ 10am-4pm Mon, Tue, Thu & Fri, 10am-5pm Wed, bureau de change 5.30am-9pm Mon-Fri, 5.30am-midnight Sat, 5.30am-10pm Sun)

Dublin Airport Pharmacy (☎ 814 4649; ⊙ 6.30am-6.30pm Mon-Thu, 9am-10.30pm Fri-Sun)

Dublin Tourism Office (⊙ 8am-10pm)

Greencaps Left Luggage & Porterage Office (☎ 814 4633; left luggage per 24hr €5-11; ⊙ 6am-11pm)

International Currency Exchange (⊙ 5.30am-midnight)

Nursery (⊙ 9am-10pm)

Post Office (⊙ 9am-5pm Mon-Fri, 9am-12.30pm Sat)

BICYCLE

Despite the intermittent presence of rust-red cycle lanes throughout the city centre, getting around by bike can be something of an obstacle course as cyclists have to share roads with buses and indifferent motorists. Bike theft is a major problem, so be sure to park on busier streets, preferably at one of the myriad U-shaped parking bars, and lock it securely. Never leave your bike on the street overnight or it may just be gone in the morning. The following cycle-orientated shops may come in handy for pedal pushers.

Cyclelogical (Map p102; ☎ 872 4635; www.cyclelogical-bikes.com; 3 Bachelor's Walk) A shop for serious enthusiasts. It has all the best equipment and is a good source of information on upcoming cycling events. It does not, however, do repairs.

DUBLIN BY BIKE

Since their introduction in September 2009, the blue bikes of Dublinbikes (www.dublinbikes.ie) have become a ubiquitous presence around the city centre, making this scheme one of the most successful transport initiatives of recent years. The pay-as-you-go service is exactly like the Parisian Vélib system: cyclists purchase a €10 Smart Card (as well as put a credit-card deposit of €150) – either online or at any of the 40 stations throughout the city centre – before 'freeing' a bike for use, which is then free of charge for the first 30 minutes and €0.50 for each half-hour thereafter.

MacDonald Cycles (Map p68; ☎ 475 2586; www.macdonaldcycles.ie; 38 Wexford St) Does repairs, and will have your bike back to you within a day or so (barring serious damage).

Bikes are only allowed on suburban trains (not the DART), either stowed in the guard's van or in a special compartment at the opposite end of the train from the engine. There's a flat €4 charge for transporting a bicycle up to 56km.

Hire

Bike rental has become increasingly difficult to find because of crippling insurance costs. Typical rental for a mountain bike is between €12 and €30 a day, or up to €150 per week. Raleigh Rent-a-Bike agencies can be found through Eurotrek (☎ 456 8847; www.raleigh.ie).

GETTING INTO TOWN

There is no train service to and from the airport. It takes about 45 minutes to get there by bus or taxi. For details of car hire, see p244. Transport options are as follows:

Bus

Aircoach (☎ 844 7118; www.aircoach.ie; one way/return €7/12) Private coach service with two routes from the airport to 18 destinations throughout the city, including the main streets of the city centre. Coaches run every 10 to 15 minutes between 6am and midnight, then hourly from midnight until 6am.

Airlink Express Coach (☎ 872 0000, 873 4222; www.dublinbus.ie; adult/child €6/3) Bus 747 runs every 10 to 20 minutes from 5.45am to 11.30pm between the airport, central bus station (Busáras) and Dublin Bus office on Upper O'Connell St; bus 748 runs every 15 to 30 minutes from 6.50am to 10.05pm between the airport, and Heuston and Connolly Stations.

Dublin Bus (Map p102; ☎ 872 0000; www.dublinbus.ie; 59 Upper O'Connell St; adult/child €2.20/1) A number of buses serve the airport from various points in Dublin, including buses 16A (Rathfarnham), 746 (Dun Laoghaire) and 230 (Portmarnock); all cross the city centre on their way to the airport.

Taxi

There is a taxi rank directly outside the arrivals concourse. A taxi should cost about €25 from the airport to the city centre, including a supplementary charge of €2.50 (not applied when going to the airport). Make sure the meter is switched on.

THINGS CHANGE...

The information in this chapter is particularly vulnerable to change. Check directly with the airline or a travel agent to make sure you understand how a fare (and ticket you may buy) works and be aware of the security requirements for international travel. Shop carefully. The details given in this chapter should be regarded as pointers and are not a substitute for your own careful, up-to-date research.

Cycleways (Map p102; ☎ 873 4748; www.cycleways. com; 185-186 Parnell St) Dublin's best bike shop, with expert staff who pepper their patter with all the technical lingo. Top-notch rentals.

MacDonald Cycles (Map p68; ☎ 475 2586; www. macdonaldcycles.ie; 38 Wexford St) Friendly and helpful, perfect for the amateur enthusiast.

BOAT

Dublin has two ferry ports. The Dun Laoghaire ferry terminal (Map p225; ☎ 280 1905; Dun Laoghaire), 13km southeast of the city, serves Holyhead in Wales; and the Dublin Port terminal (off Map p115; ☎ 855 2222; Alexandra Rd), 3km northeast of the city centre, serves Holyhead in Wales and Liverpool in England.

From Holyhead to Dublin and Dun Laoghaire, the ferry crossing takes just over three hours and costs around €25 for foot passengers or €95 for a medium-size car with two passengers. The fast-boat service from Holyhead to Dun Laoghaire takes a little over 1½ hours and costs €25 or €130 for the same.

Between Liverpool and Dublin the ferry service takes 8½ hours and costs €25 (foot passenger) or €180 (car with two passengers). Cabins on overnight sailings cost more. The fast-boat service takes four hours and costs up to €40 or €240 respectively.

There are several ferry companies that run services to and from Dublin:

Irish Ferries (Map p80; ☎ 1890 313 131; www.irish ferries.com; 2-4 Merrion Row, Dublin 2) Ferry and fast-boat services from Holyhead to Dublin.

Isle of Man Steam Packet Company/Sea Cat (☎ 836 4019; www.steam-packet.com; Maritime House, North Wall, Dublin 1) Offers ferry and fast-boat services travelling from Liverpool to Dublin via Douglas on the Isle of Man.

Norfolk Line (☎ 819 2999; www.norfolkline.com; Alexandra Rd Extension, Dublin Port) Ferry services from Liverpool to Dublin.

P&O Irish Sea (☎ 407 3434; www.poirishsea.com; Terminal 3, Dublin Port) Ferry services from Liverpool to Dublin.

Stena Line (☎ 204 7777; www.stenaline.com; Ferry Terminal, Dun Laoghaire) Ferry and fast-boat services from Holyhead to Dun Laoghaire.

To & From the Ferry Terminals

Buses from Busáras are timed to coincide with arrivals and departures from the Dublin Port terminal. For the 9.45am ferry departure from Dublin, buses leave Busáras at 8.30am; for the 9.45pm departure, buses depart from Busáras at 8.30pm. For the 1am sailing to Liverpool, the bus departs from Busáras at 11.45pm. All buses cost adult/child €2.50/1.25.

To travel between Dun Laoghaire ferry terminal and Dublin, take the DART to Pearse Station (for south Dublin) or Connolly Station (for north Dublin). Or take bus 46A to St Stephen's Green, or bus 7, 7A or 8 to Burgh Quay.

BUS
To & From the UK

Busáras (Map p102; ☎ 836 6111; www.buseireann.ie; Store St) is just north of the river behind Custom

ALTERNATE ARRIVAL PLANS

Although the vast majority of visitors will enter and exit Dublin's fair city via the airport, you can do your bit for the environment and arrive by boat – and have a bit of an adventure along the way. From Britain it's a cinch: you can buy a combined train-and-ferry ticket for a fraction of what you'll pay in airfare (yes, even in these budget airline times; see www.irishrail.ie for travel from Ireland or www.thetrainline.co.uk for travel from the UK) or, if you're really on a budget, get a bus-and-ferry ticket – from London it won't cost you more than the price of a meal. See p243 for details.

You can also arrive at another Irish port. Rosslare in County Wexford has ferry services from France and southwestern Britain while Larne, a short hop outside Belfast, is served from Stranraer in Scotland. Not only will you get to Dublin easily enough, but you can do some exploring on the way.

House; it has a left-luggage facility costing €2.50 per item per day.

It's possible to combine bus and ferry tickets from major UK centres to Dublin on the bus network. The journey between London and Dublin takes about 12 hours and costs around €34 return. For details in London, contact Eurolines (☎ 0870 514 3219; www.eurolines.com).

Around Dublin

The Dublin Bus Office (Map p102; ☎ 872 0000; www.dublinbus.ie; 59 Upper O'Connell St; ☾ 9am-5.30pm Mon-Fri, 9am-2pm Sat) has free single-route timetables for all its services.

Buses run from around 6am (some start at 5.30am) to about 11.30pm. Fares are calculated according to stages:

1-3 stages €1.15

4-7 stages €1.60

8-13 stages €1.80

14-23 stages €2.20

More than 23 stages €2.20 (inside Citizone; outer suburban journeys cost €3.50 or €4.50)

If you're travelling within the designated bus corridor zone (roughly between Parnell Square to the north and St Stephen's Green to the south) you can avail of the €0.50 special City Centre fare. You must tender exact change when boarding; anything more and you will be given a receipt for reimbursement, only possible at the Dublin Bus main office. To avoid this, the smartcard tickets are your best bet (as well as offering some good savings on fares), which you can purchase at most Spar or Centra shops.

The smartcard tickets on offer include:

Adult (Bus & Rail) Short Hop (€10.20) Valid for unlimited one-day travel on Dublin Bus, DART and suburban rail travel, but not Nitelink or Airlink.

Bus/Luas Pass (1/7 days €7/29) One day unlimited travel on both bus and Luas.

Family Bus & Rail Short Hop (€15.60) Valid for travel for one day for a family of two adults and two children aged under 16 on all bus and rail services except for Nitelink, Airlink, ferry services and tours.

Rambler Pass (1/3/5 days €6/13.30/20) Valid for unlimited travel on all Dublin Bus and Airlink services, except Nitelink.

Smartcard 10 Travel 90 (adult/child €18/6.50) Valid for 10 90-minute journeys on all Dublin Bus and Airlink services, except Nitelink.

NITELINK
Nitelink late-night buses run from the College, Westmoreland and D'Olier Sts triangle (Map p87). On Fridays and Saturdays, departures are at 12.30am, then every 20 minutes until 4.30am on the more popular routes, and until 3.30am on the less frequented ones; there are no services Sunday to Thursday. Fares are €5. See www.dublinbus.ie for route details.

CAR & MOTORCYCLE
Driving
The Automobile Association of Ireland (AA; Map p70; ☎ 617 9999, breakdown 1800 667 788; www.aaireland.ie; 56 Drury St) is located in the city centre.

Traffic in Dublin is a nightmare and parking is an expensive headache. There are no free spots to park anywhere in the city centre during business hours (7am to 7pm Monday to Saturday), but there are plenty of parking meters, 'pay & display' spots (€2.70 to €5.20 per hour) and over a dozen sheltered and supervised car parks (around €5 per hour).

Clamping of illegally parked cars is thoroughly enforced, and there is an €85 charge for removal. Parking is free after 7pm Monday to Saturday, and all day Sunday, in all metered spots and on single yellow lines.

Car theft and break-ins are a problem, and the police advise visitors to park in a supervised car park. Cars with foreign number plates are prime targets; never leave your valuables behind. When you're booking accommodation, check on parking facilities.

ROAD SAFETY RULES IN DUBLIN
- Drive on the left, overtake to the right.
- Safety belts must be worn by the driver and all passengers.
- Children aged under 12 aren't allowed to sit on the front seats.
- Motorcyclists and their passengers must wear helmets.
- When entering a roundabout, give way to the right.
- Speed limits are 50km/h or as signposted in the city, 100km/h on all roads outside city limits and 120km/h on motorways (marked in blue).
- The legal alcohol limit is 80mg of alcohol per 100mL of blood, or 35mg on the breath (roughly two units of alcohol for a man and one for a woman).

Hire

Car rental in Dublin is expensive, so you're often better off making arrangements in your home country with some sort of package deal. In July and August it's wise to book well ahead. Most cars are manual; automatic cars are available but they're more expensive to hire. Motorbikes and mopeds are not available for rent. People aged under 21 are not allowed to hire a car; for the majority of rental companies you have to be at least 23 and have had a valid driving licence for a minimum of one year. Many rental agencies will not rent to people over 70 or 75.

Nova Car Hire (www.rentacar-ireland.com) acts as an agent for Alamo, Budget, European and National, and offers greatly discounted rates. Typical weekly high-season rental rates are around €150 for a small car, €185 for a medium car and €320 for a five-seater people carrier.

The main rental agencies, which also have offices at the airport (6am-11pm), include the following:

Avis (Map p91; ☎ 605 7500; www.avis.ie; 35-29 Old Kilmainham Rd)

Budget (Map p64; ☎ 837 9611, airport 844 5150; www.budget.ie; 151 Lower Drumcondra Rd)

Europcar (Map p119; ☎ 648 5900, airport 844 4179; www.europcar.com; 29 Parkgate St)

Hertz (Map p91; ☎ 709 3060, airport 844 5466; www.hertz.com; 151 South Circular Rd)

Thrifty (Map p115; ☎ 844 1944, airport 840 0800; www.thrifty.ie; 26 Lombard St East)

TAXI

All taxi fares begin with a flag-fall fare of €4.45, followed by €1.03 per kilometre thereafter from 8am to 10pm (€1.45 10pm to 8am). In addition there are a number of extra charges – €1 for each extra passenger and €2 for telephone bookings. There is no charge for luggage.

Taxis can be hailed on the street and found at taxi ranks around the city, including on the corner of Abbey and O'Connell Sts (Map p102), College Green in front of Trinity College (Map p70) and St Stephen's Green at the end of Grafton St (Map p70). Numerous taxi companies dispatch taxis by radio. Some options:

City Cabs (☎ 872 2688)

National Radio Cabs (☎ 677 2222)

Phone the Garda Carriage Office (☎ 475 5888) if you have any complaints about taxis or queries regarding lost property.

TRAIN
DART

The Dublin Area Rapid Transport (DART; ☎ 1850 366 222; www.irishrail.ie) provides quick train access to the coast as far north as Howth (about 30 minutes) and as far south as Greystones in County Wicklow. Pearse Station (Map p80) is convenient for central Dublin south of the Liffey, and Connolly Station (Map p115) for north of the Liffey. There are services every 10 to 20 minutes, sometimes even more frequently, from around 6.30am to midnight Monday to Saturday. Services are less frequent on Sunday. Dublin to Dun Laoghaire takes about 15 to 20 minutes. A one-way DART ticket from Dublin to Dun Laoghaire or Howth costs €2.30; to Bray it's €2.75.

There are also suburban rail services north as far as Dundalk, inland to Mullingar and south past Bray to Arklow.

CLIMATE CHANGE & TRAVEL

Every form of transport that relies on carbon-based fuel generates CO_2, the main cause of human-induced climate change. Modern travel is dependent on aeroplanes and while they might use less fuel per kilometre per person than most cars, they travel much greater distances. It's not just CO_2 emissions from aircraft that are the problem. The altitude at which aircraft emit gases (including CO_2) and particles contributes significantly to their total climate change impact. The Intergovernmental Panel on Climate Change believes aviation is responsible for 4.9% of climate change – double the effect of its CO_2 emissions alone.

Lonely Planet regards travel as a global benefit. We encourage the use of more climate-friendly travel modes where possible and, together with other concerned partners across many industries, we support the carbon offset scheme run by ClimateCare. Websites such as climatecare.org use 'carbon calculators' that allow people to offset the greenhouse gases they are responsible for with contributions to portfolios of climate-friendly initiatives throughout the developing world. Lonely Planet offsets the carbon footprint of all staff and author travel.

DART passes include the following:

Adult (Bus & Rail) Short Hop (€10.20) Valid for unlimited one-day travel on Dublin Bus, DART and suburban rail travel, but not Nitelink or Airlink.

Family Bus & Rail Short Hop (€15.60) Valid for travel for one day for a family of two adults and two children aged under 16 on all bus and rail services except for Nitelink, Airlink, ferry services and tours.

Irish Rail

All rail information, including timetables and ticket and pass sales, is available from the Rail Travel Centre (Iarnród Éireann; Map p102; ☎ 836 6222; www.irishrail.ie; 34 Lower Abbey St). The city has two main train stations: Heuston Station (Map p91), on the western side of town near the Liffey; and Connolly Station (Map p115), a short walk northeast of Busáras, behind Custom House. Heuston Station has left-luggage lockers of three sizes, costing €2 to €6 for 24 hours. At Connolly Station the facility costs €3.

TRAM
Luas

The Luas (www.luas.ie) light-rail system has two lines: the green line (running every five to 15 minutes) connects St Stephen's Green with Sandyford in south Dublin via Ranelagh and Dundrum; and the red line (every 20 minutes) runs from Lower Abbey St to Tallaght via the north quays and Heuston Station. There are ticket machines at every stop or you can buy a ticket from newsagents in the city centre; a typical short-hop fare (around four stops) is €1.90. Services run from 5.30am to 12.30am Monday to Friday, from 6.30am to 12.30am Saturday and from 7am to 11.30pm Sunday.

BUSINESS HOURS

The standard business hours in relatively late-rising Dublin are as follows:

Banks 10am to 4pm Monday to Friday (to 5pm Thursday).

Offices 9am to 5pm Monday to Friday.

Post offices 9am to 6pm Monday to Friday, 9am to 1pm Saturday.

Pubs 10.30am to 11.30pm Monday to Thursday, 10.30am to 12.30am Friday and Saturday, noon to 11pm Sunday (30 minutes 'drinking up' time allowed). Pubs with bar extensions open to 2.30am Thursday to Saturday, pubs with theatre licences open to 3.30am; closed Christmas Day and Good Friday.

Restaurants Noon to 10.30pm; many close one day of the week.

Shops 9.30am to 6pm Monday to Saturday (until 8pm on Thursday and sometimes Friday, to 9pm for the bigger shopping centres and supermarkets), noon to 6pm Sunday.

CHILDREN

Dublin is a very child-friendly city. Hotels will provide cots at no extra charge and most restaurants have highchairs. Overall, restaurants and hotels go to great lengths to cater for children, although some restaurants lose their interest in kids after 6pm. Children are not allowed in pubs after 7pm. Children under five years of age travel free on all public transport.

Family tickets are available to most attractions; many tourist sites have made exhibitions more child-friendly, creating interactive spaces for kids to play (and learn) in.

Although breastfeeding in Dublin is not a common sight (Ireland has one of the lowest rates of it in the world), you can do so with impunity pretty much everywhere without getting so much as a stare. There are virtually no nappy-changing facilities in Dublin, so you'll have to make do with a public toilet. For more information and inspiration on how to make travelling with children as hassle-free as possible, check out Lonely Planet's *Travel with Children*. Two great websites are www.eumom.com for pregnant women and parents with young children, and www.babygoes2.com, which is an excellent travel site about family-friendly accommodation worldwide.

Babysitting

Many hotels can provide babysitting on request (normally €8 to €13 per hour). There are agencies that provide professional nannies. It's up to you to negotiate a fee with the nanny but €15 per hour is the average, plus taxi fare if they aren't driving. You'll need to sign a form beforehand that the agency will fax to your hotel. Agencies include the following:

Belgrave Agency (☎ 280 9341; www.nanny.ie; 55 Mulgrave St, Dun Laoghaire; per hr €10-12 plus 21% VAT)

Executive Nannies (Map p102; ☎ 873 1273; www.executivenannies.com; 43 Lower Dominick St; per hr €18-21)

CLIMATE

Dublin enjoys a milder climate than its northerly position might indicate, largely thanks to the influence of the North Atlantic Drift, or Gulf Stream. The warmest months of the year are July and August, when temperatures range from 15°C to 20°C, while the coldest months – January and February – see the thermometer drop to between 4°C and 8°C. It never gets too cold (major snowfalls are a rarity) but it never gets too hot either; even in summer you're better off carrying a sweater or a light jacket.

Dublin is one of the drier parts of Ireland, but in a typical year it still rains on 150 days. Summers are a meteorological lottery: it's impossible to predict whether it'll be a wet one or not, making forecasting a favourite subject of amateurs throughout the city ('Well, it rained all of April, so that means we'll have a good June'). Bring an umbrella. What is a certainty is the long summer day; in July and August there are about 18 hours of daylight and it's only truly dark after about 11pm. For weather forecasts, dial ☎ 1550 123 822.

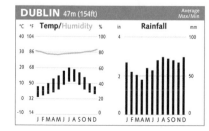

COURSES

Dublin is well known for its English-language schools. For a list of these and other courses, get a copy of the yearly *Dublin's Evening Classes* (Oisín Publications; €4.99), available at most bookshops (also check out www.eveningclasses.ie). Most courses run for extended periods, ranging from four or six weeks to a year and more.

CUSTOMS REGULATIONS

Duty-free sales are not available when travelling within the European Union (EU). Goods for personal consumption bought in, and exported within, the EU incur no additional taxes if duty has been paid somewhere in the EU. Over certain limits you may have to show they are for personal use. The amounts that officially constitute personal use are 800 cigarettes, 400 cigarillos, 200 cigars or 1kg of tobacco; 10L of spirits, 20L of fortified wine, 60L of sparkling wine, 90L of still wine or 110L of beer.

Travellers coming from outside the EU are allowed to import, duty-free, 200 cigarettes, 1L of spirits or 2L of wine, 60mL of perfume and 250mL of toilet water.

It is illegal to bring into Ireland meat, meat products, plants and plant products (including seeds). Dogs and cats from anywhere outside Ireland and the UK are subject to strict quarantine laws. The EU Pet Travel Scheme, whereby animals from certain countries *might* be allowed into the country (as long as they're fitted with a microchip, vaccinated against rabies and blood-tested six months prior to entry), came into force in the Republic of Ireland in mid-2004. Otherwise animals arriving into Ireland are quarantined for six months unless they first pass through the UK and meet British criteria for entry. Do not just try and travel with your animals. Contact the Department of Agriculture, Food & Rural Development (☎ 607 2877; www.agriculture.gov.ie) for further details.

When leaving the country, non-EU visitors can take the equivalent of US$4000 worth of goods per person (see p136).

DISCOUNT CARDS

Senior citizens get discounts on public transport and museum fees (with proof of age), and students and under-26s are entitled to a variety of discounts, from admission fees to cinema tickets, so long as they have the appropriate card (International Student Identity Card, International Youth Travel Card or European Youth Card/Euro<26). Here are a couple of local discount cards worth checking out:

Dublin Pass (www.dublinpass.ie; adult/child per day €35/19, 2 days €55/31, 3 days €65/39, 6 days €95/49) Not only do you get free entry into 30 attractions, but you can skip whatever queue there is by presenting your card. The card is available from any of the Dublin Tourism offices (see p256).

Heritage Card (☎ 647 2461; www.heritageireland.ie; adult/child & student €21/8) This card entitles you to free access to all OPW-managed sights in and around Dublin. You can buy it at OPW sites or Dublin Tourism offices.

ELECTRICITY

The standard electricity supply in Dublin is 220 volts AC, and all sockets fit a three-pin plug. Pin converters are available in all electrical suppliers.

EMBASSIES

Countries with diplomatic offices in Dublin include the following:

Australia (Map p80; ☎ 664 5300; www.ireland.embassy.gov.au; 7th fl, Fitzwilton House, Wilton Tce, Dublin 2)

Canada (Map p80; ☎ 234 4000; 7-8 Wilton Tce, Dublin 2)

France (Off Map p122; ☎ 277 5000; www.ambafrance.ie; 36 Ailesbury Rd, Dublin 4)

Germany (Off Map p122; ☎ 269 3011; www.dublin.diplo.de; 31 Trimleston Ave, Booterstown, Blackrock, County Dublin)

Italy (Map p122; ☎ 660 1744; www.ambdublin.esteri.it; 63-65 Northumberland Rd, Ballsbridge, Dublin 4)

Netherlands (Off Map p122; ☎ 269 3444; www.netherlandsembassy.ie; 160 Merrion Rd, Ballsbridge, Dublin 4)

UK (Map p122; ☎ 205 3700; www.britishembassy.ie; 29 Merrion Rd, Ballsbridge, Dublin 4)

USA (Map p122; ☎ 668 8777; www.usembassy.ie; 42 Elgin Rd, Ballsbridge, Dublin 4)

EMERGENCY

For emergency assistance, phone ☎ 999 or ☎ 112. This call is free and the operator will connect you with the type of assistance you specify: fire, police (*gardaí*), ambulance, boat or coastal rescue. There are *garda* stations at Fitzgibbon St (Map p102; ☎ 836 3113), Harcourt Tce (Map p80; ☎ 676 3481), Pearse St (Map p115; ☎ 677 8141) and Store St (Map p102; ☎ 874 2761).

A full list of all emergency numbers can be found in the front pages of the telephone book.

Alcoholics Anonymous (Map p91; ☎ 453 8998, after hr ☎ 679 5967; 109 South Circular Rd, Dublin 8)

Confidential Line Freefone (☎ 1800 666 111) *Garda* confidential line to report crime.

Drugs Advisory & Treatment Centre (Map p115; ☎ 677 1122; Trinity Ct, 30-31 Pearse St, Dublin 2)

Rape Crisis Centre (Map p80; ☎ 1800 778 888, 661 4911; 70 Lower Leeson St)

Samaritans (Map p102; ☎ 1850 609 090, 872 7700; 112 Marlborough St) For people who are lonely, depressed or suicidal.

Senior Helpline (☎ 1850 440 444) For senior citizens with any kind of problem.

Women's Emergency Hostel (Map p102; ☎ 873 2279; Haven House, Morning Star Ave, Dublin 7)

GAY & LESBIAN TRAVELLERS

Dublin's not a bad place to be gay. Most people wouldn't bat an eyelid at public displays of affection between same-sex couples, or cross-dressing in the city centre, but discretion is advised in the suburbs. If you do encounter any sort of trouble or harassment call the Gay & Lesbian Garda Liaison Officer (☎ 666 9000) or the Sexual Assault Unit (☎ 666 000) at the Pearse St Garda station (Map p115).

There are several useful organisations, publications and online resources:

BeLonG To (Map p87; ☎ 01-670 6223; www.belongto. org; 13 Parliament St) Advice and support for young members of the LGBT community.

Gaire (www.gaire.com) Online message board and resource centre.

Gay Community News (www.gcn.ie) A free news and issues-based monthly paper.

Gay Men's Health Project (☎ 660 2189) Practical advice on men's health issues.

Gay Switchboard Dublin (☎ 872 1055; www.gay switchboard.ie; ☼ 7.30am-9.30pm Mon-Fri, 3.30-6pm Sat) A friendly and useful voluntary service that provides information such as legal issues and where to find accommodation.

Ireland's Pink Pages (http://pinkpagesireland.com) A free directory of gay-centric and gay-friendly services.

Lesbian Line (☎ 872 9911; ☼ 7-9pm Thu)

National Lesbian & Gay Federation (Map p87; NLGF; ☎ 671 9076; 2 Scarlet Row, Temple Bar, Dublin) Publishers of *Gay Community News*.

Outhouse (Map p102; ☎ 873 4932; www.outhouse.ie; 105 Capel St) Gay, lesbian and bisexual resource centre. Great stop-off point to see what's on, check noticeboards and meet people. It also publishes *Ireland's Pink Pages*.

Panti's Blog (www.pantibar.com) Excellent, up-to-date blog by one of Dublin's most active members of the gay community.

Queerid (www.queerid.com) Listings, events and social networking site for the gay community.

HOLIDAYS

The only public holidays that will impact on you are Good Friday and Christmas Day, the only two days in the year when all pubs close. Otherwise, the half-dozen or so bank holidays (all of which fall on a Monday) mean just that – the banks are closed, along with about half the shops.

Public Holidays

The following are national holidays:

New Year's Day 1 January

St Patrick's Day 17 March

Easter (Good Friday to Easter Monday inclusive) March/April

May Holiday 1 May

June Holiday First Monday in June

August Holiday First Monday in August

October Holiday Last Monday in October

Christmas Day 25 December

St Stephen's Day 26 December

St Patrick's Day, May Day and St Stephen's Day holidays are taken on the following Monday should they fall on a weekend.

INTERNET ACCESS

Nearly all but the smallest, shabbiest hotels offer some kind of internet access, whether

WI-FI HOT SPOTS

Many public places offer access to wi-fi networks so that customers can use the internet on the move. Try the following hotspots for free access: Chester Beatty Library (p72), Solas (p175), Market Bar (p173), Ron Black's (p174) and the Globe (p174).

through ethernet cables, terminals or, increasingly, wi-fi – although most lodgings will charge you for the privilege. If you've packed your laptop, note that Ireland uses a square-pinned, three-pronged power plug and most hotel fittings take RJ-11 phone jacks.

Major internet service providers (ISPs) such as AOL (www.aol.com), CompuServe (www.compuserve.com) and AT&T Business Internet Services (www.attbusiness.net) have dial-in nodes in Ireland. If you access your email account through a home-based ISP, your best option is to open an account with a local, global ISP provider: the most reliable ones are Eircom (☎ 702 0022; www.eircom.ie) or O2 (☎ 1800 924 924; www.o2.ie).

For hassle-free internet access, your best bet is to rely on internet cafes, which are everywhere in Dublin. Connections are usually quick, and should be no more than €5 per hour. The following city-centre internet cafes offer quick, reliable connections:

Central Internet Café (Map p70; ☎ 677 8298; 6 Grafton St; ⏰ 9am-10pm Mon-Sat, 10am-8pm Sun)

Global Internet Café (Map p102; ☎ 878 0295; 8 Lower O'Connell St; ⏰ 8am-11pm)

Internet Exchange (Map p87; ☎ 670 3000; 1 Cecilia St; ⏰ 24hr)

Alternatively, the two main mobile phone companies offer pay-as-you-go mobile broadband service via a portable USB key modem (aka dongle), with speeds of up to 7MB. Buy a dongle from Vodafone (www.vodafone.ie; modem €39.99) or O2 (www.o2.ie; modem €59-99) at any of their outlets, register online and off you go; all you have to do is top up online whenever you need. You'll pay about €3 to €4 per day or you can buy a monthly pack for around €20.

LEGAL MATTERS

If you need legal assistance contact the Legal Aid Board (☎ 1890 615 200). It has eight offices spread throughout Dublin; the central operator will direct you to the one most convenient to you.

The possession of small quantities of hash or marijuana (deemed Class C drugs) attracts a fine or warning, but harder drugs are treated more seriously. Cocaine, ecstasy and heroin are considered Class A drugs; if you're caught in possession you can count on being arrested and prosecuted. The consumption of alcohol on the street and public drunkenness are both illegal, but the police are usually pretty lenient and at worst will issue a verbal warning and confiscate your booze.

FOR THE RECORD
- The legal age to vote is 18.
- You can leave school when you're 16.
- The legal drinking age is 18.
- Smoking is legal at 16.
- The heterosexual and homosexual age of consent is 17.
- You can get married at 16, with consent of court.
- You can ride a moped when you're 16.
- You can drive a car when you're 17.

MAPS

The free maps of Dublin are usually quite adequate, at least for the major sites in the city centre. The Dublin Tourism Centre has a basic map of the city centre (€1), which covers the major sights, but it also has fairly detailed maps for hotels and restaurants.

If you prefer an indexed street directory, the *Dublin Street Guide* (€9.99; scale 1:15,000, city centre 1:10,000), published by Ordnance Survey Ireland (OSI; see the boxed text, p120, for their retail outlet details), is the best. A handy pocket-size version of the same (€4.99; 1:10,000) is also available, but it does not include the outlying suburbs.

The OSI also publishes a *Map of Greater Dublin* (€7.99; scale 1:20,000), which includes a street index and details of bus routes. The *Collins Streetfinder Map* (€9.99; scale 1:15,000) is also pretty good, with easy-to-use laminates that won't get damaged in the (inevitable) rain.

You can buy a limited selection of maps in most bookshops and some newsagents, but the National Map Centre (Map p68; ☎ 476 0471; www.mapcentre.ie; 34 Grafton Hall, Aungier St; ⏰ 10am-6pm Mon-Sat) has a comprehensive selection of all OSI maps and other geographic sundries.

MEDICAL SERVICES
Dentists

Dental care is a costly business in Dublin. Unless you have a medical card (only available to registered residents), you can expect to pay from €60 for a basic check, about €75 for a cleaning and €90 for a filling. There are several reliable city-centre dentists:

Anne's Lane Dental Centre (Map p70; ☎ 671 8581; 2 Anne's Lane; ⏰ 9am-6pm Mon-Fri, by appointment Sat)

Dame House Dental Surgery (Map p70; ☎ 670 9256; 24-26 Dame St; ⏰ 9am-6pm)

Gallagher & Associates (Map p80; ☎ 670 3735; 38 Fenian St; ⊙ 9am-8pm Mon, 8am-8pm Tue & Wed, 9am-5pm Thu & Fri, 9am-4pm every 2nd Sat)

Doctors

If you don't have a medical card you'll have to pay for all visits to a doctor. Charges begin at €45 for even a cursory examination. You can request a doctor to call out to your accommodation at any time on the 24-hour private Doctors on Call (☎ 453 9333) service line.

The Health Service Executive (HSE; Map p91; ☎ 679 0700, 1800 520 520; www.hse.ie; Dr Steevens' Hospital, Steevens' Lane, Dublin 8) has a Choice of Doctor Scheme, which can advise you on a suitable general practitioner (GP) from 9am to 5pm Monday to Friday. The HSE also provides information services for those with physical and mental disabilities.

Your hotel or embassy can also suggest a doctor, but there are two good walk-in doctors' clinics in town:

Grafton Medical Practice (Map p70; ☎ 671 2122; www.graftonmedical.ie; 34 Grafton St; ⊙ 9am-6pm Mon-Fri)

Mercer Medical Centre (Map p70; ☎ 402 2300; Johnston Pl, Lower Stephen St; ⊙ 9am-6pm Mon-Thu, 9am-5pm Fri)

Hospitals

EU citizens are encouraged to obtain a European Health Insurance Card (EHIC) before they leave home, which will cover hospital costs should they require hospitalisation. This card, which provides cover for a year, is easily obtained from a local health authority or, in the UK, the post office. The main city-centre hospitals are the following:

Baggot St Hospital (Map p122; ☎ 668 1577; 18 Upper Baggot St)

Mater Misericordiae Hospital (Map p102; ☎ 830 1122; Eccles St) Off Lower Dorset St.

St James's Hospital (Map p91; ☎ 453 7941; www.stjames.ie; James St)

Pharmacies

All pharmacies in Dublin are clearly designated by a green cross. There are branches of the English chain pharmacy, Boots, spread throughout the city centre. Most pharmacies stay open until 7pm or 8pm, but the following city-centre chemists stay open until 10pm:

City Pharmacy (Map p68; ☎ 670 4523; 14 Dame St)

O'Connell's Late Night Pharmacy Grafton St (Map p70; ☎ 679 0467; 21 Grafton St); O'Connell St (Map p102; ☎ 873 0427; 55-56 O'Connell St)

MONEY

Ireland's currency is the euro (€), which is divided into 100 cents. While the notes are all the same throughout the 12 countries of the euro zone, the Irish coins feature a harp on the reverse side – but all non-Irish euro coins are also legal tender. For information on Dublin's economy and costs, see p19.

See the inside front cover for a list of exchange rates at press time.

ATMs

Most banks have ATMs that are linked to international money systems such as Cirrus, Maestro or Plus. Each transaction incurs a currency conversion fee and credit cards can incur immediate and exorbitant cash-advance interest-rate charges. We strongly recommend that if you're staying in the city centre, you get your money out early on a Friday to avoid the long queues that can form after 8pm.

Changing Money

You'll get the best exchange rates at banks. Bureaux de change and other exchange facilities usually open for more hours but the rate and/or commission will be worse. Many post offices have a currency-exchange facility and are open on Saturday morning. There's a cluster of banks located around College Green opposite Trinity College and all have exchange facilities.

Allied Irish Bank (Map p70; ☎ 679 9222; Westmoreland St; ⊙ 10am-4pm Mon-Wed & Fri, 10am-5pm Thu)

Bank of Ireland (Map p70; ☎ 677 6801; 2 College Green; ⊙ 10am-4pm Mon-Wed & Fri, 10am-5pm Thu)

First Rate (Map p87; ☎ 671 3233; 1 Westmoreland St; ⊙ 8am-9pm Mon-Fri, 9am-9pm Sat, 10am-9pm Sun Jun-Sep, 9am-6pm Oct-May)

Thomas Cook (Map p70; ☎ 677 1721, 677 1307; 118 Grafton St; ⊙ 9am-5.30pm Mon, Tue, Fri & Sat, 10am-5.30pm Wed, 9am-7pm Thu)

Credit Cards

Visa and MasterCard are more widely accepted in Dublin than Amex or Diners Club, which are often not accepted in smaller establishments. You can also use credit cards to withdraw cash, but be sure to obtain a PIN from your bank before you leave. This service usually carries an extra charge, so if you're withdrawing money, take out enough so that you don't have to keep going back.

If a card is lost or stolen, inform the police and the issuing company as soon as possible; otherwise you may have to bear the cost of the thief's purchases. Here are some 24-hour hotlines for cancelling your cards:

Amex (☎ 1800 282 728)

Diners Club (☎ 0818 300 026)

MasterCard (☎ 1800 557 378)

Visa (☎ 1800 558 002)

Travellers Cheques

Most major brands of travellers cheques are accepted in Ireland. Amex and Thomas Cook travellers cheques are widely recognised and branches don't charge commission for cashing their own cheques. Travellers cheques are rarely accepted for everyday transactions so you'll need to cash them beforehand.

Eurocheques can be cashed in Dublin, but special arrangements must be made with your home bank before you travel if you are thinking of using personal cheques.

NEWSPAPERS & MAGAZINES
Newspapers

Dubliners are avid consumers of the printed word. There are newspapers and magazines to suit virtually every taste and interest. All the main English newspapers are readily available. News Corp, the Rupert Murdoch–owned media group that publishes the *Times* and the *Sun*, has an Irish office that's responsible for an Irish edition of their papers – basically a section of Irish news and sport inserted into the English version.

DAILY NEWSPAPERS

The following are Dublin's main daily local newspapers:

Evening Herald (www.herald.ie; €1.30) Available from just after lunchtime, this tabloid is a bit of a scurrilous rag specialising in shock-horror headlines about government wastage, heartless killers and immigrant scams. No one takes it all that seriously and it usually makes for good bus-journey reading on the way home. It is, however, the best newspaper for finding a flat, and its Thursday entertainment listings pages are pretty thorough.

Irish Examiner (www.examiner.ie; €1.80) A solid national newspaper with more of a non-Dublin slant than others, probably because it used to be the *Cork Examiner*. Good features and well-written stories make for a dependable read.

Irish Independent (www.independent.ie; €1.80) Ireland's most widely read broadsheet is great for breaking domestic stories, as its journos usually have one up on every other hack for stories of national importance. It has good features on all facets of Irish current affairs, but its foreign coverage is appalling: limited to the back page, the content is usually reliant on stories about Russian women who've given birth to eight children, the break-up of Hollywood marriages and other 'you'll never believe this' titbits.

Irish Times (www.irishtimes.com; €1.80) The country's oldest and most serious daily newspaper; the most liberal broadsheet published in Ireland. In recent years its reputation for excellent journalism has been somewhat tarnished by the fact that it picks up far too many of its stories from its liberal British counterparts (most notably the *Guardian*) and the news wires, with the result that it doesn't break as much news as it used to. Many non-Dubliners dismiss it as an Anglo-centric newspaper that devotes too much space to issues that aren't pertinent to the country; it is, however, still an excellent read.

Irish Daily Mail (www.dailymail.co.uk; €1) The Irish edition of the popular English newspaper prides itself on making waves by attacking anyone or anything not seen to be acting in the public interest as defined by the *Mail's* largely reactionary, right-wing view of the world – or any kind of misbehaving celebrity.

Star (www.thestar.ie; €1.20) Ireland's answer to the English *Sun,* this tabloid is pretty much what you'd expect: plenty of celebrity pictures and very little news. Most of the stories are blatant exaggerations and simplistic takes on what's really going on.

SUNDAY PAPERS

Most Dubliners buy English Sunday papers, as the Irish equivalents just can't match their size and content. Our list covers the Irish newspapers:

Irish Daily Star Sunday (€2) The usual tabloid nonsense, with plenty of juice and very little news. If you want a salacious tabloid, buy the *Sunday Mirror;* at least the sports pages are better.

Sunday Business Post (www.sbpost.ie; €2) If you want to know what makes the Irish economy tick, then this superb financial paper is for you; if not, buy something else.

Sunday Independent (www.independent.ie; €2.50) A Sunday edition of the daily broadsheet, with similar news content but plenty more lifestyle sections, restaurant reviews and social gossip.

Sunday Tribune (www.tribune.ie; €2.50) Although its content pales in comparison to its English rivals, this is the best Irish Sunday paper. It offers the best summary of the week's events, has good features and also breaks its fair share of pertinent stories.

Sunday World (€2) A fairly low-brow tabloid paper with the usual fare about celebrities and their misdoings, politicians and their backroom deals, and oodles of sport. The paper's crime correspondent, Paul Williams, is the country's foremost authority on the criminal underworld; his two books on the subject, *The General* and *Gangland*, are bestsellers.

Magazines

Generic international magazines aside, there are many local publications:

Dublin Event Guide (www.eventguide.ie; free) The best weekly listings magazine, it has film, theatre and music reviews, a feature or two and a comprehensive guide to what's on and where.

Hot Press (www.hotpress.com; €3.95) The first, and once the best, guide to the city's music scene, this fortnightly publication is a bit like the Rolling Stones: once a cutting-edge force that shaped musical minds, today it's stuck in the past and is reluctant to come to terms with modern times. Its reputation and prestige ensures that it is still the most widely read of the city's music mags.

Image (www.image.ie; €4.25) Ireland's version of the glossy woman's magazine. Aside from the usual focus on beauty tips and fashion hints, what we really love about this monthly mag is its vain attempt to turn the country's B-list celebs into international superstars. *Puh-lease.*

In Dublin (free) A monthly ad-rag disguised as a listings magazine, its over-reliance on ads means that the listings are hardly objective…but it is free.

Phoenix (€2.25) A fortnightly magazine that specialises in clever political satire. The problem for non-nationals is that many of the references are strictly insider, so you'll have to know your current affairs to get the jokes.

Village (www.villagemagazine.ie; €3.50) Edited by veteran journalist Vincent Browne, this is a weekly hard stare at the major issues of the day, both local and international. The quality of the writing is good and the editorial line is uncompromising in its efforts to uncover the truth behind the issues, no matter how uncomfortable it may be.

For information on gay- and lesbian-specific publications, see p248.

ORGANISED TOURS

Dublin isn't that big, so a straightforward sightseeing tour is only really necessary if you're looking to cram in the sights or avoid blistered feet. What is worth considering, however, is a specialised guided tour, especially for those of a musical, historical or literary bent.

Boat

Liffey River Cruises (Map p102; ☎ 473 4082; www.liffeyrivercruises.com; Bachelor's Walk; adult/student/child €14/10/8; ☽ 9am-5.30pm Mar-Oct) Cruise up and down the Liffey in a comfy air-conditioned, all-weather vessel that accommodates up to 48 passengers. Gen up on Dublin's history as seen from the river, from the Viking raids to the recent dockland development.

Sea Safaris (Map p61; ☎ 01-668 9802; Pigeon House, Poolbeg; per hr €25) If you fancy seeing a bit of Dublin from the sea, Sea Safaris runs speedboats from the edge of the South Wall into Dublin Bay as far south as Dalkey and back.

Viking Splash Tours (Map p91; ☎ 707 6000; www.vikingsplash.ie; adult/child/family from €20/10/60; ☽ 9am-5.30pm Mar-Oct, 10am-4pm Tue-Sun Nov, 10am-4pm Wed-Sun Feb) Go on, what's the big deal? You stick a plastic Viking's helmet on your head and yell 'yay' at the urging of your guide, but the upshot is you'll get a 1¼-hour semi-amphibious tour that ends up in the Grand Canal Dock. 'Strictly for tourists' seems so…superfluous.

Bus

Dublin Bus (Map p102; ☎ 872 0000; www.dublinsightseeing.ie; 59 Upper O'Connell St), the city's bus company, runs a variety of tours, all of which can be booked at its office, or at the Bus Éireann counter at Dublin Tourism (Map p70) in St Andrew's Church, Suffolk St.

The Dublin Tour (adult/child/student €15/6/13; ☽ tours every 15min 9am-5pm) is a 1½-hour hop-on-hop-off tour you can join at any of the 23 designated stops covering the city centre's major attractions; admission to the sights isn't included. The Ghost Bus Tour (adult €25; ☽ tours 8pm Mon-Thu, 8pm & 8.30pm Fri, 7pm & 9.30pm Sat & Sun) is a popular 2¼-hour tour of graveyards and 'haunted' places, while the North Coast & Castle (adult/child €25/12; ☽ tours 10am & 2pm) takes in the Botanic Gardens in Glasnevin, the Casino at Marino, Malahide Castle and Howth, all in about three hours. The South Coast & Gardens Tour (adult/child €25/12; ☽ tours 11am) takes around 4½ hours and runs along the stretch of coastline between Dun Laoghaire and Killiney before turning inland into Wicklow and on to Powerscourt Estate (admission included). Other options include the following:

City Sightseeing (Map p102; www.city-sightseeing.com; Dublin Tourism, 14 Upper O'Connell St; adult/child/family €15.50/7/38; ☽ every 8-15min 9am-6pm) A typical tour should last around 1½ hours and lead you up and down O'Connell St, past Trinity College and St Stephen's Green, before heading up to the Guinness Storehouse and back around the north quays, via the main entrance to Phoenix Park.

Dublin Rock'n'Roll Bus Tour (Map p87; ☎ 620 3929; www.dublinrocktour.ie; 3 Westmoreland St; tours €15; ⊙ noon, 2pm, 4pm & 6pm) Dublin's rich rock legacy is explored audio-visually from the comfort of a kitted-out tour bus. The bus stop is on Westmoreland St and the tour lasts about 90 minutes.

Grayline Dublin Tour (Map p102; (☎ 872 9010; www.irishcitytours.com; adult/child/student & senior/family €15.50/7/13/38; ⊙ every 15min 9.30am-5.30pm, to 6.30pm Jul & Aug) Another hop-on-hop-off tour of the city's greatest bits, with stops en route at Trinity College, the Guinness Storehouse, Dvblinia and Kilmainham Gaol. A straight-through tour without getting off takes about 1½ hours – but what's the point in that? You can also arrange tours from Dublin Tourism (Map p70), Suffolk St.

Wild Wicklow Tour (☎ 280 1899; www.discoverdublin.ie; Dublin Tourism Centre, St Andrew's Church, 2 Suffolk St; adult/child €28/25; ⊙ 9.10am) Award-winning and lots of fun, this 8½-hour top tour does a quick spin of the city's main attractions before heading southwards along the coast to County Wicklow, bringing its high-energy buzz to Glendalough and the Sally Gap. Book at Dublin Tourism (Map p70) in St Andrew's Church, Suffolk St.

Carriage

Is there anything more romantic than a horse-drawn carriage clippity-clopping around the city centre? Now add the groups of drunken stag weekenders shouting at passers-by as the carriage driver laughs resignedly at their terrible jokes…you get the picture. Half-hour tours cost up to €60, but different length trips can be negotiated: fix a price *before* the driver says giddy-up. Carriages take four or five people and are found primarily at the top of Grafton St, by St Stephen's Green.

Private Tours

Accredited guides can be contacted via the tourist board (☎ 602 4000). They cost an average of €100 per day for an English-speaking guide and €125 for other languages. A reputable firm that hires out guides is Meridien Tour Guides (Map p70; ☎ 677 6336; 26 South Frederick St).

Walking

1916 Rebellion Walking Tour (Map p70; ☎ 676 2493; www.1916rising.com; adult/child €12/free; ⊙ 11.30am Mon-Sat, 1pm Sun Mar-Oct) The Easter Rising was the seminal event in the struggle to establish a modern nation, and this absolutely superb 1½-hour tour – starting in

the International Bar, Wicklow St – tells it exactly as it was, with a decent sprinkling of humour and irreverence to boot. After all, what good are heroes if you can't poke some fun at them? The guides – all Trinity graduates – are uniformly excellent and will not say no to the offer of a pint back in the International at tour's end.

Dublin Footsteps Walking Tours (Map p70; ☎ 496 0641; Bewley's Bldg, Grafton St; adult €10; ⊙ 10.30am Mon, Wed, Fri & Sat Jun-Sep) Literature and Georgian architecture are woven together on this two-hour tour that departs from the Bewley's Building on Grafton St and finishes at the Powerscourt Townhouse (where you get a complimentary cup of decent Italian coffee). It covers the lives and works of the big guns: Joyce, Wilde, Shaw and Yeats, as well as a host of others.

Dublin Literary Pub Crawl (Map p70; ☎ 454 0228; www.dublinpubcrawl.com; adult/student €12/10; ⊙ tours 7.30pm daily year-round, noon Sun Apr-Nov, Thu-Sun Dec-Mar) A tour of pubs associated with famous Dublin writers is a sure-fire recipe for success, and this 2½-hour tour/performance by two actors – which includes them acting out the funny bits – is a riotous laugh. There's plenty of drink taken, which makes it all the more popular. It leaves from the Duke on Duke St; get there by 7pm to reserve a spot for the evening tour.

Dublin Musical Pub Crawl (Map p87; ☎ 478 0193; www.discoverdublin.com; Oliver St John Gogartys, 58-59 Fleet St; adult/student €12/10; ⊙ 7.30pm Apr-Oct, 7.30pm Thu-Sat Nov-Mar) The story of Irish traditional music and its influence on contemporary styles is explained and demonstrated by two expert musicians in a number of Temple Bar pubs over 2½ hours. Tours meet upstairs in the Oliver St John Gogarty pub and are highly recommended.

James Joyce Walking Tour (Map p102; ☎ 878 8547; 35 North Great George's St; adult/student €10/8; ⊙ tours 2pm Tue, Thu & Sat) Joyce lived, was schooled and lost his virginity on the north side – and he put it all down on paper with cartographical precision from his self-imposed continental exile. You can explore all of the north-side attractions associated with the bespectacled one on a 1¼-hour tour run by the James Joyce Cultural Centre (p108).

Pat Liddy Walking Tours (☎ 831 1109; www.walking
tours.ie; Dublin Tourism Centre, St Andrew's Church, 2
Suffolk St; adult €6-22, child €5-20) We highly recommend
these award-winning themed tours of the city by well-
known Dublin historian Pat Liddy, which include Viking &
Medieval Dublin (10.30am Tuesday, Thursday and Sunday,
2.30pm Saturday), the Historic Northside (10.30am
Wednesday and Friday) and Georgian and Victorian Splen-
dours (10.30am Monday, 2.30pm Friday). All tours depart
from Dublin Tourism (Map p70) on Suffolk St. He also has a
bunch of podcast walks available for download (see iWalks
boxed text, p253).

Sandeman's New Dublin Tour (Map p68; ☎ 878 8547;
www.newdublintours.com; City Hall; admission free;
🕙 11am) A high-energy and thoroughly enjoyable
three-hour walking tour of the city's greatest hits for free:
tip only if you enjoyed the tour. Spanish-language tours are
also available.

POST

The Irish postal service, An Post, is reliable, efficient and usually on time. Post boxes in Dublin are usually green and have two slots: one for
'Dublin only', the other for 'All Other Places'.
Postal rates (priority/first class) as follows:

Type	Ireland	Britain	Europe	Other
letter/ postcard	€0.55	€0.82	€0.82	€0.82 (<100g)
package	€2.70	€3.50	€3.50	€3.50 (<250g)
package	€6	€7.50	€7.50	€10.40 (<1kg)

Mail can be addressed to poste restante at
any post office; it's officially held for two weeks
only. If you write 'hold for collection' on the
envelope it *may* be kept for a longer period.

All mail to Britain and Europe goes by air,
so there is no need to use airmail envelopes
or stickers.

Post Offices

There are a couple of post offices in the city
centre:

An Post (Map p68; ☎ 705 8206; St Andrew's St;
🕙 8.30am-5pm Mon-Fri)

General Post Office (GPO; Map p102; ☎ 705 7000;
O'Connell St; 🕙 8am-8pm Mon-Sat, 10am-6.30pm Sun
& holidays)

Postal Codes

Postal codes in Dublin (presented as 'Dublin
+ number') are fairly straightforward. Their
main feature is that all odd numbers refer to
areas north of the Liffey and all even ones to
areas south of the Liffey. They fan out numeri-
cally from the city centre, so the city centre
to the north of the river is Dublin 1 and its
southern equivalent is Dublin 2.

RADIO

Radio na Telefís Éireann (RTE; www.rte.ie) is Ireland's
government-sponsored national broadcasting
body and runs four radio stations. Licensed,
independent broadcasters are gradually filling
up the airwaves, replacing the old pirate stations that are being perpetually closed down.
Most stations now have an online live stream,
so you can listen in before you get here. The
following are the big FM players:

4FM (94.9FM; www.4fm.ie) Aimed at the over-35s, it has
everything from '80s to the Great American Songbook, as
well as a bit of current affairs.

98FM (98FM; www.98fm.ie) A commercial music station
playing a predictable range of popular tunes.

FM 104 (104.4FM; www.fm104.ie) Commercial radio playing Top 40 tunes almost exclusively.

Newstalk 106-108 (106-108FM; www.newstalk.ie)
National news, current affairs and sport talk radio.

Phantom FM (105.2FM; www.phantom.ie) New alternative rock music station.

Q 102 (102.2FM; www.q102.ie) Strictly middle-of-the-road
easy listening.

Radio Na Gaeltachta (92.6-94.4FM; www.rte.ie) A
state-sponsored Irish-language station; culture, music and
current affairs.

RTE Radio 1 (88-94FM; www.rte.ie) Culture, current affairs
and music.

RTE Radio 2 (90.2-92.4FM; www.rte.ie) Commercial radio
with some evening alternative shows.

Spin 103.8 (103.8FM; www.spin1038.com) Chart music
and chat for 18 to 24 year olds.

Today FM (100-102FM; www.todayfm.com) The biggest
independent radio station, with music and current affairs.

Other smaller stations include the following:

Anna Livia (103.2FM) A community radio station that
plays mostly alternative music.

Beaumount Hospital Radio (107.6FM) A light programming schedule of talk and music.

Dublin's Country (106.8FM) Banjos, slide guitars and
doleful lyrics about 'momma'.

Dublin South FM (104.9FM) Community radio, only on
from 4pm to 9pm.

Lyric FM (96-99FM) State-sponsored classical music radio.

Mater Hospital Radio (107.4FM) Community-based hospital radio.

Premier (92.6FM) Playing mostly hits from the '70s and '80s.

Radio na Liffe (106.4FM) Irish-language radio with the best and most wide-ranging music programs on the airwaves.

SAFETY

Dublin is a safe city by any standards, except maybe those set by the Swiss. Basically, act as you would at home. However, certain parts of the city are pretty dodgy due to the presence of drug addicts and other questionable types, including north and northeast of Gardiner St and along parts of Dorset St, on the north side, and west along Thomas St, on the south side.

TELEPHONE

You shouldn't have any problems making phone calls to anyone, anywhere.

Prices are lower in the evening, after 6pm, and weekends. Phone calls from hotel rooms cost twice the standard rate. You can send and receive faxes from post offices (or most hotels). Local calls from a public phone cost €0.30 for around three minutes (around €0.60 to a mobile), regardless of when you call – if you can find a phone that works, as nearly everyone uses mobile phones.

Local and national directory enquiries can be made at ☎ 11811 or ☎ 11850. For international it's ☎ 11818.

Prepaid phonecards by Eircom and private operators are available in newsagencies and post offices, and work from all payphones. For cheap international phone calls, try the following phone centres:

Talk is Cheap (Map p102; ☎ 872 2235; 87 Capel St; ☼ 9am-midnight)

Talk is Cheap (Map p102; ☎ 874 6013; 55 Moore St; ☼ 9am-midnight)

Talk Shop (Map p87; ☎ 672 7212; www.talkshop.ie; 20 Temple Lane; ☼ 9am-11pm)

Talk Shop (Map p102; ☎ 872 0200; www.talkshop.ie; 5 Upper O'Connell St; ☼ 9am-11pm)

Direct Home Call Codes

Instead of placing reverse-charge calls through the Dublin operator, you can dial direct to your home-country operator and then reverse the charges or charge the call to a credit card. To use the home-direct service

dial the codes listed here, the area code and, in most cases, the number you want. Your home-country operator will come on the line before the call goes through.

Australia (☎ 1800 550 061 + number)

France (☎ 1800 551 033 + number)

Italy (☎ 1800 550 039 + number)

New Zealand (☎ 1800 550 064 + number)

Spain (☎ 1800 550 034 + number)

UK – BT (☎ 1800 550 044 + number)

USA – AT&T (☎ 1800 550 000 + number)

USA – MCI (☎ 1800 551 001 + number)

USA – Sprint (☎ 1800 552 001 + number)

Mobile Phones

Virtually everyone in Dublin has a mobile phone. Ireland uses the GSM 900/1800 cellular phone system, which is compatible with European and Australian, but not North American or Japanese, phones. SMS is a local obsession, especially with young people (who communic8 mostly by txt).

There are four Irish service providers: Vodafone (087), O2 (086), Meteor (085) and 3 (083). All have links with most international GSM providers, which allow you to 'roam' onto a local service on arrival. This means you can use your mobile phone to text and make local calls, but you will be charged at a much higher rate. You can also purchase a pay-as-you-go package (for around €50) with a local provider, which includes a mobile phone (you can also opt for cheaper, SIM-only packages, but make sure your own phone is 'unlocked' to handle the SIM card).

Phone Codes

The area code for Dublin is 01. When calling Dublin from abroad, dial your international access code, followed by 353 and 1 (dropping the 0 that precedes it). To make international calls from Dublin, first dial 00, then the country code, followed by the local area code and number.

TIME

In winter, Dublin (and the rest of Ireland) is on GMT, also known as Universal Time Coordinated (UTC), the same as Britain. In summer, the clock shifts to GMT plus one hour. When it's noon in Dublin in summer, it's 3am in Los Angeles and Vancouver, 7am in New York and Toronto, 1pm in Paris, 8pm in Singapore, and 10pm in Sydney.

TOILETS

Forget about the few public facilities on the street: they're dirty and usually overrun with drug dealers and addicts. All shopping centres have public toilets; if you're stranded, go into any bar or hotel.

TOURIST INFORMATION

You'll find everything you need to kick-start your visit at Dublin Tourism Centre (Map p70; ☎ 605 7700; www.visitdublin.com; St Andrew's Church, 2 Suffolk St; ☒ 9am-7pm Mon-Sat, 10.30am-3pm Sun Jul & Aug, 9am-5.30pm Mon-Sat Sep-Jun). Besides general visitor information on Dublin and Ireland, there's also an accommodation booking service, a book and gift shop, a branch of Ticketmaster (for tickets to all major events in the city, including concerts), local and national bus information, rail information, a car-hire desk, tour information and bookings, as well as a cafe.

There are several other tourism centre branches throughout the city:

14 Upper O'Connell St (Map p102; ☒ 9am-5pm Mon-Sat)

Baggot St Bridge (Map p80; foyer of Fáilte Ireland office, Wilton Tce; ☒ 9am-5.15pm Mon-Fri)

Dublin Airport (Arrivals Hall; ☒ 8am-10pm)

Dun Laoghaire (Ferryport; ☒ 10am-1pm & 2-6pm Mon-Sat)

None of these tourist information offices will provide information over the phone – they are exclusively walk-in services. All telephone bookings and reservations are operated by Gulliver Ireland (☎ 1800 668 668; www.gulliver. ie), which is a computerised information and reservation service available at all walk-in offices or from anywhere in the world. The service provides up-to-date information on events, attractions and transport, and also allows you to book accommodation. To access the service from Britain, call ☎ 00800 6686 6866; from the rest of the world, call ☎ 00 353 669 792083.

For information on the rest of the country, call into the head office of Fáilte Ireland (Map p80; ☎ 1850 230 330; www.discoverireland.ie; Wilton Tce, Baggot St Bridge; ☒ 9am-5.15pm Mon-Fri). Web-based tourist information on Dublin is available at the following sites:

Daft.ie (www.daft.ie) The best website for all kinds of house and flat rentals, including short-term leases.

Dublinks (www.dublinks.com) A catch-all website with info on things like shopping, parking, hotels, restaurants and other necessary titbits.

DublinTourist.com (www.dublintourist.com) An excellent and thorough guide to virtually every aspect of the city, from booking a room to going for a drink.

Pigsback.com (www.pigsback.com) Offers all kinds of city-wide discounts, from cinema tickets to free lunches.

Temple Bar (www.templebar.ie) Website dedicated to Dublin's cultural quarter.

TRAVELLERS WITH DISABILITIES

Despite the fact that many of the city's hotels, restaurants and sights are increasingly being adapted for people with disabilities, there's still a long way to go. Fáilte Ireland's annual accommodation guide, *Be Our Guest*, indicates which places are accessible by wheelchair. Public transport can be a nightmare, although a limited number of buses are now equipped with electronic elevators for wheelchairs, and nearly all DART stations have ramps and/or elevators.

The Access Service (Map p102; ☎ 874 7503; 44 North Great George's St), which is part of the Social Service Board (Comhairle), provides plenty of helpful information regarding Dublin's accessibility to wheelchairs.

Another useful organisation is the Irish Wheelchair Association (☎ 818 6400; Áras Chúchulain, Blackheath Dr, Clontarf, Dublin 3).

VISAS

UK nationals don't need a passport to visit Dublin, but are advised to carry one (or some other form of photo identification) to prove that they *are* a UK national. Visitors from outside the EU will need a passport, which should remain valid for at least six months after their intended arrival.

For citizens of EU states and most Western countries, including Australia, Canada, New Zealand and the USA, no visa is required to visit either the Republic or Northern Ireland. Citizens of India, China and many African countries do need a visa for the Republic. Full visa requirements for visiting the Republic are available online at www.dfa.ie.

EU nationals are allowed to stay indefinitely, while other visitors can usually remain for three to six months. To stay longer in the Republic, contact the local *garda* station, the Garda National Immigration Bureau (Map p115; ☎ 01-666 9100; www.garda.ie; 13-14 Burgh Quay, Dublin 2) or the Department of Foreign Affairs (Map p68; ☎ 478 0822; www.dfa.ie; Iveagh House, 80 St Stephen's Green, Dublin 2).

Although you don't need an onward or return ticket to enter Ireland, it could help if there's any doubt that you have sufficient funds to support yourself while in Dublin.

WOMEN TRAVELLERS

Women travellers will probably find Dublin a blissfully relaxing experience, with little risk of hassle on the street or anywhere else. Nonetheless, you still need to take elementary safety precautions. Walking alone at night, especially in less salubrious parts of the city, and hitching are probably unwise. Report serious problems to the *garda*.

There's little need to worry about what you wear in Dublin, and the climate is hardly conducive to topless sunbathing. Finding contraception is not the problem it once was, although anyone on the pill should bring adequate supplies. For female health issues, including contraceptives and the morning-after pill (€60), contact the Well Woman Centre (Map p102; ☎ 661 0083; www.wellwomancentre.ie; 35 Lower Liffey St; ☾ 8am-7.30pm); there's another office at Pembroke Road (Map p122; ☎ 660 9860; 67 Pembroke Rd; ☾ 10am-7.30pm).

In the unlikely event of a sexual assault, get in touch with the police and the Rape Crisis Centre (Map p80; ☎ 1800 778 888, 661 4911; 70 Lower Leeson St).

WORK

The global financial collapse of 2008 has made even low-paid seasonal work in the tourist industry that bit harder to come by throughout the entire country. Citizens of other EU countries are able to work legally in Dublin without a visa. Non-EU citizens require a work permit or work visa.

Visiting full-time US students aged 18 and over can get a four-month work permit for Ireland through CIEE (☎ 617 247 0350; www.ciee. org; 2nd fl, 3 Copley Pl, Boston, MA 02116, USA). Contact your local Irish embassy for more information. Work-related information can be found at the following:

Department of Enterprise, Trade & Employment (Map p80; ☎ 631 2121; www.entemp.ie; Davitt House, 65a Adelaide Rd, Dublin 2)

Nixers.com (www.nixers.com) A good online resource listing jobs in Dublin.

If you are looking for work, there are recruitment agencies that will help make an increasingly difficult task a little bit easier. These include:

Brightwater Selection (Map p80; ☎ 662 1000; 36 North Merrion Sq, Dublin 2)

Careers Register (Map p80; ☎ 679 8900; 26 Lower Baggot St, Dublin 2)

Global Partnerships (Map p80; ☎ 661 8740; 95 Lower Baggot St, Dublin 2)

Planet Recruitment (Map p102; ☎ 874 9901; 21 Eden Quay, Dublin 1)

Reed Recruitment Agency (Map p68; ☎ 670 4466; www.reed.ie; 47 Dawson St, Dublin 2)

BEHIND THE SCENES

THIS BOOK

This guidebook was commissioned in Lonely Planet's London office, and produced by the following:

Commissioning Editor Clifton Wilkinson

Coordinating Editor Katie O'Connell

Coordinating Cartographer Valeska Cañas

Coordinating Layout Designer Carlos Solarte

Managing Editors Imogen Bannister, Liz Heynes

Managing Cartographers Alison Lyall, Herman So

Managing Layout Designer Celia Wood

Assisting Editors Carolyn Bain, Helen Koehne

Cover Designer Pepi Bluck, lonelyplanetimages.com

Internal Image Research Aude Vauconsant, lonely planetimages.com

Thanks to Helen Christinis, Melanie Dankel, Mark Griffiths, Indra Kilfoyle, Lisa Knights, Susan Paterson, Trent Paton, Averil Robertson, Lyahna Spencer, Juan Winata

Cover photographs Ha'penny Bridge, Enrique Algarra/ Photolibrary (top); facade of Cassidy's Pub, Eoin Clarke/ Lonely Planet Images (bottom).

Internal photographs

All images are copyright of the photographer unless otherwise indicated. Many of the images in this guide are available for licensing from Lonely Planet Images: www. lonelyplanetimages.com.

THANKS

FIONN DAVENPORT

Thanks to all the usual suspects, without whom this book just wouldn't have happened. Helen James, Una Mullally, Aingeala Flannery and Niamh Kiernan were instrumental in giving the book a more personal touch. At Lonely Planet, thanks to Clifton Wilkinson, Imogen Bannister and Katie O'Connell for their help, and to Herman So and his carto team for all their mapping work. And lastly, thanks to Caroline for all of her love and support.

OUR READERS

Many thanks to the travellers who used the last edition and wrote to us with helpful hints, useful advice and interesting anecdotes:

Kaia Arthur, Katie Bale, Megan Bell, Daniela Brummer, G Cadogan, Shane Cahill, Justyna Drogomirecka, Regina Fogarty, Christian Heller Jensen, Joe Holland, Cristian Ignat, Jose Kawas, Keith Kenney, Johanna King, Kim Kinsella, Marieke Koets, Outi Kyytsönen, Julie Manahan, Sara Marley, Ruth McDermott, James Moran, Sven Naumann, Chris Nivard, Kate O Reilly, Ollie Otter, Colm Patton, Declan Quinn, Sally St Clair, Niki Stavridi, Amy Townsend, Harvey & Valerie Turer, An-Sofie Van Den Noortgate, Melanie Wright, Kristie Zacher

ACKNOWLEDGMENTS

Dublin Transit Map © Irish Rail 2006–2010

THE LONELY PLANET STORY

Fresh from an epic journey across Europe, Asia and Australia in 1972, Tony and Maureen Wheeler sat at their kitchen table stapling together notes. The first Lonely Planet guidebook, *Across Asia on the Cheap*, was born.

Travellers snapped up the guides. Inspired by their success, the Wheelers began publishing books to Southeast Asia, India and beyond. Demand was prodigious, and the Wheelers expanded the business rapidly to keep up. Over the years, Lonely Planet extended its coverage to every country and into the virtual world via lonelyplanet.com and the Thorn Tree message board.

As Lonely Planet became a globally loved brand, Tony and Maureen received several offers for the company. But it wasn't until 2007 that they found a partner whom they trusted to remain true to the company's principles of travelling widely, treading lightly and giving sustainably. In October of that year, BBC Worldwide acquired a 75% share in the company, pledging to uphold Lonely Planet's commitment to independent travel, trustworthy advice and editorial independence.

Today, Lonely Planet has offices in Melbourne, London and Oakland, with over 500 staff members and 300 authors. Tony and Maureen are still actively involved with Lonely Planet. They're travelling more often than ever, and they're devoting their spare time to charitable projects. And the company is still driven by the philosophy of *Across Asia on the Cheap*: 'All you've got to do is decide to go and the hardest part is over. So go!'

BEHIND THE SCENES

SEND US YOUR FEEDBACK

We love to hear from travellers – your comments keep us on our toes and help make our books better. Our well-travelled team reads every word on what you loved or loathed about this book. Although we cannot reply individually to postal submissions, we always guarantee that your feedback goes straight to the appropriate authors, in time for the next edition. Each person who sends us information is thanked in the next edition and the most useful submissions are rewarded with a free book.

To send us your updates – and find out about Lonely Planet events, newsletters and travel news – visit our award-winning website: lonelyplanet.com/contact.

Note: We may edit, reproduce and incorporate your comments in Lonely Planet products such as guidebooks, websites and digital products, so let us know if you don't want your comments reproduced or your name acknowledged. For a copy of our privacy policy visit lonelyplanet.com/privacy.

Notes

Notes

Notes

INDEX

See also separate
indexes for:

Drinking	p269
Eating	p270
Nightlife & the Arts	p271
Shopping	p271
Sights	p272
Sleeping	p273
Sports & Activities	p274
Top Picks	p274

A

Abbey Theatre 107
accommodation 210-22,
    see also Sleeping subindex
    booking services 212
    costs 19, 211
    long-term rentals
        211-12
Act of Union (1801) 27
activities 202-8, see also
    individual activities,
    Sports & Activities
    subindex
Ahern, Bertie 55
Ahern, Cecelia 37
air travel 240-1
ambulance services 247-8
Anglo-Irish Treaty 30-1
Áras an Uachtaráin 118-19
Arbour Hill Cemetery 110
architecture 48-53
    Anglo-Dutch 48-9
    Georgian 49-50, 79-80,
        84, 111
    medieval 48
    modern 51-3
    Regency & Victorian
        50-1
    Royal Institute of the
        Architects of
        Ireland 80
area codes 255, see also
    inside front cover
Ark Children's Cultural
    Centre 88-9

000 map pages
000 photographs

arts 33-48, 186-200, see
    also architecture, books,
    film, literature, music,
    theatre
    Dublin Electronic Arts
        Festival 18
    Dublin Fringe Festival
        18, 198
    Dun Laoghaire Festival of
        World Cultures 18
    visual arts 45-7
ATMs 250

B

babysitting 246
Bacon, Francis 45, 46, 105
Bank of Ireland 75
bars, see Drinking subindex
bathrooms 256
Battle of the Boyne 26, 229
Beckett, Samuel 34, 41-2,
    199
beer 170-1, see also
    drinking
    beer gardens 175
    Guinness 90-3
beyond the Grand Canal
    121-3, **122**
    accommodation 220-2
    drinking 182-3
    food 167-8
    shopping 146-7
beyond the Royal Canal
    124-7, **125**
    accommodation 222
    drinking 183
bicycle travel 241-2
Binchy, Maeve 37
blogs 55
Bloody Sunday (1920)
    30, 125
Bloody Sunday (1972)
    29, 79
Bloomsday 17, 35
boat travel 242
Bono 39, 40, 194, 230
Book of Kells 24, 45, 66,
    69, 72
books 33-7, see also
    literature, Ulysses, writers
    Dracula 34
    Dubliners 35

Gulliver's Travels 33
    history 32
    Portrait of the Artist as a
        Young Man, A 35
Boomtown Rats, the 39
Boyzone 40
Brú na Bóinne 230-3
bureaux de change 250
bus travel 242-3
business hours 246, see
    also inside front cover
    clubs 189
    pubs 171
    restaurants 151
    shops 136
buskers 5, 74, **5**
Byrne, Jason 47

C

cafes, see Eating subindex
car travel 243-4
castles, see Sights
    subindex
Castletown House 238-9
cathedrals, see Sights
    subindex
Catholicism 26, 27, 31, 32
cell phones 255
Celtic Tiger 3, 23, 32
Chester Beatty Library 72-3
Chieftans, the 38
children, travel with 246,
    see also Sights subindex
    accommodation 216
    activities 17, 19
    babysitting 246
    cultural centres 88-9
Christ Church Cathedral 48,
    50, 96-7, 129, **96**
Christianity 24
    Catholicism 26, 27,
        31, 32
    Protestantism 25-6
Christmas Dip at the Forty
    Foot 17
churches, see Sights
    subindex
cinemas 191-2
City Hall 50, 77
Clayton, Adam 40
climate 16, 246
climate change 244

clubbing 186-90, see also
    Nightlife & the Arts
    subindex
    business hours 189
coffee 159
Collins, Michael 30-1, 125
comedy 47, 190-1
    Bulmers International
        Comedy Festival 18
Connolly, James 28, 29, 98
Convergence Festival 17
costs 19-20, 136-7, 247
    accommodation 19,
        211
    free attractions 17,
        20, 90
    courses 247
Cowan, Brian 54-5
credit cards 250-1
credit crunch, see global
    financial crisis
Croke Park 6, 124-5, 206, **6**
Cromwell, Oliver 22, 26,
    94, 110
Custom House 114-16
customs regulations 247
cycling, see bicycle travel

D

Dalkey 229-30
dance 47-8
DART 244-5
day trips 224-39
De Valera, Éamon 29-31
dentists 249-50
disabilities, travellers
    with 256
discount cards 247
Diversions 17
Docklands 114-17, **115**
    accommodation 220
    architecture 52
    drinking 182
    food 166
    shopping 146
doctors 250
Dowth 232-3
Dracula 34
drinking 170-84, see
    also Drinking subindex
    beer gardens 175
    business hours 171

costs 19
  tipping 172
drinks 170-1
  beer 170-1
  coffee 159
  Guinness 90-3
  whiskey 105-6, 171
Dublin Castle 76-7, 130, **76**
Dublin City Gallery – the
  Hugh Lane 4, 104-5
Dubliners 35
Dubliners, the 38
Dun Laoghaire Festival of
  World Cultures 18
Dvblinia & the Viking
  World 97, 129

E
Easter Rising (1916) 28, 29
  exhibition 107
  sites 69, 73, 77, 97,
    107, 111
  walking tour 253
economy
  global financial crisis
    22, 23
  Celtic Tiger 2, 23, 32
Edge, the 40
Electric Picnic 18
electricity 247
embassies 247
emergencies 247-8, *see
  also inside front cover*
entertainment 186-200,
  see also Nightlife & the
  Arts *subindex*
  bookings 186
environmental issues 20-1,
  53-4
  climate change 244
  Convergence Festival 17
Enya 39, 230
events 16-19
exchange rates, *see inside
  front cover*
excursions 224-39

F
Famine, the 27
  Jeanie Johnston ship
    116-17
  memorial 116
Father Ted 47
ferry travel, *see* boat travel
festivals 16-19
  Anna Livia International
    Opera Festival 192

Bulmers International
  Comedy Festival 190
Dublin Fringe Festival
  18, 198
Dublin Theatre Festival
  18, 198
Jameson Dublin
  International Film
  Festival 16-17, 192
Taste of Dublin 161
Temple Bar Trad Festival
  196
Fianna Fáil 31, 54-5
film 42-4
  cinemas 191-2
  Dublin International
    Film Festival 192
  French Film Festival 19
  Jameson Dublin
    International Film
    Festival 16-17
  Junior Dublin Film
    Festival 19
Fine Gael 55
Finnegans Wake 35
fire services 247-8
Fitzwilliam Sq 84-5
folk music 38-9, 195-7
food 150-68, *see also*
  Eating *subindex*
  business hours 151
  costs 19, 151-2
  reservations 152
  self-catering 152
  shops 140
  specialities 150-1
  Taste of Dublin 161
  tipping 152
  vegetarian travellers
    164
football 204-5, 206
Four Courts 108
Frames, the 40
free attractions 17, 20, 90
Funderland 19

G
GAA Museum 124-5
Gaelic, *see* Irish language
Gaelic football 205-7
  All-Ireland Finals 17
galleries 46, *see also* Sights
  subindex
gardens, *see* Sights
  subindex
Gardens of Remembrance
  111

gay travellers 176, 248, *see
  also* Drinking *subindex*
International Dublin Gay
  Theatre Festival 17
Mardi Gras 18
Geldof, Bob 39
genealogy 84, 85
General Post Office (GPO)
  29, 50, 107
Georgian architecture
  49-50, 79-80
  Henrietta St 111
  Number Twenty-Nine 84
Glasnevin Cemetery 5,
  125-6
Glendalough 233-5
global financial crisis 22,
  23, *see also* Celtic Tiger
Gogarty, Oliver St John 34
Goldsmith, Oliver 34, 41
golf 203-4, *see also* Sports
  & Activities *subindex*
Gonne, Maud 30
government 54-5
  buildings 83-4
Grafton St area 5, 66, **68,
  70, 5**
  accommodation 212-15
  drinking 172-7
  food 152-9
  shopping 136-7
greyhound racing 207, *see
  also* Sports & Activities
  subindex
Griffith, Arthur 28
Guinness 90-3
Guinness, Arthur 92
Gulliver's Travels 33
gyms 202-3

H
Hallowe'en 18
Handel, George Frideric
  17, 193
Hansard, Glen 40-1, 44
Ha'penny Bridge 133, **2**
Heaney, Seamus 37
history 22-33
  1916 Easter Rising 29
  Bloody Sunday (1920)
    30, 125
  Bloody Sunday (1972)
    29, 79
  Civil War 30-1
  Famine, the 27, 116-17
  Georgian Dublin 26
  Home Rule 28

IRA (Irish Republican
  Army) 29-32, 125, 238
Viking era 24
War of Independence
  29-30
holidays 248
Home Rule 28
horse racing 19, 207
  Dublin Horse Show 18
  Leopardstown Races 19
hospitals 250
Howth 5, 227-8, **227, 5**
Huguenot Cemetery 73
hurling 205-7
  All-Ireland Finals 17

I
internet access 248-9
internet resources 20, 21
  blogs 55
  entertainment 187
  shopping 138
IRA (Irish Republican Army)
  29-32, 238, *see also*
  Sinn Féin
  hunger strike
    memorial 125
Ireland's Eye 226
Irish language 56-7
Irish Museum of Modern
  Art 4, 98-9, **4**
Irish Volunteer Force (IVF)
  28-9
Irish-Jewish Museum 77-8
itineraries 15, 62-3
Iveagh Gardens 12, 78, **12**
Iveagh House 74

J
Jameson whiskey 105-6
jazz 193
Joyce, James 34, 35, 108,
  see also Ulysses
  Bloomsday 17, 35
  cultural centres 108-9,
    129
  Dubliners 35
  Finnegans Wake 35
  museums 12, 230, **12**
  *Portrait of the Artist as a
    Young Man, A* 35
  walking tour 253

K
karaoke 192
Kavanagh, Patrick 11, 34,
  121, 123, 133, **11**

Keating, Ronan 40
Kelly, Luke 38
Keyes, Marion 37
Killiney 11, 230
Kilmainham 90-100, **91**
  drinking 180
  food 163
  shopping 144
Kilmainham Gaol 29, 97-8
Kilmainham Gate 99
Knowth 232

L
Lane, Hugh 105
language 56-8
  courses 247
Larkin, Jim 28, 108, 125
legal matters 249
Leinster House – Irish
  Parliament 8, 83-4
Leopardstown Races 19
leprechauns 107-8
lesbian travellers 176,
  248, see also Drinking
  subindex
  International Dublin Gay
    Theatre Festival 17
  Mardi Gras 18
Liberties, the 90-100, **91**
  drinking 180
  food 163
  shopping 144
libraries, see Sights
  subindex
Liffey, River 60, see also
  north of the Liffey
Liffey Swim 17
literature 33-7, see
  also writers, books
  Nobel laureates 34
  walking tours 128-9, **128**
Long Room 67, 69
Luas 245
Lynott, Phil 39, 195

M
magazines 56, 252
Malahide 228-9
Mansion House 78
maps 249
marathons 17
Mardi Gras 18
markets **7**, see also Eating
  and Shopping subindexes

000 map pages
000 photographs

Markievicz, Countess 30
Marsh's Library 12, 49,
  95-6, 130, **12**
McAleese, Mary 55
measures, see inside front
  cover
medical services 249-50
Merrion Sq area 79-85, **80**
  accommodation 215-16
  drinking 177-8
  food 159-61
mobile phones 255
money 19-20, 247, 250-1,
  see also inside front cover
  ATMs 250
  bureaux de change
    250
  credit cards 250-1
  travellers cheques 251
Moore, Thomas 34
Moran, Dylan 47
motorcycle travel 243
Mullen, Larry 40
museums, see Sights
  subindex
music 37-41, see also
  Shopping, Drinking and
  Nightlife & the Arts
  subindexes
  classical 192-3
  Electric Picnic 18
  folk 38-9, 195-7
  Hard Working Class
    Heroes 18
  opera 192
  Oxegen 18
  popular 39-41
  Temple Bar Trad Festival
    196
  traditional 38-9, 195-7
musicians 38-41
  Bono 39, 40, 194, 230
  Enya 39, 230
  Handel, George Frideric
    17
  O'Connor, Sinéad 39
  Lynott, Phil 39, 195
  Thin Lizzy 39, 195
  U2 39, 40, 194
My Bloody Valentine 39

N
National Gallery 4, 82-3, **4**
National Leprechaun
  Museum 107-8
National Library &
  Genealogical Office 85

National Museum
  Archaeology 80-2
  Decorative Arts & History
    8, 106-7, **8**
  Natural History 83
National Photographic
  Archives 89
New Year's celebrations 16
Newgrange 231-2
Newman House 74-5
Newman University
  Church 75
newspapers 55-6, 251-2
nightlife, see entertain-
  ment, drinking, Nightlife
  & the Arts and Drinking
  subindexes
north of the Liffey 101-13,
  102-3
  accommodation 218-20
  drinking 180-2
  food 163-6
  shopping 144-6

O
O'Briain, Dara 47
O'Casey, Sean 41
O'Connell, Daniel 27, 82,
  108, 125
O'Connell St area 101-13,
  102-3
  accommodation 218-20
  drinking 180-2
  food 163-6
  shopping 144-6
O'Connor, Sinéad 39
Old Jameson Distillery
  105-6
Old Library 69
opening hours, see business
  hours
Original Print Gallery 89
Oxegen 18

P
painting 45-7
parks, see Sights subindex
Parnell, Charles Stewart 28,
  108, 125
Pearse, Pádraig 29
  museums 122-3
Pearse, Willy 29
pharmacies 250
Phoenix Park 5, 11, 118-20,
  119, **5**
  drinking 182
  food 167

planning 16-21, 187
police services 247-8
politics 54-5
Poolbeg Lighthouse 114
Portrait of the Artist as a
  Young Man, A 35
postal services 254
Powerscourt Estate 236-7
Powerscourt Townhouse
  Shopping Centre 77
Protestantism 25-6
public holidays 248
pubs 170, see also Drinking
  subindex
  business hours 171
  etiquette 170
  tipping 172

R
radio 56, 254-5
responsible travel 20-1,
  244, 275
Riverdance 38, 48
road rules 243
Robinson, Mary 55
Royal Barracks 48
Royal Hibernian Academy
  (RHA) Gallagher Gallery 85
Royal Hospital Kilmainham
  8, 48, 98-9, **4**
Royal Irish Academy 78
rugby 207-8
  Six Nations Rugby 17
Russborough House 4,
  237-8, **4**

S
safety 255
Sandycove 230
Shaw, George Bernard 12,
  34, 41, 77
shopping 136-48, see
  also Shopping subindex
  business hours 136
  internet resources 138
  taxes & charges 136-7
Sinn Féin 28, 29-30, 55, see
  also IRA (Irish Republican
  Army)
Six Nations Rugby 17
slang 56
smoking 172
spas 202-3
Spire, the 110, 132
sports 202-8, see also
  individual sports, Sports &
  Activities subindex

St Audoen's Churches 99, 129
St George's Church 113
St Kevin 234
St Mary's Abbey 112
St Mary's Church 112
St Mary's Pro-Cathedral 112
St Michan's Church 110
St Patrick 24
St Patrick's Cathedral 8, 48, 50, 93-5, 130, **93**, **8**
St Patrick's Festival 17
St Stephen's Green 73-4
St Stephen's 'Pepper Canister' Church 85
St Werburgh's Church 99-100
statues, *see* Sights *subindex*
Stoker, Bram 34, 129
Strawberry Beds 126
sustainable travel 20-1, 244, 275
Swift, Jonathon 33, 94, 193
swimming 17
Synge, John Millington 41

T
Taste of Dublin 161
taxes 136-7
taxis 244
telephone services 255
television 45, 56
Temple Bar 11, 86-9, **87**, **3, 11**
  accommodation 216-18
  drinking 178-80
  festivals 196
  food 161-3
  shopping 143-4
Temple Bar Gallery & Studios 88
theatre 41-2, 197-9, *see also* writers, Nightlife & the Arts *subindex*
  contemporary scene 42
  Dublin Fringe Festival 18, 198
  Dublin Theatre Festival 18, 198
  International Dublin Gay Theatre Festival 17
Thin Lizzy 39, 195
time 255-6
tipping 152, 172
Tóibín, Colm 36
toilets 256
tourist information 256

tours 252-4, *see also* walking tours
  boat 252
  bus 252-3
  Dublin Castle 76
  horse-drawn carriage 253
  Kilmainham Gaol 98
  Leinster House 8, 83-4
  National Museum of Ireland – Archaeology 80
  Royal Hospital Kilmainham & Irish Museum of Modern Art 98-9
train travel 244-5
tram travel 245
transport 240-5
travellers cheques 251
Trinity College 66-7, 69-70, 72, **67**
  architecture 50
  Book of Kells 24, 45, 66, 69, 72
TV 45, 56

U
U2 39, 40, 194
Ulster Volunteer Force (UVF) 28
Ulysses 35
  Bloomsday 17, 35
  sites 85, 96, 109, 125, 172-3, 180, 230
unemployment 23
University College Dublin (UCD) 74, 206
urban planning 54

V
vegetarian travellers 164
Vikings 24, 97
visas 256-7
visitors centres, *see* Sights *subindex*
visual arts 45-7

W
Waiting for Godot 42
walking tours 128-34, 253-4
  Glendalough 235
  Grand Canal area 133-4, **134**
  literary-themed 128-9, **128**
  north of the Liffey 132-3, **133**

pub-themed 131-2, **131**
  Trinity College 66
  Viking and medieval themed 129-30, **130**
War Memorial Gardens 12, 100
War of Independence 29-30
weather 16, 246
websites, *see* internet resources
weights, *see* inside front cover
Westlife 40
whiskey 105-6, 171
Whitefriars Street Carmelite Church 78
wi-fi 248
Wilde, Oscar 34, 41, 82, 129
William of Orange 26
women travellers 257
Women's Mini-Marathon 17
working 257
writers, *see also* Joyce, James
  Ahern, Cecelia 37
  Beckett, Samuel 34, 41-2, 199
  Binchy, Maeve 37
  festivals 17
  Gogarty, Oliver St John 34
  Goldsmith, Oliver 34, 41
  Heaney, Seamus 37
  Kavanagh, Patrick 11, 34, 121, 123, 133, **11**
  Keyes, Marion 37
  Moore, Thomas 34
  museums 109-10
  O'Casey, Sean 41
  Shaw, George Bernard 12, 34, 41, 77
  Stoker, Bram 34
  Swift, Jonathon 33, 94, 193
  Synge, John Millington 41
  Tóibín, Colm 36
  Wilde, Oscar 34, 41, 82, 129
  Yeats, William Butler 34, 82, 111, 128, 129

Y
Yeats, Jack B 46, 82
Yeats, William Butler 34, 82, 111, 128, 129

Z
zoos 118

DRINKING

CONTEMPORARY BARS
Bailey 172
Bank 172
Bar With No Name 173
Café en Seine 172
Dakota 172
Davy Byrne's 172
Dicey Reilly's 173
Fitzsimons 178
Gravity Bar 92
Horseshoe Bar 173
Ice Bar 182
Kiely's 183
Jameson Bar 106
Market Bar 173
Mercantile 173
Messrs Maguire 178
Morrison Bar 180
Octagon Bar 178
Odeon 173
Porterhouse Brewing Company 178
Pravda 180
Purity Kitchen, the 179
Pygmalion 174
Ron Black's 174
Samsara 174
Sycamore Club 179
Thomas Read's 179
Turk's Head 179

DJ BARS
Anseo 174
Bernard Shaw 174
Bia Bar 174
Dice Bar 180
Globe 174
Hogan's 174
No 4 Dame Lane 174
Sin É 181
Solas 175
South William 175
Village 175

GAY BARS
Dragon 175
Front Lounge 179
George 175
Pantibar 181

TEAHOUSES
Tea Garden, the 181

TRADITIONAL PUBS
Auld Dubliner 179, **3**
Brazen Head 180
Brogan's 179
Bruxelles 175
Dawson Lounge 175
Doheny & Nesbitt's 177
Fallon's 180
Flowing Tide 181
Gill's 181
Gravediggers (aka Kavanagh's) 10, 183
Grogan's Castle Lounge 10, 175
Hartigan's 177
International Bar 176
James Toner's 177
Kavanagh's 10, 183
Kehoe's 10, 176, **10**
Kennedy's 182
Long Hall 10, 176, **10**
Long Stone 176
McDaid's 176
Mulligan's 10, 176, **10**
Nealon's 181
Neary's 176
O'Brien's 183
O'Donoghue's 178
Old Stand 177
Oliver St John Gogarty 179
Oval 181
Palace Bar 179
Patrick Conway's 181
Peter's Pub 177
Ryan's 182
Sackville Lounge 181
Sean O'Casey's 182
Searson's 183
Stag's Head 177
Swan 177
Temple Bar 11, 180, **11**
Welcome Inn 182
Whelan's 9, 177, **9**

WINE BARS
Ely 161
La Cuvee @ Eno Wine Bar 182

EATING

AMERICAN
Shanahan's on the Green 152

ASIAN
Diep Le Shaker 160-1
Saba 155

BELGIAN
La Peniche 167

BURGERS
Bobo's 158
Gourmet Burger Kitchen 158, 163
Jo'Burger 168

CAFES
Avoca 157
Brown's Bar 159
Butler's Chocolate Café 159
Cobalt Café & Gallery 165
Coffee Society 159
Grangecon Cafe 238
Honest to Goodness 159
Milk & Honey 159
Milk Bar 159
Panem 165
Phoenix Park Tea Room 167
Poppies Country Cooking 237
Queen of Tarts 163
Simon's Place 159

CHINESE
Good World 156-7
Imperial Chinese Restaurant 155
Melody 165

CREOLE & CAJUN
Tante Zoé's 162

CREPERIES
Lemon 159

DELIS
Listons 158

FISH & CHIPS
Leo Burdock's 163

FRENCH
Balzac 153
Chez Max 155, 161
Chez Sara 229
Dax 160
Dobbins 160
Expresso Bar 167
French Paradox 167
Green Hen 157
La Maison 156
L'Ecrivain 160
L'Gueuleton 155
Pichet 154
Restaurant Patrick Guilbaud 160
Thornton's 152

INDIAN
Jaipur 155
Mohana 239

INDONESIAN
Chameleon 162

INTERNATIONAL
Dublin City Gallery - the Hugh Lane 165
Epicurean Food Hall 166
Herbstreet 166
Larder, the 163
Sixty6 155
Trocadero 153

IRISH
Gibney's 229
House, the 228
Juniors 167
Kehoe's 239
Kimchi/The Hop House 165
Pichet 154
Thornton's 152
Wicklow Heather Restaurant 235

ITALIAN
Ar Vicoletto 162
Bar Italia 165
Bottega Toffoli 158
Café Bardeli 157, 167
Dunne & Crescenzi 156
Emilia's Ristorante 237
Il Baccaro 162
La Taverna di Bacco 166

Sale e Pepe 229
Taste of Emilia 165
Unicorn 160

JAPANESE
Wagamama 157
Yamamori 154
Yamamori Sushi 164

KOREAN
Bon Ga 165
Kimchi/The Hop House 165

LEBANESE
Cedar Tree 155

MARKETS
Coppinger Row Market 7, 154
Dublin Food Co-op 7, 154, **7**
Harcourt St Food Market 154
Howth Fishermen's & Farmers' Market 7, 228
Meeting House Square Market 7, 145, **7**
People's Park Market 154

MEDITERRANEAN
Coppinger Row 156
Odessa 154
Seagrass 154

MIDDLE EASTERN
Silk Road Café 157
Zaytoon 163

MODERN EUROPEAN
Bang Café 161
Eden 161
Ely Chq Bar & Brasserie 166
Ely HQ 166
Fallon & Byrne 153
Quay 16 166
Town Bar & Grill 153

MODERN IRISH
Chapter One 164
Halo 164
Itsa4 167
Lennox Cafe Bistro 156
Pig's Ear, the 157
Tea Rooms 161
Winding Stair 164

MOROCCAN
El Bahia 155

NEPALESE
Monty's of Kathmandu 162-3

ORGANIC
Ely 161
Green Nineteen 158
Organic Life/Marc Michel 237

PASTRIES
Cake Cafe 158

SANDWICH BARS
Nude 159

SEAFOOD
Aqua 228
Caviston's Seafood
    Restaurant 230
Guinea Pig 230
Mermaid Café 161
Oar House, the 228

SOUP BARS
Soup Dragon 166

STEAKHOUSES
Marco Pierre White
    Steakhouse & Grill 153

TAPAS
Market Bar 158

TEA ROOMS
Boyle's Licensed Tea Rooms
    233
THAI
Café Mao 156
Chilli Club 156

Siam Thai Restaurant
    229
Tiger Becs 153

VEGETARIAN
Blazing Salads 164
Cornucopia 164
Fresh 164
Govinda's 164
Juice 157

VIETNAMESE
Café Mao 156

WINE BARS
Ely 161
La Cuvee @ Eno Wine
    Bar 182

NIGHTLIFE & THE ARTS
CINEMAS
Cineworld Multiplex 191
Irish Film Institute 191
Lighthouse Cinema 191
Meeting House Sq 191
Savoy 191
Screen 191

CLASSICAL MUSIC
Bank of Ireland Arts Centre
    192
Dublin City Gallery – the
    Hugh Lane 192
Gaiety Theatre 192
Grand Canal Theatre 193
Helix 193
National Concert Hall 193
Royal Dublin Society
    Showground Concert
    Hall 193

CLUBS
Academy, the 187
Andrew's Lane Theatre 187
Button Factory 188
Copper Face Jacks 188
Good Bits, the 189
Hogan's 188
Krystle 188
Lillie's Bordello 188

PoD 188
Rí Rá 188-9
Spy/Wax 189
Think Tank 189
Tripod 189
Twisted Pepper 9, 189
Village 189
Wright Venue, the 189

COMEDY
Banker's 190
Comedy Dublin 190
Ha'penny Bridge Inn 190
International Bar 190
Laughter Lounge 190

JAZZ
Globe 193
JJ Smyth's 9, 193, **9**

KARAOKE
Ukiyo 192
Village 192

POPULAR MUSIC
Academy, the 194
Ambassador Theatre 194
Button Factory 194
Crawdaddy 194
Marlay Park 194
O2 195
Olympia Theatre 194
Sugar Club 195
Tripod 195
Vicar Street 9, 195
Village 195
Whelan's 9, 195, **9**

THEATRES
Abbey Theatre 197
Ark 197
Bewley's Café Theatre
    197
Civic Theatre 198
Crypt Arts Centre 197
Draíocht Theatre 198
Gaiety Theatre 198
Gate Theatre 198
International Bar 197
Lambert Puppet Theatre
    197
New Theatre 198
Olympia Theatre 198

Pavilion Theatre 198
Peacock Theatre 198
Project Arts Centre 199
Samuel Beckett Theatre
    197
Tivoli Theatre 199

TRADITIONAL & FOLK MUSIC
Cobblestone 9, 196, **9**
Comhaltas Ceoltóirí
    Éireann 196
Devitt's 196
Ha'penny Bridge Inn 196
Hughes' Bar 196
Oliver St John Gogarty
    196
Palace Bar 197

SHOPPING
ANTIQUES
Fleury Antiques 144
O'Sullivan Antiques 144
Oxfam Home 144

BEAUTY
Blue Eriu 137

BOOKS
Cathach Books 137
Dubray Books 137
Eason's 144
Gutter Bookshop 143
Hodges Figgis 137
Murder Ink 137-8
Stokes Books 138
Waterstone's 138
Winding Stair 144

CAMPING & OUTDOORS
Great Outdoors 138

CIGARS
Decent Cigar Emporium
    138

DEPARTMENT STORES
Arnott's 144
Avoca Handweavers 138
Brown Thomas 138
Clery's & Co 145

Debenhams 145
Dunnes Stores 138
Marks & Spencer 139
Penney's 145

EYEWEAR
Optica 139

FASHION & DESIGNER
Alias Tom 139
Bow Boutique 139
BT2 139
Costume 139
Design Centre 139
Havana 146
Kilkenny Shop 139
Louis Copeland 139
Smock 140
Tommy Hilfiger 140
Urban Outfitters 143

FOOD & DRINK
Asia Market 140
Bretzel Bakery 140
Fallon & Byrne 140
Magills 140
Sheridan's Cheesemongers 140

IRISH CRAFTS
Avoca Handweavers 138
Blarney Woollen Mills 141
Designyard 141
H Danker 141
House of Names 141
Kilkenny Shop 139
Knobs & Knockers 141
Tower Craft Design Centre 146

JEWELLERY
Angles 141
Appleby 141
Barry Doyle Design Jewellers 141
Designyard 141
Rhinestones 141
Weir & Son's 142

000 map pages
000 photographs

MARKETS
Blackberry Fair 145
Blackrock Market 145
Book Fair 145
Cow's Lane Designer Mart 145
Meeting House Square Market 7, 145, **7**
Merrion Sq art market 82
Moore Street Market 7, 145, **7**
Smithfield Fish Market 145
Toejam Carboot Sale 145

MUSEUM SHOPS
Chester Beatty Library 146
Dublin City Gallery - The Hugh Lane Shop 146
Irish Museum of Modern Art 146
National Gallery 146
Trinity Library Shop 146

MUSIC
Claddagh Records 143
HMV 142
Road Records 142
Urban Outfitters 143
Walton's 142, 146

PHOTOGRAPHY
Dublin Camera Exchange 142

SHOES
Clark's 146
Schuh 146

SHOPPING ARCADES
George's St Arcade 142
Westbury Mall 142

SHOPPING CENTRES
Dundrum Town Centre 147
Jervis Centre 146
Powerscourt Townhouse Shopping Centre 142
St Stephen's Green Shopping Centre 142

VINTAGE CLOTHING & ACCESSORIES
Flip 144
Harlequin 143
Jenny Vander 143

SIGHTS

ANCIENT SITES
Brú na Bóinne 230-3
Dowth 232-3
Knowth 232
Newgrange 231-2

BREWERIES & DISTILLERIES
Guinness Storehouse & St James's Gate Brewery 90-3
Old Jameson Distillery 105-6

CASTLES
Corr Castle 227
Dalkey Castle 229
Dublin Castle 76-7
Howth Castle 227
Malahide Castle 228
Rathfarnham Castle 123

CEMETERIES
Arbour Hill Cemetery 110
Glasnevin Cemetery 5, 125-6
Huguenot Cemetery 73

CHILDRENS' VENUES
Ark Children's Cultural Centre 88-9
Dvblinia & the Viking World 97, 129
Newgrange Farm 232

CHURCHES & CATHEDRALS
Christ Church Cathedral 48, 50, 96-7, 129, **96**
Newman University Church 75
St Audoen's Churches 99
St George's Church 113
St Mary's Abbey 112, 227

St Mary's Church 112
St Mary's Pro-Cathedral 112
St Michan's Church 110
St Patrick's Cathedral 8, 48, 50, 93-5, 130, **93**, **8**
St Stephen's 'Pepper Canister' Church 85
St Werburgh's Church 99-100
Unitarian Church 73
Whitefriars Street Carmelite Church 78

GALLERIES
Douglas Hyde Gallery 4, 70
Dublin City Gallery - the Hugh Lane 4, 104-5
Gallery of Photography 88
Irish Museum of Modern Art 4, 98-9, **4**
National Gallery 4, 82-3, **4**
Original Print Gallery 89
Royal Hibernian Academy (RHA) Gallagher Gallery 85
Temple Bar Gallery & Studios 88

HISTORIC & NOTABLE BUILDINGS
Áras an Uachtaráin 118-19
Bank of Ireland 75
Belvedere House 111
Berkeley Library 8, 70, **8**
Casino at Marino 126-7
Castletown House 238-9
City Hall 77
Custom House 114, 116
Farmleigh House 119
Four Courts 108
General Post Office (GPO) 107
Government buildings 84
Iveagh House 74
Kilmainham Gaol 97-8
Leinster House - Irish Parliament 8, 83-4
Long Room 69
Mansion House 78
Newman House 74-5
Number Twenty-Nine 84
Old Library 69
Powerscourt Estate 236-7
Powerscourt Townhouse Shopping Centre 77

INDEX

Rotunda Hospital 111-12
Royal College of Surgeons 73
Royal Hospital Kilmainham 8, 48, 98-9, **4**
Russborough House 4, 237-8, **4**
Shaw Birthplace 12, 77
Trinity College 66-7, 69-70, 72

LIBRARIES & ARCHIVES
Berkeley Library 8, 70, **8**
Chester Beatty Library 72-3
Marsh's Library 12, 95-6, **12**
National Library & Genealogical Office 85
National Photographic Archives 89
Old Library 69
Royal Irish Academy 78

LIGHTHOUSES
Poolbeg Lighthouse 114

MONUMENTS, STATUARY & GATES
Children of Lir statue 111
College Green statuary 75
Essex Gate 129
Famine Memorial 116
Figure of Justice 77
Fusiliers' Arch 73
Kilmainham Gate 99
O'Connell St statuary 108
Phoenix Park 120
Spire, the 110
St Stephen's Green statuary 73

MUSEUMS
Dublin Writers Museum 109-10
GAA Museum 124-5
Garda Museum 76
Glasnevin Cemetery museum 125
Irish-Jewish Museum 77-8
James Joyce Cultural Centre 108-9
James Joyce Museum 12, 230, **12**
Jeanie Johnston 116-17

National Leprechaun Museum 107-8
National Museum – Archaeology 80-2
National Museum of Ireland – Decorative Arts & History 8, 106-7, **8**
National Museum of Ireland – National History 83
National Print Museum 121
National Transport Museum 228
Pearse Museum 122-3

PARKS & GARDENS
Castle Gardens 227
College Park 72
Fitzwilliam Sq 84-5
Garden of Remembrance 111
Iveagh Gardens 12, 78, **12**
Larchill Arcadian Gardens 239
Merrion Square 79-80
National Botanic Gardens 126
Phoenix Park 5, 11, 118-20, 119, **5**
St Stephen's Green 73-4
War Memorial Gardens 12, 100

SHOWGROUNDS & STADIUMS
Croke Park 6, 124-5, **6**
Royal Dublin Society Showground 6, 121-2

VISITOR CENTRES
Brú na Bóinne Visitor Centre 230
Glendalough Visitor Centre 234
Phoenix Park Visitor Centre 119
Waterways Visitor Centre 117

WATERFALLS
Powerscourt Waterfall 237

ZOOS
Dublin Zoo 118

SLEEPING
APARTMENTS
Clarion Stephen's Hall 215
Home From Home Apartments 215
Latchfords 215
Oliver St John Gogarty's Penthouse Apartments 215

B&BS
Ariel House 222
Coolakay House 237
Dublin City University (DCU) 222
Glebe House 233
Glendale 235
Griffith House 222
Haylands House 238
Newgrange Lodge 233
Rossnaree 233
Tinode House 222

BOUTIQUE HOTELS
La Stampa Hotel 213
Merrion Hall 221
Morgan Hotel 217
Number 31 216
Pembroke Townhouse 221
Schoolhouse Hotel 221
Townhouse 218

CAMPUS RESIDENCES
Mercer Court Campus Accommodation 215
Trinity College 215

GUESTHOUSES
Aberdeen Lodge 221
Anchor Guesthouse 219
Clifden Guesthouse 219
Eliza Lodge 217-18
Grafton Guesthouse 214
Harrington Hall 214
Staunton's on the Green 214

Trinity Lodge 213
Waterloo House 221

HERMITAGES
Glendalough Cillíns 236

HOSTELS
Abbey Court Hostel 219
Ashfield House 217
Avalon House 215
Barnacles Temple Bar House 218
Globetrotters Tourist Hostel 220
Gogarty's Temple Bar Hostel 217
Isaacs Hostel 220
Jacob's Inn 220
Kinlay House 218
Newgrange Lodge 233

HOTELS
Academy Hotel 219
Brooks Hotel 213
Brown's Hotel 219
Buswell's Hotel 214
Camden Court Hotel 214
Carton House 239
Castle Hotel 219
Central Hotel 214
Clarence Hotel 217
Clarion Hotel 220
Conrad Dublin International 216
Croke Park Hotel 222
Davenport Hotel 216
Dublin Citi Hotel 217
Dylan 221
Fitzwilliam Hotel 213
Four Seasons 220
Gibson Hotel 220
Glendalough Hotel 235
Grafton Capital Hotel 215
Grand Canal Hotel 222
Gresham Hotel 219
Herbert Park Hotel 221
Hilton 212-13
Jury's Inn Parnell St 219
Kildare Hotel & Golf Club 239
Maldron Hotel Cardiff Lane 220
Maldron Hotel Smithfield 218
Mercer Hotel 214

Merrion 216
Morrison Hotel 218
Paramount Hotel 217
Radisson Blu Royal Hotel
  213
Rathsallagh House &
  Country Club 238
  Shelbourne 212
Stephen's Green Hotel
  213
Summerhill House Hotel
  237
Walton's Hotel 218-19
Westbury Hotel 212
Westin Hotel 212

SELF-CATERING
Irish Landmark Trust
  216

SPORTS &
ACTIVITIES
GOLF COURSES
Carton House 203
Deer Park Golf Course 228
Druid's Glen 203
K Club 203
Kildare Golf Club 239
Killeen Castle 204

GYMS & SPAS
Bellaza Clinic 202
Dublin Spa @ Four Seasons
  202
Mandala Day Spa 202
Markievicz Leisure Centre
  202
Melt 202-3
Wells Spa 203

HORSE &
GREYHOUND
RACING TRACKS
Curragh 207
Fairyhouse 207, **6**
Harold's Cross Park 207
Leopardstown 207
Punchestown 207
Shelbourne Park 207, **6**

**SPORTING
GROUNDS**
Aviva Stadium 205, 208
Parnell Park 206
Royal Dublin Society
  208

TOP PICKS
accommodation 217

bars
  DJ bars 172
  hotel bars 218
  Temple Bar 86
blogs 55
club nights 188
free attractions 90
galleries 46
history books 32
Irish cuisine 160
Irish-made goods 137
Merrion Sq area 79
music
  contemporary
    albums 39
  songs 41
  traditional albums
    38
sporting moments
  203

000 map pages
000 photographs

GREENDEX

ACCOMMODATION
Coolakay House 237
Glendalough Cillíns 236

ATTRACTIONS
Larchill Arcadian Gardens 238

EATING
Avoca 157
Coppinger Row Market 154
Dublin Food Co-op 154
Grangecon Cafe 238
Green Nineteen 158
Harcourt St Food Market 154
Herbstreet 166
Honest to Goodness 159
Howth Fishermen's & Farmers' Market 228
Juice 157
Larder 163
Lennox Cafe Bistro 156
Meeting House Square Market 145
Nude 159
Organic Life/Marc Michel 237
People's Park Market 154
Poppies Country Cooking 237
Russborough Farmers Market 238
Seagrass 154
Wicklow Heather Restaurant 235

SHOPPING
Blackberry Fair 145
Blackrock Market 145
Book Fair 145
Bow Boutique 268
Cow's Lane Designer Mart 145
Moore Street Market 145
Toejam Carboot Sale 145

MAP LEGEND
ROUTES

............Freeway	...........Mall/Steps
............Primary	...........Pedestrian Overpass
............Secondary	...........Walking Tour
............Tertiary	...........Walking Path
............Lane	

TRANSPORT

.........Rail	........Tram

HYDROGRAPHY

.........River, Creek	.........Water

AREA FEATURES

...........Building	...........Mall
...........Campus	...........Park
...........Cemetery, Christian	...........Sports
...........Land	...........Urban

POPULATION

☼ CAPITAL (NATIONAL)	● ....Town
● ....City	

SYMBOLS

Information
- ⑤ ....Bank, ATM
- ⑳ ....Embassy/Consulate
- ✛ ....Hospital, Medical
- ⓘ ....Information
- ⓦ ....Internet Facilities
- ⓟ ....Police Station
- ⓟ ....Post Office, GPO
- ⓣ ....Telephone
- Ⓣ ....Toilets

Sights
- 🏰 ....Castle, Fortress
- ✝ ....Christian

- ⚑ ....Monument
- 🏛 ....Museum, Gallery
- ● ....Point of Interest
- ✠ ....Ruin
- 🦜 ....Zoo, Bird Sanctuary

Shopping
- 🛍 ....Shopping

Eating
- 🍴 ....Eating

Drinking
- ☕ ....Drinking

Nightlife & the Arts
- 🎭 ....Nightlife & the Arts

Sports & Activities
- ⬛ ....Pool
- ● ....Other

Sleeping
- 🛏 ....Sleeping

Transport
- 🚌 ....Bus Station
- 🚕 ....Taxi Rank

Geographic
- 🔭 ....Lookout
- ▲ ....Mountain
- 🌲 ....National Park, Forest
- 💧 ....Waterfall

Published by Lonely Planet Publications Pty Ltd
ABN 36 005 607 983

Australia (Head Office)
Locked Bag 1, Footscray, Victoria 3011,
☎03 8379 8000, fax 03 8379 8111

USA 150 Linden St, Oakland, CA 94607,
☎510 250 6400, toll free 800 275 8555,
fax 510 893 8572

UK Media Centre, 201 Wood Lane, London
W12 7TQ
☎020 8433 1333, fax 020 8702 0112

Contact talk2us@lonelyplanet.com
lonelyplanet.com/contact

MIX
Paper from
responsible sources
FSC™ C021741
www.fsc.org